Southern Crucifix,
Southern Cross

RELIGION AND AMERICAN CULTURE

Series Editors

David Edwin Harrell Jr.
Wayne Flynt
Edith L. Blumhofer

Southern Crucifix, Southern Cross

Catholic-Protestant Relations in the Old South

Andrew H. M. Stern

THE UNIVERSITY OF ALABAMA PRESS
Tuscaloosa

Typeface: Caslon

Cover photographs: Clockwise from top left: Thyatira Church, Salisbury, Rowan County, North Carolina, 1938. Catholic Church, Milledgeville, Georgia, 1939 or 1944. St. Paul's Church, Edenton, Chowan County, North Carolina, 1937. Old Frame Episcopal Church, Greensboro, Greene County, Georgia, 1939 or 1944. Photographs by Frances Benjamin Johnson. Courtesy of the Library of Congress Prints and Photographs Division.
Cover design: Todd Lape / Lape Designs

∞

The paper on which this book is printed meets the minimum requirements of American National Standard for Information Sciences—Permanence of Paper for Printed Library Materials, ANSI Z39.48-1984.

Library of Congress Cataloging-in-Publication Data

Stern, Andrew H. M., 1977–
Southern crucifix, southern cross : Catholic-Protestant relations in the old south / Andrew H. M. Stern.
p. cm. — (Religion and American culture)
Includes bibliographical references and index.
ISBN 978-0-8173-1774-4 (trade cloth : alk. paper) — ISBN 978-0-8173-8629-0 (ebook) 1. Southern states—Church history. 2. Protestant churches—Relations—Catholic Church. 3. Catholic Church—Relations—Protestant churches. I. Title.
BR535.S74 2012
277.5'08—dc23

2012016469

For Gretchen, Nicholas, and Charlie, whose naps gave me time to write and whose waking hours fill me with joy.

Contents

Acknowledgments

This work would not have been possible without the advice and support of many people and organizations. Emory University provided several grants for research and conference travel, as well as a fellowship that allowed me to focus on this project. One of the great pleasures of the project was the opportunity to explore archives across the South. I am very grateful to the archivists of the Diocese of Charleston, the Archdiocese of Baltimore, the Archdiocese of Mobile, Spring Hill College, the University of Notre Dame, and the Southern Historical Collection at the University of North Carolina–Chapel Hill. In particular, I would like to thank Mary Giles of Charleston, Michael King and Sr. Mary Elizabeth Cullen of Mobile, and Jessica Deese of Fairhope. I am especially grateful to the Filson Historical Society of Louisville for financial assistance, as well as for the support and encouragement I received from the society's excellent staff during my research there.

Parts of this work appeared in the journal *Religion and American Culture,* published by the Center for the Study of Religion and American Culture and the University of California Press, and in the *Encyclopedia of Religion in America,* published by CQ Press. I am grateful to those publishers for allowing me to use this material, to the editors for their suggestions, and to the anonymous reviewers for their insights. I am also very grateful to The University of Alabama Press. It was a pleasure to work with my editor, Daniel Waterman, and I am deeply indebted to the press's anonymous reviewers, who provided remarkably detailed and insightful evaluations of the manuscript.

Over the years, I have presented parts of this project at several conferences, and I am grateful to all those respondents who raised questions and made suggestions. I also benefited greatly from the opportunity to participate in two A. Worley Brown Southern Studies seminars at Emory. I am grateful to my fellow participants and to Merle Black for facilitating one of the seminars and for providing valuable suggestions for the chapter on slavery. I am deeply indebted to the late Elizabeth Fox-Genovese, not only for leading the other seminar, but also for being an inspiring teacher and a wonderful source of insight and support. I am also grateful to Eugene Genovese for several stimulating discussions and for guiding me to many valuable resources, and to Patrick Allitt for his suggestions.

I am particularly grateful to two wonderful mentors for their guidance and encouragement. Over the years, James Roark read and edited numerous drafts of this work with endless patience, graciousness, and insight. His affirmation that this project was worth exploring has always meant a great deal to me. My greatest debts are to Brooks Holifield, who first suggested this topic and who over the years provided unflagging support and encouragement. This work would not have been possible without his generosity and insights. Whatever is of value in the following pages belongs at least as much to him as it does to me.

On a personal note, I wish to thank the people of Leasburg United Methodist Church, who demonstrated that good Catholic-Protestant relations continue to this day, and Homer Simpson, whose good humor and perspective were constant inspirations. I am also extremely grateful to Grant Wacker for the interest he took in this project and for all the ways he has advised and assisted me, as well as to Katherine Wacker for all her support and kindness over the years. I have also been fortunate to receive support from my parents, Krisztina Krivátsy Stern and Henry Stern, who taught me to see wonders in different cultures and to hear wisdom in the voices of the past. And, in this as in all my endeavors over the past ten years, I owe a great deal to Laura. I cannot thank her enough so I will simply say—*Ich liebe Dich.*

Southern Crucifix,
Southern Cross

Introduction

In 1842, the citizens of Charleston, South Carolina, lamented the passing of a great public figure. Across the city, church bells tolled; ships in the harbor flew their flags at half-mast; and politicians, journalists, and religious leaders added their voices to the chorus of dismay. The man the city mourned was not a politician, low-country grandee, or military hero. Instead, he was John England, the first Catholic bishop of Charleston.[1]

John England was born in Cork, Ireland, in 1786. He was ordained in 1808 and proved to be an energetic priest, founding a Catholic monthly in Cork and serving as president of the diocesan seminary, inspector of the poor schools, and secretary to the fever hospital in addition to his other priestly duties. He was also an Irish patriot, opposing the English government's claim to veto rights over the appointment of English and Irish bishops. In 1820, in a service in St. Finbar's Cathedral in Cork, he was consecrated bishop of Charleston, South Carolina. He declared it "idle and useless" to take the customary oath of allegiance to the British Empire, noting that his first act upon arriving in America would be to renounce it.[2]

Even in an era of missionary bishops who built a church from the ground up, England distinguished himself as a dynamo. In Rome, he earned the moniker "*il vescovo a vapore*"—the steam bishop. He was an outstanding preacher, perhaps the greatest in the American Catholic Church of his time, although some auditors found him too theatrical. England's combativeness and willingness to speak his mind won him admirers and enemies, even among his fellow bishops, several of whom resented his unsolicited advice, found him too receptive to American culture, or distrusted him simply for being Irish.

But if England and his episcopal colleagues did not always see eye-to-eye, many non-Catholics loved him. A Protestant merchant from South Carolina described him as "beloved by all the cultured people of the State" and recalled many pleasant evenings spent in conversation with him "over a glass of Irish whiskey or a bottle of Madeira, with which his cellar was kept well stocked by his numerous friends."[3] When England died in 1842, these friends of all denominations joined in mourning. Jewish, Lutheran, Episcopalian, Presbyterian, Baptist, Congregationalist, Universalist, Methodist, and Unitarian representatives gathered in the cathedral of Charleston for the burial service. Thousands of mourners filed past his casket. As the *Charleston Patriot* noted, "the Church was thronged by persons of every rank and denomination."[4] The *Charleston Courier* commented on the ecumenical significance of the event, hoping that the representatives gathered "to bury with him . . . in one common grave, their memories of past dissensions and antipathies."[5]

This incident—and many like it—suggests that cooperation, not conflict, marked relations between Catholics and Protestants in at least some regions of antebellum America. To be sure, the antebellum South produced striking incidents of Catholic-Protestant animosity, and those incidents have loomed large in American religious historiography.[6] Too large. More often than not, southern Protestants supported Catholics, particularly in building hospitals, schools, and churches. Catholics reciprocated when they could. Bishop England contributed to a Protestant-run school in Savannah, and his colleague in Kentucky, Bishop Benedict Joseph Flaget, promised to help two Protestant missionaries distribute Bibles.[7] But because Catholics were chronically short of resources, Protestants normally assisted them without expecting or receiving anything material in return.

In the South, Protestant support continued throughout the antebellum period. One of the most striking aspects of this support is how little it changed over the decades. This work does not adopt a chronological approach for precisely this reason. The motives behind Protestant support for Catholics may have varied by time and place, but the support itself was remarkably consistent. Elsewhere in America, in contrast, attitudes toward Catholics hardened as immigration spiked. Some southerners were also antagonistic, but overall Protestant generosity counterbalanced—and even surpassed—the hostility. This striking amicableness had multiple sources. It emerged, in part, because of Catholics' loyalty as southerners, especially their support for slavery. But other factors reinforced Protestant openness. Civic pride prompted some to contribute to Catholic institutions. Curiosity led others to admire Catholic worship. Similarities between Catholic and southern culture also improved relations. The reasons were complex, but they led to a remarkable outcome: tolerance and cooperation, more than violence and animosity, marked Catholic-Protestant relations in the antebellum South.

Historiography

Maria Monk and her "exposé" of convent life enliven almost every survey of American religious history. The burning of the Charlestown convent consistently occupies a prominent place in studies of American Catholicism, and the anti-Catholic Know-Nothing Party casts a wide shadow in every discussion of nineteenth-century interfaith relations. The historiography abounds with attacks on convents, riots, and nativist politics. Such events merit attention, for they were part of the story, but other patterns, although not appearing as brightly in the historical record as a burning convent, marked the day-to-day relationships of Protestant and Catholic laity and clergy.

Hostility occupies an even more central position in surveys of American Catholicism. Some authors see nativism and anti-Catholicism as decisive themes even before the massive influx of immigrants in the 1840s.[8] Others discover anti-Catholicism lurking below the surface of American society even when all seemed calm.[9] In some recent surveys, Protestant hostility is taken as evidence that Catholicism was foreign to republican governance, political and ecclesiastical. The dominant narrative in such works tells how Catholics became Americans by altering patterns of authority in the church and diffusing power from the hierarchy to the laity. The nineteenth-century Know-Nothing complaint that an undemocratic Catholic Church stood in tension with political democracy became, ironically, a favored theme of twentieth-century American Catholic historians. A reassessment of Catholic-Protestant relations in the antebellum period can at least complicate the story.

Some historians have recognized the complexities, even accenting the more positive relations. John R. Dichtl's *Frontiers of Faith* focused on Catholic clerical leadership and documented numerous cases of Protestant support for Catholics. Dichtl's analysis of this support is illuminating, but he limited his study to the Diocese of Bardstown, and he argued that relations between Catholics and Protestants deteriorated after 1830, concluding that the moments of cooperation "were ephemeral and did little to change either group."[10] Other historians have noted parallels between anti-Catholic, anti-Masonic, anti-Mormon, and anticult literature and have argued that anti-Catholicism often had less to do with Catholics than with Protestant social strains.[11] Or they have observed the fascination with Catholicism that often lingered beneath the surface of anti-Catholicism.[12] Others have emphasized that Catholics and Protestants cooperated at least in the decade after the American Revolution.[13] Even in the darkest moments of anti-Catholicism, some Americans felt ill at ease with what they saw as a betrayal of national principles. Condemnation invariably followed the most heinous incidents of violence against Catholics.

Such correctives cannot alone subvert the dominant view of Catholic-Protestant hostility. Anti-Catholicism indeed served multiple social functions, but one of them was to marginalize Catholics. Maria Monk's "disclosures" may have testified to uncertainty about changing gender roles, but the success of her work also disclosed genuine hostility to Catholicism. And scholars who emphasize post-Revolutionary cooperation concede that it was brief and anomalous. Anti-Catholicism returned, arguably in a more virulent form, as Irish and German immigrants poured ashore. Protestants might have been embarrassed by convent or church burnings, but that did not mean that they liked Catholics. The ideals of the Declaration of Independence and the Bill of Rights, "promissory notes of religious pluralism," might have circulated through the public, but the historiographical consensus is that these notes remained unredeemed for decades.[14] As a result, the story of cooperation still needs a hearing.

In part the dominant assumptions stem from limits in the sort of Catholics historians have studied. Few have focused on the South, mainly because the immigrants who swelled the ranks of the church settled primarily in the urban North.[15] But for much of the antebellum era, northern dominance of the American Catholic Church lay in the future. By some estimates, even in 1840, a majority of the nation's Catholics lived in the South.[16] Before the Civil War, the church was, ecclesiastically if not in sheer numbers, as southern as it was northern. In 1789, Baltimore became the first episcopal see in the nation, and in 1808, it also became the nation's first archdiocese with the creation of four new dioceses, including Bardstown, Kentucky. As late as 1840, southern dioceses outnumbered northern nine to seven, and in 1860, the North outnumbered the South only by seven dioceses (twenty-two to fifteen).[17]

Southern Catholicism is significant in the history of American Catholicism in more than just an ecclesiastical sense. Some of the earliest Catholic institutions in the country took root in southern soil. The first Catholic colleges appeared in Maryland, Kentucky, Missouri, and Alabama.[18] The first Catholic paper was the *United States Catholic Miscellany* in 1822 in Charleston. Several early religious orders in the country, including the Sulpicians, Ursulines, Sisters of Mercy, Sisters of Charity, and Sisters of Loretto, either originated in the South or came there from Europe. The South produced notable nineteenth-century Catholic leaders, including the Carrolls, the Spaldings, and the Fenwicks. It became home to important foreign-born clerics, most notably John England and Benedict Joseph Flaget.

The South never experienced the deluge of Catholic immigration that threatened to overwhelm northern cities such as Boston and Philadelphia. It was easier for southern Catholics to assimilate because there were fewer of them. But demographics alone are an insufficient explanation for Protestant openness. Small Catholic populations did not necessarily ensure Protestant acceptance, as the anti-Catholic sentiment of the colonial period demonstrates. Moreover, Catholic communities in many southern cities, although smaller than in the North, were still sizeable. Most large southern cities were home to thousands, and sometimes tens of thousands, of Catholics. During the antebellum period, immigrants, including many Catholics, helped shape urban life in the South. Irish immigrants formed a large part of urban workforces. In 1860, they accounted for roughly 30 percent of the free workingmen in Charleston and Mobile. That same year, over one-third of Louisville's population was foreign-born, with a large Catholic contingent.[19] Southern Protestants did not fear being overrun by Catholics, but neither could they ignore them. Nor did they wish to. The relatively low numbers of Catholic immigrants may help explain Protestant tolerance, but they do not explain why so many Protestants decided to help build Catholic institutions.

Just as studies of American Catholicism slight southern Catholics, so too do studies of southern religion. In his introduction to *Religion in the Southern States: A Historical Study,* Samuel Hill identified white Protestant hegemony as the source of southern cultural identity, and the book's following essays fell prey to the same assumption, paying little attention to exceptions to Protestant dominance.[20] Randall Miller's essay in *Varieties of Southern Religious Experience* spent more time on Catholics but concluded that they legitimated an evangelical culture to which they could never fully belong. As a result, they "perhaps deservedly, passed into historical obscurity."[21] In these and other works on southern religious history, the modest number of Catholics in the South is taken to signify modest influence.[22] But Catholics clustered in the urban economic, cultural, and political centers, and in those places, they made a difference, working alongside Protestants to build southern society.

Charleston, Louisville, and Mobile

To the extent that historians have considered southern Catholicism, they have focused on Baltimore and New Orleans. Those cities were the sites of the oldest major Catholic communities in the United States and also contained the largest Catholic populations in the South. For these reasons, however, they are anomalous. Smaller cities such as Louisville, Kentucky; Charleston, South Carolina; and Mobile, Alabama, in contrast, hosted

Catholic communities that were sizeable yet not large enough to separate from the Protestant majority. Catholic populations in those cities were too large to escape the notice of Protestants but too small to build networks of institutions without Protestant support. In this way, they represent the Catholic experience in the South better than Baltimore or New Orleans do. Each city, moreover, was the see of an early diocese (dating from 1808, 1820, and 1829), which together encompassed the majority of the territory that would become the Confederacy. Considering not merely cities but dioceses incorporates evidence from neighboring smaller cities and the southern hinterland and thus addresses the question of whether or not there was an urban-rural divide in the experiences of southern Catholics. Finally, these three cities represent southern diversity. In important ways, they and their patterns of Catholic settlement varied. The fact that similar forms of interfaith cooperation existed in such different contexts suggests that local conditions alone are insufficient explanations—the real causes of Protestant support for Catholics lie in the nature of southern culture and society.

In Kentucky, Catholics arrived with the first Protestant settlers, and the two communities grew side by side. Catholics settled in Kentucky's handful of towns and in tiny communities throughout the central and northern parts of the territory (see map 1). The first center of Kentucky Catholicism was Bardstown, named the see when the area became a diocese in 1808. The diocese originally included the states of Tennessee, Kentucky, and Ohio, and the territories of Indiana, Illinois, and Michigan. Over time, the church carved new dioceses out of this area.[23] By 1841, when the see transferred from Bardstown to Louisville, only Kentucky remained. The diocese's jurisdiction contracted further with the creation of the Diocese of Covington (1853).

Like most early Kentuckians, Catholic settlers made their livings from farming and hunting. They settled along creeks and rivers or near salt licks, often in groups so that they could build a church or at least attract an itinerant priest. By the 1820s, however, Louisville began emerging as the state's economic and cultural center, and it soon became the center of Kentucky Catholicism as well. Situated along the Ohio River, where a series of falls blocked navigation and made portage necessary until the opening of a canal and locks in 1830, the city was ideally positioned to benefit from the nation's westward expansion. The city's location also ensured that commerce and manufacturing would drive its growth and that merchants and industrialists, rather than aristocratic planters, would guide it. In the mid-antebellum period, Louisville was a boomtown, its population more than

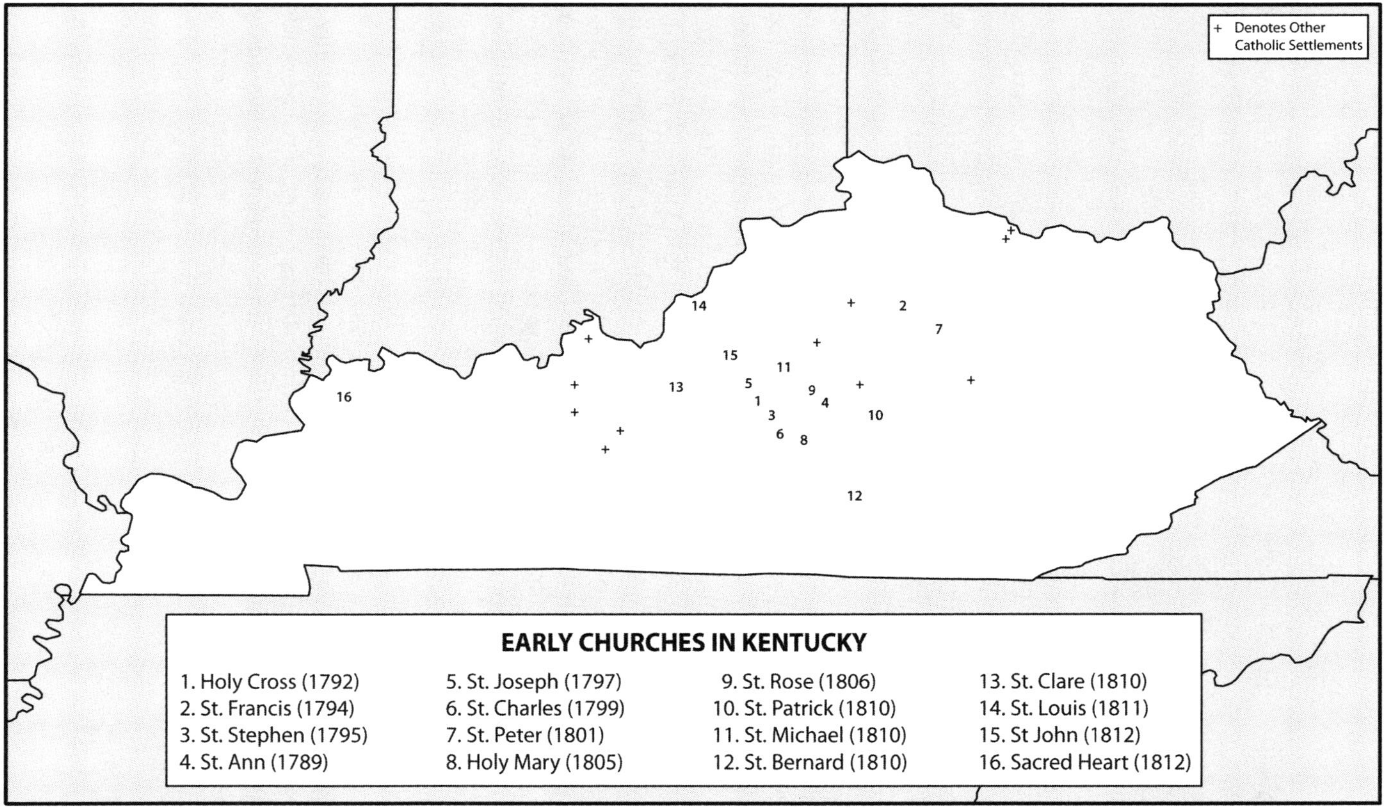

1. Locations of early Catholic churches in Kentucky.

Table 1. Charleston, Louisville, and Mobile populations, 1790–1860

	1790	1800	1810	1820	1830	1840	1850	1860
Charleston	16,359	18,824	24,711	24,780	30,289	29,261	42,985	40,522
Louisville	200	359	1,357	4,012	10,341	21,210	43,194	68,033
Mobile				2,672[a]	3,194	12,672	20,515	29,258

[a]Mobile County
Source: US Bureau of the Census

doubling each decade between 1800 and 1850. By 1830, it had overtaken Lexington as the most populous city in Kentucky and had transformed itself from a small frontier trading post to the twelfth largest city in the country. (See tables 1 and 2.)

Immigration accounted for a large part of Louisville's growth, and many of the immigrants were Catholic. The Catholic community had an early presence in the city; only a Methodist church, built in 1809, predated the Church of St. Louis, built two years later. As the church's name suggested, many of these early Catholics were of French stock. Within a few decades, however, the source of immigration had shifted to Ireland and Germany. Refugees from poverty and politics flooded the Ohio Valley. Nationwide, the Irish were the largest group, but in Louisville, the Germans dominated. By 1850, the city was home to roughly 7,500 German-speaking immigrants and about 3,100 Irish immigrants. The Germans belonged to several faiths—in 1836, the Catholics among them established the city's second parish, St. Boniface, and six years later the Protestants established a German Methodist church and St. John's Evangelical Church—but the Catholic percentage was substantial.[24] It was not until 1853 that Irish Catholics built their first church in the city, St. Patrick's. Catholic immigrants tended to settle in certain areas of the city—the Irish occupied the Eighth Ward and the Germans filled the First and Second wards on the city's eastern end. Their churches reflected this pattern of settlement, but the city had other Catholic churches in the heart of downtown, some very close to prominent Protestant churches (map 2).[25] The locations of these churches reveal the difficulty of generalizing about the Catholics of Louisville. Many were poor immigrants, but others occupied the highest echelons of society.

Established in 1820, the Diocese of Charleston originally included the Carolinas and Georgia, "a measureless extent of insalubrious swamps" in the words of Bishop England.[26] Despite this grim appraisal, the diocese included a number of important cities, most notably Charleston. The dio-

Table 2. Charleston's, Louisville's, and Mobile's rank among the largest urban places in the United States, 1790–1860

	1790	1800	1810	1820	1830	1840	1850	1860
Charleston	4	5	5	6	6	10	15	22
Louisville				44	22	16	14	12
Mobile					80	30	32	27

Source: US Bureau of the Census

cese's Catholics clustered there and in other cities such as Columbia, Savannah, Augusta, and Wilmington. By the 1830s, they appeared throughout the diocese, and indeed throughout the South, wherever there were canals to dig or railroad tracks to lay.

Built at the southern tip of a peninsula where the Ashley and Cooper rivers flowed into a large harbor, Charleston grew northward. Although the city was always the queen of the South, at least in the minds of its citizens, population growth slowed by the 1820s and 1830s and upstart cities such as Richmond, Louisville, and St. Louis caught and then surpassed it. The city remained an important transit point for cotton and other goods, but ports such as Savannah and Mobile won an increasing percentage of trade. The city boasted some important industries, but shortages of labor and expertise hindered their growth. Perhaps most importantly, Charleston's aristocracy never accepted trade and industry as legitimate occupations. Their attitude helped ensure that Charleston would remain a planters' city, a fact that accounted for both its charm and its deficiencies. The city never became a hub of industry, but it continued to serve as a center of southern intellectual and cultural life.[27]

In Charleston, the Catholic community achieved a significant presence only through immigration in the nineteenth century. Unlike the Catholics in Kentucky, Catholic Charlestonians had to find a niche in a well-established, Protestant-dominated social order. They benefited from the fact that Charleston had a long tradition of religious diversity. In the seventeenth century alone, Episcopalians, Huguenots, Baptists, Presbyterians, Congregationalists, Quakers, Lutherans, Jews, and Catholics all established places of worship. Episcopal planters and lawyers controlled the city's government but not its religious life.[28]

Catholic immigration, especially from Germany and Ireland, increased during the 1840s. Despite the fact that Charleston was perhaps the least industrialized of America's major cities, immigrants continued to arrive looking for work. By 1855, the Irish and Germans alone composed roughly

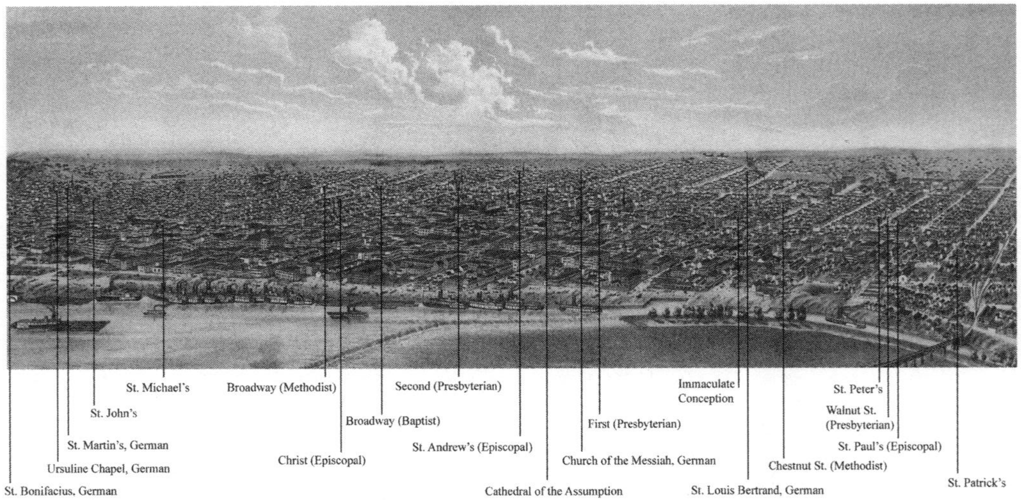

2. Bird's-eye view of Louisville, Kentucky, 1876. [By] A. Ruger. Chas. Shober & Co., props. Chicago Lith. Co. Courtesy of the Library of Congress.

40 percent of the white population.[29] Many of these immigrants could only afford lodging in the poorest neighborhoods. By 1850, the city filled its peninsula with the rich claiming the waterfront property and the poor clustering in the interior.[30] As in Louisville, Catholic immigrants were prominent among the urban poor, but other Catholics—especially the descendants of French refugees from Santo Domingo—occupied much higher places on the social ladder. The locations of Catholic churches demonstrated the community's economic diversity (see map 3).

The oldest of the three Catholic communities, Mobile was the last to receive its own diocese. The Alabama and the Floridas Vicariate was established in 1825 and became a diocese, with Mobile as the see, four years later.[31] Mobile was home to the largest Catholic community, although Pensacola and St. Augustine also had significant populations. Catholics settled in other parts of Alabama, most famously at Demopolis, where a group of French Bonapartists launched an ill-conceived attempt to grow grapes and olives, but in general their communities remained confined to cities such as Montgomery, Huntsville, and Tuscaloosa and grew slowly.

Like Louisville and Charleston, Mobile made its living largely through trade, but unlike the other cities, it depended almost exclusively on a single good: cotton. One visitor described the city as a place where "the people live in cotton houses and ride in cotton carriages. They buy cotton, sell cotton, think cotton, eat cotton, drink cotton, and dream cotton."[32] When the price of cotton was high, the city boomed, and when the price collapsed, it suffered. But the booms outnumbered the busts during the antebellum period and the city prospered, its population increasing almost twenty-fold between 1820 and 1860. Dependence on the cotton trade hampered industry, however, and among southern cities only Charleston showed less interest in manufacturing.[33]

Mobile's Catholic community traced its roots to the Spanish and French colonial periods and so predated the American takeover and the gradual emergence of a Protestant majority. These roots made the community even more diverse than the communities of Louisville and Charleston. The city attracted large numbers of Catholic immigrants from Germany and Ireland in the 1840s and 1850s, some of them recruited by industrialists hampered by labor shortages.[34] But although the Irish were the largest segment of the Catholic population by 1850, Catholics could still hear preaching not only in English but also in German and French.[35] Parishes sprung up in immigrant neighborhoods and followed the city's westward spread, but as in Louisville and Charleston, the earliest churches—most notably the Cathedral of the Immaculate Conception—occupied prime real estate in the heart of the city.

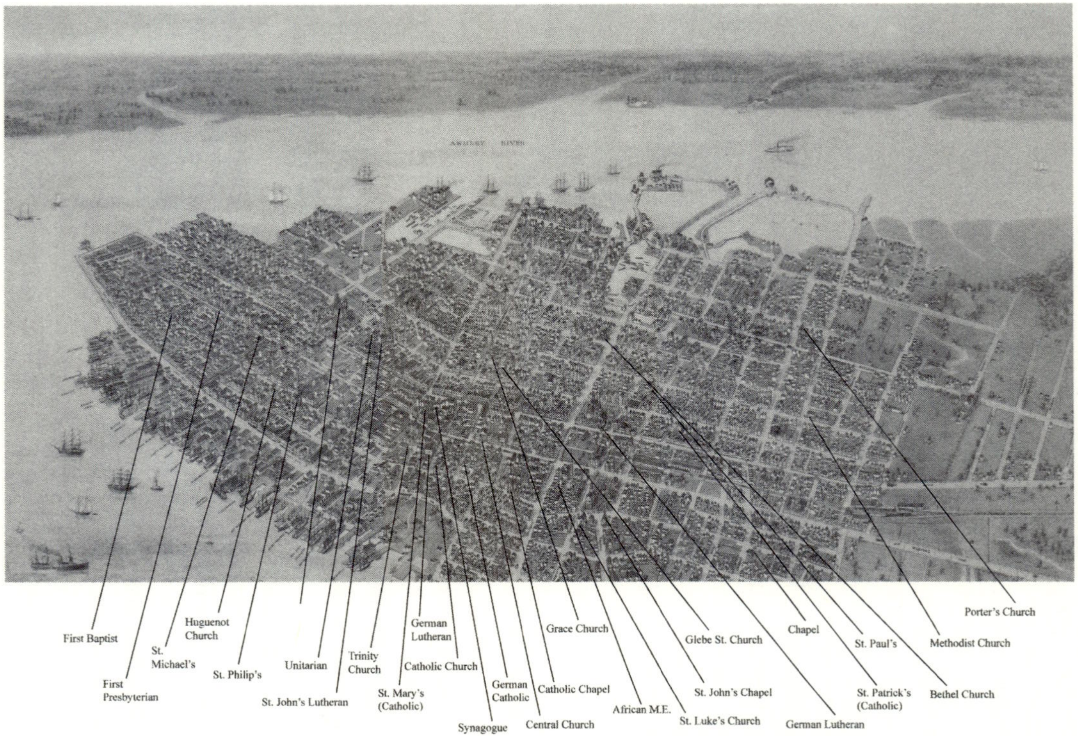

3. Bird's-eye view of the city of Charleston, South Carolina, 1872. C. Drie, lithographer. Courtesy of the Library of Congress.

The statistics on the numbers of Catholics in Charleston, Louisville, and Mobile are elusive. Catholic leaders conducted no systematic census in the antebellum period. Individual prelates occasionally offered estimates, but whether because they lacked the resources to survey their vast dioceses or because they had an eye on soliciting donations, these are often wildly unrealistic. Historians' estimates are also imprecise because they have to rely on unreliable sources. Further complicating the matter, it is often unclear whether estimates refer to communicants, formal members, or believers. Nor is it always clear whether they refer to cities, states, or dioceses. In the case of the dioceses, statistics are often misleading because the creation of new sees repeatedly siphoned believers from established dioceses. Despite these difficulties, however, considering the estimates in aggregate allows for some general conclusions. Most sources agree that the Catholic population in the Carolinas grew from a few hundred in the early 1800s to at least ten thousand by 1860 (with roughly an equal number in Georgia). The Diocese of Mobile began with slightly more Catholics and grew to between ten and twelve thousand. During the same period, Kentucky's Catholic population increased from roughly six thousand to between fifty and sixty thousand.[36] These numbers represent a small fraction of each state's overall population, but because Catholics tended to cluster in urban areas, their influence there was greater. By 1855, for example, Catholics made up over 60 percent of Mobile County's 10,355 church members. The next largest group, the Methodists, could claim scarcely 20 percent. At roughly the same time in Louisville, Catholics nearly matched the membership of all Protestant denominations combined.[37]

The dioceses of Charleston, Louisville, and Mobile contained large and varied Catholic populations. The task of considering in detail whether conclusions drawn about these dioceses also apply to the southern cities with larger Catholic populations—Baltimore and New Orleans—is an important one for future historians. However, in situating the three dioceses in the broader southern context, I will offer evidence from the larger cities to suggest that they do.

The stories of the Catholic communities of Charleston, Louisville, and Mobile shed light on the shape of antebellum Catholic-Protestant relations, illuminate an overlooked chapter in American Catholic history, and offer a new way of understanding the Old South. Considering how a foreign minority carved a place for itself in a new and strange society reveals a great deal about both the minority and the host society. The history of Catholics in the South demonstrates that Catholics and southerners made an earnest effort to accommodate each other, largely because they had a great deal in common.

The Colonial and Revolutionary Contexts

The antebellum religious climate did not develop in a vacuum; rather, it evolved out of a centuries-long encounter between Catholics and Protestants in both Europe and the Americas. Antebellum relationships showed clear vestiges of this legacy, with older attitudes lingering in the region. But some of those attitudes faded after the Revolution. To a striking degree, early nineteenth-century southern Protestants departed from their ancestors' attitudes toward Catholicism.

The colonial period was difficult for Catholics in almost every colony. Few Catholics settled in British North America for the simple reason that Britain, the origin of most immigrants, was an overwhelmingly Protestant nation. Nor did the colonies welcome Catholics who did attempt to emigrate. Protestant settlers imported anti-Catholicism as part of their cultural heritage. Isolation made it worse. Over time, politics added further anti-Catholic strains, as colonial attitudes shifted in accord with relations with Catholic powers. Wars with France and Spain in the 1690s intensified anti-Catholic sentiment, and South Carolinians engaged in brutal warfare against the Spanish and their Native American allies in Florida for much of the early eighteenth century. Although loyalty to Britain and religious sentiments could reinforce each other, anti-Catholicism also heightened support for independence. Protestants saw the Quebec Act of 1774, by which Britain extended tolerance to Catholics in Quebec and incorporated French settlers in Ohio, as a popish plot and a betrayal.[38]

Anti-Catholicism permeated the colonial legal system. By 1700, only Rhode Island offered Catholics full civil and religious rights. Most colonies established one or another Protestant church, usually Congregationalist or Anglican, and over the course of the eighteenth century, proscriptions against Catholics tightened in almost all the colonies. In South Carolina, a system of oaths blocked Catholics from political offices and from religious exercise.[39] Some colonies required public office seekers to swear test oaths, which excluded Catholics by including clauses declaring the truth of the Protestant religion. Other colonies restricted Catholics and Protestant dissenters by requiring anyone wishing to preach to obtain a license from the state.

Anti-Catholicism spilled over the boundaries of law books into the streets. Each year, Protestant colonists celebrated Pope Day, devised by the Puritans as the equivalent of Guy Fawkes Day, which celebrated the failure of a small group of English Catholics to blow up the houses of Parliament. Crowds paraded effigies of the pope and the devil through the streets. Initially confined to New England, Pope Day spread throughout the colonies in the wake of the Quebec Act. In 1774, the citizens of Charleston burned an effigy of the pope on a pile of English tea.[40] Such activities sometimes encouraged spontaneous violence, as when a mob in Charleston, in 1775, tarred, feathered, and banished two Irish Catholics.[41]

Despite such animosity, Catholics made an early entry into the colonies. In Maryland, a large group of Catholics settled under the leadership of Cecil Calvert, Lord Baltimore, and there they first enjoyed religious freedom. Calvert's "Maryland Design" issued in a form of toleration that both ensured the rights of Catholics and conceded that Protestants would always compose the majority. The Maryland Assembly enshrined Calvert's intentions in law in 1639 and ten years later in the Act Concerning Religion, or the Toleration Act, which stands as one of the earliest official expressions of religious liberty in America. Many moderate Protestants supported it because they recognized the importance of peace and stability. Such practical considerations, rather than any abstract ideal of religious liberty, produced the Toleration Act. The act asserted that intolerance had proven dangerous to commonwealths, and it required that no one "professing to believe in Jesus Christ, shall from henceforth bee any waies troubled . . . in respect of his or her religion nor in the free exercise thereof . . . nor in any way compelled to the beliefe or exercise of any other Religion." It also prohibited reproachful language about the Virgin Mary, the Apostles, or Evangelists; it forbade derogatory names for religious groups; and it ordered respect for the Sabbath.

Despite an auspicious beginning, Maryland enjoyed little peace. From the granting of the charter, Catholic control of the colony depended on royal support, and the turbulence of English politics led to instability. The spread of Puritanism in the colony and a decline in royal authority in England helped pave the way for a series of attacks in the mid-1640s by Richard Ingle, the captain of a Chesapeake tobacco ship, and a gang of Virginia Protestants. In 1654, with Puritans in control of Parliament in England, Maryland Protestants repudiated the Toleration Act, and they proceeded to outlaw Catholicism, plunder Catholic property, and kill or exile the colony's priests. Even following the Restoration of royal authority in England in 1660, Catholics in Maryland had a precarious status. Four revolts, which reflected both economic and religious tensions, disrupted the colony in the seventeenth century and with the Glorious Revolution in England in 1689, Protestants took control of the colony. In 1691, William III made Maryland a royal province, although he allowed the Calverts to keep their property. The following year, Maryland's fragile history of religious liberty came to an end with the establishment of the Church of England.[42] Over time, anti-Catholic legislation grew so onerous that Catholics dispatched Charles Carroll to French Louisiana in an unsuccessful search for a refuge.[43]

By the early 1700s, Maryland resembled every other southern colony, but it continued to serve as a symbol for Catholics. Baltimore was the see of the first American Catholic bishop, making the city the church's ecclesiastical center. The old Catholic families of Maryland continued to provide the church with leaders, and even in the mid-nineteenth century, when dioceses had cropped up across the country and the Catholic planter families had either died out or moved to other states, Maryland symbolized for American Catholics the first fulfillment of the promise of religious liberty. Throughout the antebellum period, Catholics invoked Maryland to remind Protestants that they had helped forge American principles.

Maryland remained the center, but colonial Catholics also migrated west into Kentucky, precursors of a larger movement after the Revolution, and they journeyed into South Carolina, where Protestants worried about papist treachery.[44] The Catholic population in South Carolina grew in the winter of 1755–1756 with the arrival of almost a thousand Acadians exiled from Nova Scotia, who also drew anxious Protestant attention, although most of them died of disease or left the colony within a decade.[45] Antebellum Catholics there would build their church from scratch, bearing the memory of ostracism by the Protestant majority.

The Revolution marked a moment of transition. Although antipathy lingered, colonial patriots encouraged unity, and George Washington forbade his soldiers to celebrate Pope Day, an example of restraint that helped end the practice. With the French alliance in 1778, patriot sentiment shifted in favor of Catholics, and revolutionary rhetoric made talk about the dangers of popery seem paranoid.[46]

Most Catholics favored independence and many fought for it.[47] The few prominent Catholic leaders were patriots. Charles Carroll signed the Declaration of Independence as a delegate for Maryland. Two years later, he traveled with the priest John Carroll, Benjamin Franklin, and others to Canada to win support for the war. Two Catholic laymen, Daniel Carroll and Thomas Fitzsimmons, served on the Constitutional Convention. Following the Revolution, many Catholics—lay and clerical—wanted to enhance their integration into American society by creating an American Catholic Church with an American bishop elected by the American clergy, seminaries to train American priests, and freedom for the church from foreign oversight.

The first clerical election of a bishop, however, was also the last, and as priests and bishops continued to arrive from overseas and the bishops opposed lay trusteeship over church property, some of the old fears returned. Some historians have argued that a return to a more traditional, ultramontane form of Catholicism was a mistake that intensified Protestant hostility.[48] But despite occasional outbursts of anti-Catholic feeling, many Protestants cooperated with Catholics throughout the antebellum period, even if the bishops were increasingly traditional and ultramontane.

In the early nineteenth century, most state constitutions favored Protestantism and some barred Catholics from office. Even though all five southern states disestablished Anglicanism, only North Carolina refused to grant special privileges to Protestants. South Carolina was one of seven states that limited office holding to Protestants.[49] And yet more liberal sentiments also found expression when the federal Constitutional Convention proposed to forbid Congress from imposing any religious test on officeholders and the first amendment to the Constitution prevented Congress from passing laws regarding the establishment of religion or prohibiting free exercise. The new states disestablished Protestant churches and removed restrictions on Catholics. They still faced some legal disabilities, but they enjoyed more freedom than in any other Protestant nation.[50]

At the outset of the antebellum period, however, little in the history of Catholic-Protestant relations would have suggested that the two faiths could coexist peacefully, let alone cooperate. The temporary harmony during the Revolution seemed in danger of fading away as Catholic immigration stirred Protestant unrest. Who could have predicted that within a few years a significant number of Protestants would be sending their children to Catholic schools, donating money to build Catholic churches, and praising Catholics for their patriotism, valor, and honesty? It might have appeared that Catholics could hope, at best, for a measure of tolerance from their Protestant neighbors. In fact, they received that and a great deal more.

1

Living Together

In 1782, a French immigrant to America named Hector St. John de Crèvecoeur published his *Letters from an American Farmer.* Crèvecoeur had arrived in North America in the 1750s and traveled throughout the colonies before settling in New York. A keen observer of American life and a nominal Catholic, he was no doubt aware of the discriminatory laws under which his coreligionists suffered. But Crèvecoeur's depiction of religious life in America suggested that law did not necessarily reflect common practice. "When any considerable number of a particular sect happen to dwell contiguous to each other," he explained, "they immediately erect a temple, and they worship the Divinity agreeably to their own peculiar ideas. Nobody disturbs them." After all, "if they are peaceable subjects, and are industrious, what is it to their neighbours how and in what manner they think fit to address their prayers to the Supreme Being?"[1]

Crèvecoeur asked his readers to imagine walking with him down an ordinary American country lane. On one side, they would pass a Catholic farmer who prayed to God, believed in transubstantiation, raised wheat, and offended no one. A mile later, they would pass a German Lutheran who prayed to the same God, believed in consubstantiation, tended his fields, and likewise scandalized no one. Further on, they would pass a "seceder," a Calvinist, and an array of believers in any number of other sects. The one thing these people had in common was that they were all too busy to worry about the theology of their neighbors. They patronized whatever place of worship happened to exist in the area, even a Quaker meeting house, and socialized without discrimination.[2]

Crèvecoeur's vision of American religious life was too idyllic. In his time, as throughout American history, many people were passionately interested in what their neighbors believed and how they worshipped. Crèvecoeur's assumption that American tolerance grew from religious indifference also ignored deep currents of religiosity, manifest in awakenings and revivals. As a rough sketch, however, Crèvecoeur's depiction of the American farmer has much to recommend it. Discriminatory laws and religious violence may stand out in the historical record, but tolerance and even friendships figured much more prominently in the everyday lives of countless Americans. And what Crèvecoeur observed in 1750 would be equally true a century later, at least in the South.

Elite Catholics

In the South, most Catholics toiled anonymously as laborers in cities and along the railways and canals, but a few made their way into the upper echelons of society. There they enjoyed not only acceptance but also warm and enduring friendships with their Protestant peers. Among the affluent and the educated, religious differences often faded into the background and ancient prejudices lost their power to divide.

One of the leading Catholics of Charleston, South Carolina, was Joanna England, who had accompanied her brother Bishop John England from Ireland in 1820. She assisted her brother in his ministry, taking over the last page of his diocesan newspaper, the *United States Catholic Miscellany,* and providing many translations for its pages. A devout Catholic, she befriended prominent Charlestonians of all faiths and helped ease her brother's entry into society. Charleston's second bishop, Ignatius Aloysius Reynolds, later complained of his predecessor, with a hint of envy, that "*he* had an accomplished sister to introduce into society, for this and other reasons *he* was, as far as possible for him as a bishop, a man of the fashionable world."[3] South Carolinians mourned when Joanna died of fever in 1827, at only twenty-seven years old. An obituary published in the *Courier* bemoaned that "we have lost an ornament to our communion, and to society in general," and it praised the departed as "pious, without pretension; religious, without bigotry; learned, without pedantry; dignified, without ostentation."[4] The *Mercury* eulogized her "youth, grace and intelligence" and mourned the silencing of a heart that had "throbbed with the finest impulses."[5]

Another young Catholic lady Pauline DeCaradeuc enjoyed similar esteem. DeCaradeuc's paternal ancestors had arrived in Charleston in 1792 as refugees from Santo Domingo, and her maternal grandfather had emigrated from Italy in 1809. In 1840, her father purchased a 450-acre plantation named Montmorenci near Aiken. Pauline grew up in affluence, received her education from nuns, and regularly attended Most Holy Trinity

Church in Augusta, Georgia. Her family's wealth, status, and culture earned them the respect of upper-class Protestants, and Pauline's wide circle of friends and admirers included such luminaries as the future Confederate general John Bell Hood. Pauline was intensely devoted to her faith—she almost decided to join the Ursuline order—but like her father, who regularly conversed with the local Episcopal priest, she had a host of Protestant friends. Her religion proved to be a hindrance only when it came time to marry. "My faith has kept back a good many from seriousness," she noted in her diary, but "all this only increases my ardent love for it." She viewed the hesitation of her Protestant beaux with humor: "what a romantic struggle between love & religion, I could have, if the affair were only mutual," she wrote after being informed that one prominent suitor intended to propose if only she would convert. In the end, love conquered even that obstacle, and in 1866, Pauline married a non-Catholic named Guerard Heyward, the scion of one of South Carolina's oldest families.[6]

Elite Catholic women claimed a place in southern society and helped make Catholicism respectable. The Catholic community in Washington, Wilkes County, Georgia, owed its existence largely to the intercession of Kate Teliaferro Semmes, the wife of the planter Thomas G. Semmes. Thomas Semmes had received his education at Georgetown College, while Kate had studied with the Sisters of the Visitation in Georgetown. Upon settling in Washington, Kate offered her home for Mass in 1835, and several years later, her family donated a lot for a stone church, which they populated with family members, many of them converts. But she not only helped Catholics create a spiritual home, she also helped them feel at home in a new land. Wilkes County was a bastion of aristocratic Protestantism, but Kate won a place in society. Largely through her patronage, other Catholics, many from Ireland, also gained acceptance. In 1840, when Bishop England came to town to lay the church's cornerstone, a large crowd of non-Catholics appeared at the ceremony and invited him to preach in the local Methodist church. Over a decade later, Bishop Francis Gartland of Savannah visited Washington and noted in the parish registry that he had lectured to a largely non-Catholic audience. Kate Semmes was gone by that time, having moved with her family to Mississippi, but the relations she had helped forge between Catholics and Protestants endured.[7]

Wealthy Catholics won praise for their refinement and generosity. Mary Boykin Chesnut of South Carolina complimented a play that the Semmes and Ives families of Richmond put on as "beautiful beyond words." Noting that both families were Catholic, she added that they "understand how to get up that sort of thing."[8] A Protestant minister in New Orleans praised Stephen Poydras, a patron of the city's orphan asylum, as a "pious, upright, self-denying, humble, generous man." He described in similar fashion a member of a respected Creole Catholic family: "I have not seen, in the whole course of my life, a more charming woman."[9] At the death of Julia Rowan Sneed, the daughter of Chief Justice John Louis Taylor of North Carolina, the local paper in Salisbury described her as an "intelligent, accomplished, and highly esteemed lady," praising her for the religious training she imparted to her children and concluding that "a purer spirit has seldom breathed on earth, or winged its triumphant flight to the bosom of God."[10] Obituaries revealed disregard for ecclesiastical differences. Non-Catholic papers eulogized Catholics, and the *Miscellany* reciprocated for Protestants. Two editions in 1826, for example, ran an obituary and tribute for William Crafts, a Protestant lawyer, author, and politician, who had supported the Catholic-run Philosophical and Classical Seminary in Charleston.[11]

Friendship and prejudice could coexist. In 1828, Bishop England noticed that the Female Episcopal Society had published a "Protestant Catechism shewing the principal errors of the Church of Rome." England observed, however, that many of the women had Catholic friends. In an open letter to Episcopal Bishop Nathaniel Bowen, he wondered whether they really believed what they had published. If they did, "how could they associate with Roman Catholics?" If they did not, how could they publish material "of the most defamatory nature, and the most insulting and degrading to the great majority of the Christians now in the Universe?"[12] England suggested that he was confident that mutual respect would overcome the prejudice.

Ordinary Folks

Southern Protestants extended their welcome to ordinary Catholics. Mary-Anne McManus, for example, was a native of Ireland who had immigrated to Kentucky in the late eighteenth century. After Indians killed her husband, she managed to raise four children by herself, giving each an education and turning them into "respectable citizens and exemplary Christians." When she died, "persons of all religious denominations, and every rank, assisted at the long and august ceremony of her obsequies" at Bardstown's cathedral.[13] The outpouring of affection reflected broader patterns of mutuality that transcended religious differences.

Even Irish Catholics—often stereotyped by Protestants as ignorant, superstitious, and violent—attracted favorable comment. "The Irish race are endowed with eloquence, courage, enthusiasm, reverence, and sensibility," a Methodist bishop from North Carolina declared.[14] A Protestant minister in New Orleans praised the Irish for their "many generous and noble traits of character" and blamed British oppression for any flaws in their national character. He argued that America had nothing to fear from the growth of Catholicism and that immigrants such as the Irish fueled the nation's prosperity.[15] A paper in Alabama recommended a book entitled *Sketches of the Irish Character* as a Christmas present for its readers, praising the author for her "fine appreciation of the feelings of her country people as well as the wit and humor which sparkle on their surface."[16] The paper reported that Irish workers in New York had raised $80,000 for the starving in Ireland: "What a fact is this! and what volumes does it speak in favor of the strong indications and generous hearts of the Irish!" The paper urged its readers to remember such generosity whenever they should hear "of excesses committed under the impulse of despair or starvation by the wretched peasantry of Ireland."[17] Of course not all Irish immigrants were Catholic, but in the popular imagination Irish and Catholic were largely synonymous, so praise of Irish virtue invariably elevated Catholic immigrants.

Catholics and Protestants formed such intimate relationships that intermarriage posed a conundrum for Catholic priests, who did not always know what to do when Catholics wanted to marry non-Catholics or to celebrate their marriages before non-Catholic ministers.[18] Was it proper, moreover, to deny Christian burial to someone who had "knowingly and very willingly, married an infidel or non-baptized person; who passed all his life in such concubinage, and, at the death, at his own request, asked for absolution"? "These cases," one priest reported, "are not rare."[19] During the Jubilee of 1827, church officials reported that many Catholics "who in the heat of passion had transgressed the laws of the church, by sacrilegious contracts of marriage" presumably had returned "sincerely penitent."[20] But what should priests do when Catholics' non-Catholic spouses died? One bishop came up with a solution by blessing each grave individually rather than consecrating the entire cemetery. He recognized that this was not ideal but concluded that because mixed marriages were so common, it would be "unpleasant and odious" to end the practice.[21]

The church registers reveal that intermarriage was indeed common. The Cathedral of the Assumption in Louisville, for example, recorded 299 marriages between 1835 and 1843, and 57 of them involved a non-Catholic.[22] The register of Spring Hill College, a Catholic college just outside Mobile, recorded the church affiliations of students and sometimes of their parents, who were often of mixed denominational allegiance.[23] Southern Catholics often counted many Protestants among their friends and even their relations. In fact, whenever Catholics and Protestants happened to be neighbors, they generally got along "as happily . . . as if they were all of the same creed."[24]

Common Causes

In March 1827, the courthouse of Augusta, Georgia, filled with people who gathered to discuss the suffering of the Irish. Mayor Robert Raymond Reid opened the meeting, which passed a resolution denouncing "such a system of persecution for conscience' sake" as existed in Ireland. Bishop England detailed the persecution suffered by the Irish while "doing ample justice to the liberal portion of the Protestants of Ireland, who have deprecated the continuance and frequently defeated the operations of the atrocious code of penalties."[25]

Southerners raised money for the Irish. Several cities established chapters of the "Friends of Ireland." In six months, Charleston raised almost $2,000 for Irish emancipation and aid for Irish emigrants, whereas a chapter in Savannah voted to give money to an Irish school. The Savannah Friends of Ireland publicized the ecumenism of their efforts. "There are among us people of all denominations; Jews as well as Christians; Protestants as well as Catholics; members of the Episcopal Church as well as those denominated dissenters in England," they proclaimed, all united in "the *great* and *common cause* of charity and religious toleration *throughout the whole world.*"[26]

Catholics were grateful for Protestant support. In September 1828, the *Miscellany* announced: "We find the genuine spirit of Carolinian liberty in full vigor regarding the state of Ireland." The paper saw the religious dimension of humanitarian aid: "The descendants of the exiled Hugunots [*sic*] advocating the cause of Catholics! This is an example of a most praiseworthy description; this is indeed taking a lead in the race of genuine liberality."[27] The Irish members of the Charleston Friends of Ireland expressed "their deep feelings of gratitude to the native citizens of these United States . . . for the cheering encouragement, liberal aid, and benevolent sympathy exhibited by them," and they pledged to repay the debt by always supporting civil and religious liberty.[28] Such support presented to the world "the very gratifying spectacle of Protestant liberality and kindness" toward Catholics.[29]

In early 1847, a women's society in Mobile held a public dinner with entertainment as a fundraiser for Ireland. The Mobile papers published, free of charge, a priest's offer to transfer donations to Ireland, and one paper endorsed him: "those who are disposed to contribute may rely on their charities being forwarded safely and promptly."[30] That winter, citizens of New Orleans imposed on Henry Clay, who was visiting the city, to address a meeting held for the relief of the Irish. Clay noted that any suffering people had a claim to Americans' sympathies, but particularly the Irish, who had been America's friends "in all the vicissitudes of our national existence," whose sons had fought shoulder to shoulder with Americans in every battle "from Quebec to Monterey," and whose nation was "so identified with our own as to be almost part and parcel of ours—bone of our bone and flesh of our flesh."[31] Ireland became a cause célèbre in the South. A thief who stole $260 from a business in Charleston left a note claiming that he intended to send the money to Ireland.[32]

Catholics and Protestants joined in support of other causes. In 1824, they raised money for the Greek rebellion against the Turks. Bishop England spoke at Charleston's city hall and earned the assembly's thanks with a donation of $50 from the Philosophical and Classical Seminary. A few days later, a collection at the cathedral netted $93.[33] A Methodist writer praised England's support for the Greeks: "No address that in the course of a long life I have ever heard, afforded me such heartfelt satisfaction."[34] Sixteen years later, Catholics rallied along with Protestants behind a similar cause, this time in defense of the Jews facing persecution in the Ottoman Empire. At a public meeting, England helped pass a resolution calling for an end to the Jews' oppression and asking the president to intervene with other world leaders.[35]

Standing side by side with Protestant reformers, Catholics combated southerners' vices. Some took part in opposition to dueling. Bishop England helped frame the Anti-Dueling Association's charter along with Episcopal Bishop Nathaniel Bowen and several other Protestant clergymen, who unanimously chose England to give the annual address.[36] A few Catholics joined the temperance movement, especially after the Irish crusader Fr. Theobold Mathew arrived in America in 1849. Viewed with suspicion in the South because of his support for abolition, Mathew managed to calm southern fears, and the citizens of Augusta welcomed him with a torchlight parade. Mathew organized Catholic Total Abstinence societies and held meetings in Charleston, Richmond, Augusta, Columbus, Montgomery, Mobile, and New Orleans.[37]

Catholic leaders also shared the ascetic Protestant distaste for excessive revelry. In 1810, the American bishops warned the laity against attending dances or the theater too frequently, and they attempted to impose this discipline in their dioceses.[38] Bishop Benedict Joseph Flaget of Bardstown forbade Catholics to attend balls, singling out those who hosted them.[39] Fr. Stephen Theodore Badin adopted a different tactic, appearing at homes during dances and announcing that it was time for evening prayers. On one occasion, he rounded up a group of dancers, sat them down, and gave them a catechism lesson.[40] Priests disciplined their flocks with one eye on Protestant reactions. Badin cautioned that the Baptists "consider dancing as an abomination, & this is a grand objection they have against Catholics."[41] He thought it unfortunate that Catholics danced at all hours, even on Sundays, and gave "general scandal to the Baptists, Methodists, Presbyterians, &c., who abominate the practice."[42] Fr. Charles Nerinckx, a severe disciplinarian, told young ladies preparing for their first communion that "to attend a dance, or to be unbecomingly dressed, is punished by refusal of admission" to the sacrament. "I succeed wonderfully well in abolishing these abuses," he boasted.[43] Such discipline met with resistance among the laity and even some clergy, but it defused charges that Catholics threatened the moral regime of the evangelical Protestants.

Catholics even helped Protestant mission work and Bible distribution. Around 1812, two New England missionaries arrived in Louisiana. Seeking permission to circulate Bibles, they approached a Spanish Capuchin named Fr. Antonio de Sedilla who conveyed their request to Bishop William DuBourg, who not only gave his consent but also promised to make a donation. Both he and Fr. de Sedilla voiced their support for the project and for the establishment of the Louisiana Bible Society.[44] A few years later, another party of missionaries encountered Bishop Flaget who promised to support the distribution of French editions of the New Testament, provided that he could examine them first. When the missionaries arrived in New Orleans, Fr. de Sedilla again proved eager to help and took "an active part in aiding the circulation of the New Testament among the Catholics."[45]

Catholics and Protestants worked together to address a multitude of social needs. Archbishop John Carroll set the tone, serving on the boards of numerous institutions including St. John's College in Annapolis, the Library Company of Baltimore, the Humane Impartial Society, the Baltimore General Dispensary, and Baltimore College, often hosting board meetings in the cathedral rectory.[46] In New Orleans, members of all faiths established a home for widows.[47] In Mobile, Catholics joined firefighting companies. In 1860, half of the men in one of the companies, Mechanics Number 7, had Irish surnames.[48] Fires were a big concern in the city, with arsonists destroying roughly $2 million worth of property in 1839 alone. The firefighters not only endured considerable danger, but they also paid most of their own expenses because the city purchased only the larger pieces of equipment.[49] Whether aiding the needy in distant lands or making life better closer to home, Catholics and Protestants found common ground.

They also served together in government. After the annexation of Mobile by the United States, the board of commissioners included a refugee from Santo Domingo named Samuel H. Garrow. Miguel Eslava, an official under the Spanish regime, remained in office as assessor.[50] In Kentucky, the state constitutional convention included several Catholics. Others served in the state legislature throughout the antebellum period. James Twyman, who had fought with Daniel Boone at the disastrous Battle of Blue Licks during the Revolution, converted to Catholicism and served Kentucky as a prominent judge and Catholic apologist. On one occasion, he silenced a crowd denigrating Catholics in a tavern by loudly identifying himself as a convert.[51] In South Carolina, an Irish-born merchant named William McKenna, who had once studied for the priesthood, served as state representative, state senator, and commissioner of free schools.[52] By far the most famous Catholic politician in the South was William Gaston of North Carolina. Gaston served in the state legislature or as a US congressman almost continuously from 1800 to 1832. The General Assembly of North Carolina elected him chief justice in 1833, a position he held until his death in 1844.

Gaston served North Carolina despite the state constitution's restrictions against Catholics. "It is strange," noted the *Miscellany,* "that although Mr. Gaston has presided in the legislature of his native state, and represented one of her districts in Congress; still by her Constitution, that State, North Carolina, could not invest him with any office even one as low as that of Constable."[53]

Common Enemies

Catholics and Protestants served together in times of war. Catholics reminded Protestants of their contributions and of the assistance given by France during the Revolution. Following George Washington's election in 1788, a group of Catholics sent their congratulations and expressed their pleasure at the nation's bright prospects. They hoped that Catholics would soon receive the full rights of citizens "*as the price of our blood spilt under your eyes.*" Washington assured them that Americans would not forget "*the patriotic part*" played by American Catholics in the Revolution or "the important assistance" of Catholic France.[54]

After independence, Catholics continued to offer martial service to the country. In 1798, Charles Carroll of Maryland wrote George Washington to tell him that Carroll's son wished to serve as Washington's aide de camp so that "he may early in life be useful to his country."[55] Over the subsequent decades, Catholics formed militia companies in several southern cities. Mobile alone had companies for natives of Germany, France, and Ireland—the German Fusiliers, the Lafayette Guards, the Mobile Grenadiers, and the Irish Independent Greens.[56] A northern visitor to South Carolina estimated that immigrants, many of them presumably Catholics, formed the majority of the state militia.[57] During the War of 1812, the Catholics of New Orleans rallied around Andrew Jackson during the battle for the city. Jackson commended Bishop DuBourg for the support and later attributed his victory in large part to the piety of a local priest.[58] America's Irish Catholics in particular celebrated the nation's rising power relative to that of Great Britain, but Britain was not the only common enemy.[59] In the 1830s, the Irish in South Carolina volunteered to serve in the Seminole Wars. England contrasted their loyalty with the treachery of Protestant missionaries and abolitionists who, it was rumored, incited Indians to resist removal.[60]

In Kentucky, as well, Catholics fought the Indians. On the frontier, a near-constant state of war existed between settlers and Indians until General Anthony Wayne's victory at the Battle of Fallen Timbers in 1794. Catholics filled the companies and expeditions formed to defend the settlements.[61] The danger decreased after 1795, but Catholic commitment to military service persisted. In an 1805 report to the Sacred Congregation for the Propagation of the Faith, also known as Propaganda, Fr. Badin reported that Catholics participated regularly in the "political, civil, and military activities of the State."[62] Catholic clergy blessed the soldiers and prayed for their victory.[63]

The war with Mexico in 1846, a war against a Catholic nation, had the potential to intensify anti-Catholicism, and American propagandists stereotyped Catholics in rallying support. The Mexicans were a "corrupt," "superstitious," and "priest-ridden" people. This rhetoric stimulated animosity against American Catholics, and Senator John C. Calhoun of South Carolina worried that annexing a nation of eight million Catholics, "all concentrated under a powerful and wealthy priesthood," would provoke religious violence and ultimately Catholic dominance of the government.[64] A correspondent from South Carolina argued that annexation would gain the United States nothing but "a worthless, idle & insubordinate Catholic population."[65] Another South Carolinian argued that Mexicans could never live under a republican government because their priests "forbade them to use the grand means by which God himself has given for the improvement of their morals & intellect . . . thus training them to the way of impiety, immorality & servility."[66]

Americans who viewed Catholic immigrants as potential subversives found a warrant for their fears in the defection of hundreds of American Catholic soldiers. These defectors, primarily immigrants, formed what became known as the Saint Patrick's Battalion of the Mexican army, which first fought as a distinct unit at the Battle of Monterey (September 21, 1846). Loathed by American forces, they endured brutal treatment if captured. The defectors' motives varied, but sympathy for fellow Catholics often played an important role. So too did resentment against the treatment of Catholics in the American army. Some Irish immigrants in particular felt that the war was "not entirely free from the machinations of Protestants" and that the Irish soldiers had been "ill *used*" by Protestant generals.[67]

Recognizing the potential for divisiveness, President James Polk encouraged the recruitment of Catholic immigrants to the army, appointed the first Catholic chaplains, and ordered the army to treat Mexican Catholicism with respect. Military officers, therefore, ordered soldiers to remove their caps in the presence of priests. Dr. J. G. M. Ramsey of Tennessee, a Presbyterian elder, reported that "along the track of our armies the padre (priest) was unmolested. His sacerdotal garments gave him the amplest protection from insult or aggression."[68] Such steps helped integrate Catholic soldiers and kept the war from becoming a religious crusade.[69]

The war enabled Protestants to meet Catholics, often for the first time, and soldiers of different faiths even worshipped together. The *Daily National Intelligencer* recorded in 1846 that at Mass in the town of Parras "the building was crowded with visitors from the camp . . . Protestant and Catholic, realizing for once the equality of man in the temple erected to the worship of his Creator."[70] The aesthetics of Mexican Catholicism, in particular the architecture and decoration of the churches, sometimes captivated Protestants.[71] Even the *Baptist Banner and Western Pioneer* noted that the beauty of a cathedral "cannot fail to impress the most insensible."[72]

Most Protestants seem to have ascribed the "objectionable" aspects of Mexican religious life to national and racial rather than religious sources. "The Catholic Church of Mexico is no more to be compared to the Catholic Church of the United States than the Methodist Episcopal church is to be compared to the Mormon church," claimed one Protestant soldier.[73] A Kentuckian wrote from Mexico City that "the Roman Religion here is not what it is with us in the U. States. If it is was [*sic*] not for some of its forms & ceremonies, and its professions, it might as well be call[ed] by any other name."[74] Catholics in the army and on the home front downplayed the faith they shared with Mexicans and emphasized the republicanism that they shared with other Americans.

To view the Mexican War as a source of increased tension and hostility is not so much incorrect as incomplete.[75] The religious press seized on the war to promote a religious agenda. At the same time, the war unified the country against an external enemy. Immigrant Catholic companies fought well and received a hero's welcome. Protestant and Catholic soldiers came to know one another. Protestants realized that Catholicism did not supplant national loyalty—"American Catholic" was no contradiction. War with a Catholic nation enabled American Catholics to prove their loyalty.[76] In the face of shared experiences, religious differences faded.

Priests

Protestants often had no idea that their neighbors, colleagues, or comrades-in-arms were Catholic. Priests, however, were the symbols of Catholicism in the South, and they too enjoyed the esteem and affection of many Protestants. The Catholic Church, in its ecclesiology and self-conceptions, was a hierarchy not unlike that of southern society. The clergy generally spoke for the laity and represented them as a community of believers. When Protestants accepted the heads of the church, they signaled their support for the body as well.

Non-Catholics frequently praised Catholic priests for virtues ranging from courage, devotion, and honesty to an admirable work ethic. "No Protestant ministers in the United States, of any denomination, accomplish as much hard service as they do," noted one Protestant minister.[77] In Portsmouth, Virginia, and Natchez, Mississippi, papers praised local priests for their preaching, liberality, manners, and care for members of all denominations.[78] A European traveler in Pensacola noted that the resident priest, originally from Flanders, was "universally esteemed and loved on account of his exemplary conduct and learning."[79] In New Orleans, Fr. de Sedilla preached on the anniversary of Jackson's victory, prompting the general to reply that the priest inspired him "with increased reverence" for the Catholic faith and to pray that his ministry would continue to flourish.[80]

Methodist Bishop Oscar Penn Fitzgerald, a native of North Carolina, found that priests, like the clergy of all denominations, varied "in gifts and graces," but he thought that most were good men. He criticized people who used the examples of a few unworthy priests to besmear the entire faith. Fitzgerald reserved special praise for the Irish priests. Although he found some to be "ascetics, austere and rigid," and a few others to be "by visible tokens rather over-jolly," most "went about doing good, placing their feet where they saw the footprints of their Lord." He admired their eloquence and devotion: "they were ready to expend their enthusiasm, their eloquence, their money, and even their lives for any cause that was dear to them or a friend they loved."[81]

Respect led to friendships. "I will always bear a grateful remembrance," wrote Fr. Francis Boland of Savannah, "not only of the Catholics, but of many of my respected Protestant acquaintances."[82] When Fr. Joseph Stokes left his church in Columbia, South Carolina, his parishioners praised him for having "not only gained on the hearts of your own congregation; but even those of every other denomination."[83] In turn, Stokes testified to the "liberal and friendly dispositions" of Columbia's non-Catholics, and he said that the friendships he had enjoyed reflected "great credit" on people who had often been raised with the most unfavorable impressions of Catholicism.[84]

Prelates also garnered respect. Even in the midst of a controversy over Catholic schools, Maryland Presbyterians praised Archbishop Carroll. They noted that Protestants of all denominations had "long borne witness to his liberal and dignified deportment in the walks of social intercourse." Carroll later reported to Rome, with perhaps a touch of hyperbole, that the Catholic Church was "venerated" in America.[85]

Among the most esteemed prelates was Bishop Flaget. Flaget was born at Contournant, France, in 1763. His parents were humble but respectable farmers who died by the time he was two. At age seventeen, he received a scholarship to the seminary at Clermont. He soon joined the Sulpicians, and in 1792, he set sail for America. Flaget was not known for his erudition, but like many of his fellow exiles, he was a man of determination, energy, and administrative skill. Over the course of more than half a century of ministry in America, the "Patriarch of the West" established dozens of churches and schools, ordained numerous priests, consecrated five bishops, and helped train several others. His achievements are all the more notable given that he had a nervous disposition and an extreme sensitivity that made conflict with others almost painful to him. He also labored under self-doubt, bordering at times on depression. When Archbishop Carroll informed him of his appointment as bishop of Bardstown, he begged Carroll to change his mind and even returned to France to implore the superior of the Sulpicians to intervene. Carroll described Flaget as a man of "tender piety" and "bland manners" who was "if not profoundly, at least sufficiently imbued with theological knowledge," and Carroll was astute enough as a judge of character to refuse Flaget's protestations. Indeed, Carroll rightly recognized that Flaget more than compensated for his weaknesses with his piety, warmth, and compassion.[86] These characteristics would serve him well in Kentucky. Colonel John Johnson, who cared for Flaget when the bishop attended a negotiation between the government and several Indian tribes in 1818, later remembered him fondly. "His conduct throughout his sojourn with us was so marked by the affability, courtesy, and kindness of his manners, with the dignity of the christian and gentleman, that he won all hearts," recalled Johnson. He added that Flaget's admirers raised a collection of $100, but that he refused to take it.[87]

Even critics of Catholicism could admire the bishops. Two New England missionaries claimed that the people of Louisiana were "entirely ignorant of divine things, and have been taught only to attend mass, and count their beads," but they conceded that Bishop DuBourg "appears to be a man of piety."[88]

Some Protestants voiced respect for the supposed archnemesis of their faith—the pope. The *Alabama Planter* reported that Pope Pius IX had released a man caught distributing leaflets attacking the papacy. The paper viewed the incident as "one of the most touching instances of character exalted and elevated by purity and christian love, that we ever remember to have seen." It added that crime in Rome had plummeted since Pius's accession.[89] Senator Calhoun praised Pius before the Senate as "a very wise and liberal reformer."[90] The American ambassador, Daniel Jenifer, wrote to Calhoun about a pleasant audience with Pius's predecessor, Gregory XVI. "His Holiness was unreserved in the expression of the most cordial sentiments towards us," reported Jenifer. Gregory had spoken of "the kind and liberal reception which was invariably given to the Roman Catholics who emigrated from Europe: of the growing prosperity of the Country and his gratification in giving audiences to Americans."[91]

By the mid-antebellum period, rising levels of immigration led to nativist reaction, but in the South, the priests continued to profess affection for America: "I was an American in feeling and conviction long before I became a naturalized citizen," said one French Catholic priest. "I would now die, with a devotion next to that I owe my God, for the country of my choice."[92] Bishop England stated that America had on him "every claim which kind partiality, warm affections, tender solicitude, and pastoral attachment could create."[93] Other priests and bishops pledged their loyalty to the South. On the eve of the Civil War, Bishop Augustin Verot of Savannah proclaimed himself a "sincere and devoted friend of the South." He was willing to undergo "any hardship—to make any sacrifice—for the true welfare of the people among whom I live."[94]

Foreign-born priests and bishops often pointed out that they had chosen America as their home. "My zeal for the Country which I have freely & deliberately adopted is unrelenting," wrote Bishop Flaget.[95] He boasted to a crowd that he was "more of an American than those who surrounded him; whose birth in the country was only the result of accident, while he had . . . after mature deliberation . . . freely sworn allegiance to this Republic."[96] In 1808, Flaget, prone at times to homesickness, wrote to his brother that he would not return to France, for "it is very difficult to uproot a tree which has been for seventeen years in a good soil." America had become his home, and he resigned himself to never seeing his family again.[97] Flaget worried that "the principles of liberty and independence are carried to such extremes" and that a schismatic "finds support and protection in the very Constitution of the Republic and has unbridled liberty to write and say whatever he pleases."[98] But for the most part, he found America to be a congenial place.

"We wear . . . the clerical dress in public, without ever receiving the slightest insult," noted a priest in Mobile. He explained that Americans "do not claim tolerance in order to be able to persecute. They love freedom, but not license."[99] A French priest in Kentucky remarked that he and his colleagues met with "great respect in social life; for the Americans are very fond of the French, whose politeness and gayety they try to emulate."[100] Another Kentucky priest reported to colleagues in Europe that Protestants would "do all in their power" to assist Catholic missionaries, "though the best fare that he can expect consists of nothing but some cornbread very badly baked, salt pork, potatoes and water."[101]

Early in his American ministry, Bishop Flaget spent six months in Pittsburgh, where a French Huguenot married to an American Protestant invited him to board with them and permitted him to say Mass in their house.[102] Years later, during one of his trips through Kentucky, the Protestant wife of a family with whom he dined treated him with such "extreme kindness" that he hoped she would allow him to baptize her children.[103] During Flaget's visit to Nashville in 1821, "the Protestants of the city vied with one another in showing every polite attention," and a Presbyterian minister invited him to tea.[104] When he transferred his see from Bardstown to Louisville in 1841, he found that the non-Catholics there were as favorably disposed to him as those of Bardstown had been.[105]

Traveling through the South Carolina upstate in 1823, Bishop England received an invitation to stop at the home of a Presbyterian who also rounded up the local Catholics for him.[106] Two years later, when Fr. Stokes passed through the area, the Presbyterian minister in Camden treated him "with great kindness."[107] On a later missionary tour across South Carolina, Stokes again spoke of "the kind reception he has met with from many protestant friends."[108] In 1824, England visited Augusta, Georgia, where he received "marked attention" from people of "every creed and country," including a public dinner in his honor.[109] In Charleston, England wrote an oration for a volunteer militia company that had long treated him with "respect and kindness" although there were rarely more than a handful of Catholics among its hundred-odd members.[110] England remarked that Protestants in South Carolina "uniformly manifested kind and friendly dispositions towards any of the clergy that have either been resident or visiting in their vicinity."[111]

Sometimes priests and ministers became good friends. Theodore Clapp, a New Englander who served a Presbyterian and later Unitarian church in New Orleans, recalled that acquaintances had warned him about the Catholics but that when he met several priests at a dinner soon after his arrival, he found them to be "intelligent, enlarged, refined, and remarkably interesting in conversation." Clapp expressed in the warmest possible terms his affection for a priest he identified only as "Father K." "A better man I have not known," he recalled. He said that there was no clergyman of his own faith whom he loved "with a purer, intenser affection."[112]

Priests could share these sentiments. Fr. Stephen Theodore Badin was born in Orleans, France, in 1768, the third of fifteen children. In 1789, he entered the Sulpician seminary, and two years later, he left for America aboard the same ship as Flaget. On May 25, 1793, he became the first priest ordained in the United States, and soon afterward, he left for Kentucky. For years, Badin labored virtually alone in the wilderness, but despite his dedication—he sometimes funded new parishes out of his own pocket—he never won the affection of his people. He had been trained in an austere form of Catholicism (tinged, some suspected, with Jansenism), and his rigorous discipline alienated some believers. Most respected him, but few loved him.[113] But even Badin managed to make friends with Protestants. He noted that a Presbyterian minister serving as president of Transylvania Seminary had lent him some treatises of St. Chrysostom "which might make him as friendly to the Catholic doctrine as he is to me."[114]

Like elite lay Catholics, priests and bishops formed friendships with Protestants in high places. Among Bishop England's Protestant friends were Judge James Louis Pettigru and former governors Robert Y. Hayne and James Hamilton Jr., who helped him when he aroused public displeasure for agreeing to serve as papal legate to Haiti.[115] Hayne and Hamilton escorted England when the bishop arrived in Washington to address Congress—the first Catholic priest ever to do so.[116]

In Kentucky, Fr. Badin enjoyed the friendships of several Protestant judges, General Robert Todd, Senator William T. Barry, and Joseph Hamilton Daviess, a US district attorney for Kentucky and commander of the Indiana militia.[117] Bishop Flaget counted William Clark, the explorer and later governor of Missouri, among his friends.[118] Another friend was Felix Grundy, a US congressman, senator, and attorney general who treated Flaget with kindness during the bishop's visit to Nashville in 1821. Early in Grundy's career, he had served as a member of the Kentucky Constitutional Convention of 1799. When a former Presbyterian minister tried to insert a clause barring Catholics from office, Grundy threatened to add another clause that "no broken-down Presbyterian preacher" be eligible either.[119]

Flaget had warm relations with Secretary of State Henry Clay, who offered Flaget the use of his house and a loan of $4,000 when Flaget passed through Washington. Flaget cherished their "warm friendship."[120] Clay would write to another Catholic friend, Demetrius Gallitzin, that he had the "highest respect" for the Catholic religion and counted among its adherents "some of my best and truest friends."[121] Six years later, he reacted adamantly to the charge that the Whigs opposed Catholic immigration and wanted to repeal the naturalization laws: "Without regard to Country or their particular Religion, I judge of men by their conduct & character. I have many friends among the Catholics, and some that I highly esteem among their clergy."[122] In 1832, Clay joined forces with another of Flaget's powerful friends, Congressman Charles Wickliffe of Kentucky, to pass a bill absolving Flaget from having to pay duties on several valuable items imported from Europe.[123]

Clergy sometimes got along better with Protestants than with their fellow Catholics. In 1825, Bishop Flaget consulted a magistrate friend named Badolet regarding tensions in one of Flaget's parishes. Many of the parishioners had taken a deep dislike to their priest and threatened to go into schism if Flaget did not remove him. In an anguished letter, Flaget complained about "nominal Catholics," who cared no more for their church than Flaget cared for the dust of his shoes, and begged Badolet for his assistance. What made this appeal notable was that Badolet was not Catholic. Flaget recognized the incongruity of asking a non-Catholic to help resolve such an issue, but Badolet was an "intimate friend" and Flaget judged him more Catholic in spirit than many of his disloyal parishioners.[124] Flaget was not alone in looking to non-Catholics for support. "If all the Catholics are not my friends, I am amply compensated by the friendship of many non-Catholics," Fr. Badin, who had his share of conflicts with parishioners, once remarked.[125] In Alabama, Bishop John Quinlan complained that a priest with whom he was at odds spent his time gossiping with Protestants and "infidels" instead of working.[126] Priests and laity squabbled over finances, control of church property, and ethnic prejudices. Priests wrestled with bishops over property and episcopal authority. Bishops fought with the laity, their priests, and one another. When tensions within the church rose, Catholic leaders were no doubt especially grateful for their Protestant friends.

Such friendships could receive symbolic confirmation at moments of grief and loss. The deaths of leaders became occasions for friendly exchanges. When Bishop England died in 1842, church bells tolled across Charleston and ships in the harbor lowered their flags to half-mast.[127] The *Daily Mercury* of Mobile eulogized Bishop Michael Portier as "one of those kind, loving, sincere, single-hearted, generous-minded beings the like of whom is rarely given us to see again in the lapse of a generation."[128] When Fr. George Elder, president of St. Joseph's College in Kentucky, died in 1838, citizens attended "without distinction of creed or sect" and formed a funeral procession over half a mile long.[129]

Catholics returned the warm sentiments when Protestant leaders passed away. The *Miscellany* republished a poem from the *Charleston Courier* commemorating the death of Episcopal Bishop Theodore Dehon, and it published obituaries for prominent Protestant ministers from across the South.[130] When Bishop Nathaniel Bowen died in 1839, Bishop England ordered his seminarians to wear badges of mourning.[131]

Conclusion

Friendships between Catholics and Protestants, often born of shared experiences, suggest that religious toleration was at least as important as antipathy in the Old South. But southern Protestants went a step further than simply tolerating Catholics or describing them as decent people; they encouraged Catholics to participate in the public life of the South. Protestants not only welcomed Catholics as individuals, but they also welcomed Catholicism as a faith by building the institutions—charities, schools, and churches—on which it relied.

The reasons Protestants befriended Catholics help explain their generosity toward Catholic institutions. These reasons varied widely, but they tended to crystallize around four themes. First, class solidarity blurred distinctions between faiths. Although working-class Protestants often saw Catholic laborers as unwelcome competitors, elite Protestants recognized themselves in the wealth and social graces of planter Catholics and appreciated the learning and culture of impoverished prelates. Only elite Protestants, by and large, had the money to help build Catholic institutions, which they did to suit their own tastes. Class consciousness bound Catholics and Protestants in friendship and in institution building.

Religion is a second explanation for Protestant kindness toward Catholics. Religion divided, but it could also unify. Christianity dictated kindness towards others, regardless of their backgrounds. When First Lady Varina Davis and other prominent Protestant women of Richmond came to pay their respects at the home of a young Catholic woman who had just lost her infant child, many motives may have driven them, but they no doubt included simple charity and compassion.[132] In countless cases, Protestants reached out to Catholics because their faith taught them that love of neighbor was the will of Christ. Sometimes this expressed itself in openness toward individual Catholics and sometimes in support for a community struggling to take root.

Christianity also provided a shared identity between Catholics and Protestants, some of whom recognized Catholics as fellow Christians, although perhaps misguided in specifics. "I believe the Catholic Church a truly Christian Church in all the main essentials of religion—its belief in the regeneration of the heart and in being saved through faith in Christ," explained a Louisiana man, going on to list a host of specific Catholic beliefs and practices with which he disagreed.[133] But for him, and for many others, the commonalities outweighed the differences. There was thus no reason not to befriend Catholics and to support the spread of a religion that was at least better than no religion at all.

Christian faith did not preclude hatred and even violence. Christians often treated each other quite cruelly. Catholics notably complained that the fiercest opposition they faced came from Protestant ministers. No doubt many Catholics and Protestants harassed and reviled each other one day and piously worshipped in their separated enclaves the next. Religion was a double-edged sword. Whether it united or divided depended on time, place, and individual inclination.

In addition to a common faith, common enemies also drew Catholics and Protestants together. In the colonial period, southern Protestants had viewed the Catholic powers of France and Spain as their mortal enemies, which heightened their antagonism to Catholics in general. In the antebellum period, however, Catholics and Protestants in the South generally found themselves on the same side. The enemies varied over time and place—Indians, British, Mexicans, rebellious slaves—but in each case, Protestants discovered that Catholics were reliable allies. Eventually, the North became the South's greatest enemy, and once again Catholics and Protestants faced the threat standing shoulder to shoulder.

A final explanation for Protestant support of Catholics, either individually or as a community, is sheer practicality. For many, the South was a hostile and unforgiving environment, rife with disease, poverty, and isolation. Whether in urban shanties or remote plantations, southerners needed the support of their neighbors, both as individuals and as groups. For environmental and demographic reasons, southern governments were slow to build institutions such as hospitals, orphanages, and schools. The need still existed, however, so southerners supported whoever was willing to meet it. Just as a planter surrounded by potentially mutinous slaves would have counted on his white neighbor, whether or not the neighbor happened to believe in transubstantiation, a laborer dying of yellow fever would not have let his objection to vows of celibacy keep him from receiving aid in a hospital run by nuns. Protestants who could find no other reason to cooperate with Catholics could at least appreciate their usefulness to society.

Protestants rarely explained why they befriended Catholics, and they almost never articulated their reasons for generosity to Catholic institutions. Even if they had tried, it is doubtful that they would have identified one predominant motive. Protestants gave money and time to Catholic institutions for different reasons and sometimes for several reasons at once. Only the confluence of numerous motives can explain the striking degree of religious harmony that the Old South attained.

2

Healing Together

Yellow fever struck Augusta, Georgia, in June 1839. The epidemic began as a few isolated cases along the city's riverfront, but it quickly spread. By mid-August, with over forty confirmed cases and more being reported each day, Mayor Alfred Cumming convened the city's physicians to discuss remedies. Their efforts had little effect, however, as the disease continued to spread, overwhelming the city's health-care resources. By the time it abated in early November, 1,500 to 2,000 people had fallen ill and 240 had died.[1]

Catholics throughout the region responded to Augusta's suffering. The congregation of the Church of the Purification of the Blessed Virgin Mary at Locust Grove, Georgia, contributed about $200 for the relief of fever victims. Fr. John Barry, pastor of the Church of the Holy Trinity in Augusta, transformed his residence into a temporary hospital.[2] He opened it to the sick of all faiths and invited Methodist minister Augustus Longstreet, the sole remaining Protestant minister in the city, to tend to the spiritual needs of Protestant patients.[3] In response to a request from Mayor Cumming, Barry also wrote to Bishop John England in Charleston, asking for Sisters of Our Lady of Mercy to come serve as nurses. England dispatched three sisters, along with Fr. T. J. Cronin. The sisters immediately went to work and labored in Augusta until the end of October. During that time, they cared for almost seventy patients, fifty of whom they nursed back to health.

The people of Augusta appreciated the Catholic exertions, especially the work of the sisters. "If the world ever produced a more kind, attentive, patient, indefatigable set of nurses than these, I never saw them," remarked Longstreet.[4] Civic officials treated the sisters with utmost solicitude. A committee of the Board of Health formally greeted them upon their arrival, and Cumming offered them the hospitality of his home. The city council determined to defray their travel expenses, in addition to providing for them during their stay.[5] At a meeting in early November, the Board of Health unanimously resolved to thank England for his liberality and Barry for the use of his parsonage and his devotion to the patients. The board particularly commended the sisters, who labored "with such constant care, skill and kindness." Cumming forwarded the board's resolutions to England and enclosed his own thanks. He commended England's kindness and Barry's "Christian spirit," but like the board, he reserved his highest praise for the sisters. He contrasted them with the pastors of the city who had fled and noted that "their disinterested devotion to the claims of suffering humanity, presented a beautiful moral spectacle, which made a deep and lasting impression."[6]

Catholics reciprocated these warm sentiments. Upon returning to Charleston, the sisters expressed gratitude for the kindness shown them in Augusta. The Catholics of Charleston instructed Barry to decline the Board of Health's offer of reimbursement for the sisters' travel expenses, explaining that they could not accept money for an act of charity. England himself replied to Cumming, thanking him and the board for their letter of appreciation. He spoke of his attachment to Augusta and of Barry's report of the assistance rendered him by the mayor, the board, and the doctors of the city. He also expressed his gratification at the sisters' usefulness and at their reports of the kindness shown to them. He concluded by assuring Cumming that the mayor's own "noble conduct amidst the afflictions and desolation of your fine city" had elevated him in England's esteem. England believed that the epidemic had been a chastisement from God. Like a loving father, God punished His children, although often in ways they could not immediately understand. England hoped that God would spare Augusta in the future, but he assured the people that, if the fever returned, "to the best of our power we shall be ready to prove not in word but in work the sincerity of our affection to all indiscriminately of what creed or colour soever to whom our exertions or sacrifices may be useful."[7]

Diseases and epidemics ravaged the South throughout the antebellum period. In response, Catholics made good England's promise of care for all, regardless of religious difference, and they found many Protestants eager to help.

Southern Health Care

Catholic charity, whether in individual ministry or in institutions, emerged within a broader context of southern health care. The late eighteenth and early nineteenth centuries were times of optimism about the future of

American health care. Southerners shared the sense of headiness. In 1801, for example, Dr. Ramsey Clark of Charleston hailed advances in hygiene and the prospects for improving health. This confidence was grounded in real improvements, including better medical training, discoveries in Europe, and a decrease in child mortality. Within a few decades, however, the mortality rates made it clear that earlier expectations had been unrealistic. Though based on some real advances, faith in American health care had also sprung from a blind confidence in science and an unwarranted optimism about the nation's destiny.[8]

Throughout the antebellum period, southern health care fell short of expectations. As one historian has noted, "the gap between medicine in the antebellum South and the medical practices of the far removed medieval period is not nearly so great as the lapse of several centuries would indicate." Science advanced, but medicine remained stagnant, and southerners suffered as a result.[9] In the earliest years of settlement, some southern cities enjoyed reputations for good health, but contaminated water, infectious mosquitoes, and deplorable social conditions favorable to the spread of disease shattered those unrealistic fantasies. Charlestonians, for example, boasted of their healthfulness in 1666, but within twenty years, they uprooted the city in search of a safer location.[10] The South shared many diseases with the rest of the nation but experienced them in more virulent form because of its hot, muggy climate. It also bore the burden of imported African diseases.[11] The climate, coupled with underdeveloped economic, social, and educational conditions, also subjected southerners to epidemics, initially smallpox and malaria and then, from the early nineteenth century, cholera and yellow fever. Fever became the scourge of the South, ravaging at least one seaboard city each year in the 1840s and 1850s.[12] Epidemic and endemic illnesses, to which southerners hardly knew how to respond, made life in the South less healthy, and shorter, than life in the North.[13] By the 1820s and 1830s, the South had gained an unenviable reputation for ill health, a reputation that in part explains the low levels of immigration to the region.[14] Even southern partisans who attempted to vindicate their region from charges of unhealthiness had to face the uncomfortable truth. A researcher in New Orleans hoped to use statistics to prove that his city was not "the Golgotha which it was every where represented to be," but when the numbers came in, he discovered that New Orleans "has manifestly been the most unhealthy city in the civilized world."[15] When it came to medical care, the South needed all the help it could get, whatever the source.

With the exception of New Orleans and a few other cities, the South lacked major urban areas, and their absence made a difference in southern health. In some respects, it helped. The absence of dense populations and urban slums discouraged certain diseases. The isolation of rural southern doctors may have sharpened their skills and opened them to innovation.[16] But the absence of urban cultural centers made it hard to build medical schools and form professional organizations.[17]

Although the South could not match the North, the region had some resources, and during the eighteenth century it made progress. Even before the Revolution, southerners traveled abroad for the medical training they could not get at home. At one time, Charleston had more alumni of European medical schools than any other city in the colonies.[18] After 1730, increasing numbers of Americans published articles in European medical journals. The names of Charlestonians appeared regularly, and the city compared favorably with all other British provincial cities.[19] After 1800, southern aspirants to the medical profession often went north for their training and then brought their knowledge back home.

The region eventually formed its own institutions. In 1823, Charleston opened the Medical College of the State of South Carolina. Soon after, similar schools opened at the University of Virginia and in the cities of Augusta, New Orleans, and Richmond. By 1839, Transylvania Medical College at Lexington, Kentucky, had 257 students; only one other American school had more. The medical college at Louisville ranked third with 204.[20] Cities vied with one another for medical schools, with Charleston and Mobile gaining renown for the facilities they offered for clinical education.[21] Once schools were in place, medical journals followed. The *Southern Journal of Medicine and Surgery* appeared in Augusta in 1836, and Charlestonians promptly added the *Southern Journal of Medicine and Pharmacy.* The South remained rural, but the growth of roughly a half dozen cities by 1840 produced new cultural and scientific institutions, including medical societies.[22] Soon the region was laying claim to some of the best doctors and surgeons in antebellum American.[23]

The growth of a distinct southern identity stimulated southern medical education and health care. Southerners believed that northern medical schools could not train people for southern conditions. Practitioners in other regions also believed that regional needs should shape the approach to health care, but southerners made the argument with unusual vehemence.[24] Samuel Cartwright, for example, argued that Hippocrates had written his doctrines with a southern climate in mind, specifically the Aegean island of Cos. Only those living in similar climates, for example in the Deep South, could fully understand and apply his teachings.[25]

By the 1840s and 1850s, debates over the relative salubrity and the competency of medical professionals of various regions developed an acrimonious tone that both reflected and contributed to the worsening relations between North and South.[26] In the winter of 1859–1860, in an ominous portent of things to come, three hundred southern medical students in Philadelphia and fifty in New York seceded from their schools and transferred en masse to southern institutions. By this time, the cause was not belief in southern medical distinctiveness so much as a rejection of what was perceived to be the poisonous political and moral atmosphere of the North.[27]

The argument for medical distinctiveness largely reflected southern physicians' economic self-interest, hopes for elevating their profession's social status, and sensitivity to disparagement by northern colleagues. But it was also part of a much broader movement toward economic, cultural, and political regionalism.[28] As southerners began to assert their cultural independence, and to resent their reliance on northern schools for their doctors and surgeons, they began to call for their own medical institutions. Indeed, coherent arguments in favor of southern medical distinctiveness generally emerged as justifications for establishing separate institutions. In Mobile, for example, advocates for a local medical school argued not only that it would keep students and their tuition money at home and allow future doctors to study the diseases peculiar to the region, but also that it would make Alabama less dependent on the North. Advocates would train a generation of southern doctors for a distinctly southern culture.[29]

Catholics shared this southern pride in the quality of the region's health care. Following an account of the opening of a medical college in Charleston, the *Catholic Miscellany* boasted that "few cities in the Union" could provide "better opportunities for Medical proficiency than Charleston is likely to create."[30] Years later, the paper praised the city for its "well deserved character for affectionate benevolence to the sick and the indigent."[31]

The South boasted of its medical schools, but many were of dubious quality.[32] Aspiring doctors could generally attend medical school and become physicians without ever having gone to college. Many medical schools had virtually no admissions requirements. Some were essentially "diploma mills" with no campuses, labs, or faculties.[33] A student at the East Alabama Male College (later Auburn University) noticed that many of his friends were rushing to Mobile to become doctors without sufficient preparation. "The majority of them, when they graduate will not be competent to wait on a sick horse. They are not competent to read medicine, as it should be read," he complained.[34]

Reformers struggled to raise the standards of medical education, but even more glaring problems hindered southern health care. The region found it almost impossible to care for the health of the poor and to cope with epidemics. The burden of charity toward the poor fell largely on overworked doctors. Southerners assumed that doctors would pass on to their paying patients the expense of caring for the poor, but even wealthy clients treated their medical bills as a low priority. Some cities established almshouses, which soon required infirmaries, and they became the first municipal hospitals. Such public efforts on behalf of the sick poor made little lasting difference, and many of the poor refused to avail themselves of the services. They felt that accepting charity demeaned them. As a result, health care for the poor continued to devolve largely on individual doctors.[35] During epidemics, care for the poor became not only a burden on doctors but also a grave danger to them. Doctors consistently suffered high mortality rates. During the 1854 yellow fever epidemic in Savannah, for example, 10 of the roughly thirty physicians attempting to care for the city's 18,000 inhabitants died within a few weeks.[36] Catholics proved eager to care for the poor, even during epidemics, and so filled a void in southern health care.

State and local governments were largely to blame for the South's inability to cope with epidemics, particularly yellow fever. No statewide board of health existed in the antebellum South, and although boards of health did appear in various cities, including Charleston (1808) and Mobile (1841), they generally came into being only when a fever was already in full force and then dissolved as soon as the danger passed. Powerful business lobbies hindered the boards' work, keeping them from warning the public about epidemics out of fear of harming commerce. Business interests also helped render quarantine systems, which most cities had on the books by 1850, ineffective, viewing them as restraints on trade. Demands for hygienic reform occasionally goaded the boards into action; for example, Charleston enjoyed improvements in drainage and cleanliness by the 1850s, but such progress was atypical. Hogs, cows, and packs of stray dogs plagued Mobile as late as the 1850s, the beneficiaries of unenforced, or nonexistent, health codes. City governments typically confined improvements to business districts where they would bring the highest returns. Sanitation also fell prey to the spoils system, with street-cleaning contracts often going to political cronies who, not surprisingly, took little interest in the work. Most states even refused to collect the vital statistics necessary to track and study disease. Only South Carolina, Virginia, and Kentucky required the registration of such statistics, and each began only in 1853 to collect them.[37] Lawmakers hesitated largely because southern doctors could not agree on the most effective means to combat disease. Baffled by debates and by myriad proposals, legislatures chose inertia, leaving the task of caring for their citizens to others.

The failings of southern health care also stemmed from its openness and lack of uniform standards. These were lamentably familiar problems. On the eve of the Revolution, the colonies were home to roughly 3,500 medical practitioners. Only four hundred had any formal medical training, and only about two hundred held medical degrees. These "doctors" often farmed, practiced law, or preached. The line between lay practitioner and medical professional was vague, if it existed at all. Results, not training, earned one the status of a doctor. Clergymen often enjoyed public esteem for their medical prowess, and even slaves often had the reputation of being healers.[38]

One clergyman who tried his hand at medicine was Fr. John Baptist Mary David. Born in Brittany in 1761, David joined the Sulpicians in 1783 and received ordination two years later. Under pressure during the French Revolution, he fled to America, where he arrived in 1792. Although inclined to corpulence, he was an intellectual in appearance and in fact, and he delighted in composing both theological treatises and sacred music. Described by Archbishop Carroll as "eminent in prudence, constancy, ecclesiastical learning, piety, zeal for instruction," he was considered for the sees of New Orleans and Philadelphia, but he successfully begged to be allowed to remain in Kentucky. He proved well-suited for mission work in Kentucky, taking an active role in teaching, ministering to the sick, and engaging in controversies with Protestants.[39] Among his many roles, David assumed that of doctor when several of his seminarians fell sick in 1813. Seemingly stretching church regulations that allowed clergy to practice medicine only if they had training and as a last resort, he used a medical guide and basic supplies, and he wrote another priest to ask for suggestions. Only when his own efforts failed did David call for a more qualified doctor.[40] Necessity prompted David to pick up his medical bag, but he did so with the belief, common among southerners, that he was as good as any doctor.

Southerners eschewed doctors not only because they were often unavailable, ineffective, or expensive, but also because an entire industry existed to support domestic medicine. Like Fr. David, many southerners employed their own resources first and only called a doctor if their own efforts failed. By the early nineteenth century, a flourishing market in medical manuals offered Americans an array of techniques to protect and restore their health. Information and remedies also circulated through journals and newspapers and by word of mouth. Southerners could choose from a variety of medical sects or schools of thought. Many did so in reaction to mainstream medicine's emphasis on harsh drugs and copious bloodletting. Dr. Edward H. Barton, a southern leader of the public health movement, typified attitudes to heroic measures when he wrote that "heroism in war is built upon the slaughter of our fellow creatures; it is little less in physic."[41] As alternatives to painful and often fatal healing techniques, many southerners turned to hydropathy, homeopathy, or whisky. A sect known as the Thomsonians, who advocated domestic botanic remedies, drew large numbers of southern adherents thanks in part to their founder's motto: "Every man his own physician." In some respects, this innovation was a product of necessity in a largely rural society where many people lived far from a professional physician. But it was also due to a deeply rooted belief about the nature of medicine. As one manual writer put it, any man could amputate a limb "unless he is an idiot or an absolute fool."[42]

Population growth, westward expansion, and the democratic ethos of the post-Revolutionary period made it difficult to remedy this situation. As early as 1760, reformers had sought to raise requirements. The effort continued for 150 years, continually banging against the wall of laissez-faire competition. By the 1820s, some states passed legislation requiring the MD degree for practitioners. But the states proved far more willing to pass such legislation than to enforce it and although laws requiring medical degrees helped medical schools, they did little to ensure their quality.[43] Within a few decades, the futility had become apparent. By 1845, ten states had repealed their licensing laws. Only three had even pretended to enforce them, and eight had never implemented laws at all. By defeating such laws, Jacksonian Democrats asserted "their inalienable rights to life, liberty, and quackery."[44] This ethos, prevalent on the southern frontier, devalued professional training and saw attempts to impose uniform standards as an elite conspiracy. Nationwide the abolition of licensing laws and the growth of medical sects marked a decline in the prestige of the medical profession.[45] At the same time, disease and rising populations increased demand for doctors and made it impractical to restrict supply. By the late antebellum period, despite real gains in medical knowledge and training, virtually anyone could practice medicine.[46]

Protestant gratitude for Catholic health care makes sense within this context. Catholics specialized in the two areas where southern health care was weakest: care for the poor and responses to epidemics. Although some lay Catholics practiced medicine by profession, the priests and nuns who cared for the sick did so purely out of charity.[47] Care for those most in need was part of their vocation. Because they administered care in private homes, or in hospitals independent of almshouses, their services did not carry the stigma attached to public hospitals for the indigent. Even the Catholic religious who did not focus on health care served as a ready pool of volunteers during epidemics, able to relocate at short notice when necessary. Catholic caregivers were able to adapt to sudden demands more quickly than other institutions, and Protestants were impressed.

Protestant support reflected the fluidity of antebellum medicine. The absence of uniform standards for doctors and nurses hindered professionalization, but it created space for others to practice, including clergy and women. Clergy had practiced medicine in colonial America because they stood among the most educated. They continued to practice medicine until the 1820s, and reformers were still complaining about their "presumption" as late as 1850. Even when they withdrew from the practice, clergy raised money and advocated for hospitals.[48] When Catholic priests rushed to aid epidemic victims or tend to the dying, they were following well-worn paths. Southerners were accustomed to the overlap of physical and spiritual care.

Women religious had to live with more ambiguity. Like the clergy, women figured prominently in colonial health care. By the early eighteenth century, however, the public turned away from women as professional healers. Women retreated to the margins of medical practice, but they refused to disappear. After 1850, they began to claim anew a place in medicine, but their efforts created a backlash. Their critics argued that they were unfit, mentally and physically, for medical work. Many viewed it as absurd that a woman should be a doctor.[49] But a few welcomed women's services, and some even compared them favorably to their male counterparts. One Catholic traveler in Kentucky told the *Miscellany* that his male physician proved utterly useless but that a woman's potion quickly cured him.[50] Immigrants turned often to women for care, recalling perhaps the importance of midwives in Europe.[51] Americans may have rejected women as professional physicians, but they did not discriminate when it came to domestic medicine. Whether in the plantation house or the slave quarters, women often took responsibility for nursing, administering medicine, and deciding when to call for a doctor.[52] The history of women in American health care shaped southerners' reception of Catholic women religious. Those willing to turn to women for care were grateful for the aid of nuns. Even the critics of women as doctors recognized that the work of female Catholic orders continued a long tradition. It was no bizarre innovation.

Although nuns could clash with male medical authorities, they had a reputation as caregivers that even the doctors could not ignore.

The Origins of Catholic Charities

Catholic clergy devoted themselves to caring for the sick. In Kentucky, Fr. David ministered to the infirm immediately upon his arrival in 1811.[53] Another of the first priests in Kentucky, Fr. Stephen Badin, noted that missionaries in Kentucky "are obliged to ride on horseback nearly every day of the year, and to brace often alone the solitude of the forests, the darkness of night, and the inclemency of the seasons, to minister to the sick and to visit their congregations."[54] In one typical month in 1812, Bishop Flaget traveled almost two hundred miles, largely to visit the sick.[55] In Alabama, Jesuits from Spring Hill College exchanged their classrooms for the bedsides of epidemic victims.[56] In Charleston, diocesan officials curtailed publication of the *Miscellany* in order to devote themselves to caring for the stricken during epidemics.[57]

Priests cared for their flocks and for Protestants as well. Bishop Flaget kept a journal in which he recorded visits to sick Protestants as well as to "a professed infidel, who has lost his mind, and in his ravings sometimes calls for a priest."[58] Ministry across denominational lines was by no means unusual. "'I spend all my time among the sick, irrespective of their character or creed,'" explained a New Orleans priest to a Protestant colleague. Prohibited from offering the sacrament of extreme unction to non-Catholics, this priest had even devised a separate rite to soothe the consciences, and hopefully save the souls, of those dying outside the church.[59]

Priests cared for the sick wherever they found them. In 1792, Flaget nursed smallpox victims in Pittsburgh while waiting for the river to rise so that he could make his way west.[60] Fr. Simon Bruté, a confidant of several Kentucky priests and first bishop of Vincennes, cared for an injured sailor on a voyage to Bordeaux. Bruté was eminently qualified for such work, having received a doctorate in medicine in Paris, where he finished first among over a thousand students.[61] Not all excelled at pastoral care. One Kentucky priest scandalized both Catholics and Protestants by inquiring of the dying whether they had made provisions for the church, and for him, in their wills.[62] But most southern priests were adept at ministering to the ill.

Care for the sick had long been a part of the church's mission, but the canon law of the late Middle Ages and the decrees of the Council of Trent (1545–1563) prohibited priests from practicing medicine. Some ignored the restrictions, especially missionaries in remote regions, and in 1641, the Sacred

Congregation for the Propagation of the Faith permitted priests to practice medicine as a means of facilitating conversions. Even then, they could practice only if they had medical training and their mission had no other physician, and they could not perform surgery or receive compensation.[63]

Catholics in the South could follow the example of the Jesuits of colonial Maryland in formulating their approach to health care. The most prominent of these early Jesuits was their superior, Fr. Andrew White (1579–1656). White was born to an English family, possibly in London, and studied at Douai College, where he matriculated in 1593. He received ordination in 1605 and promptly returned to England, flouting a law that made it an act of treason for a priest to enter the country. Soon after, he entered the Jesuit novitiate at Louvain, returning to England on several occasions to conduct missions. White's "daring and impetuous personality" provoked conflicts with his superiors, but it encouraged the Calverts to entrust him with spiritual guardianship of their new Maryland colony.[64] White arrived with the first colonists in 1634 and immediately set to work tending to the people's spiritual and medical needs. A report to the Jesuit provincial for 1639 included an account of White's ministering to a sick Piscataway leader named Tayac. He gave him "a certain powder of known efficacy mixed with holy water," and the following day, he performed a bloodletting. Tayac recovered, embraced Catholicism, and urged all the Piscataways to do likewise.[65] In another incident three years later, White was more restrained. When called to an injured Piscataway seemingly on the brink of death, he summarized the core articles of the Catholic faith, heard the man's confession, recited passages from the Gospels and a litany to Mary, and applied a cross to the man's wounds. Again the victim recovered.[66] Such exploits became part of Catholic lore and helped make care for the sick, whether Catholic or non-Catholic, a part of ministry.

Southern clergy constantly referred in their letters and diaries to caring for the sick. Most seem to have followed the dictates of the church, and of common sense, and abstained from surgery or specialized forms of medicine. Often they performed traditional rituals. When four Kentucky children fell into convulsions—and one issued streams of profanity—the priests used holy water and scapulars and contemplated an exorcism.[67] Priests' first concern was always to administer the sacraments to the dying. They tried to convey the "consolations of religion" and lamented if they arrived too late.[68]

Like priests, nuns cared for the spiritual and psychological needs of the sick, but they also nursed their bodies. This was particularly true during times of great demand, such as epidemics or war, or in Catholic hospitals.

The Catholic religious specialized in pastoral rather than medical care. The line between the two often blurred, however, in the frontier conditions of much of the antebellum South, where there was often little that anyone could do for the sick beyond trying to make them comfortable in body and spirit.

In part to provide regular care for the sick, priests and bishops helped establish religious orders of women. In Kentucky, Fr. David, along with several laywomen, established the Sisters of Nazareth in 1812, urging them to succor the sick and destitute.[69] The sisters based their constitutions on the rules written in the early 1630s by St. Vincent de Paul for the French Daughters of Charity.[70] St. Vincent recognized that cloistral regulations, common to female orders, would hinder his order's focus on works of charity. He declared that his sisters would have "no monastery but the houses of the sick, no cell but a hired room, no cloister but the streets of the city or the wards of hospitals."[71] One of the first acts of charity of the sisters in Kentucky was to shelter elderly men and women in cabins near their house.[72] Fifteen years later, the *Miscellany* described the order as an "association of ladies of all religious denominations for the benevolent purpose of aiding the aged poor." It noted that the order assisted the poor "without sectarian distinction or preference or intrusion."[73]

The sisters cared for the suffering, regardless of creed, during Kentucky's numerous epidemics. During the cholera epidemic of 1832, in Louisville, they nursed the sick alongside the city's pastor and Bishop Flaget, who returned from a visitation to aid the victims. The following spring, Fr. David was celebrating Mass in Bardstown when he received word that cholera had broken out at the home of a non-Catholic family nearby. Interrupting his homily, he informed the newly elected superior, Mother Frances Gardiner, who summoned two other sisters and flew to the stricken family. At the home, they met two sisters of another order. Flaget soon joined them, only to encounter a scene of utter desolation. Several slaves lay dead or dying in a single room, along with a son and daughter of the family. The sisters took the mother and father from the house to avoid infection and nursed them in the home of state senator Benjamin Hardin. Throughout the epidemic, they labored there and wherever they encountered the sick.[74]

Like the Sisters of Nazareth, the Sisters of Our Lady of Mercy in Charleston came into being when church leaders encouraged aspirants to religious vows to form a congregation to teach, practice charity, and care for the sick. In 1829, three Irish women living in Baltimore moved to Charleston and formed the core of the new order.[75] These sisters also based their rule on St. Vincent de Paul's. In 1840, Bishop England laid the cornerstone for the sisters' new academy and restated their mission: "to cherish the orphan, to console the afflicted, to teach the ignorant and to solace and minister to the victim of disease."[76] This was by no means easy work. One sister recalled that it was almost laughable to see her colleagues "wade through the mire, with large boots, their habits and cloaks tied up, and lugging along their baskets, which seemed twice as large as themselves, that they might bring relief to the sick in the poor quarter of the town."[77] During epidemics, the sisters traveled to Augusta and other afflicted cities. In 1855, they assisted during outbreaks in Norfolk and Portsmouth, Virginia, nursing in homes, hospitals, and aboard ships. Their efforts won them wide renown. In the 1850s, the sick in Charleston often called them before summoning a doctor. City officials took over the debt the sisters assumed in their ministries, and a relief society run by prominent Protestants gave them alms to distribute.[78]

Bishop England expressed a conviction "that Charleston will bountifully sustain and enlarge" so useful an institution, and he voiced confidence, "that the trust thus placed in the community . . . will not be disappointed."[79] The church praised—and advertised—their usefulness. An announcement for a fundraising fair in 1841, reminded Charlestonians that during epidemics, the sisters "regard not the creed or the country of the patient: his distress and bereavement are the best titles to their attention." The announcement urged support for the sisters as a sound investment: while hoping to avoid an epidemic, "we desire to have amongst us the power of alleviating its infliction and of healing its wounds, should we be again subjected to its severity." The fair netted $4,000.[80]

In addition to establishing orders, bishops recruited communities. In Mobile, Bishop Michael Portier, at the urging of a society of lay women, invited Sisters of Charity from Maryland to care for the diocese's sick and poor.[81] The sisters became a source of "non interrupted consolation" for Portier.[82] On a journey to Europe in 1832, England sought additional women religious to supplement the work of the Sisters of Mercy in Charleston. In a letter to the American bishops, he outlined his plan to bring Ursulines from Ireland.[83] The following January, he reported to Propaganda that he had succeeded in attracting Uruslines from the community of Cork and had already bought them a house in Charleston, a property that cost him $12,000, only $4,000 of which he had on hand.[84] In October 1834, Srs. M. Charles Moloney, Borgia McCarthy, and Antonia Hughes, along with a postulant, joined England on the *Pocahontas,* bound from Liverpool to Philadelphia. Along with them came five young Irish women who intended to join the Sisters of Mercy of Charleston.[85] England later reminded a convention of Georgia Catholics that he had tried for years to secure women religious who would be devoted "to the instruction of the ignorant . . . to the protection of the orphan . . . to the care of the despised and the neglected, and to smoothing the pillow of disease, encouraging those who languish in sickness, endeavoring to restore them to health or to cheer them on towards heaven." Thanks to the Sisters of Mercy and Ursulines, it had "pleased God to bless those efforts."[86] Women religious attained a reputation throughout the South as nurses for the sick.

Catholic Hospitals

The church in the antebellum South continually suffered shortages of personnel and funds. At first, it could merely extend charity through individual acts of ministry. But gradually some Catholic communities established hospitals and orphanages. Protestants were happy to assist.

In establishing hospitals, southern Catholics continued a centuries-old tradition. The Sisters of the Holy Ghost founded the city hospital in Rome in 1204, which became a model for almost one thousand city hospitals across Europe, most established by religious orders, especially of women. Over four centuries later, the Catholic Reformation led to another boom in hospital building, including the French Hôtels-Dieu for the care of the sick poor. The building impulse crossed the Atlantic. In Spanish and French colonies, the church established and ran hospitals that also received support from the state. These included the first Spanish hospital in Santo Domingo (1503), the Hospital de Jesus established by Cortez in Mexico City (1524), and the Hôtel Dieu de Precieux Sang of Quebec (1639).[87] Southern Catholics could also find a precedent for hospital work closer to home. The Ursulines of New Orleans, who established the first permanent settlement of nuns in what would become the United States, took charge of the city hospital upon their arrival in 1727. Receiving subsidies from the civil authorities, they ran the hospital until early 1770, when other demands and a shortage of personnel compelled them to resign.[88]

Diocesan officials and women's religious orders, including the Ursulines, Dominicans, and Sisters of Mercy, built permanent institutions across the South.[89] In Louisville, in 1836, the Sisters of Nazareth opened St. Vincent Infirmary in two rooms of their orphanage. Its purpose was to both address a pressing need in the city and provide a regular source of revenue for the orphanage. This hospital came into existence thirteen years after the Louisville Marine Hospital but operated for half a century before the first Protestant hospital opened its doors.[90]

In Charleston, a Catholic hospital arose from the combined efforts of

Bishop England, the Sisters of Mercy, and an association of lay Catholics. In July 1838, England called a meeting to discuss the needs of newly arrived Catholic laborers, many of whom had come to rebuild the city after a disastrous fire the previous April. In response to his call, a group of lay people established the Brotherhood of San Marino, the first society of workers under Catholic auspices in the United States. The choice of St. Marino as patron reflected admiration for his work in establishing "a community upon the principles of pure democratic republicanism, strict frugality, healthful temperance and exemplary virtue." The brotherhood's constitution made clear that it welcomed Protestant participation. It named England president and only Catholics as officeholders, but it opened membership to all regardless of faith. It prohibited discussion "of politics, elections, religious controversy, national or sectional distinctions, or of any other description which may tend to destroy harmony."[91] Fr. William Burke, the chairman, explained that one of its chief purposes was to allow working men to fulfill their religious duties, "whatever religion they profess." Another objective was support for a small hospital for its members, located in a house converted for that purpose. A year later, the brotherhood received another house, rent free, from the Sisters of Mercy.[92]

The hospital of San Marino immediately went into use, thanks to the prevalence of yellow fever in the summer of 1838. Weeks of oppressive heat and days of incessant rain created an environment in which the fever thrived. Two Sisters of Mercy, Sr. M. Vincent Mahoney and Sr. M. Veronica Cagney, and volunteer nurses staffed the hospital, which cared for about thirty poor laborers and strangers to the city. Despite their labors, 125 Catholics died of fever in less than three months, including 83 natives of Ireland, 11 of Germany, and 13 of the United States. Of those cared for in the hospital, twelve died.[93] Catholics also contributed to a new hospital established at the medical college. England served as a commissioner for the hospital, along with several Protestant ministers and leading citizens, and Catholic parishes joined the city's Protestant and Jewish congregations in sending representatives.[94] The following summer, the sisters reopened the hospital of San Marino during a new outbreak and extended their efforts to Savannah, sending three members in response to an epidemic in that city. The hospital seems to have disbanded soon after the fever, but fourteen years later, in response to another epidemic, Fr. Patrick Lynch opened Roper Hospital where the Sisters of Mercy once again practiced their healing arts.[95]

In Mobile, Catholic hospital work began in the city-run institution. Although the city periodically supported a "pest house" for smallpox victims, for many years its only permanent publicly supported health-care facility was the City Hospital. This hospital began as a one-room house, but, by 1837, it had expanded to accommodate 150 people. The city's mayor and alderman initially managed the hospital until it was decided that contracting the work to private groups would be more economical. Among the groups that took a turn managing the hospital were the Samaritan Society, a nondenominational benevolent association, the Alabama Medical College, and the Sisters of Charity, all of whom agreed to treat paupers without charge.[96] The sisters initially enjoyed good relations with the hospital's governors and had a great deal of independence because there was no resident physician.[97] They ran the institution for several years, losing two of their members during the plague of 1853. When the plague subsided, anti-Catholic and nativist politicians ousted the sisters on the grounds of mismanagement and proselytizing. An investigating committee declared the charges groundless, but the sisters, nonetheless, felt compelled to withdraw. In response, both Catholics and non-Catholics donated money for the sisters to build their own hospital. By May 1855, Providence Infirmary received its first patients. Civic authorities asked the sisters to return to the City Hospital in 1860 and offered "additional securities and advantages" to ensure that they would never again be driven off.[98]

Protestants recognized the value of Catholic hospitals, and Catholics realized that the hospitals helped win them a place in southern society. In one sense, the institutions were evangelical, with priests and nuns encouraging conversion experiences among Catholics and Protestants. But Catholics also tried to respect religious difference. In regions like the South, where Catholics composed a small minority, Catholic caregivers felt pressure to privatize their faith. Such signs of devotionalism as crucifixes, statues, and images, so common in Catholic hospitals in the North, tended in the South to appear in the priests' and sisters' private residences.[99] Religious pluralism engendered in Catholic hospitals "both a self-consciously Catholic attitude and a consideration of Protestant sensibilities."[100]

Catholic views about proselytism in hospitals found expression in a handbook for the Sisters of Charity of Emmitsburg. It dates from 1796 and includes instructions from a French priest to the Daughters of Charity about catechesis for the sick poor. Its "Instructions for the Care of the Sick by M.X." probably came from Mother Mary Xavier Clark, a refugee from Santo Domingo who served as superior general from 1839 to 1845.[101] She encouraged the sisters to care for spiritual needs, but only with Catholic patients. They were first to provide patients with all physical comforts and then to ask "'of what religion are you my good friend?' If he says: 'I am a

Protestant'—she should say nothing more but give him all the temporal assistance he needs." Clark recognized that even patients in Catholic hospitals could have anti-Catholic prejudice. Sisters should avoid discussion of Catholicism with their patients, "because some of these poor creatures are very bitter against our holy religion." This did not mean that sisters should disregard Protestants' souls. Clark instructed each sister to "offer silent supplications to the father of mercies for a deathbed conversion, for a special act of infinite goodness, like that exercised on the penitent thief." All care included a spiritual component: "your charity to their bodies will aid them to raise their minds to God."[102] In all likelihood, members of other orders shared Clark's views. Catholics may have used their hospitals to change Protestants' minds, but they did not use them to win Protestant souls.

Catholic Orphanages

Epidemics and disease left scores of orphans in their wakes. For most of the eighteenth and nineteenth centuries, the public saw care of orphans as a task for religious and philanthropic groups, and Catholics accepted the responsibility. Female religious orders took the lead in running these institutions, often building on years of experience. The Ursulines, who arrived in New Orleans in 1727, not only ran a hospital but also cared for orphans. Decades earlier, Ursulines and Daughters of Charity accompanied girls who left their families in France to become wives of settlers in colonies along the Gulf Coast. One such band arrived in Mobile in 1704, and another in Biloxi in 1721. In both cases, the sisters cared for the girls until they married.[103] Care for orphans flowed from the same Gospel imperatives as care for the sick. In both cases, Catholics, particularly women religious, provided the charity on which southern society relied.

In Kentucky, the Sisters of Nazareth opened Louisville's first orphanage in response to the cholera epidemic of 1832. In the fall, the sisters received word of a destitute family of non-Catholic emigrants, recently arrived from Pennsylvania. Mother Catherine Spalding visited the family and found the mother dead, the teenage daughter severely ill, the father, and two other children, including a small baby. Although the teenage girl resolved to care for the family, she died within two weeks. The father asked the sisters to take charge of the two surviving children, who became the nucleus of St. Vincent's Orphan Asylum. Mother Spalding no doubt had a special interest in caring for orphans. Born in Maryland to one of the first families of the state, the descendants of a prominent English Catholic family, she had lost both of her parents by age ten. Upon her election, at the tender age of nineteen, as the first superior of the Sisters of Nazareth, she devoted herself to care for the vulnerable. By the end of 1832, the sisters had taken in four additional young girls, and within a year, they had charge of nearly thirty more. The sisters purchased a lot on which to build an orphanage and held a fair that raised $1,150. In the spring of 1833, the orphanage was complete. It relied from the outset on donations, proceeds from the sale of articles produced by the orphans and sisters, and the generosity of local farmers and merchants. By 1836, the sisters had to buy a hotel for space. The three-story brick building, with four and a half acres of grounds, provided space for the orphans, whose numbers had grown to between forty and fifty.[104]

The church plunged into the building of orphanages. In 1843, the Sisters of the Good Shepherd, invited from France by Bishop Flaget, opened one, and they also aided delinquent girls in Louisville and six other cities. The sisters relied largely on Protestants, who not only furnished them with gifts but also purchased the needlework that provided the sisters with the bulk of their income.[105] In 1850, the male component of St. Vincent's separated to form a new orphanage, St. Thomas's, at the seminary in Nelson County. That same year, an association of German Catholics in Louisville established the St. Joseph Orphan's Asylum. With the exception of the Protestant Episcopal Orphan Asylum, established in 1835, no Protestant orphanages existed until the 1850s, and no state-run orphanages until after the war.[106] Female Catholic orders in Kentucky also cared for orphans through their schools, often waiving tuition for as many as they could afford to accept, and often lodging them with the boarding students.[107]

Mobile and Charleston became sites for even more homes for orphans. In Mobile, Bishop Portier began to care for them soon after his arrival in 1830. Portier was born in France in 1795. He received his first impressions of the priesthood from fugitive clerics who tutored him while seeking refuge in his parents' home. He entered the seminary at Lyon soon after the Napoleonic Concordat permitted its reopening. While a student there, he heard an appeal from Bishop DuBourg of Louisiana who was in France seeking recruits. DuBourg described the privations and dangers that awaited missionaries to the South; Portier was among the first to volunteer. He arrived in Maryland in 1817, received ordination at St. Louis in 1818, served as vicar-general of New Orleans, and received consecration as vicar-apostolic of Alabama and Florida in 1825. Four years later, he became the first bishop of Mobile.[108]

Care for orphans was one of Portier's top concerns. Two of his servants fed them and collected donations of food and clothing from city merchants. This ad hoc system proved inadequate after the yellow fever epidemic of 1837, so Portier called a meeting of laywomen to devise a permanent solution. These women soon formed the Catholic Female Charitable Society of Mobile for the care of orphans and the relief of the destitute. It probably cared from the outset for the needy of all faiths, because no mention of religion appears in its mission statement. Laywomen ran the society, electing nine managers and various officers, who charged yearly dues of $6.00 plus donations from each member. In 1838, Portier proposed that the society open an orphanage. He offered the use of a three-story brick building, contingent on the society's willingness to make $1,500 worth of repairs. The women unanimously accepted the offer and set to work preparing the building. Within five months, St. Mary's Home, also known as the "Asylum," opened its doors. The society funded a full-time superintendent to run the facility and teach and care for the children.[109]

The orphanage required more funds than the society could provide solely from dues, so in 1839, the women sponsored a fair. The owner of the Alabama Hotel in Mobile, a member of the Alabama House of Representatives, offered the use of its grand room. The fair raised over $2,000, and it became an annual event for decades. A Mobile paper wished its readers "hearts open as day to the calls of the Orphan Fair."[110] The orphanage received bequests and legacies, including an 1840 donation of $5,000. In September, the society received the lot of land behind the orphanage as a gift, and in 1841, donations came in from as far away as Montgomery and Tuscaloosa. Two local doctors provided free medical care for a number of years. A local funeral home buried without charge an infant who had died at the orphanage after being found abandoned on a road outside Mobile. The owner of the city waterworks provided free water. In 1840, the state of Alabama incorporated the Catholic Female Charitable Society of Mobile, and six years later, the managers of the orphanage petitioned the legislature to change the charter to allow them to receive funds from the county of Mobile. The lawmakers acquiesced, and the orphanage received its first payment of $500 in 1846.[111] Non-Catholics were pleased with the results of this generosity. "The system adopted is paternal, and its effects are seen in the cheerful and contented faces of these poor, helpless orphans," noted a visitor to the public exhibition, adding that "if all the children were members of the Bishop's own household, he could not have displayed more gratification when one of them exhibited superior culture."[112]

Support from the community allowed for expansion. In 1839, the society paid for a dining hall. Several years later, it erected a new brick building using not only financial donations but also volunteer supplies and labor.

In subsequent decades, the society acquired even more property and expanded the physical plant, making it possible to accept more children. The number of children increased from three to thirty-one in less than a year. Such growth required the assistance of trained workers, so in 1840, the society asked Portier to request the Sisters of Charity of Emmitsburg to send three or four sisters. Within a year, the society collected $432.00 to send to Emmitsburg, and in 1841, four Sisters of Charity arrived in Mobile to assume control of the orphanage. By 1845, 88 children lived at the orphanage, a number that grew to 102 in a year and increased, by 1853, to 200, ranging in age from three months to thirteen years.[113]

In the year that St. Mary's opened, Portier founded an orphanage for boys. The Catholic Male Orphan Asylum of Mobile received on average fifteen boys a year, a number that almost always included Protestants.[114] In 1847, the decision by the Sisters of Charity to cease tending to male orphans led to the opening of a second facility for boys. The previous year, aware of the sisters' impending policy change, Portier had arranged for members of a French order called the Brothers of the Sacred Heart to come to Mobile and take charge of orphan boys.[115] He promised to provide lodgings and funds to cover expenses, and five brothers arrived in Mobile in 1847. After a few weeks to learn English, they took charge of eighteen boys in a house rented for the purpose. By September, the orphanage had a permanent home on land purchased by the female society.

In Charleston, a Catholic orphanage came into being in an atmosphere of religious controversy. England objected when the city-run orphanage refused to allow Catholics to teach religion to the Catholic orphans. In 1825, he wrote to its commissioners to explain his position, making it clear that he had no intention of interfering with non-Catholics. He insisted that Catholics be taught only by Catholics, who should have a fair opportunity to offer instruction. England appealed to the liberality and benevolence of the commissioners, but they were unmoved. The chairman merely pointed out that the church attached to the orphanage was open to priests in rotation with other clergy every Sunday afternoon.[116] England lost this battle, but years later, when three women asked to take religious vows, he urged them to form a congregation to care for Catholic orphan girls, "whom heretofore I have been constrained to see collocated in places where they lose their faith and their morals." In 1830, the Sisters of Mercy began to care for the orphans, and by 1841, when they acquired a new house, ten of them cared for seventy orphans and twenty poor students.[117]

Although Catholics in Charleston cared for orphans to protect their own, they also assisted non-Catholic agencies. In 1824, England lectured in Augusta at a fundraiser for the education of orphaned girls in the city. Members of all denominations attended and made donations. According to the *Miscellany,* the program held up a vision of ecumenical harmony, seeking to educate orphans "of every religious denomination, who are not obliged to learn the catechism of a church to which they do not belong, but are placed under the religious care of their own pastors."[118] The *Miscellany,* under England's editorship, had a motive to overstate the success of such events and Catholics' good relations with Protestants. However, it was also quick to note and condemn instances of prejudice against Catholics. The paper walked a fine line in claiming a public voice for Catholics without antagonizing the Protestant majority, but its outspokenness in the face of anti-Catholic hostility lends credence to its descriptions of interfaith cooperation.

Catholic Sacrifice

Care for the sick took a heavy toll on the Catholic religious. In Kentucky, Bishop Flaget sent a young priest named Philip Horstman to Louisville to minister to the sick during a typhoid fever outbreak in 1822. Horstman contracted the disease and soon died, along with a Catholic layman who had been caring for him. At the funeral, Flaget was overcome with grief and could not finish his homily.[119] Over a decade later, Sr. Patricia Bamber died while nursing victims of the 1833 cholera epidemic as did three other Sisters of Nazareth and Fr. William Byrne, who expired after administering the sacraments to a sick black woman.[120] Flaget reported the stress of caring for the sick on the Dominicans of Kentucky: "For more than three weeks, night and day, they were constantly employed in fulfilling their ministry among the sick, taking rest only half-clothed, and I would say almost all their meals on horseback." Despite this, "a holy joy all the same appeared on their visages because their ministry had been blessed by the happiest success both among Catholics and among Protestants."[121] Other dioceses endured similar losses. In Charleston in 1838, an outbreak of fever left only Bishop England and a priest fit for duty, prompting them to ask the public to leave the names of the sick at the cathedral so that they could minister more efficiently.[122] In Mobile, the first sister superior of the Sisters of Charity died of yellow fever in 1849. She had spent over seven years laboring among the poor in Mobile; in the weeks before her death, she nursed fever victims.[123]

Bishops labored alongside priests and nuns, and they too paid a heavy price. Flaget traveled throughout Kentucky during the 1833 epidemic, administering the sacraments and nursing the sick. Laid low by the disease, he hovered on the brink of death for three days. This was not his first brush with death. Forty years earlier, he had contracted smallpox while ministering to sick slaves, Indians, and parishioners in Vincennes, Indiana. Several months before Flaget's narrow escape from cholera, Edward D. Fenwick, the scion of an old Maryland family who had established the Dominicans in Kentucky and labored there for years before becoming bishop of Cincinnati, died of the disease while on a visitation of his diocese.[124] In Savannah, Bishop Francis Gartland died during the yellow fever epidemic of 1854 when he refused to flee the city and instead went door-to-door assisting the sick.[125]

The Catholic religious sacrificed themselves on behalf of the sick throughout the antebellum era. Before becoming bishop of Mobile, Portier fell sick while caring for fever victims at Natchez in 1819.[126] In Baltimore, fever killed eight priests between 1793 and 1800, and it incapacitated six others. The losses were so severe that Bishop John Carroll worried for the future of the church in America, and he asked Catholics to use prudence when calling for priests.[127] The parish of Fell's Point, just outside Baltimore, was particularly hard-hit. Fr. John Floyd, the parish's second priest and a member of the first seminary class in the United States, became infected in 1797 while administering the sacraments to a fever victim. He died four days later at the age of twenty-nine. Seven years later, Floyd's successor, Fr. Michael Cuddy, died after contracting fever in the course of his duties. The parish's fifth pastor, Fr. John Francis Moranvillé, served during the city's worst yellow fever epidemic from 1819 to 1821. Many residents fled, but Moranvillé remained, visiting the sick and arranging for food, medicine, and nurses. Struck twice with fever, he never completely recovered, and he died three years later.[128] Few areas suffered like Fell's Point did, but Catholics gave their lives caring for the sick in many other southern cities. In Norfolk, Virginia, in 1855, a yellow fever epidemic killed two thousand people, including half the city's physicians. While many Protestant ministers fled the city, Fr. Matthew O'Keefe stayed, even after he contracted the disease twice. O'Keefe ministered to people "of all classes and creeds" alongside a Presbyterian minister named George Armstrong, with whom he made a pact that if either died, the other would celebrate his funeral. That same year in Portsmouth, Virginia, the Irish-born Fr. Francis Devlin labored throughout the three months that yellow fever raged in the city's "Irish Row" ghetto in 1855. He worked ten to twelve hours a day, praying with the afflicted, bringing them food, and often digging their graves when others feared to risk contagion. Devlin contracted the fever three times. The third time, he died. When the epidemic finally ended, the people of Portsmouth constructed a monument in his honor.[129]

Even the strongest priests were often no match for disease. Fr. Charles Nerinckx was born in Belgium in 1761. He received ordination in 1785, and he quickly rose through the clerical ranks. When the French Revolution erupted, Nerinckx's prominence made him a prime target, and he spent seven years in hiding in a hospital run by an aunt. Eventually, he resolved to escape to America, where he arrived in November 1804. After just a few months studying English at Georgetown College, Nerinckx, following instructions from Bishop Carroll, headed for Kentucky.[130] Nerinckx was an austere man whose rigorous discipline led to conflicts both with his parishioners and with other clergy. But he compensated for his failings with unusual physical strength, seemingly endless energy, and the ability to endure hardship. According to Kentucky lore, he once rode straight through the night to elude a pack of wolves in the wilderness. On another occasion, when a man, who felt slighted by Nerinckx, waylaid him, the priest calmly subdued the attacker and held him until he promised to repent. Nerinckx not only organized the construction of many of Kentucky's first churches but also took part in the labor himself. It was said that when he lifted one end of a log, it took two or three men to lift the other end.[131] Nerinckx seemed immune to persecution, the dangers of the frontier, and hard labor, but he could not escape the ravages of disease-carrying microbes. In 1824, he traveled to Missouri, where he died of fever contracted while ministering to an isolated Catholic settlement.[132] The *Miscellany* expressed confidence that the people of Kentucky would long remember him for his willingness "night and day—all seasons . . . to fly to the call of the distressed," even at the cost of his own life.[133]

Clergy traveled far from home to reach the suffering. Four Sisters of Charity traveled from Maryland to St. Louis to take charge of a hospital in 1828. In 1849, during one of numerous epidemics, they cared for nearly 1,500 cholera victims, losing 500 patients and 2 of their own number.[134] Joseph Adams, a Kentuckian ordained in 1840, became a Jesuit at Spring Hill College in Mobile. Although he taught at the college for a while, by the 1850s, he was in Baton Rouge, caring for victims of yellow fever. In 1855, he died in that ministry.[135] The Catholic religious in the South devoted themselves to caring for the sick. Few escaped from these labors unscathed.

The demands of ministry to widely scattered congregations, often in difficult environments with little assistance, drained the strength of the

Catholic religious and left them vulnerable to disease. In 1803, the death of Fr. Michael Fournier, an energetic and popular French priest who ruptured a vessel while lifting beams of wood, left Fr. Badin alone in Kentucky.[136] The following year, he reported to Bishop Carroll that he had been "attacked with a transient fever and quinsy caused by habitual fatigues and too great an exercise of speaking." He noted that even his hair was beginning to turn gray.[137] Four years later, Badin attempted to regulate sick calls in order to conserve his strength. After Fournier's death, he found himself responsible for six thousand people spread over eight hundred square miles, "all liable to die with sickness, and likely except infants to send for me . . . at any time of day and night, by all seasons and weathers, and from any distance." Finding that "more than once I have mounted my horse in the greatest anguish of body, fits of fever, colds, insuperable sleepiness (caused by excessive fatigues) to visit persons less sick than myself," Badin asked for a donation of a dollar for each visit so that he could buy a new horse, and he required that a physician certify that the patient was near death. Badin's parishioners accused him of greed, leading him to defend himself indignantly to Archbishop Leonard Neale of Baltimore.[138]

Constant travel, often on horseback in heat, rain, or cold, sapped the health of the Catholic religious. Flaget contracted fever after months of "traversing immense prairies, exposed to legions of flies and musquitos [*sic*], who covered both travelers and horses with blood," during a visitation to Illinois and Missouri in the summer of 1814.[139] Not only did the travel drain his strength, but at each stop, he preached once or twice a day, up to four times on Sundays, and heard confessions for hours, very often late into the night and beginning again at three o'clock in the morning.[140] Later in life, Flaget observed that in reflecting on his early years in the diocese, he could scarcely remember having spent four days continuously under one roof.[141] Mother Catherine Spalding of the Sisters of Nazareth died in 1858 from bronchitis. Bishop Martin John Spalding attributed her illness to getting her feet wet while visiting a poor family.[142] Travel posed numerous hazards. In 1818, while on a visitation to Michigan, Flaget was pitched from a carriage, down a slope and into a river. He survived but suffered an injury to his shoulder that would bother him the rest of his life.[143] England suffered a similar injury on the road to Madison, Georgia, in the middle of the winter of 1829.[144] Years earlier, Fr. Anthony Salmon, a French priest who arrived in Kentucky in 1799, had met a worse fate. Riding in bad weather to visit a Protestant whom he was preparing for baptism, he fell from his horse and died of his injuries after several hours.[145] The vast sizes and primitive transportation networks of southern dioceses, coupled with the necessity of traveling to Baltimore for councils and to Europe to raise funds, meant that most Catholic religious expended great energy on travel. Continually they placed themselves in harm's way by traveling to reach the sick.

Healing the Sick Together: Cooperation and Mutual Admiration

Protestants admired these sacrifices. A correspondent for the Society for the Propagation of the Faith noted that Protestant gratitude for the work of Bishop Gartland and a missionary bishop, who died during the fever in Savannah: "All the Protestant journals have done justice to their memory, by giving publicity to their heroic devotedness."[146] Following Fr. Moranvillé's death in Fell's Point, the trustees of his parish sent the news to Bruté. They noted that the Protestants of the city "speak of him in the most unqualified terms of approbation and admire those heroic virtues which he so long practiced among them."[147] Priests' sacrifices even inspired Protestant emulation. The Rev. Sylvester Larned, the first Presbyterian minister in New Orleans, recalled that he had heeded his friends' advice and left the city during a yellow fever epidemic. In his absence, the newspapers "'inquired if it were consistent with the character and obligations of a *Protestant* clergyman to desert his people in periods of calamity,'" pointing out that "'Catholic priests always remain at their posts, whatever perils assail them.'" Larned took the comparison to heart and resolved to stay through any future epidemics. Like many of his Catholic counterparts, he soon lost his life ministering to the sick and dying.[148]

Many Protestants echoed the gratitude of Augusta's Mayor Cumming for the work of Catholics and especially for women religious. In Charleston, a Catholic-run organization of workers praised the Sisters of Mercy for laboring wherever "the poverty or affliction of individuals required them," and it noted its satisfaction that the community shared its high opinion of them.[149] A Baltimore weekly remembered Sr. M. Frances Boarman, who served in a cholera hospital and died of the disease in August 1832, as "one of those ministering angels who had volunteered their services . . . to nurse the sick and comfort the dying." Less than three weeks later, a daily paper eulogized another nun, Sr. Mary George Smith, as "one of those admirable ladies, who are truly denominated Sisters of Charity."[150] The *Presbyterian* went even further, editorializing that "no ministers possess so much learning or display so much disinterested zeal, as those of the Church of Rome," singling out the Sisters of Charity for praise as the only women who could fearlessly tend to the sick in the midst of cholera.[151] In Louisiana, the legislature expressed its gratitude by granting the Sisters of Charity property for a novitiate in Donaldsonville. Less formal signs of appreciation came from railroad and steamboat operators who often waived the sisters' fare.[152] A Protestant minister in New Orleans, witnessing four Sisters of Charity, along with thirteen priests, die during the epidemic of 1853, marveled that "the word *fear* was not in their vocabulary." He prayed that all American women would be like them who alone exhibited "that living and most perfect exemplification of a Christian spirit."[153]

A Protestant Englishwoman named Sarah Mytton singled out for praise the hospital work of women religious in the South. Complimenting American hospitals for their achievements despite scant resources, she identified the hospitals of the Sisters of Charity in New Orleans and St. Louis as "the most admirable, clean and extensive," and she observed that they were staffed by "excellent women."[154] A Presbyterian minister from Scotland also lavished praise on the Sisters of Charity hospital in St. Louis. "Any thing neater and better than the arrangements of this Hospital cannot be conceived," he effused, adding that he was not alone in his sentiments: "the gentle manner and self sacrificing spirit of these Sisters, have secured for them throughout the valley of the Mississippi . . . an affectionate respect which is reflected back on the Church to which they devote their services."[155] Methodist Bishop Oscar Penn Fitzgerald perhaps best articulated the view of those who had been "won" by nuns in their ministry to the sick. He praised the work of Irish women religious in tending to the sick, suffering, and dying: "should I reach heaven and not meet there the Sisters of Mercy and the Sisters of Charity whom I have met in the hovels of want, the abodes of sickness, and the chambers of death . . . I should feel that I was in the wrong place."[156]

Protestants reserved their most vocal outpouring of appreciation for the medical work of the Ursulines of New Orleans. During the Revolution, some colonial soldiers had formed positive impressions of the Ursulines in Canada after nuns cared for them during the Battle of Three Rivers.[157] Such sentiment became widespread during the War of 1812. After the Battle of New Orleans, Ursulines in that city nursed the wounded of both armies, often for months. For years afterward, former soldiers from Kentucky and Tennessee sent the convent gifts of thanks. General Andrew Jackson visited the convent to express his gratitude, and he enjoyed a close relationship with the nuns after becoming president.[158] When Jackson visited New Orleans for the anniversary of the battle in 1828, the Ursulines gave $50 to the fund set up to welcome him. The *Louisiana Advertiser* praised their gift as the most moving of the many tributes to Jackson, given "the sanctity of the place whence it comes, and the purity of the hands by which it is rendered." It praised the Ursulines for their devotion to education and charity and recalled the "Christian benevolence" they had demonstrated by caring for the wounded of both armies during the battle.[159] In Washington, Congressman Edward Livingston of Louisiana, a former mayor of New York City, who had moved to New Orleans and served under Jackson during the battle, recalled in a public speech how the Ursulines had "implored the God of Battles to nerve the arm of their protectors, and turn the tide of combat against the invaders of their country."[160] Even though many Americans viewed nuns as a potentially dangerous foreign influence, the sacrifices of the sisters helped to dispel prejudices and win respect for women religious and for Catholics.[161]

Lay Catholics were among the earliest physicians in the South and earned renown for their services.[162] Bishop Fitzgerald reminisced that the second Irishman he ever met was a physician who cared for him during a long illness: "it gave me a very distinct impression that a man might be a Roman Catholic and at the same time a follower of Him who called Luke, 'the beloved physician,' to be one of the Twelve."[163] Louis Alexander Dugas, the son of a refugee from Santo Domingo, rose to become one of the most prominent doctors in Georgia. Having studied at the University of Maryland Medical School and in Europe, he returned home and established a practice in Augusta in 1831. He later served as editor of the *Southern Medical and Surgical Journal* and as a consulting surgeon at the Augusta hospital during the Civil War. His reputation won him an appointment to the Medical College of Georgia, and in 1834, he received a commission to purchase a library and museum for the college in Europe.[164] Other lay Catholics, although not trained as physicians, won similar accolades. In an obituary for the wife of a prominent Catholic merchant, the *Paducah Journal* praised her home as "not only the abode of elegance, but true charity went forth from it on many a ministration of good to the haunts of the poor and the suffering." Among the woman's accomplishments, the obituary noted her "practical Christianity, which spread its genial influence, like sunshine, over all her duties and associations."[165]

Catholics admired Protestants who showed similar courage. In a letter describing the 1836 cholera epidemic in Charleston, Bishop William Clancy spoke of the high number of deaths and also noted that "parsons of the different persuasions attended rather fearlessly throughout the pestilence."[166] Catholics thanked Protestants for their medical assistance. The South Carolina Convention of 1827 issued public thanks to doctors who aided the seminarians of Charleston during a fever.[167] Over a decade later, the *Miscellany* lavished praise on Protestant efforts during another outbreak: "The charitable exertions of our fellow-citizens, the benevolent activity of the Mayor, seconded by the wise liberality of the council; added to the untiring charity of our medical men, are effecting much in the way of relief."[168] Epidemics ravaged southern societies but also helped unite the survivors.

Catholic efforts to care for the sick did not always unfold as Catholics expected. A Protestant lady in Kentucky once sent for Fr. Edward Fenwick, who rushed four miles on foot in the dark to her aid only to discover that she was not ill but simply wanted to buy some tobacco from him.[169] Such care across confessional lines could also produce religious tensions. During a yellow fever outbreak in 1824, an open letter in the *Miscellany* criticized a local merchant "who states that HE has been justified some years since, and that the prayers of a JUST MAN availeth much, and that Bishop England can not save a man's soul." The writer asked the man "not to torment the sick Roman Catholics, as they are fully satisfied with the attendance of there [*sic*] own clegy [*sic*]."[170] Some Protestants imputed base motives to Catholics' charity, claiming that they cared for orphans only in order to put them to work and tended to the dying only to convince them to bequeath the church their money.[171] Errands of mercy also produced theological disagreements. The *Charleston City Gazette* mocked the Catholic sacrament of extreme unction, prompting the *Miscellany* to complain of gross misrepresentation.[172]

Despite the lingering hostility, acts of charity improved Catholic standing in southern society. A Scotsman in the South noted Catholic work among the suffering and bemoaned that Protestantism, in contrast, "could draw her sword, but, until of late years, had not learned to draw her purse for Christ."[173] A Protestant minister in New Orleans put the matter more succinctly: "the Roman Catholic church is infinitely superior to any Protestant denomination in its provisions of mercy and charity for the poor," he argued.[174] Another Protestant, stopping outside the cathedral of New Orleans, recoiled from the sight of a priest "with a face in which the expression of an owl and an ape are combined," but welcomed his presence for the sake of the Sister of Charity who followed him "probably to some death-bed, with a corpse-like face herself, haggard but composed, pensive and absorbed, and with the eyes of a broken heart." Speculating that he might meet the two again, "looking down compassionately and soothingly, in some far distant pestilent or war-hospital," he threw some money in the offering box.[175]

Catholic charity even reconciled some Protestants to clerical celibacy. Sarah Maury praised priests' work among the sick, attributing their dedication to the fact that "they do not fear to carry sickness to the wife of their bosom, or the children of their hearth; they have renounced domestic ties, that they may open their hearts more fully to those extended sympathies which include the whole human race."[176] A Catholic traveler in Kentucky caused a stir at an inn in Elizabeth by requesting a meal appropriate for a fast day. When another guest, overhearing the request, voiced his disapproval of Catholic clerics and clerical celibacy, another stranger said that he "defied any Preacher encumbered with the cares of a family to make the heroic exposure of health which the Catholic ministry required, in the constant visiting of the sick."[177] Both comments suggest the extent to which clerical care for the sick strengthened Catholicism's place in southern society.

Catholics recognized the benefits of their dedication. "The Sisters of Charity have won the people of all creeds by their charity," wrote Mother Rose Philippine during the 1832 epidemic in St. Louis.[178] It is less clear whether they saw health care as a means of winning converts. Propaganda viewed the practice of medicine by priests "as a means of aiding the conversion of unbelievers."[179] The report of Fr. Andrew White's care for the Indian chief Tayac stressed his conversion to Catholicism.[180] Bishop Flaget observed that Fr. Bruté had "begun to practice medicine on the foot of a sailor, while waiting to practice it on his soul."[181] In the obituary of a Protestant Irishman named Joseph Skerrett, the *Miscellany* noted that "like many of his brethren on the approach of that awful moment which tries men's souls, he chose to die in the Catholic faith, and ardently desired the spiritual aid of a Priest." Although he lived in a remote corner of North Carolina, a priest named Andrew Byrne managed to visit him on the very day that he died.[182] The possibility of conversion did not escape notice.

Whether intended or not, care for the sick won converts. Bishop Clancy noted several deathbed conversions from Protestantism during a cholera epidemic in Charleston.[183] During the epidemic of 1832, Bishop Joseph Rosati of St. Louis recorded in his diary that both dying and healthy Protestants called for priests and converted.[184] A Kentuckian who had married a Catholic, converted, but lapsed, called for a priest and received the sacraments after falling dangerously ill. After his recovery, he invited the priest to teach Catholic doctrine to his neighbors.[185] Catholic care for the sick brought some of them into the church.

Catholic health care defused the charge that Catholics burdened society. In early America, some Protestants saw disease as a "scourge of the sinful" and claimed that impoverished Catholic immigrants suffered more than others.[186] By 1820, medical theorists suspected environmental causes for higher urban mortality among the poor. L.R. Villermé's research in France confirmed this hypothesis, and in the 1840s, medical theorists in the United States linked disease and epidemics to poor sanitation.[187] Because bad conditions often existed in urban slums populated largely by Catholic immigrants, enemies of Catholicism continued to charge that their behavior caused disease. Bishop John Baptist Purcell of Cincinnati argued that poverty and disease were simply signs of one's place among the elect, but nativists charged that disease struck "only the unworthy immigrants who were polluting the pure streams of American life." Epidemics were not punishment for society's insensitivity to the poor, as Purcell argued, but the fruit of misdeeds.[188] Catholic immigrants were spreading disease and overburdening hospitals. Whether they suffered disproportionately from disease because their sins invoked God's wrath or because their bad habits provided breeding grounds for germs made little difference. Such scapegoating could have violent consequences. In 1855, a mob in Norfolk blamed an outbreak of yellow fever on the squalid living conditions of Irish immigrants and burned their slums in anger.[189]

Nativists also argued that immigrants undermined temperance and education and increased pauperism and crime. Some saw immigration as a weapon wielded by European monarchs against America's republican institutions. "For a series of years, Foreign Governments have been engaged in deporting thousands and tens of thousands of their paupers from their Alms houses and Hospitals, as well as convicted felons and chained cut-throats from their Jails and Penitentiaries," a nativist broadside in Kentucky complained.[190] The Know-Nothing Party introduced legislation in Congress to outlaw immigration by paupers, criminals, the insane, and the blind.[191] It was true that immigrants put a strain on public institutions. By 1850, only 1 in 317 natives required public support, whereas among foreign-born populations, the ratio was 1 for every 32. At that time, in Charleston, the immigrants outnumbered natives in the city's poor house by a ratio of seven to one.[192] Even Catholics acknowledged the cost. Bishop England speculated that the fever of 1838 arose less from the weather than from "the predisposition of many persons newly arrived in the city, and from the wretchedness and want of suitable accommodation in some of their boarding houses, as well as from their own great imprudence."[193]

England's observation that disease struck immigrants who indulged in the "habitual use of great quantities of ardent spirits" and lived in filthy conditions echoed the nativist views. But unlike the nativists, England pointed out that cities like Charleston "can not dispense with the services of the persons thus liable." His solution was not to restrict immigration but to build institutions "by which the services and comparative safety of this class of industrious persons may be secured."[194] The hospital of the Brotherhood of San Marino was one such institution. Fr. William Burke of the brotherhood noted that immigrants wanted to "aid in sustaining that country which had received them." The brotherhood would not coddle the lazy or irresponsible but rather would "secure the health of the *industrious and well-conducted* working men of this city."[195] Catholics would help society cope with its problems.

In individual ministry, hospitals, and orphanages, Catholics cared for southerners without distinction of creed. They lessened individual suffering and eased the social burden of immigration. They used their institutions to integrate themselves into a Protestant-dominated society, and the institutions helped reshape public conceptions of Catholicism. One nineteenth-century historian noted that the "active orders" in the church—visible "in the streets, in the hospitals, in the schools, in the stores"—produced an "impression on the public mind in favor of Catholicity."[196] Protestants testified to this effect. Reflecting on his years in Augusta, Augustus Longstreet recalled a moment during the fever of 1839 when his friend Fr. Barry informed him of a dying Methodist patient at Barry's hospital. The priest and the minister hurried to the hospital, knelt by the sick man's side, and prayed together. Having described the scene, Longstreet concluded: "Now if there is a member of any Church of Christ who is not tenderly and pleasantly touched with this picture, he is out of his place and a disgrace to any place."[197] Many would have found the image of Catholics and Protestants working side by side for the betterment of southern society to be quite pleasant indeed.

3
Educating Together

A few days before Christmas 1831, a correspondent for the *New Orleans Bee,* on his way to Mobile, stumbled on an astonishing sight. On a hill a few miles outside the city, where the year before he had seen just a scattering of ramshackle buildings in various stages of completion, stood a college of lawns and gardens arranged around "a noble structure, towering over the loftiest tress . . . fronted by a bold and massive colonnade of the Tuscan order." This was Spring Hill College, founded in 1830 by the Catholic bishop of Mobile, Michael Portier. The *Bee*'s correspondent arrived just in time for the school's first public examination, and he was impressed by what he saw. Although the students had only recently begun their studies, "the degree of self-confidence with which the questions were answered, the order and decorum which strongly characterized the exercises" demonstrated "the zeal, method and assiduity of the teacher." He was delighted to find such excellence so close to New Orleans.[1]

Spring Hill College shared one surprising trait with other Catholic schools that emerged across the South during the antebellum period: it relied on the combined efforts of Catholics and Protestants. Southern Protestants contributed financially to its founding and continued to give as it grew. They welcomed a Catholic college and integrated it into their society. On the occasion of the college's first public examinations, the school invited the community to attend, and scores accepted the invitation. In later years, as exams and commencements became elaborate events with dramas, orations, discourses, and music, the crowds likewise grew. Protestants came not simply for the spectacle, but also because they had enrolled their sons. Their support solidified the college's position, and Catholic standing, in Mobile. Students from other regions—which as early as 1831 included New Orleans, Pensacola, New York, Philadelphia, and even

Mexico—extended its influence. They exemplified a pattern of Protestant and Catholic cooperation that left its mark on education throughout the South.

We Don't Need No Education: Schooling in the South

Catholic education made a difference because the South had few schools. Alabama, like the rest of the South, lagged behind in establishing public systems. Unlike the New England states, southern states rarely mentioned education in their constitutions. They were equally lax about state school laws. New England states amply provided for schools, whereas southern states either cared only for parochial and pauper schools or ignored schooling altogether.[2] Legislative inaction crippled education. The first free school in Charleston opened in 1710, but South Carolina as a whole instituted no public schools until 1811, when the legislature established free schools in each district and parish.[3] Two years later, the legislators threatened to repeal the act, and although it survived, the system it created suffered from poor organization, little oversight, and severe underfunding. "In no country is the necessity of popular education so often proclaimed, and in none are the schools of elementary instruction more deplorably neglected. They are entirely without organization, superintendence, or inspection of any kind," bemoaned Governor George McDuffie in 1835.[4] Some lawmakers tried to remedy deficiencies but with little effect. In 1839, an investigative committee noted that the scattered population and the need for children as farm laborers—common throughout the South—posed the greatest obstacles. Critics charged that the schools had too little money, too little oversight, and too few books. In 1840, one estimated that only one child in nine attended school.[5] In an 1847 report to the legislature, Henry Summer voiced the lament of education reformers: "It was declared on the floor of this hall during the last session of this body that the free school system was a failure; and no one contradicted it; it seemed to be conceded by all."[6]

Other states fared even more poorly. Kentucky waited until 1853 to establish a school in each county, and Alabama had no meaningful school law until 1854. Kentucky passed its first law aiding common schools in 1821, but more than three decades of squabbling passed before the money appeared. Not content to wait, Louisville established public schools in 1819 and made them free a decade later.[7] Upon admission to the Union in 1819, Alabama reserved a section of each township for support of a school. Mobilians went further, receiving permission from the state in 1826 to establish and run their own school system. The statute provided for new sources of revenue, but collection proved difficult. As a result, city officials chose to subsidize private schools rather than establish a public system. In exchange, private schools would educate poor children gratis. In 1846, an act allowed taxpayers to designate their school taxes for institutions run by their religious denominations. Methodist and Presbyterian schools benefited first, but by 1851, Catholic and Episcopal schools also received public funds. Despite these provisions, the money did little for the poor. In 1851, nearly 42 percent of Mobile's children did not attend school. Not until the mid-1850s would Mobile enjoy an efficient public school system and eventually goad the rest of the state into action.[8]

The census of 1850 revealed how far southern education had come, and how far it still had to go (see table 3).

By 1850, South Carolina boasted close to a thousand public schools, academies, and other schools; Alabama claimed over a thousand and Kentucky over two thousand. But these schools tended to be very modest, with only thirty students on average. Few had more than a single teacher. By even the most generous estimate, only half the states' white children spent time in school, and the percentage of those attending regularly was probably closer to one-third.[9]

The notion that government had little role to play in education hindered southern school systems. Even when sentiment favored schools out of a desire to raise good citizens or a fear of falling behind the rest of the nation, money rarely followed. Even Virginia struggled to educate its children. In 1847, college president John B. Davis urged the Virginia Synod of the Lutheran Church to assume the burden: "It behooves us to take up the subject of education, and urge it upon the attention of our people. The State, to her dishonor be it said, will not do it."[10] The regions west of the Appalachians lagged even further behind. "An inhabitant of the Eastern States can have no adequate conception of the want of schools in this country," reported two New England missionaries traveling through the Southwest in 1814.[11]

Despite the failings, some southerners attained a good education.[12] Elite families in the colonies often sent their sons to England. After the Revolution, affluent southerners continued to study abroad or to go north for schooling. The South could also boast of educational innovations. The first manual labor schools appeared in South Carolina in 1796, anticipating by thirty years a trend that would sweep the country.[13] Academies for secondary education flourished. By 1830, South Carolina had at least one in almost every county.[14] And southerners established some of the nation's first colleges, public and private. Georgia chartered the first public univer-

Table 3. Education statistics for the South, 1850

	Alabama	Kentucky	South Carolina
Number of colleges	5	15	8
Students	567	1,873	720
Teachers	55	100	43
Annual Income	$26,250	$131,461	$104,790
Number of public schools	1,152	2,234	724
Students	28,380	71,429	17,838
Teachers	1,195	2,306	739
Number of other schools	166	330	202
Students	8,290	12,712	7,467
Teachers	380	600	333
Public libraries	56	80	26
Volumes	20,623	79,466	107,472
White adults unable to read or write	33,757	66,687	15,684
Percentage of total adult white population[a]	15	16	10
White children attending school[b]	62,846	130,917	40,293
Percentage of white population age 5–15 attending (based on parents' reporting)	50	60	52
Percentage of white population age 5–15 attending (based on census estimates of enrollment)	29	39	33

[a]Adult = Sixteen years old and older; all percentages rounded.
[b]Reported by families. These numbers are significantly higher than the census's recorded enrollment of public and private schools and probably include children who attended sporadically.

Source: Seventh Census of the United States (1850)

sity, whereas North Carolina's was the first to open its doors to students. Between 1820 and 1860, churches built over twenty-five colleges in the South, offering low-cost alternatives to the state institutions and attracting students of all denominations. Some of these "colleges" provided only a basic level of education, but the best ones dispelled "the facile observation that the early-nineteenth-century colleges tended to be pedagogically unimaginative and disconnected from the major social and political trends of the era."[15] Nor were they any less rigorous than their northern equivalents. They too modeled their curricula on the medieval liberal arts, gradually adding natural sciences and modern languages. Admissions requirements included knowledge of Latin and Greek and proficiency in mathematics. To compensate for the absence of standardized testing, students seeking admission normally had to pass oral exams.[16]

To extend the benefits of education, cities established public libraries; Charleston had one in 1700. By 1850, Alabama had fifty-six public libraries, Kentucky had eighty, and South Carolina had twenty-six.[17] Literary societies also attested to desires for intellectual improvement. A foreign visitor to Charleston praised the library of its literary society as the best in the country.[18]

Such achievements touched the lives of pitifully few southerners. Emphasizing private over public schools, southern states limited opportunities for the masses. Free schools labored under social stigmas. A commentator in South Carolina, in 1839, noted that the wealthy would not permit their children to attend and that even the poor "from pride and delicacy of feeling, will rather keep their children at home altogether than, by sending them to the free school, attach to them, as they think and feel, the stigma of being poor, and of receiving an education as paupers."[19] Stephen Elliott Jr. and J. H. Thornwell complained to Governor Patrick Noble of South Carolina, in a report on the free school system, that "foolish pride" kept many poor "from receiving that as a bounty which they cannot procure in a better way."[20] Preference given to the poor undermined the schools by making them appear as charity institutions. College building commanded more energy and resources, but only the wealthy could afford a college education; tuition at the University of Virginia was the highest in the country. Southerners designed their colleges not as vehicles for upward mobility but as agencies to "socialize the planter aristocracy's scions into a tradition of leadership."[21] They left the mass of southerners behind. The *Miscellany* noted, in 1829, that while New England could claim one college student for every two thousand inhabitants and the Mid-Atlantic states one for every four thousand, the states south of Pennsylvania had only one college student for every six thousand people.[22]

Women found educational opportunities severely limited. In one respect, the South surpassed other regions by establishing more than its share of female colleges. Whereas northern men worried that highly educated women would threaten professional segregation, southern men had no such fears. Safely confined to their separate sphere, southern women's education was a mark of gentility that heightened their husbands' status, not threatened it. This mentality allowed southerners to build female colleges designed to be the equivalents of male institutions. In the 1850s, according to one estimate, the South had thirty-two of the nation's thirty-nine chartered female colleges. In 1860, North Carolina had over twice as many colleges for women as for men.[23] But assessment of the schools requires a sense of perspective. Many ridiculed higher education for women. In 1831, the *Raleigh Register* ran a mock ad for a female college offering classes in "scolding and fretting," "talking idly, and dressing ridiculously," and "how to keep from work when you return home."[24] The women's colleges reached an even smaller portion of the population than their male counterparts did. Only the daughters of the wealthy could attend, a restriction that made the schools palatable. Wealthy women would not enter the professions, and an education designed to reinforce gentility buttressed a hierarchical society. The women's colleges also rested on a pitifully weak foundation. They struggled to find enough women with the elementary and secondary education to pursue advanced learning.[25]

The reformers who sought solutions included Catholic priests and laity. They helped build one school in Kentucky after a priest found that children preparing for their First Communion could not read their catechisms.[26] Bishop Flaget lamented "the great and almost barbaric ignorance" of the children in his diocese.[27] So the church built schools. Catholic education, like Catholic charities, met a need in southern society. The best known Catholic schools enjoyed elite patronage, but Catholics also attended to the lower end of the social spectrum. Bishop Rosati of St. Louis noted, in 1832, that "here the idea of free public schools does not exist. The idea of a free school is that of a charity school. . . . Even the poor do not like to send their sons to such a school, for they consider it a disgrace."[28] Catholic schools offered an alternative, charging a low tuition made possible by the supply of free labor from priests and nuns. Some school administrators used tuition from the wealthy to subsidize the poor. Although orders in Europe often ministered only to the poor, the American orders saw that the wealthy lacked schooling and decided that their tuition fees could fund work among the less affluent. Indeed, some orders found that their schools could not survive without fees from wealthy students.[29] The schools were not egalitarian. Some separated wealthy and poor students, both to preserve social distinctions and to accommodate varying educational needs.[30] Nonetheless, they made an effort to teach the poor as well as the well-connected and rich.

Catholic educators lavished attention on young women. When the Ursulines arrived in Charleston, Bishop England rejoiced that their school for young ladies would fill a void.[31] Schools for women catered to the rich and poor. He later expressed satisfaction that they had erected "one of the best schools for the education of young ladies in the useful and ornamental acquirements that befit those of their sex who are to decorate the most polished circles of society."[32] But he also charged the Sisters of Mercy with the education of poorer girls. In Kentucky, Catholics established orders of women to educate girls even as they postponed plans for male orders to educate boys.[33] Because religious orders of women ran so many of the schools in the South and typically educated only girls, the young women benefited disproportionately.

Not all Protestants welcomed the proliferation of Catholic schools.[34] Ancient prejudices and new fears greeted the growth of Catholic institutions, in the North and the South, but Catholics also found defenders among southern Protestants. Speaking to Congress in 1832, Representative Charles Wycliffe of Kentucky offered a litany of reasons to support Catholic schools. He pointed out that the Catholic college in Bardstown relied solely on private support, accepted students of all denominations, and waived fees for orphans and the destitute. Above all, it offered instruction in "all those branches of useful knowledge and of science which qualify men for the duties of life" and through its discipline provided "a perfect guaranty for the preservation of the morals of our young men."[35] Each of these reasons underlay Protestant support for Catholic education across the antebellum South. Elsewhere, Catholics and Protestants fought over schools. Education in the South was, on the whole, a matter of cooperation, not contestation.

The Spread of Catholic Education

Catholics educated southern children in non-Catholic institutions. In South Carolina, Fr. Simon Gallagher, an Irish priest educated in Paris, taught mathematics at the new College of Charleston in the early 1790s and also served as the school's headmaster. Another South Carolina priest, Fr. James Wallace, ministered in Columbia but supported himself by teaching mathematics at South Carolina College, later the University of South Carolina.[36] Lay Catholics also took a leading position in southern education. Patrick Walsh, an Irish Catholic, became head of the Beaufort District Academy in the 1820s.[37] In 1847, Abbott Hall Brisbane, a graduate of West Point, took office as Professor of History, Belles Lettres, and Ethics at the Citadel.[38] Bishop England supported non-Catholic education by making a donation to the Protestant-run Savannah Free School.[39] In Kentucky, Fr. Badin regretted that he could only contribute moral support, instead of money and books, to Transylvania Seminary. Other Kentucky Catholics took more concrete action. In 1775, an emigrant from Maryland named Jane Coomes established a school at Harrod's Station; she was among the first schoolteachers in Kentucky. Another Maryland émigré, Zachariah Riney, who arrived in Kentucky in 1795, opened a school in Hardin County that might have counted a young Abraham Lincoln among its students. Two Catholics served as trustees of another early school, Washington Academy, and a third rose to become superintendent of Kentucky Academy at Frankfort by 1812.[40] A few years later, the Catholic president of the University of Frankfort helped Flaget secure a teaching position for a former seminarian.[41] In a region struggling to establish schools, Protestants welcomed Catholic assistance, both clerical and lay.

As soon as they could, Catholics built their own schools. The expansion of Catholic education, like that of Catholic charities, resulted largely from the work of religious orders, particularly of women. Some orders, both European and American in origin, chose teaching as a core responsibility. Others, particularly European contemplative orders, had teaching thrust upon them. Without endowments or large dowries from new members, both common in Europe, such orders turned to teaching and nursing as means of support.[42] Bishops encouraged them, realizing that they had few other resources. John Carroll urged a group of Carmelites who arrived in Maryland in 1790 to add active works such as teaching to their traditional focus on prayer. Although they declined his request, most orders were open to teaching.

At times, the addition of teaching to a contemplative life caused serious problems. The Poor Clares, who arrived in Maryland three years after the Carmelites, opened a school in Georgetown but closed it within a few years when they found teaching incompatible with austere contemplative practice. Yet several women who had assisted at the school became the nucleus for a more lasting institution. In 1795, they banded together under a rule devised by future archbishop Leonard Neale, and four years later, they opened an academy and free school in Georgetown. Over time, the community affiliated itself with the French Visitandine Order, receiving permission from the papacy to adapt parts of the rule to fit the American context. The academy became the most prestigious Catholic school for girls in America.[43]

By the time women religious established schools in Maryland, the Ursulines of New Orleans had been educating southern daughters for decades. From their arrival in 1727, they ran a boarding school and academy for the upper classes and a day school for poor children of all races. Although several sisters left when Spain ceded New Orleans to France in 1803, others continued to run schools there.[44] Women religious filled the vast territory between Maryland and Louisiana with schools. Orders established in Maryland, Kentucky, and South Carolina supplemented the efforts of Visitandines, Ursulines, and others arriving from Europe. Most female religious orders in America taught, both from a sense of mission and for reasons of economic necessity. For many, teaching became even more important than care for the sick, although the two responsibilities commonly existed side by side. The sisters attained a reputation as both nurses for the sick and teachers of the ignorant.

Orders of men undertook much of the early Catholic educational work. Members of the Society of St. Sulpice, founded in France in 1641, in large part to train priests, figured prominently in education.[45] Joining the waves of priests and nuns driven from Europe by the French Revolution, the first band of four priests and five seminarians reached Baltimore in July 1791, and within three months, they opened a seminary in the city. Several taught at Georgetown College, which was established through John Carroll's efforts in 1789. In 1808, a group under the direction of Fr. John Dubois opened Mount St. Mary's College at Emmitsburg, Maryland.[46] Sulpicians spread across the continent, establishing seminaries and colleges as they went.

Bishops, several of whom were Sulpicians, focused their energies on men's colleges. They wanted to alleviate one of the church's most pressing problems—the shortage of priests—and to fulfill the mandate of the Council of Trent, which, in 1563, decreed that each diocese establish a seminary.[47] In the absence of a native priesthood, bishops had to rely on Europeans. Many immigrant priests were excellent, but America also became a refuge for clergy fleeing Europe, and it was hard to assess the qualifications of these "*rambling clergymen*."[48] Some were not clergy at all. In 1822, a man claiming to be a priest arrived in Louisville. Bishop Flaget was wary, for the man's dress and demeanor created a stir. The man's landlady observed that he looked nothing like a priest and that he spent little time in prayer. When Flaget invited him to a retreat, he disappeared.[49] Two years before, a man claiming to be a priest said Mass in Kentucky but gave himself away by omitting prayers and key words of the consecration.[50] Con artists even impersonated bishops. In 1827, a man claiming to be Bishop Portier preached in Kentucky wearing a pectoral cross and bishop's ring.[51]

A few poorly qualified clergy, or outright imposters, could wreak havoc in a diocese. Fr. Badin thought that bad priests had "done more harm to the Church here than its declared enemies."[52] Indeed, many Protestant enemies of the church delighted in the scandal caused by Fr. Charles Coomes of Kentucky, who, in 1827, ran off with a former Sister of Charity.[53] In Martinsburg, Virginia, a priest named Fr. William Kenny placed a pistol on the altar before Mass and threatened to shoot a prominent layman with whom he was feuding. When the bishop removed Kenny's faculties, Kenny tried to excommunicate his enemies, stole a chalice, and threatened the deputy sheriff who eventually arrested him, leading to an embarrassing public trial.[54] In Charleston, Bishop England complained that the vices of one or two priests drove people from the church. He saw "bad clergy" as his most daunting obstacle.[55] Bishops intended Catholic colleges to alleviate these problems. Bishop Carroll, for example, intended Georgetown to be a "nursery" for a national seminary, educating young men who would enter the priesthood. On the school's ability to fulfill this role, he wrote, "is built all my hope of permanency and success to our holy religion in the United States."[56] Other bishops followed his lead in establishing colleges, some of the earliest of which took root in Kentucky, Missouri, and Alabama. Like Carroll, later bishops intended colleges to prepare students for seminary and to underwrite the seminaries' budgets, but Catholic colleges also benefited southern society. Using unsalaried seminarians as teachers, they could offer high-quality, low-cost education to the public. Even though they hoped to draw future priests, they also accepted non-Catholic students.[57]

Few regions in the antebellum South could boast Catholic school systems as extensive as Kentucky's. Several of its first priests came from a background in education. Fr. David began his ministry by teaching philosophy, scripture, and theology at the preparatory seminary at Angers, France. There he came to know Flaget, who made David his assistant upon being appointed superior. Little could the two have suspected, when the Revolution drove them apart, that their collaboration would resume on the Kentucky frontier. David continued to teach after coming to America, first at Georgetown College, then at St. Mary's seminary.[58] Like David, Flaget engaged in teaching soon after arriving in America, opening a trade school for boys in Vincennes, Indiana. For three years after he left Vincennes, he taught and served as vice president at Georgetown, but in 1798, he and three other Sulpicians established a college in Havana, Cuba. Hindered by bureaucratic obstacles, he ended up as a private tutor for a wealthy family until 1801, when he returned to Baltimore and taught in the seminary for the next seven years. Flaget believed that Catholic educators would "be a great acquisition" for America and would "render important services to the community at large," and he dedicated much of his career to proving it.[59]

Many French priests, refugees from the French Revolution, turned to teaching to support themselves in exile. Fr. Michael Fournier, a native of Blois, France, spent four years teaching in London after the French Revolution. Ordinary in appearance but possessing seemingly limitless energy, he became fluent in English and sailed to America, where he served under Bishop Carroll. After arriving as a missionary in Kentucky in 1797, he urged Fr. Anthony Salmon, a friend from his seminary days also teaching in England, to join him.[60] The priesthood in Kentucky grew through clergy networks that were often rooted in educational ventures.

As Sulpicians, Flaget, David, and other priests in Kentucky stressed education, particularly seminary education. Three seminarians accompanied Flaget on his first journey from Maryland to Kentucky in 1811 and formed the nucleus of St. Thomas's Seminary, the first seminary west of the Alleghenies and the second in the nation after that of Baltimore. A local Catholic named Thomas Howard had left the church his plantation of over three hundred acres just outside Bardstown, which became the site of the seminary.[61] By the beginning of 1812, St. Thomas housed six students, ranging in age from thirteen to over thirty years.

One of St. Thomas's first students, Robert Abell, was probably the first native Kentuckian to enter the seminary. Like many Kentucky Catholics, the Abells traced their roots to Maryland. Robert Abell's grandfather was a Protestant who served as sheriff of St. Mary's County. His grandmother was an Irish Catholic who insisted on raising the family's daughters in her faith. The family's eldest son, Philip, grew up Protestant but upon being chosen to serve as sheriff, refused to take the state's anti-Catholic test oath. Eventually the entire family converted, and the second son, Robert Senior, followed the stream of Catholic emigrants to Kentucky in 1788. He helped frame the state's constitution, which excluded any restriction on religious liberty, and became an influential figure in the state's political and religious life. In 1792, Robert Abell's wife gave birth to a son, Robert Junior, whom she would raise alone, along with the rest of the large family, after the death of her husband a few years later. Robert's mother provided his basic education and then sent him to the Dominican College of Kentucky. In 1812, Robert entered the seminary. Upon his ordination, he began a career of ministry that would last for fifty years. Standing almost six and a half feet in height, Abell was an imposing figure in the pulpit and quickly earned a reputation as a gifted orator for his almost always extemporaneous addresses. On one occasion, when Flaget and David asked to inspect one of his sermons before he delivered it, he explained that his handwriting was virtually illegible and instead offered to preach it to them. His words deeply moved the men, who never realized that the manuscript from which he was "reading" contained only the roughest of outlines.[62]

The seminary where Abell and others studied was a single, two-story log house, thirty by eighteen feet. The large downstairs room served as a study hall, refectory, and church for the neighboring Catholics. Upstairs, David occupied one room, the six seminarians another, and visiting priests slept in a tiny room off the hall or in the hall itself. David and his students immediately embarked on a building project to alleviate the cramped conditions. Like other settlers, they struggled to meet their daily needs, cultivating an extensive garden, raising livestock, and tapping trees for syrup. They relied often on neighbors who brought food or household articles. The manual labor of the seminarians was part of a rigorous daily schedule. The community rose at 5:00 a.m. for Mass, prayers, study, and a class in theology, all before breakfast at 8:00. Classes in Latin and philosophy began at 8:30, manual work from 9:30 until prayers and lunch at 12:45 p.m. After lunch there was more work until 4:45, then rosary, study, and an hour-long Latin class at 6:00. Reading and supper followed at 7:00, then recreation, prayers, reading, and sleep.[63] When authorities in Baltimore expressed skepticism about the quality of education at the frontier seminary, Flaget could reply that his students followed the same routine and rules as seminarians in Paris.[64]

By 1814, the number of seminarians had increased to nine, and two years later to twelve, seven of whom were Kentucky-born. They completed several buildings and began the foundation for a brick chapel to measure sixty-five by thirty feet. Completing the chapel in 1816, they turned their attention to the main seminary building. Its construction took just three months, and when they finished it by the end of November, it included a basement with a refectory, fruit cellar and storage, ground floor rooms for study and exercises, and a top floor of sleeping rooms. Within two years, the seminarians laid the foundation for another, larger building on a donated plot of land in Nelson County near Bardstown. In 1819, they left this home and moved to Bardstown to live in a still-unfinished building adjacent to the cathedral that would serve as their seminary and the episcopal residence. The new institution became St. Joseph's Seminary, and St. Thomas continued to function as a preparatory seminary until 1839.[65] Within five years of the move, Flaget could boast that, given sufficient funds, "not only can I educate a sufficient number of priests for my own diocese, but I can supply the neighboring dioceses with them."[66] Although adequate funding remained elusive, Kentucky produced numerous priests and religious.[67]

Other orders joined the Sulpicians in educating Kentucky's first settlers. A community of Trappists ran a school for boys at Pottinger's Creek, the first Catholic school in Kentucky, before adversity and a desire to work among the Indians pushed them further west.[68] Nearly half a century later, Trappists returned to Kentucky and opened a free school where they soon taught over sixty children.[69] The Dominicans, who like the Trappists were refugees from the French Revolution, began educating youths in their homes in 1806. Two years later, they established the College of St. Thomas Aquinas at St. Rose.[70] In 1824, female members of the Dominican third order opened a school for children of the local parish.[71]

Several Catholic schools in Kentucky resulted from initiatives of forceful personalities. Among the most prominent was St. Mary's, near Lebanon. The driving force behind St. Mary's was a priest named William Byrne. Born in Ireland around 1780, Byrne early on resolved to enter the priesthood but had to delay this ambition when his father died, leaving him to care for his mother and younger siblings. He arrived in the United States while still in his twenties and studied in Maryland before assuming parish and mission work in Kentucky. Appalled by the ignorance he found, he applied to Bishop Flaget for permission to establish an elementary school. Flaget gave him a farm that another priest had purchased with a vague idea of forming an industrial school. Byrne labored through much of 1821 at converting an old distillery into a facility suitable for a school. He set tuition as low as possible and accepted payment in produce. By February 1822, he was training about sixty students in arithmetic, grammar, and English. Fire consumed the building four months later, but Bryne constructed a larger and sturdier building of brick. He served as the president and sole teacher, although he received some assistance from older students, one of whom, Martin John Spalding, would become Bishop of Louisville and Archbishop of Baltimore.[72]

It was at St. Mary's that the premier Catholic teaching order, the Jesuits, began their work in Kentucky. Flaget had long attempted to secure their services for Kentucky, but his efforts proved unsuccessful until June 1831, when two French Jesuits arrived in Bardstown.[73] Flaget cast his eye on St. Mary's as a potential field for their labors. Byrne initially resisted, but eventually he offered Flaget the school with a plantation of 310 acres and other property. He intended to create a similar school near the confluence of the Ohio and Tennessee Rivers, but he died in 1833, before he could do it. In the fall of 1831, St. Mary's passed into the hands of the Jesuits, who soon faced a severe challenge as fire once again destroyed the school's main building. After a rapid rebuilding effort, the school prospered, with enrollment soon hitting its maximum of 127 students. In 1837, the state legislature granted a charter, elevating the institution to the level of a university.[74] The following year, the Jesuits opened a novitiate on an adjoining farm, and in 1842, they sent priests to Louisville, where they opened Saint Ignatius Literary Institution. But in 1846, they fell into conflict with diocesan clergy, who struggled to support their own institutions and viewed the Jesuits as rivals; the Jesuits withdrew from Louisville, transferred St. Mary's back to the diocese, and left Kentucky for New York, where they took over Bishop Hughes's institution that became Fordham University.[75]

The exodus of the Jesuits was a blow to education in Kentucky, but other schools flourished. Foremost was St. Joseph's College, which had opened in Bardstown in 1819. Fr. George Elder, a native of Kentucky educated at St. Mary's in Baltimore, ran the school. Classes met in the seminary basement, and the seminarians did the teaching. The college set its sights high, aspiring to offer—Flaget boasted—"an education as complete as can be obtained in the colleges in France." Under Elder's administration, the college grew rapidly. By the end of 1820, a separate building opened to accommodate the increased enrollment, which soon stood at forty-two students. Shortly after, the first boarding students arrived, some from as far away as St. Louis.[76] By May 1823, the college's growth necessitated construction of an additional wing.[77]

Although the college's growth had been steady, its enrollment exploded in the early 1820s when a Catholic college in New Orleans failed and its director, searching for an alternative for his students, received permission to transfer them to St. Joseph's. In 1824, the first contingent of twenty students settled in Kentucky. After a year, the school had about ninety boarders and one hundred day students. To accommodate the boarders, school officials constructed a large, central building.[78] The campus compared favorably to other colleges, most of which consisted of little more than a multipurpose main building, a residential building, and perhaps a chapel.[79]

The influx of students from Louisiana helped spread St. Joseph's reputation across the South.

After a devastating fire in January 1839, the school had to rebuild, and it lagged under the weight of its debts.[80] In 1848, the college's president, Fr. Edward McMahon, announced its transfer to a group of Jesuits from Missouri.[81] Flaget had tried for almost a decade to place an order in charge of the college, appealing without success to both the Lazarists and the Holy Cross Fathers. He was pleased when the Jesuits finally accepted his offer, for their work at St. Mary's was well known.[82]

Although diocesan priests and male religious orders ran the most prominent schools, female orders established and administered a greater number. The Friends of Mary at the Foot of the Cross, often known as the Sisters of Loretto, excelled as school builders. Even before Flaget's arrival in Kentucky, Fr. Nerinckx and Fr. Badin had tried to form a sisterhood, but their project collapsed before it began when a fire destroyed the motherhouse. Several years later, a second attempt proved more lasting. The Sisters of Loretto originated after Mary Rhodes, a convent-educated emigrant from Maryland, collaborated with Nerinckx in opening a school in an abandoned cabin near Hardin's Creek. The school drew so many children that Nerinckx arranged for another young woman, Christine Stuart, to assist Rhodes. The two women lived in a cabin near the school and followed a religious routine. When Anne Havern joined them, they proposed establishing a religious community. With Flaget's approval, the three received the veil in 1812, and two other women joined as postulants. The women improved the facilities and devised a system to store beds in the attic and lower them in the evenings to accommodate boarding students. The rule Nerinckx devised for the order affirmed the primacy of education.[83] Within four years, the sisters opened a second school at Holy Mary's, and two years later, they formed still another one at Gethsemane.[84] Their schools spread across the state and, in 1823, into Missouri, where twelve sisters settled at the Barrens in Perry County in response to Bishop DuBourg's request. By the following year, the sisters counted 103 members educating over 250 tuition-paying girls plus orphans at six schools.[85]

Founded just a few months after the Sisters of Loretto, the Sisters of Nazareth undertook to support the seminary at St. Thomas by making clothes for students, then by caring for the sick, giving charity, and teaching. Within a year, they were instructing two boarding and several day students, a number that increased rapidly.[86] Early in 1814, Ellen O'Connell, a native of Maryland and the well-educated daughter of a professor of languages and rhetoric, offered her services to the sisters. While she and

David trained them, the seminarians built a log schoolhouse. Within four years, the increase in students required a new brick building, large enough to accommodate fifty boarders. O'Connell directed the school for twenty years.

At Flaget's request, the sisters also opened in 1819 a day school called Bethlehem Academy in Bardstown, the order's first branch house. The following spring, four sisters established a school in Breckinridge County, and in December, another group founded St. Vincent's Academy in the southwestern part of the state.[87] By 1820, Flaget could boast of six girls' schools in his diocese that were educating almost two hundred young women.[88] Some survived only a few years, but by 1821, the Sisters of Nazareth routinely sent groups throughout Kentucky to establish schools and convents.[89]

By 1816, the order had fourteen members educating thirty-one students, and the Bardstown school had become so popular that it lacked space to accommodate all the applicants.[90] In the early 1820s, the sisters discovered that the land did not belong to them, so in 1822, the thirty-eight boarders and the nuns moved to a house three miles outside Bardstown. The house had been owned by a Presbyterian minister, who was well known for his debates with Badin and other priests.[91] By 1825, the school had sixty boarders, and the sisters had to construct a larger building. In just over a year, the number increased to seventy-six, requiring yet another building and additional property. By that time, sixty sisters ministered and educated at Nazareth, Bardstown, St. Thomas, Union County, Scott County, and Vincennes, Indiana.[92] In 1837, the school at Nazareth alone housed 112 boarders.[93] By 1842, the sisters reached into Tennessee, establishing a school in Nashville that soon attracted over sixty students. Spalding estimated the total enrollment of the sisters' schools at 447 students, including 40 orphans.[94]

Catholic schools educated orphans and sought creative ways to care for the disadvantaged. In Kentucky, the church opened a free school for poor boys, teaching them reading and writing and employing them on a farm to cover the cost of their board.[95] Other Catholics educated the handicapped. In the late 1830s, Eulalie Flaget, the niece of the bishop, opened a school for the deaf and dumb in Bardstown. Born in France in 1789, she had suffered, as a young girl, an attack of yellow fever that left her frail and slightly deaf. For years, she begged her mother to allow her to follow her missionary uncle to America. When she finally arrived in Kentucky, she joined the Sisters of Nazareth. In 1835, a trip to France with her uncle gave her an unplanned opportunity to visit a school for the deaf, where she remained to receive training, and on her return to Kentucky, she opened the Loretto Deaf and Dumb Asylum. Enjoying a long career as a religious, she nursed her uncle during his final days and retired to the Convent of the Sacred Heart in Sault au Recollet, Canada, where she died in 1883.[96]

In Kentucky, Catholic schools gave the church a distinctive public presence in the midst of the Protestant majority. In Louisville, especially, several orders built schools. Among their Louisville ventures, the Sisters of Nazareth opened Presentation Academy in 1831, and a free school in 1843. The Sisters of Loretto opened Cedar Grove Academy in Portland, just outside Louisville in 1842, whereas the Jesuits built a free school and the College of St. Aloysius. Xaverian Brothers, who arrived from Belgium in 1854, and Ursulines, who arrived from Bavaria in 1858, contributed additional teachers. But the orders had no monopoly on the creation of Catholic schools. The mainly German parish of St. Boniface created the city's first parochial school. By 1863, Bishop Spalding reported twenty Catholic schools in Louisville alone.[97]

The reputation of Kentucky's Catholic schools drew students, Catholic and Protestant, from other states, mostly in the South. The southern educators also extended their organizing efforts to other parts of the nation, including Notre Dame, which Fr. Badin was instrumental in supporting, and New York, where the transplanted Jesuits from St. Joseph's took over John Hughes's college, soon to be Fordham.[98]

Catholics in Mobile could not match the number of Kentucky's schools, but at least one of their institutions outlasted all of Kentucky's. Like Flaget, Bishop Michael Portier had experience in education before he came to Mobile. Completing his studies at St. Mary's in Baltimore, he admired the model DuBourg implemented at Georgetown and in Baltimore, catering to American tastes in courses and discipline, welcoming non-Catholics, and appealing to influential families.[99] He put these lessons to good use in his successful school for boys in New Orleans.[100] In 1829, he became bishop of the newly created see of Mobile, and within a year, he had purchased land for a college west of the city. He selected a hill with ample woods, sufficient elevation to offer protection from disease, and a spring from which its name derived. In April 1830, he purchased 222 acres for $2,100.[101] Spring Hill College set up temporary accommodations in a hotel with six teachers and thirty students, but in July, the completion of two frame buildings, each two stories high, allowed the fifty students to move to the campus.[102]

Portier chose July 4 to lay the main cornerstone, signifying that the college would serve not merely the church, but also the nation.[103] With the priests doing much of the labor and Portier, axe in hand, helping clear the forest, the group completed the main building by the following May. Built of brick, it stood four stories high, one hundred by forty-four feet, with a front adorned with twelve Tuscan columns supporting a gallery opening on each floor. A large belvedere, offering views of Mobile Bay, crowned the structure, making it, "without question, one of the finest structures in the Floridas," in one priest's estimation. The campus had attractive yards, orchards, vineyards, and gardens. In December, the community laid the foundation for the college chapel and parish church.[104]

Because Spring Hill suffered from shortages of teachers and funds, Portier transferred control in 1844 to the Fathers of Mercy and three years later to the Eudist Fathers. Neither group proved adept at running a college, and when fever and financial crisis struck Mobile, Portier suspended operations in 1845.[105] In 1847, the Jesuits agreed to resuscitate it, though the transfer, like so many interactions between orders, produced friction. Portier complained that the Jesuits "have screwed me pretty tight," taking over not only a building and bit of land as originally agreed, but also a larger piece of land, the library, the furniture, the "philosophical apparatus," and a chapel ornament. Still, he conceded that the college's prospects looked brighter and that the Jesuits would "bring blessing to my poor diocese."[106] So they did. By 1850, Spring Hill educated one-third of all the college students in Alabama. It had more teachers and a higher annual income than the state's four other colleges combined.[107]

Mobile Catholics built other schools for younger and poorer students. The Catholic Female Charitable Society, which had already underwritten health care, voted to fund the education of up to sixteen poor children, eight male and eight female. Woman religious added their energies. In 1832, four Visitandines from Georgetown opened a school for girls in Summerville, outside Mobile. The Sisters of Charity who came from Emmitsburg to run the orphanage also opened free and pay schools, including schools for orphans and a free day school for girls. Within a year, they taught ninety orphans and sixty tuition-paying girls. Four years later, the sisters and the society built a $1,000 brick addition to the orphanage as a schoolhouse for poor children. The Brothers of the Sacred Heart also took up the cause, opening a boarding and free school for boys shortly after their arrival in 1847. By the late 1840s, Catholics in Mobile had six schools: two free ones for male students, two for female students, and two for orphans. Alongside Spring Hill College, they furnished a comprehensive system of Catholic education and enrolled more students than any other schools.[108]

In South Carolina, John England announced that Catholic education was "the pastors' most pressing and elevated duty."[109] Like other bishops, he sought mainly to train priests; for throughout his tenure, he decried the shortage of clergy, occasionally chiding his flock: "As a body you have done nothing towards securing for yourselves a ministry." But he held out hope, noting that plenty of men sought admission to holy orders and that it only remained to train them.[110] Given his meager resources, England envisioned a combined college and seminary as the best solution. On January 5, 1822, the Philosophical and Classical Seminary and Seminary of St. John the Baptist opened their doors in Charleston. England assumed that the general diocesan fund and the college fees—a $5 entrance fee and tuition of $12 per quarter for the course in English, and $20 for the courses in belles lettres, classics, mathematics, and philosophy—could support the seminary, with seminarians teaching in the college.[111] In later years, the "St. John the Baptist Society" and the "Ladies Society in Aid of the Seminary" provided support.[112] By 1822, the college enrolled thirty students, and in about a year, the number tripled. England rejoiced at the progress in preparing men for ordination.[113]

His educational enterprises depended heavily on the work of women religious. The Sisters of Mercy founded the Academy of Our Lady of Mercy in 1830, a few months after their founding. Within two years, they moved to a larger house, where they accepted boarders and orphans as well as day students. A decade later, they moved again, taking with them seventy orphans and twenty-four boarders, and they soon expanded into Savannah and Columbia.[114] They owed much of their success to Julia Datty, who was the daughter of wealthy parents in Santo Domingo and had been educated in Paris. A refugee to Charleston during the French Revolution, Datty joined the Sisters of Mercy and underwrote teaching for young girls in Charleston for almost fifty years, ministering also to the sick in hospitals and private homes, regardless of "peculiarities of creed, or caste, or colour, or country." Datty was the superioress of the order from 1834 until her death from cholera in 1836, and her funeral at St. Mary's Church proceeded "amidst the blessings, prayers, and tears of the rich, and poor, of the young, and old—of Protestants and Catholics."[115] In 1854, some of the sisters moved to Columbia, opening St. Peter's school for children to complement the program at St. Mary's College, opened by Fr. Jeremiah O'Connell two years earlier.[116]

Like the Sisters of Mercy, the Ursulines, whom England recruited from Europe, viewed education as even more crucial than health care. Soon after they arrived in Charleston, the *Miscellany* announced their intention to educate young ladies "in all the becoming accomplishments of their sex, in the principles of pure religion and the practice of solid and unostentatious piety." England explained to a convention of South Carolina Catholics that he had long viewed the education of young women as a priority and that the Ursulines would meet this need. The delegates to the convention promptly marched to the convent to welcome the sisters, who announced in 1835 that they were ready to receive students.[117] England continually praised their labors, promising a friend that newcomers in Charleston could be assured of "the best education in virtue & religious and scientific information and ladylike accomplishments" for their daughters.[118]

A third female order made a temporary impression on schooling in Charleston. The Dames de la Retraite traced their roots to seventeenth-century Brittany. Persecuted during the French Revolution, the order took up teaching after its restoration in 1805, and in the 1830s, a small group under Madame Hery du Jarday came to Philadelphia, where they opened a school. By the end of 1833, they added an academy in Charleston. England welcomed them, but requested letters testifying to their standing with the order in France, not an unusual request at a time when the rejects of European dioceses sometimes made their way to America. When the women failed to produce the letters, England asked them to leave. They opened an academy in St. Augustine, but they also returned to Charleston in 1839 for a fund-raising fair.[119]

Although the Diocese of Charleston never had a Catholic school system as extensive as Bardstown's, or as lasting as Mobile's, in 1835, the city housed the Philosophical and Classical Seminary for boys, a diocesan seminary, an elementary school for girls run by the Sisters of Mercy, the Ursuline Academy for the higher education of girls, and the school for young ladies of the Dames de la Retraite. The host of religious women as teachers especially privileged Catholic girls. By 1839, England could assure the First General Convention of the Diocese that no other diocese could surpass them "in the possessions of a good institution for the perfect education of young ladies."[120]

Catholics in Charleston tried to identify themselves with intellectual progress. England joined the literary society as a charter member who presented papers. Despite diocesan debts, he hoped to establish a museum as an answer to charges that Catholics opposed science.[121] His *Miscellany* published accounts of scientific discoveries, historical essays, literary reviews, and poetry. He also gave lectures that publicized Catholic interest in learning.

Southern colleges proved to be open to the ideas of learned Catholics. During a visit to Columbia in 1825, England preached in the chapel of South Carolina College "at the request of the students, and with the consent of the respectable President."[122] The Dialectic and Philanthropic Society at the University of North Carolina opened its lecture platform to William Gaston, a well-known Catholic layman in North Carolina. Bishop Spalding of Louisville later addressed the Maryland Institute on "the thousand years' struggle between the Crescent and the Cross."[123] Such invitations gave Catholics a chance to showcase their value to southern education.

"The Hardest Work I Ever Undertook": Education's Costs

Because Catholic communities were small and often poor, the schools required sacrifices. A few wealthy Catholics could help. Ann Rhodes, a member of the Sisters of Loretto, sold her possessions to buy the land for the sisters' school. The youngest member of the order, she won election as superior before dying of consumption in a bare cabin.[124] The Sisters of Nazareth benefited when a wealthy postulant—the daughter of a non-Catholic and the widow of a prominent physician—joined the community and donated $3,000, a family of slaves, and valuable property.[125] Edward Fenwick used his patrimony to establish the Dominican house and College of St. Thomas Aquinas at St. Rose, Kentucky, and the Gardiner family gave three hundred acres of land in Kentucky for a girls' school in 1821.[126] But few Catholics could give such substantial donations.

Maintaining the schools required vast expenditures of time and energy. Bishop England complained that having to teach three to four hours each day impeded his other duties.[127] The struggle to cover the seminary's expenses and to pay down its debt also generated unending anxiety. In frontier Kentucky, the rigors could be even more taxing. A community of Trappists ran a school at Pottinger's Creek even after several of them succumbed to the hardships of the wilderness.[128] Resources were scarce. A seminarian traveling to Baltimore asked Flaget for pocket money. The bishop declined the request: "in the circumstances in which I am, to touch my purse, is to wound me to the heart . . . I wish my priests to make their delights in poverty."[129] Catholics sometimes had to delight in poverty, especially if they wanted to support the schools.

It was also no easy undertaking to teach southern students. Conflicts between students and faculty erupted because of student immaturity and the dictates of southern honor.[130] Flaget implied that students from the Deep South were especially difficult: "Although I complain rather often about my Kentuckians, they are Angels compared to the inhabitants especially of lower Louisiana."[131] The college register for 1847–1849 at Spring

Hill recorded expulsions for offenses that ranged from circulating naughty songs to "insubordination" and association with "scamps" in the college. College authorities also expelled one student for wounding classmates and another for threatening a servant with a knife.[132] At St. Joseph's, a student waylaid a priest he believed had offended him, grabbing him by the throat and beating him over the head with a hickory club.[133] Fr. Nerinckx, who had escaped the French Revolution, labored alone in the wilderness, and built numerous churches, described preparing ninety teenage girls for their First Communion as "the hardest work I ever undertook."[134] Jefferson Davis recalled that one night during his school days in Kentucky, a group of boys extinguished the candle in a priest's room and then pelted the man with "cabbages, squashes, biscuits, potatoes, and all kinds of missiles."[135] Non-Catholics, especially those with school-aged children, could appreciate that Catholics endured far more than merely financial hardships in their educational missions. For Catholics, the demands posed by education in terms of time, energy, money, and sometimes physical safety made outside aid essential.

Southern Catholics appealed to Europe for help, and aid came primarily from three missionary societies: The Society for the Propagation of the Faith, established at Lyon in 1822; the Leopold Foundation, organized in Vienna in 1828; and the Ludwig Mission, founded by Louis I of Bavaria in 1838. Prelates traveled to Europe to make appeals to these societies, but England found a more convenient route. The nephew of the head of the Lyon Society lived in Savannah, and his intervention helped secure Charleston's first donation in 1829.[136] In the 1840s, Portier received several hundred thousand francs from the society. The foundations of Spring Hill College rested on a gift of 30,000 francs from a friend whom Portier visited in Rome in 1829.[137] The oldest of the dioceses, Bardstown was the first to obtain assistance from the society, receiving $1,300 in 1823.[138] The Lyon Society was so generous that the first Provincial Council of Baltimore in 1829 sent a letter of thanks written by Bishop Flaget.[139]

Aid from Europe came with a price. Overseas appeals demanded considerable effort and produced only sporadic assistance, and they drew Protestant criticism. They stoked fears that European despots would undermine American institutions. Catholics could only wish that Protestant conspiracy theories were true. "We should feel happy, if it were true that there had arrived in the United States, a corps of Jesuits. . . . We should feel doubly gratified, if it were true that the Pope could spare $24,000 yearly, for any mission," noted the *Miscellany* in response to a Protestant journal's "exposé" of Catholic plans to take over the West.[140] The absence of evidence for Catholic plots did nothing to dampen Protestant suspicions. Samuel F. B. Morse, whose *Foreign Conspiracy Against the Liberties of the United States* epitomized the anti-Catholic impulse in the 1830s and 1840s, argued that the Austrian crown controlled the papacy and covertly tried to destroy American democracy through the Leopold Foundation.[141] But Catholics discovered a source of help closer to home.

Protestant Patronage

Catholics struggling to build schools reached beyond their meager resources, but Protestants made up the difference. In 1810, Badin noted that Protestants offered land to induce Catholics to emigrate, at times with the stipulation that they build churches and schools.[142] In 1826, the citizens of Harrodsburg, Kentucky, offered Flaget a building, farm, and lot if he would establish schools like those he had built in Bardstown.[143] In 1835, Charles Ashley, a Protestant and possibly the wealthiest man in the Arkansas Territory, offered a missionary priest named Fr. Annemond Dupuy twelve plots of land in Little Rock and $50 in cash per year for five years if Dupuy would build a school.[144] When the Sisters of Nazareth enlarged their boarding school in Bardstown in 1824, merchants allowed them to pay for supplies at their convenience.[145] In Alabama, the Diocese of Mobile purchased the site for Spring Hill College from a "kindly disposed Protestant" and friend of Portier who probably also donated twenty acres. The city of Mobile contributed another 380 acres.[146] The generosity of non-Catholics was so great that Catholics sometimes struggled to take advantage of it. In Hopkinsville, Kentucky, non-Catholics pledged four thousand acres of land for the Sisters of Loretto to establish a school, but because the sisters could not spare any members for the project, the pledge went unredeemed.[147]

Protestants entrusted their children to Catholic educators. Their tuition payments sustained school budgets. Spring Hill College recorded consistent Protestant attendance during the late antebellum period (table 4). Beginning in 1849, the register noted denominational affiliations. The major denominations were well represented (table 5).

Georgetown College educated over one thousand Protestant students between 1790 and 1859. These students formed a third of the entire student body.[148] In St. Louis, in 1844, a visitor noted that schools run by the Jesuits and the Sisters of Charity attracted more students than all the common schools combined, "so excellent is their organization, and so extensive their

Table 4. Religious affiliation of Spring Hill College students, 1847–1864

Year	Catholics	Protestants	Jews	"Infidels"
1847	43	4		1
1848	64	19		
1849	62	19	1	
1850	76	19		3
1851	55	18		9
1852	68	14		
1853	69	15		1
1854	56	3		
1855	38	9	1	1
1856	66	10		5
1857	86	6		3
1858	56	14		4
1859	101	11		5
1860	103	19		
1861	39	5		3
1862	17	8		12
1863	82	8	1	11
1864	39	17		5

Note: Statistics from this chart do not correspond precisely to statistics culled from the register. It seems likely that the register did not record all students who enrolled at the college.
Source: Spring Hill College Archives, *Historia Domus* 95.

influence."[149] In 1857, a Catholic elementary school in Jackson, Mississippi, reported that fifteen of its forty students were non-Catholic.[150] In Kentucky, Protestants attended the Dominican College of St. Thomas Aquinas and Presentation Academy.[151] Many sought admission to the school at Loretto.[152] Nazareth Academy educated over a hundred young Protestant ladies from Mississippi alone.[153] At times, Protestants constituted the majority of students in Catholic schools. During an 1839 visit, Flaget observed that less than a third of the students at St. Joseph's were Catholic and that a school run by the Sisters of Nazareth had scarcely forty Catholics out of 135 boarders.[154] Many non-Catholics attended St. Mary's College in Columbia, South Carolina.[155] In Charleston, England noted that his school had twelve Catholic students and fifty-one non-Catholics "from the most respectable families."[156]

Table 5. Protestant Spring Hill College students by denomination, 1849–1865

	1849–1854	1854–1859	1859–1865
Presbyterian	15	6	21
Methodist	14	8	21
Baptist	4	5	7
Episcopal	29	13	34
Unitarian	1	0	0
Protestant	6	2	2
Congregationalist	2	0	0
Campbellite	1	0	2
Other	16	12	31

Note: I treat students who the register lists as having received baptism in a particular denomination as members of that denomination. "Other" includes those whose affiliation is "none," "not baptized," or baptized but without affiliation and those for whom the record is inconclusive.
Source: Spring Hill College Register.

Catholic schools had long attracted students from America's elite families. "The education of all the first classes of Protestants seems to be entrusted to the Catholic priests and nuns. . . . The parents say that their children are better taught and better looked after than they would be in any other schools," noted an English traveler in the early 1850s.[157] Catholic religious and laity, often scions of Europe's aristocratic families, were among the most educated and cultured people in the South. Wealthy southerners valued the cosmopolitanism they imparted. The convent schools of the Ursulines and the Religious of the Sacred Heart in New Orleans and along the Mississippi Valley reproduced the French tradition of elite boarding schools, and their reputation for instilling ladylike virtues attracted the daughters of prominent families regardless of religion. Such elite education had its detractors. A Scottish traveler denounced the "frivolous accomplishments" associated with a Catholic women's school in Natchez, although he attested to the school's popularity by bemoaning that so many "nominal Protestants" enrolled their daughters.[158] In the East, the Academy of the Visitandines of Georgetown drew young women from Washington and throughout the South from its founding in 1799. Because of the school's proximity to the capitol, politicians enrolled their daughters, and presidents James Madison and John Quincy Adams spoke at commencements.[159] Next door to Visitation Academy, Georgetown College enjoyed similar renown, attracting students from influential families, including two close relatives of George Washington, who formally visited the school in 1797.[160] Not far from Washington, the school of the Sisters of Charity of Emmitsburg likewise attracted upper-class Protestants as well as Catholics. These elite schools benefited from the perception of Catholicism as a refined, aristocratic religion, and from the esteem of some Protestants for European religious orders.[161] The schooling perpetuated these views for future Protestant generations.

Other southern Catholic schools, although lacking the pedigree of those in New Orleans or Georgetown, attracted Protestants. "The Jesuits," noted a Scottish traveler in 1844, "have seized with equal success on the education of the future statesmen and legislators of Missouri."[162] In Kentucky, Jefferson Davis studied at the Dominican College of St. Thomas, and three of his nieces attended the school at Nazareth. St. Mary's College counted Governor J. P. Knott and Judge John E. Newman among its alumni. St. Joseph's educated two future Mississippi congressmen, Otho R. Singleton and William R. Miles, two future governors of Louisiana, and several other powerful Kentuckians, including Cassius Clay, famed as an abolitionist.[163] "I do not cease to feel much consolation," remarked Flaget, "in seeing that the richest and the most distinguished families in our regions, put themselves above all religious prejudices, and are eager to entrust the education of their children to Catholic priests."[164]

Some Catholic educational institutions enjoyed the favor of government. In 1818, Flaget reported that the legislature granted him the sizeable estate of a Trappist who had died, even though the state had legal claim to the property. He intended to use this windfall to build the seminary.[165] Six years later, St. Joseph's College received a shipment of books, scientific instruments, and ornaments from Europe. Congress passed a bill waving customs fees for the college.[166] England boasted that he could import items for his planned museum duty-free, because "the Secretary of State . . . is anxious to oblige me."[167]

Friends in high places helped Catholics win recognition for their schools. In an 1825 column in the *Miscellany,* Flaget thanked non-Catholics for their kindness, noting that the state legislature had voted almost unanimously to raise St. Joseph's College to a university.[168] Such aid persisted in Kentucky for decades. In 1830, the legislature incorporated "the female literary and benevolent institutions" of Nazareth and Loretto. (The Speaker of the House of Representatives had sent his daughter to Nazareth.) The legislator who introduced the bills in the Senate pointed out that many members knew the value of the schools firsthand because their daughters were students.[169] In 1837, a state legislator whose son attended St. Mary's College introduced a bill to grant the school a charter and empower it to confer degrees. The bill passed, and the lawmakers also invited Fr. Abell, who had gone to Frankfort to witness the vote, to preach in the State House of Representatives.[170] Two years earlier, Spring Hill College won similar support from the Alabama legislature, which unanimously approved a charter and the right to confer degrees.[171] Charters were a reward of political patronage and a prize in the spoils system, and Catholic success in getting them demonstrated respectability.[172] Fr. John Bazin, second president of Spring Hill and later Bishop of Vincennes, remarked that a major advantage of the college was that it put Catholics in touch "with all that is most distinguished and influential in the land."[173]

Non-Catholics recognized that Catholic schools enriched society. "The charitable objects of your institution . . . and its furtherance of the wholesome purpose of society, by training up its younger members . . . cannot fail to ensure it the patronage of the government," wrote Thomas Jefferson in response to a request from the Ursulines of New Orleans that their property be respected after the Louisiana Purchase.[174] In an act incorporating a Catholic college in Kentucky, the state legislature noted that "it is not less accordant to the genius of this Republic, than compatible with the sentiments of the legislature, that the dissemination of learning and morality are amongst the first attributes that should characterize its citizens," before stipulating that the school should accept students of all faiths as it had up to then.[175] After attending examinations at the Catholic school for orphans and adjacent free school for girls in Mobile, a correspondent for the *Alabama Planter* rhapsodized that "one's heart goes involuntarily to estimate the salutary fruits which such establishments provide for society—and although war has its triumphs, herein are laurels won which remain forever green."[176]

Some non-Catholics welcomed the schools as an opportunity to enrich themselves. News that a school would open in a suburb of Mobile prompted speculators to build a hotel near the site. Southerners realized that schools boosted local economies fully as much as they elevated learning. One of the first professors at Spring Hill College reported that news of its founding "delighted all, even the Protestants, who are the first to favor us."[177] Interest in education and profit converged in Nashville, leading non-Catholics to solicit a Catholic school. The city's citizens, few of whom were Catholic, raised a subscription to induce Bishop Flaget to send a priest to establish a school. "The fame of Bardstown college had led them to form high ideas of the literary acquirements of our clergy, and the great advantages which this town derived from the institution (perhaps equivalent to 50,000 dollars annually) had prevailed on speculators themselves to be generous," the correspondent explained.[178] A Kentucky legislator sponsoring a bill to charter two schools pointed out that students from other states had brought money into Kentucky.[179]

For all these reasons, the schools won support even from Protestants who did not enroll their children. A student at Nazareth, Kentucky, remembered large crowds at the 1825 public examinations, crowds that included Secretary of State Henry Clay, who presented the students' awards.[180] Protestants no doubt liked the pageantry and entertainment. The first commencement at Spring Hill under the Jesuit administration, for example, lasted several days and included public examinations, with the audience invited to add questions, discourses in English and French, plays, orations, a brass band, and the awarding of honors.[181] The schools offered other forms of entertainment. The students at St. Mary's College staged patriotic plays that drew local audiences to the outdoor amphitheater.[182] Or sometimes the occasions could be less joyful. When Fr. George Elder died in 1838 after years of teaching at St. Joseph's College, the mourners "attended without distinction of creed or sect" and formed a funeral procession over half a mile long.[183]

Indeed, Protestants could dispense lavish praise on Catholic educators. The *Mobile Times* wrote that Fr. Francis Gautrelet, president of Spring Hill College, was "as pure and learned a man as our country contains." So effective was he that "there is not a man or youth who has been under his teaching . . . but will join us in calling blessings on his venerable head."[184] England felt that he could make his Charleston schools successful because "the citizens had a greater opinion of my learning than I merited" and because they respected the Ursulines as educators.[185] In Kentucky, the *Bardstown Herald* expressed its pleasure that the Sisters of Nazareth, "with their extensive acquirements, possess a peculiar facility of communicating instruction even to the feeblest capacity, and at the same time of exciting in them a thirst for literature which so highly adorns the female character."[186] A judge hearing a case involving the sisters advised the jury that whereas most women could not manage property, Mother Catherine Spalding was "an eminent exception," adding that he had heard that "she has capacity to govern a state."[187]

Protestants praised the fruits of Catholics' labors. "Your pupils hitherto have done credit to themselves, to you, and to us," remarked Thomas Cooper, president of South Carolina College and a frequent correspondent with England.[188] After witnessing examinations at two Catholic schools in Mobile, one visitor noted that "the culture of the pupils was displayed to great advantage." He believed that their classes in needlework prepared young women "for that highest and noblest office of the sex—to be good, gentle and discreet wives."[189] The *Bardstown Herald* bragged that the recitations at Nazareth in 1827 "would have done honor to any institution in the Union," and a legislator in Kentucky praised the Sisters of Loretto and Nazareth for having "sent forth to society, some of its brightest ornaments."[190] Protestants could take pride in Catholic accomplishments.

Reading, Writing, 'Rithmatic, . . . and Religion?

Catholics, in turn, welcomed students of all faiths into their schools. In Kentucky, the Sisters of Nazareth and Sisters of Loretto educated young women without distinction of creed: "No one shall be refused for belonging to another denomination, if they have the readiness to observe the Rules of the school." The sisters would even excuse non-Catholics from chapel services, although they thought that dissenters "ought not take it ill if they are invited."[191] In Charleston, England's Philosophical and Classical Seminary served the community "without any discrimination of Catholic, Jew or Protestant."[192] The *Miscellany* noted that the Ursulines "neither seek nor invite pupils of any denomination," but it added that the nuns "can not refuse their services under the circumstances prescribed by their rule," and it summarized the conditions under which Protestants would be admitted.[193] The 1848 prospectus at Spring Hill noted that students of all denominations would be accepted "provided, for the sake of order and uniformity, they be willing to conform themselves to the others in the exterior exercises of worship."[194]

The schools invited participation from the whole community. The *Miscellany* advertised public examinations of the Philosophical and Classical Seminary and invited everyone, especially the educated, to attend. Many accepted the invitation.[195] In 1825, the school's president announced a contest, open to students of any school in the state, for the two best addresses, in English and Latin, to commemorate Lafayette's visit to the city.[196] At Spring Hill College, Fr. Pierre Mauvernay, formerly an officer in Napoleon's army, organized a military corps called the Spring Hill Lancers that marched in public parades in Mobile and "helped to make the College an integral part of public life."[197] In the North, Catholic schools often separated and protected the Catholic community from Protestants. In the South, they encouraged Catholic-Protestant interaction.

They reassured parents that teachers would not pressure Protestant students to convert. The prospectus of Spring Hill promised that "no influence will be exercised upon pupils bred in the principles of other Christian Denominations." The charter the legislature granted in 1835 reaffirmed that "no person shall be excluded from any liberty, immunity, office, or situation in said College, on account of his religious persuasion."[198] Regulations for religious exercises stipulated that Protestants memorize twelve verses of the New Testament, but they could assist at catechism only with their parents' written permission.[199] Non-Catholics suffered no discrimination. They were no more likely to be expelled or disciplined than Catholic students were, and they earned praise from school officials. "They have, as a rule, excellent characters and are remarkably kindhearted," extolled Bazin.[200]

The most famous alumnus of Kentucky's Catholic schools, Jefferson Davis, testified to the lack of proselytizing. Aware that many Americans believed that priests pressured students to convert, he recalled his experiences. Convinced that he wanted to become a Catholic, he interrupted the head of the school in the middle of a meal to inform him of his wish. "He received me kindly, handed me a biscuit and a bit of cheese, and told me that for the present I had better take some Catholic food," Davis recalled.[201] It was as close as he ever came to becoming Catholic.

In Charleston, England assured the public that at his school "the religion of the children is neither known nor inquired into." The prospectus, he observed, pledged that "no religious instruction, of any kind whatsoever, should be introduced." Protestant students had nothing to fear, he added, because he supposed that they constituted a majority of the student body.[202] In response to a letter in the *Southern Intelligencer* charging that the school aimed to win converts, England repeated his pledge that school officials would respect all faiths. He added that the school had no religious books, that Catholics would not invite Protestant students to religious services, and that the adjacent church closed during school hours. He cited a school regulation: "No pupil shall remark upon any difference of religious belief between himself and another, nor upon any such difference between any of his fellow pupils; nor in any wise converse upon the subject of religion during his attendance at any of the duties or recreations of the Seminary."[203] The disclaimers imply Protestant suspicions of Catholic schools, but Catholics nonetheless succeeded in attracting Protestant children.

Calming Protestant suspicions was particularly important in schools run by nuns, for Protestants were likely to have imbibed shocking stories of women forced into convents. Most such stories originated in the North, but the South had its own Maria Monks. In the 1830s, Millie McPherson went public with her tale of escape from a convent in Bardstown. Two decades later, Josephine Bunkley caused a sensation with her exposé of the Sisters of Charity of Emmitsburg.[204] In such tales, nuns often selected their prey from the ranks of the girls in their schools. The stories fed not only anti-Catholic inclinations but also quasi-pornographic impulses, promising forbidden glimpses of the violent and erotic, and they reflected anxieties about sexual values, women, and families.[205] Specifically, the "attack on convents in Jacksonian and antebellum America intricately voiced Protestant perplexities over the ongoing construction of the 'cult of domesticity.'" As Protestants fashioned a domestic ideal that simultaneously elevated women and confined them, Catholicism "advertised a constellation of alternative femininities" that threatened but also intrigued Protestants.[206] Neither the consumers nor the publishers of convent tales necessarily worried about Catholicism. Some authors simply espied profit in provocative writings.[207]

Just as the motives behind convent tales varied, so too did responses to the spread of convents and schools. Wealthy Protestants had long patronized convent schools, but others were suspicious. In the North, class divisions appeared in the burning of the Charlestown convent in August 1834. The mob that attacked the convent was Protestant, but so were many of the convent's students. Working-class Congregationalists made up the mob, but the students belonged to elite Unitarian families.[208] The upper classes—apart from the clergy—were generally restrained in their anti-Catholicism, but even they grew uneasy as Catholic schools proliferated. Between 1829 and 1859, thirty-nine new foundations of religious women took root in America.[209] Many Protestants of all classes worried as Catholic schools and convents sprang up in their own communities.

The most serious attacks against Catholics, especially nuns, took place in the North, but incidents also occurred in the South. News of the impending arrival of Ursulines in Charleston led one Protestant minister to call for citizens to prevent the establishment of a convent to which single women would be "either carried . . . by force, or driven . . . by disappointment of misfortune, or drawn . . . by the influence of those in whom they confide." Uneasy with the destruction of the Ursuline convent in Charlestown, the public seemed anxious to avoid further disturbance and ignored the appeal.[210] But sometimes passionate tempers prevailed. In Hannibal, Missouri, and Baltimore, rumors of women held unwillingly in convents nearly sparked mob violence. In Frederick, Maryland; New Orleans; Galveston; and Columbia, mobs damaged or destroyed convents and an orphanage.[211]

The potential for violence simmered below the surface of southern hospitality, but the region generally avoided anti-Catholic violence. In most cases, civic leaders stopped it before it got out of hand. In Baltimore, in 1839, with rumors flying about an escaped nun, the mayor visited the convent, interviewed the nuns, and announced no one lived at the convent against her will. When his words failed to assuage public worry, volunteers guarded the building for three days and nights until tensions passed. Similarly, when a mob harassed the Ursulines in Columbia, the mayor placed a guard around the convent and civic leaders called a meeting to ensure peace.[212] Leading southern Protestants denounced threats against Catholics and acted to prevent violence.

Catholic leaders also learned to defuse threats against nuns and their schools. In 1815, three young women studying with the Sisters of Loretto asked permission to join the order. Their parents protested, and accusations circulated that Fr. Nerinckx exercised hypnotic powers over young minds. Bishop Flaget promptly delivered a sermon on the religious life and assured his audience that women could enter only of their own free will and could leave whenever they desired.[213] Catholic officials tried to ensure that no one entered religious orders impulsively or with misguided notions. David asked Bruté to describe the hardships facing the Sisters of Nazareth to any young lady of Baltimore who expressed an interest in joining them. He noted that the sisters prevented entry into the novitiate without parental permission.[214] The orders assured the public that nobody would lure beloved daughters into convents.

The orders of women—to many Protestants the epitome of foreignness—strove to prove their American loyalties. Some jealously guarded their independence from European societies. The Sisters of Loretto rejected Nerinckx's urging that they affiliate with a European order, as did the Sisters of Nazareth when Flaget proposed to unite them with the French Daughters of Charity.[215] The orders adapted to American conditions, discarding impractical cloistral requirements, charging tuition in their schools, broadening their curricula, buying slaves, and modifying their dress. A laudatory chronicler of the Convent of the Visitation in Georgetown explained that they elected their superior every three years: "Thus the elective franchise in this country, in its most republican form, has found its way into 'The Convent's Shade.'"[216] Some superiors recognized that the sisters would be more useful if they could cast off European rules. Arguing for changes in the rule of the Sisters of Nazareth, Father David concluded that American conditions precluded strict adherence to the rule that bound the French counterpart.[217] Even Rome counseled sensitivity to the American context.

In 1858, Propaganda noted that "the character of the [American] people and their laws and customs favor liberty"; solemn vows were unwise because "it often happens that girls change their minds and wish to leave and cannot be detained for fear of the people."[218]

The adaptation of American values was more than expedient—it was necessary. Of the six American women's religious orders established between 1790 and 1829, all survived. Of the six imported from Europe, only one achieved stability.[219] Americanized convents challenged the preconceptions of non-Catholic visitors. A Scottish minister touring a convent of the Sisters of the Sacred Heart in St. Louis noted with surprise: "Their veils were gracefully cast behind, as the ornament, not the disguise of the person. Iron gratings I saw none. We sat on chairs face to face, like any other honest people."[220] Such convents could never be accused of subverting American liberty.

The women's orders promised also not to proselytize. The prospectus of Nazareth Academy praised liberty of conscience and assured Protestant parents that their children would face no pressure to convert.[221] Mother Frances Gardiner, principal of the school at Nazareth, testified that the academy required parental consent for any student seeking baptism, a commitment affirmed by Flaget and David.[222] The Religious of the Sacred Heart in New Orleans went even further, requiring that parents not only give permission for baptisms but also attend the ceremonies.[223] In Charleston, the Sisters of Mercy catechized Catholic students in the cathedral every Tuesday and Thursday but promised "no interference with the religious opinions of other pupils," a commitment echoed by the Ursulines.[224]

Catholics nonetheless won converts through their schools. Letters to Europe from Catholics in Kentucky mentioned students who elected to join the church.[225] Fr. Joseph Haseltine, a convert from New England, helped convert several students while he was superior of the Sisters of Nazareth. Anna Bradford, one of three nieces of Jefferson Davis to convert at the Nazareth school, admired the priest and believed that he had prayed for her conversion.[226] At least fifty-seven Protestant students at Georgetown College converted between 1790 and 1859.[227] The schools converted more than students: H. V. Brown, a New England artist who instructed sisters who wanted to teach art, became first a Catholic and then a priest.[228] The Spring Hill College register recorded nine conversions of both students and alumni between 1847 and 1862, and family members also converted. Soon after the death of a converted former student at Spring Hill, his father, an Episcopal priest, joined the church, and the fever of

1853 encouraged another father to make the change.[229] The authorities at Spring Hill refused to proselytize—and they required parental consent, recording parents' wishes about religious instruction. But some converts refused to be turned aside.

Catholic educators were certainly open to converts. The Spring Hill register recorded the religious affiliations and predilections of both students and parents. Officials identified students likely to convert: "Not a Catholic—no objection to his being received in the church."[230] Flaget acknowledged the spiritual mission, hoping that "all will turn some day to the greater glory of God and to the salvation of many souls."[231] Orders sometimes used their success at winning converts as a bargaining chip. When Flaget wanted to merge the Sisters of Nazareth with another order, the sisters wrote a remonstrance: "With due humility," they pointed out "the numbers of respectable families added to the Church by the education and religious impressions which individuals receive at Nazareth; every year brings with it conversions either in the school or after the young ladies have left our institutions."[232] The sisters kept their independence. Like the hospitals and orphanages, the schools did not press for converts, but they were happy to welcome them.

They made no secret of their ambition to remove Protestant prejudices. The Sisters of Nazareth pointed out "the immense weight of prejudice which has been removed by Nazareth's humble efforts."[233] The Sisters of Loretto aimed to improve the minds of Protestants by "removing the prejudices that may have been instilled in them against our religion."[234] Flaget wrote to Propaganda about the amelioration of prejudices as a goal of the schools, and Bazin remarked that Protestants at Spring Hill "begin to show esteem and respect for those whom they have been taught to look upon as fanatics as idolaters." Even parents could have their minds changed: one mother "said if she knew a Catholic she would cast him to the flames," but after she met the priests she enrolled her son.[235] A Baptist student at Spring Hill, anti-Catholic when he enrolled, made his First Communion in just over a year.[236] Of course, influence flowed both ways. Archbishop Samuel Eccleston speculated that contact with Protestant peers led some Catholic boys to abandon the ambition of priesthood.[237] Spalding believed that seminarians teaching at St. Joseph's College "had their vocations shaken by being thrown so much in contact with youth of the world."[238] Nevertheless, the mingling of Catholic and Protestant students probably benefited the church.

Freed from prejudice, Protestant students carried their new understanding of Catholicism into the world. "Having known themselves the false imputations charged against Catholics," church leaders hoped that they would become agents of tolerance.[239] One non-Catholic journal warned that Protestant students in Catholic schools "embrace the Catholic religion, or at least receive impressions in its favor, *which they carry into the bosom of their families.*"[240] The lines between winning converts, ameliorating prejudices, and changing society's views of Catholicism could blur. England favored the admission of Protestants to the Ursuline school for multiple reasons: "their prejudices will be removed and many conversions will follow; or at least the way will be opened through the good ladies educated by the nuns to exercise a very powerful influence on the whole mass of society."[241] It is impossible to quantify any decline in southern prejudice, but Protestant students from influential families must have at least helped integrate the church into southern society.

Other Protestants remained suspicious. Some objected to the reciprocal relationship between colleges and seminaries. In Charleston, Protestant ministers warned that England used tuition from his school to subsidize the training of priests, and several Protestants withdrew their children. They accepted Catholic teachers but balked at educating priests.[242] England attributed this to jealousy: "it is acknowledged that we make the best scholars, yet as our opponents see the use to which our funds would be converted, they will not send their children to us." But he had to concede that the Catholics' increase "of numbers, of respectable standing & of influence in this place, is too striking to pass unobserved & to leave us without the annoyance of those who would prefer its being otherwise."[243]

A more serious problem than educating priests was the education of blacks. Catholic teaching of blacks, both free and slave, stoked fears of Catholic disloyalty. Badin insisted that masters allow their slaves to receive instruction in the catechism, and Catholics also offered blacks a secular education. The Ursulines taught them almost immediately after arriving in New Orleans, and other orders followed their lead.[244] England charged the Sisters of Mercy with educating black girls and hoped to establish a male order to teach black boys "free and slave."[245] Such initiatives met resistance. In 1835, in Charleston, suspicions about black education nearly exploded into violence. Abolitionist societies and firebrand politicians had put the city on edge, and in late July, a shipment of abolitionist tracts aroused a mob to sack the Charleston post office. Suspicious of England for serving as papal legate to Haiti, the mob turned on Catholics. Rumors of impending danger led England to station an armed guard of Irish volunteers. Protestant civic leaders joined them, and the danger passed. But England, under pressure, closed the school run by the Sisters of Mercy.[246]

The Tip of the Spear?

The gravest charge leveled against Catholic schools was that they spearheaded a plot against American liberty. This was the argument of Lyman Beecher's *A Plea for the West.* A celebrated Congregationalist minister, who in 1832 accepted the presidency of the newly formed Lane Theological Seminary in Cincinnati, Beecher fretted about the expansion of Catholicism in the West. Drawing on Samuel F. B. Morse's "disclosure" of a Catholic plot, Beecher's 1835 tract warned that Catholic infiltration represented "one department of a comprehensive effort to maintain despotic government against the march of free institutions."[247] The forces of despotism pursued their nefarious designs through schools. Education would guide the ship of state, so the right people needed to control the rudder. Catholic schools were dangerous because they were antirepublican: "I am pressing upon republican America that it is better for her to educate her population by her own sons and money, than to rely on the school-masters and charitable contributions of the despotic governments of Catholic Europe."[248] If loyal Americans did not build schools, "the Catholic powers of Europe" would "make up our deficiencies" until Catholic power was "sufficient to embarrass our republican movements."[249] Even Beecher conceded that the "self-denial and good deeds" of some priests and nuns "in the visitation of the sick and the education of the poor" were "worthy of imitation," but he had no doubt that Catholic education writ large was dangerous.[250] Beecher's incendiary sermons in Boston in 1834 helped inspire the attack on the Ursuline convent in Charlestown.[251] *A Plea for the West* had the potential to prove even more damaging.

Beecher was by no means alone. The *Quarterly Register of the American Education Society* saw the Catholic schools establishing "THE SUPREMACY OF PAPAL ROME" in the West, and it issued a warning: "It becomes THE FRIENDS OF EDUCATION among us, *who are yet Protestants,* to look well to that great concern."[252] Foreign observers seconded such arguments. A Scottish visitor to New Orleans noted that Rome recognized the significance of the Mississippi Valley and "thither it has sent its agents in great numbers, and planted its colleges and nunneries . . . through the instrument of education to proselytise all to Rome."[253] The Jesuits bore the brunt of Protestant fear and hatred. One anti-Catholic association in Kentucky referred to them as a threat to "civil and religious institutions, and the moral and intellectual development of our youth." The association solicited contributions for an exposé of Jesuitism by an alleged former member.[254] Political nativism and anti-Catholicism increased in the 1850s, emboldening opponents of Catholic schools. In Columbia, South Carolina, threats against St. Mary's College became so troublesome that school officials contemplated shutting down.[255]

If Catholics were using schools for a papal takeover of America, Protestants who supported the schools were complicit in the effort. During the 1830s, Protestant nativists began to caution their coreligionists against collaboration with Romanism. A Missouri correspondent to the *Home Missionary* warned in 1829 that contributions from Protestants facilitated an ominous spread of Catholic institutions, especially schools, across the West.[256] Lyman Beecher alerted his readers that Catholics kept their tuition low specifically to attract Protestants, "calculating that for a morsel of meat we shall sell our birth-right" as Americans, republicans, and Christians.[257]

In the face of such conspiracy theories, Catholics insisted that their schools buttressed American liberty, and they used public events to highlight their patriotism. In Kentucky, Fr. Peter Chazelle, the head of St. Mary's, wrote patriotic dramas entitled *Red Hawk* and *The Treason of Arnold* that the students performed for their neighbors.[258] St. Joseph's commemorated Independence Day with processions, orations, a banquet, and the firing of cannons.[259] In addition to holidays mandated by the bishop, the faculty and students at Spring Hill celebrated such national holidays as Washington's Birthday, the anniversary of Jackson's victory at New Orleans, and the signing of the Declaration of Independence. An invitation to a Fourth of July celebration, addressed to parents and supporters, promised a reading of the Declaration, speeches, discourses, lectures, a play, and refreshments. The *Mobile Tribune* recorded large crowds at the 1852 celebration of Washington's Birthday and noted that the institution "continues to sustain its reputation, and even to increase in public favor."[260] Catholic schools became advertisements for Catholic patriotism.

The schools ensured that their teachers were loyal Americans regardless of their origins. The *Miscellany* responded to a rumor that Georgetown's faculty was entirely foreign by announcing "not without pleasure . . . that the *entire Faculty without exception* consists of native Americans."[261] Other schools had to establish their Americanness in other ways. Fr. Peter John Mathias Loras, a native of Lyon who served as president of Spring Hill from 1833 until becoming first Bishop of Dubuque in 1837, told his teachers that in America "to be French is the original sin." Fr. Francis Gautrelet, the first Jesuit president of Spring Hill, sent the French members of his faculty to cities in the North and West where they could quickly learn to speak English and to observe American customs. Gautrelet himself traveled to Kentucky, where he learned how to run an American college from the Jesuits at St. Mary's. Spring Hill's foreign teachers raced to apply for citizenship.[262] In Charleston, England urged that Catholic teachers be fully American. In recommending a foreign-born teacher to an academy in North Carolina, he praised the man's virtue but added one reservation: "It were to be wished he could unlearn his Irish accent."[263] If Catholic schools colluded in a papist plot to undermine American society, southern Catholics had not been informed.

It became a Catholic commonplace that their seminaries produced loyal citizens. The European origins of many priests and seminarians lent credence to anti-Catholic claims about foreign plots. The church in America could not produce enough priests, but it required European imports to sever ties with their native lands. "I cannot help expressing a wish that your Clergymen may be entirely independent of . . . any foreign prince," stressed Archbishop Carroll in reply to a 1790 report that Catholics in Charleston might receive much-needed funds from Spain and France.[264] All Catholic leaders recognized that "one of the strongest topics of prejudice against our Religion is that it is a foreign Religion,"[265] and that priests and bishops would therefore need to assimilate in order for the faith to find a home in America.

None was more vocal than John England in calling for an American priesthood. In the Pastoral Letter of the Second Provincial Council of Baltimore, written by England, the prelates thanked foreign nations for supplying priests but declared that "we cannot be always, we should not be, when we can avoid it, dependent upon other nations for our ministry."[266] In virtually every public mention of the diocesan seminary, England stressed its indispensable role in training priests suited for America. Only priests educated in America could possess "knowledge of American laws, intimacy with American people, the attachment to American institutions, the habit of American discipline, the zeal for American improvement, and the devotion to American rights."[267] The lay delegates at the fourth South Carolina convention echoed England's sentiments, noting that their republican spirit recoiled at dependency on foreign priests and that the local seminary would satisfy their desire "that our clergy should be fully acquainted with the principles of our civil government, and warmly attached to the constitution of our general government and of our States." Neither the laity nor England tried to exclude foreign seminarians, but they insisted that all be educated as loyal Americans.[268] Some bishops refused to send promising American seminarians to Rome for advanced training for fear that they might develop foreign habits.[269] England even declined to send young men from his diocese to the French-controlled seminary at Baltimore.[270] He wanted to ensure that clerical influence "not be exercised by any person except one who is acquainted with the nature of our republican form of government, and attached to its institutions."[271] The schools were to be bastions of American liberty.

The schools were not the only nurseries of American values. After arriving in America, Portier spent two months in the home of Charles Carroll of Carrollton, the man who epitomized the compatibility of Catholicism and America. David also benefited from Carroll's acquaintance, formed while serving as his chaplain.[272] Bishops boarded European priests with American families to help them learn the language and customs.[273] Assimilated priests helped their newly arrived colleagues fit in. Italian-born Joseph Rosati, later Bishop of St. Louis, recalled of his training in Kentucky: "they advised us not to attack certain customs of the country which were not wrong in themselves . . . but merely different from the customs of Europe."[274] These measures were designed, as England wrote, "to raise up for America, an American clergy: for our Republic, men who love and prefer our institutions."[275]

The range of Protestant reactions to these initiatives emerged during debates in the Kentucky legislature in 1830 over chartering Catholic schools. The House of Representatives, with only one or two dissenters, passed a bill to charter Nazareth. A bill to charter Loretto met opposition when a representative warned that the pope would control the property. He declared himself nonsectarian but opposed to the charter as unconstitutional. Another legislator responded that he "thought the present request a very just one, since Catholics have done so much for education" and that the sisters deserved a charter "for the services which they have rendered . . . by diffusing the benefits of education." The bill passed in the House with only one opposing vote. The Senate required even less debate, with the supporters praising the schools as among the best in the country and pointing to Protestant schools that received charters. One of them argued that Catholics, loyal citizens, deserved the same rights as others. The bill passed thirty-one to four.[276] Throughout the antebellum South, some would always oppose the Catholic schools as cells of foreign influence, but many more welcomed them as engines of progress.

Conclusion

Southern Catholics abided by the spirit of Archbishop John Hughes's oft-repeated dictum: "build the school-house first, and the church afterwards." Their determination seemed foolhardy in light of their numbers and poverty, and they could have built little had they relied on their own resources. Without donations from Protestant citizens, tuition from Protestant students, and recognition from Protestant legislatures, Catholic education would have faltered. William H. Sparks, a planter, lawyer, and poet, represented the sentiments of Protestants who favored cooperation: "The whole system of education, as practiced by the Protestants," he wrote, "is wrong; religious prejudice prevents their learning from the Catholics . . . who are far in advance of their Protestant brethren." He added that he had never known "a vicious, bad woman, wife, or mother trained in a Jesuit convent, or reared by an educated Catholic mother."[277] Like Sparks, a host of broad-minded Protestants recognized that Catholic schools could enlighten the South. All they needed was a little help.

4
Worshipping Together

In 1830, Catholics in Louisville lay the cornerstone for a new St. Louis Church. It was an auspicious occasion, signifying growth and influence. Several bishops had traveled across the country to participate in the event. But as the crowd gathered, Catholics discovered that they were not alone—their Protestant neighbors outnumbered them. Indeed, the crowd swelled to such a size that no Catholic building could accommodate it. But the congregation of a large Presbyterian church came to the rescue by offering use of its facilities. The ceremonial foundation of a Catholic church occurred within a Protestant church before an ecumenical crowd. Bishop Flaget reflected: "What a sight for a Catholic . . . to find himself in a meeting house of the Calvinists . . . in the presence of 3 other bishops, 5 priests, 5 or 6 ministers of different sects, and an audience of which ⅔ were Protestants. Who would believe I would live long enough to witness such a triumph?"[1]

The scale of the event in Louisville was unusual, but the celebration of Catholics and Protestants together in a single house of worship was not. Throughout the Old South, Catholics and Protestants worshipped, prayed, celebrated, and mourned side by side. Divisions between the churches were real, but they were also permeable. Protestants not only participated in Catholic ceremonies and opened their doors to Catholics, but they also helped Catholics build their own churches. St. Louis was only one of many Catholic churches that enjoyed friendship and support from southern Protestants.

"The Valley of the Shadow of Death": Churches in the South

Catholic churches grew in a fluid religious landscape. One historian has argued that religious life before the Revolution, especially in the South, was heterogeneous and often shallow and that post-Revolutionary religious movements were diverse, fluid, syncretistic in belief, and locked in competition.[2] Another historian has observed that the late-eighteenth-century American colonies "were perhaps the most unchurched regions in all Christendom."[3] Such assertions may rely on a flawed definition of what it meant to be "churched." One study of Anglican parishes in 1724 has suggested that many more colonists attended churches than joined them as communicant members. It concluded that 56 to 80 percent of the population might be numbered as church "adherents," a term designating attenders and their children.[4] But even this study conceded that the religious lives of southern colonists were "disconcertingly unstable."[5] This instability might have resulted from the absence of churches—the colonial South probably had only one church for every 1,046 people, far lower than the middle colony ratio of 1:467 or the ratio of 1:606 in New England.[6] Even if more colonists were adherents than historians have assumed, southerners occupied the lowest end of the scale.[7]

Church adherence and denominational affiliation increased during the antebellum period, but very slowly. As southern evangelicals spread their message in the early nineteenth century, they engaged in a protracted negotiation with Southern culture that changed them as much as it changed the culture.[8] Churches found it particularly hard to root themselves west of the Appalachians. Kentucky's population, for example, outpaced its churches, whose leaders worried about deism, materialism, and indifference. Concerned clerics painted a picture of stagnation and decline.[9]

The camp meeting revivals, which began around 1800, seemed to increase interest in religion. The Cane Ridge revival of 1801 attracted between twelve and twenty-five thousand people, and similar meetings elicited religious preoccupations that resulted in growing churches. Methodists and Baptists tripled their membership, and new churches sprang up to consolidate these gains.[10] But the revivals had a dark side. Emotionalism and populism won converts but repelled critics. Conflict and schism roiled the Presbyterians and Baptists and produced a new denomination—the Disciples of Christ—that took members away from older churches.[11] One Kentucky woman complained that religion at the camp meetings lost "its dignity, its beauty." She wondered: "can we not worship God rationally like civilized people in our houses or in meeting houses instead of praying in the woods sleeping on the ground all together etc." She hated it that a family member, presumably her husband, neglected their farm to attend meetings, to which he carried more provisions than the family could spare. Prorevival family members referred to her, in turn, as "the greatest cross they have."[12] Church and family unity strained under the revivals. Their legacy was not a single, homogenous evangelical culture, but rather an even greater level of religious diversity.

Even after the Great Revival, New England missionaries noted that the majority of the inhabitants of Kentucky in 1812 had "no fixed opinions or principles" and lamented that "many of them are regardless of religion, while others are blown about 'by every wind of doctrine.'"[13] Colleagues evangelizing Mississippi and western Florida complained that people seemed ashamed to purchase Bibles and claimed to have encountered some "*who never saw a Bible, nor heard of Jesus Christ.*" In their eyes, the South resembled nothing more than "the valley of the shadow of death. Darkness rests upon it."[14] Almost two decades later, a Presbyterian missionary claimed that of the nine hundred inhabitants of Covington, Kentucky, only fifty professed allegiance to a denomination; that the town lacked any church or meeting house; and that "profaneness is common."[15] Another missionary claimed to have visited sixty families that, on average, attended church once every seven years. "Some grown-up youths had never heard a sermon or prayer, until my visit, and did not know of such a being as the Savior," he recalled.[16] Missionaries had an interest in emphasizing difficulties, but others confirmed their impressions.

In 1805, Fr. Badin reported that "pretty near half the settlers do not affiliate with any religion but believe in general in a confused manner in revelation, and they die without having made choice of any sect."[17] A decade later, Bishop Flaget reported that "the majority" of Presbyterians, Baptists, and Methodists were "wholly ignorant" of their denominations' doctrines. He lamented the masses "who belong to no sect at all but live in complete indifference, whose God is either Mammon or their belly."[18] An English traveler in the late 1820s noted that one "will rarely find either churches or chapels, prayer or preacher" in western villages.[19] A Catholic in South Carolina told a similar story: "The people say not a word about religion. Though Sunday is kept—no church or meeting."[20] Such reports demand caution, for apologists for a denomination often described other denominations as lacking religion, but the reports suggest, at a minimum, the absence of an evangelical hegemony.[21]

Catholics too suffered from the fluid conditions, with members prone to wander. "Not a day passes that we do not find great numbers of these strayed sheep, who, because they do not see their real shepherd, become Baptists, Methodists, etc., or at least nothingists," bemoaned Flaget.[22] A layman in Augusta warned Bishop Carroll that "a few years more without a pastor, & the R.C. of this town & the neighbourhood [*sic*] will lose even the name."[23] Another in Huntsville, Alabama, warned that the shortage of priests would impel Catholics to join other churches.[24] Like other southerners, some Catholics also refused to be bound to a single faith. Even those loyal to the church sampled other forms of worship. Pauline DeCaradeuc, a devout young lady in upstate South Carolina, visited both a Methodist meeting and a synagogue during a Holy Week trip to Augusta.[25]

Some southerners hesitated to commit themselves to one denomination. Two New England missionaries traveling through the Southwest in 1814 discovered that most of the inhabitants "although by no means regardless of religion, have not yet embraced any fixed principles or sentiments respecting it. They are ready to receive any impressions which a public speaker may attempt to make."[26] A few let whim dictate the church they would attend. Elizabeth Blackwell of Aiken, South Carolina, attended an Episcopal church one Sunday, found it uninspiring, and decided the next week to visit "a dark wooden building with little steeple, half hidden amongst the trees, that took my fancy."[27] Others viewed church going as meritorious, regardless of the church. A judge in Tuscaloosa told his wife that he had heard an Episcopal bishop one day and a Presbyterian minister the next, so that "having gone twice to church I feel absolved from sin in going to the ball tonight."[28] The ecumenical spirit found expression in the will of the eminent Charleston merchant Benjamin d'Harriette, who made provisions for "the French church, the Baptist church, St. Philips, and the Protestant Dissenters."[29]

Conditions sometimes encouraged southerners' indecision. A northern visitor in the 1850s noted that many southern churches lacked regular clergymen and instead welcomed preachers of various denominations on a rotating basis.[30] An Episcopalian from Louisiana often attended and took communion at Methodist meetings, largely because her own church was often closed. She occasionally went to the local Catholic church, which offered the only regular services.[31]

The Spring Hill College Register revealed the indecision of the school's students. One was "rather at a loss to know what he is," and another did not know if he had been baptized. One had a Lutheran father but carried "his religion in his breast," and another was baptized Catholic but "left free to choose his religion." One student's religious sentiments were minimal: "not much of any," wrote the registrar. Another seemed confused: "Episcopal it seems; and perhaps baptized" but having "no sentiments scarcely of religion." One young man was "Not attached to any religious denomination" even though he had been baptized by a Methodist minister. Students could inherit indecision from parents who had no affiliation. Other parents had spouses of different faiths. A few students had to guess at their parents' faith. One father, with "predilections" toward "Catholicity" and an Episcopal wife, displayed the buffet-style approach to religion, asking that his son learn the "general principles of Christianity" in order to choose a religion for himself.[32]

Southerners who decided to go to church could choose from a wide selection. A resident of St. Louis noted that in the city of only twenty thousand people, "the number of religious sects is incredible." He listed Catholics, Episcopalians, two branches of Presbyterians and Methodists, Baptists, Unitarians, Jews, "and some others whose names I forget, besides a good number who attend no church."[33] A foreign visitor, reading a book that mentioned forty-three denominations, avowed that the list was far from exhaustive. "The right of private judgment, which, in breaking the yoke of Popery, broke loose also in Europe from all respect for authority . . . has in America run into still greater excesses," he complained.[34] An English traveler noted "an almost endless variety of religious factions," adding that there were dozens whose names she could not remember. Catholicism alone seemed "exempt from the fury of division and sub-division that has seized every other persuasion."[35] "In this state of things," asked one Kentuckian, "is not the most ancient church as good as any—perhaps nearer the truth than any?"[36]

The variety of religious institutions bewildered travelers to the South. The Reverend George Lewis, sent by the Free Church of Scotland to tour the United States in 1844, found that even small towns had so many churches that he ceased trying to count them, but he also discovered that quantity did not translate into quality. In Savannah, he learned of a Presbyterian church that had split from the national body and hired its own pastor, who wrote beautiful sermons but could not preach or pray extemporaneously and had to resign. It turned out that he had failed as a merchant, a Unitarian preacher, and a teacher, "until in an unhappy hour he was promoted to preach in the Independent Presbyterian Church."[37] In Augusta, he talked with an elderly Scotsman who announced that he viewed religion as fit "'for rogues or fools, and for the most part a scramble for power or money.'" Pressed about his beliefs, he replied: "'I am neither Roman Catholic, Presbyterian, nor Methodist, nor Baptist, nor anything at all. I am determined to live as long as I can in this world, and as for the next I don't trouble myself about it.'"[38] In Louisville, Lewis discovered that few of the leading merchants belonged to a church. By the end of his travels, he concluded that religious diversity served only to "lower the tone of ministerial feeling, to vulgarize and secularize the churches of Christ, and to diminish the moral weight and influence of the ministers of the Gospel."[39]

A steamboat trip up the Mississippi gave Lewis time to examine religious opinions. His berth-mate, a pious man, told him of a captain who railed against the Bible. Lewis commiserated: "Such are the kind of objections that are afloat in this region in the mouths of Infidels, such as Voltaire and Volney and Paine started last century."[40] The crew proved little better. The mate "swore with one breath and quoted Scripture with the next." Lewis concluded that the man was "sadly bewildered in his views." When the Scottish pastor held service on Sunday, the captain, crew, and half the passengers stayed away. His congregation seemed attentive, but he deemed it "rather an attention of novelty than of intelligent interest and sympathy with what was said."[41] Lewis's steamboat stood as a microcosm of southern society: some were pious, some were irreverent, and most were somewhere in between.

The census of 1850 reveals an evolution of religious conditions. In 1850, South Carolina had one church for every 556 people, in Alabama the ratio was 1:562, and in Kentucky, 1:532—ratios that far exceeded those of the colonial South. The ratios were even better if one excluded blacks and children. The churches varied in size, but the census reports on church capacity also suggested progress. South Carolina had one church seat for every 1.45 people, Alabama, a seat for every 1.76 people, and Kentucky, one for every 1.46. Every white southerner had a seat. Not everyone attended, but the churching of the South had progressed since the mid-eighteenth century, and two denominations had made the greatest strides. Baptists and Methodists claimed 3,564 of 4,400 churches, and roughly 73 percent of the church capacity, in the three states. But this still left nearly a thousand churches in the hands of other denominations, of which the census listed eleven, plus Jews and the so-called "Minor Sects." Evangelicals' share in the overall value of church property was much lower—Baptists and Methodists, by far the leaders among the evangelicals, owned only 39 percent. Kentucky had eleven Methodist churches for every Catholic church, but the value of Methodist property was only 27 percent greater. In Alabama, the Catholic Church was the wealthiest according to the census estimate of property values.[42]

Over time, evangelical Protestantism claimed the lion's share of the South's churchgoers and put its stamp on southern culture. But its dominance was never complete. Other religious groups also staked out territory in the South, and many southerners refused to be pinned down by denominational allegiances. Catholicism did not struggle to make itself heard alongside a single evangelical chorus but contributed one among a cacophony of voices, each trying to attract an often skeptical audience.

Religious Controversy in the South

The large number of souls up for grabs bred competition and contentiousness in southern religion. "It is the misfortune of our position in this country, to be constantly tempted to undervalue the saving truth in which we are all agreed, and to magnify the importance of the metaphysical opinion, or external practice, in which we differ," an Episcopal bishop in Kentucky complained.[43] Southerners magnified their differences on a scale that shocked visitors. A northern traveler in the 1850s noted that churches carried on their rivalries "with a bitterness and persistence" unlike anything he had ever seen.[44] Catholics were not the only objects of criticism and even violence. Methodists and Baptists faced persecution in the colonial period. Physical threats—like the ones directed by a Savannah mob against Methodist Hope Hull in 1790—were common.[45] Methodists and Baptists encountered civil persecution and harassment by individuals and mobs. When they refused to return violence for violence, detractors condemned them as unmanly.[46] Conditions improved slowly after the Revolution. Methodists continued to draw condemnation for threatening familial unity, and the exclusive Methodist class meetings and love feasts led outsiders to gossip about mischief behind closed doors. "Rowdies" disrupted camp meetings by drinking, shouting, and threatening the pious.[47] Methodists, in turn, could be "most bitter against the Calvinists" and they railed "against the practice of the Presbyterians receiving pay for preaching, calling them hirelings," or depicted Baptists as "unfeeling monsters who blithely consigned their children to hell"—a reference to the Baptist embrace of Calvinism.[48]

Churches savaged each other but saved their fiercest salvos for dissenters within their ranks. A Presbyterian missionary bemoaned that "members of the . . . Presbytery accuse each other of everything that is mean, unchristian, and knavish" and denounced their coreligionists from the East as "New Lights," a reference to those who embraced the revivalism, emotion, and zeal of the Great Awakenings.[49] A Kentucky Presbyterian concluded with disgust that "the Bible only is the word of God—its expounders in all ages (with now and then an exception . . .) are wolves in sheep's clothing."[50]

Catholics were not immune to infighting. In some communities along the Gulf Coast, laymen refused to assist at masses in the homes of people they disliked.[51] In Kentucky, a feud between two of the leading families of the parish in Scott County threatened to split the church and required Flaget and Badin to intervene.[52] They did so with the memory that a quarrel between two parishioners years earlier had escalated to the point that one tried to shoot the other.[53]

Catholics worried that internal divisions eroded the church's standing. The laity in England's diocese were mostly poor: "their previous dissensions had so lowered them in public estimation that those who wished to maintain a certain dignified position in society abandoned the Church."[54] A layman in Kentucky worried that "loos catholicks" complained about priests not only among themselves "but even among Protestants."[55] Division no doubt weakened Catholicism in the South, but it also gave Catholics something in common with every other southern church.

Some Protestants set aside differences to form a united front against Catholicism, but religious competition rarely stopped with Protestants and Catholics. Southern religion was a free-for-all. Catholics took no more abuse than the Campbellites, Mormons, Shakers, Quakers, Unitarians, or anyone else. And Catholics returned blow for blow.

Religious debates were a form of entertainment, and southerners turned out in droves.[56] A spectator at a debate in Lexington, Kentucky, between two prominent Protestants noted that "strangers are collected here not only from all parts of this state but from the states around. In spite of the continued rain, the church—a large one has been constantly filled to overflowing."[57] An 1812 debate between Presbyterians and Baptists over baptism roiled Bardstown, and Badin leapt into the fray. The crowd at the courthouse was so great that he moved outside to a platform used by Methodists for their camp meetings.[58] The contest between David and Presbyterian minister Nathan Hall over images in 1821 drew overflow crowds to the Bardstown courthouse.[59] These crowds had a chance to hear the Catholic position, often for the first time. Few individuals converted, but by gaining a hearing, Catholics had already won.

Verbal controversies continued in pamphlet form. After debating Hall, David published a sixty-four-page pamphlet, to which Hall responded, prompting from David a hundred-page reply.[60] Bishop England received requests from non-Catholics to republish a lengthy debate he had held in the pages of the *Charleston Courier* with the Rev. Richard Fuller of Beaufort.[61] Sometimes the controversies faded quickly. A year after two debates with a Methodist near Bardstown, Badin reported that "controversial engagements are over & we live in peace with Methodists." He declined a request to publish his arguments, citing "the desire of not renewing the spirit of religious discussion, & the want of time and money." Nonetheless, he warned, "I would reason differently if any public writing had taken place on the opposite side."[62]

Skirmishes continued in the press. Church leaders used letters to editors to complain of inaccuracies. In Mobile, Bishop Quinlan decried the *Tribune*'s misrepresentation of the church's role in European politics.[63] In Charleston, England countered editors who failed to print his letters by publishing them as advertisements. In 1822, he founded his own paper, the *United States Catholic Miscellany,* to harness the power of the press and a decade later thought that it had "dissipated many prejudices and . . . silenced many enemies."[64] Its purpose was to correct those who had been "misled into erroneous opinions of the principles of their neighbors," and England referred to the paper as "our sword and our shield."[65]

Catholics in other dioceses followed England's lead and established their own papers. In 1834, St. Joseph's College in Kentucky began publishing a monthly literary magazine, the *Minerva,* which was soon replaced by a weekly paper called the *Catholic Advocate.* Although priests, primarily Martin John Spalding, future bishop of Louisville and archbishop of Baltimore, exercised editorial control, the driving force was a layman, Benjamin Webb, who had worked for the *Louisville Journal* and used his expertise to sustain the *Advocate,* at great financial sacrifice, for fifteen years before it merged with a paper in Cincinnati.[66] The Catholic press remained a faint whisper relative to the roar of the Protestant and secular papers. In 1833, England estimated that only ten of one thousand journals were Catholic, a hundred of which were anti-Catholic.[67] But papers like the *Miscellany* and *Advocate* carried forward the debate with Protestants.

Religious debates were often rancorous but not necessarily hostile. Southerners enjoyed the fireworks of religious controversy and appreciated the freedom of all groups to express themselves. Believers wanted to prove the superiority of their creeds by fair and open debate. "Put Methodism and Romanism upon the field of fair argument and I will stake my all upon the issue; but I am not such a coward as to flee the field of honorable warfare . . . or such a fool as to believe that a man's religion is to be reformed by harassing his person," wrote Methodist minister Augustus Longstreet.[68] Episcopal Bishop B. B. Smith of Kentucky echoed Longstreet's sentiments: "We know that we are right. And it is on this very account that I contend that we can afford to be humble, patient and magnanimous; since our cause is the cause of truth and of God."[69] Religious debates were a regional pastime in which Catholics participated along with everyone else. Some laity read books of religious controversy "in order to render themselves capable of sustaining a discussion with Protestants."[70]

And discuss they did. Pauline DeCaradeuc even recalled engaging in a "real fine" religious controversy with one of her Protestant beaux.[71] An anonymous chronicler told of a Baptist minister in South Carolina who debated infallibility, transubstantiation, and scripture with a Catholic gentleman. The chronicler described the Catholic's faith as "a system which outrages reason" and made clear that the Baptist had won the debates, but the story's conclusion was telling: "They parted in all friendliness of feeling, which they continued to maintain toward each other."[72]

Catholics hoped their ceremonies, speeches, debates, and publications would weaken anti-Catholic prejudice. As John England saw it, churches would also contribute to this goal by providing places where "our separated brethren frequently have the strange opinions which they have indulged of our belief corrected."[73] He hoped to build small churches wherever a handful of Catholics settled so that "by means of this convenience afforded them, their Protestant neighbors will learn the truths of our holy religion."[74]

The Catholic clergy felt confident that they could change negative Protestant attitudes. England traveled to North Carolina to "explain the principles of our Faith & their foundation to strangers," and he agreed to preach in a Presbyterian church to that end.[75] He saw Americans as a "well-disposed, religiously-inclined people" who "must be instructed, not abused" and who would eventually accept the truth of Catholicism. At least, they would change their misapprehensions.[76] Catholics had grounds for optimism. Badin reported to Propaganda that "the non-Catholics who live among the Catholics are less under the influence of prejudices, and they treat us generally as brothers."[77] Protestants also testified to this effect. James Graham Ramsey, a member of the North Carolina state senate and bitter enemy of "the Romish Church" complained that so many Protestants of his day accepted and even defended Catholicism as a Christian faith.[78] In the South, familiarity often bred not contempt but acceptance.

The Spread of Catholic Churches in the South

The fluidity of religious life in the South created opportunities for Catholicism, but a lack of resources hindered the church. Southern Catholic prelates were among the nation's poorest. "My diocese is one of the largest, and perhaps it is the poorest, in all Christendom," complained England. For six years, he relied financially on his sister, who had paid his way to Charleston on the condition that she could accompany him.[79] Bishop William Clancy, England's coadjutor, told a colleague in Europe that he would prefer "any diocese in America or Great Britain to my present connexion [*sic*] with Charleston."[80] Bishop Flaget contested England's claim to the title of poorest prelate. Following his consecration in Maryland, he had to take a collection just to get to Kentucky.[81] "I am the poorest of all the Bishops in the world," he wrote.[82]

The resources of the bishops were especially paltry in light of their vast territories. Southern dioceses dwarfed those of Europe. Flaget was initially responsible for the states of Kentucky, Tennessee, and Ohio and the territories of Indiana, Illinois, and Michigan.[83] England oversaw the Carolinas and Georgia, and Portier administered Alabama and Florida.

Some Catholics refused to support the church. Before moving to Kentucky, Fr. Charles Whelan, an Irishman who had served as a chaplain in the French fleet during the American Revolution, signed a contract with Catholic emigrants that guaranteed him a steady income. Within six months, he was in court seeking to prevent his parishioners from nullifying the contract.[84] Badin issued a similar complaint: "I have been sued, warranted & executed [*sic*] several times by Catholics for church affairs, many Catholic people complying not with the payments they have engaged to make to the congregation."[85] Conflict persisted even after Bishop Flaget's arrival. When dissenters opposed his plan for supporting priests, he appeared in episcopal garb and threatened excommunication.[86]

Priests battled with parishioners in court, where Protestant-dominated juries occasionally gave priests the support their parishioners hesitated to provide. In Whelan's case, the jury upheld the contract's validity, while allowing that the payment be made in produce.[87] But priests did not always win. After Fr. Whelan complained about duplicitous congregants, they charged him with slander, and the jury imposed a hefty fine.[88] Embittered, he left Kentucky and warned other priests to stay away.[89] At the northern end of the diocese, Fr. Gabriel Richard lost a lawsuit after he excommunicated a parishioner, and he served time in prison.[90] Flaget suggested denying the sacraments as a penalty for refusing to support priests, but Rome told him that his suggestion was "unworthy of a churchman."[91]

When laity did give, it often caused more problems for church leaders. The conflict had its origins in the shortage of clergy, which prompted laypeople to build churches on their own initiative. When priests and bishops later asserted their authority, lay trustees resisted, sparking a controversy known today as "trusteeism." Some lay people argued that control over the church buildings entitled them to choose their own priests. Even though the bishops often tolerated dissent over ownership, they could not allow the laity to control the appointment of priests.

The fiercest clashes between clergy and laity took place in the North, but southern dioceses were not immune. At St. Mary's in Charleston, trouble began before England's arrival. The conflict had its roots in ethnic tensions between the largely Irish trustees and French priests. The trustees so disliked one priest, Fr. LeMercier, that they threatened to tear down the church. His replacement, a monarchist named Clorivière, fared even worse.[92] The trustees wrote to Archbishop Neale that they had "an insurmountable personal dislike to the Rev. Mr. Clovierir [*sic*]" and wanted a priest who could preach clearly in English. Things got so bad that some of Clorivière's parishioners threatened to kill him at the altar.[93] In 1820, England landed in the midst of the dispute. Fr. Benedict Fenwick, who had tried to resolve it, advised him to build a new church in his own name, independent of any trustees. He warned that the trustees would oppose this plan: "they cannot bear to see even a Bp. [Bishop] independent of their interference. Base Miscreants!"[94] England accepted Fenwick's advice, dedicating the Church of St. Finbar in 1822.[95]

In Norfolk, trouble between the clergy and lay trustees began in the 1790s. The city's first priest, Fr. James Bushe, clashed with the trustees soon after his arrival. His successor, Fr. Michael Lacy (or deLacey) went to the opposite extreme, emboldening the trustees by agreeing to a series of demands, including a provision that the trustees would collect and administer all church revenue. In 1815, Archbishop Leonard Neale appointed Fr. James Lucas, a French émigré priest, to the largely Irish parish, thus adding the familiar ethnic component to the controversy. Soon, the trustees were in open revolt, and Neale placed the church under interdict. Inspired in part by allies in Charleston, the Norfolk trustees then sent a delegation to Rome and, amazingly, deceived Propaganda into endorsing the creation of a new diocese in Virginia, over the vigorous protests of the new archbishop, Ambrose Maréchal. In 1818, the leader of the trustees, Oliveira Fernandez, reached out to policy makers in the United States as well, penning a letter to Thomas Jefferson, Congress, and the governors of all the states in which he denounced Maréchal's undemocratic actions. Only after Lucas and Fernandez left the city in the early 1820s did trusteeism in Norfolk finally subside.[96]

Trusteeism threatened several southern parishes. Bishop Portier came into conflict with trustees in St. Augustine in 1832.[97] Prelates in Kentucky battled parishioners who clung to republican ideals and envied Protestant congregational autonomy. In 1807, laity at White Sulphur attempted to implement a Presbyterian church government.[98] Decades later, Holy Cross parish, the oldest in the state, demanded the right to elect an overseer for the farm that supported their church and insisted that the overseer appoint the pastor.[99] Flaget complained that parishioners in the northern end of his diocese were "so strongly republicanized or rather jacobinized that they count very much more on the authority of the people than upon that of their Bishop," and they treated their priests as employees.[100]

Control of property became a point of contention. A church in Scott County, Kentucky, became embroiled in controversy over title to the church land, and only Bishop Carroll's intervention resolved the issue. Over time, the clergy usually acquired the titles but in some cases with conditions. One parishioner offered to donate several hundred acres if the church would absolve the next four generations of his family from any obligation to contribute.[101]

Conflicts between clergy and lay trustees exposed an antidemocratic ecclesiology. Every time a bishop smashed an attempt to pass power to "the people" with the hammer of episcopal authority, it provided fodder for critics who charged that Catholicism was antithetical to Americans' most deeply cherished values.[102]

The most innovative attempt to settle trusteeism in a manner suitable to Americans' tastes came from Bishop England, who wrote what he referred to as a constitution for his diocese. "I have learned by experience that the genius of this nation is to have written laws, to have these laws at hand, and to direct all their affairs according to them," he explained.[103] The constitution's provisions were quite conservative—bishops were to be obeyed in ecclesiastical affairs; the laity were to honor priests "as the legates of God, not as servants of the people"; and although churches could keep their trustees, the priest was to be the president of the board—but the act of codifying these rules, and England's deliberate usage of the term "constitution," made them more palatable. So too did the process of ratifying the constitution through conventions of clergy and lay delegates, each side being careful, in the words of the *Miscellany,* "to avoid the semblance of interference with the rights of others."[104] Many of England's colleagues viewed the constitution with displeasure, considering it far too democratic, but England seemed more concerned with what non-Catholics would think: "Our brethren of other denominations who may peruse it, will probably find that they have too often attributed to us tenets and principles which are not ours."[105]

The ties that bound the Catholic Church in the South often seemed in danger of fraying. The size of the dioceses, the sparse populations, and internal divisions meant that Catholic churches, like hospitals, orphanages, and schools, had to depend on resources from outside the Catholic community. It was support from outsiders that held things together.

Protestant contributions revealed a community open not only to Catholics as citizens but also to Catholicism as a faith. From the start, Catholic churches relied on Protestants. When Catholics purchased their first permanent church in Charleston in 1789, Protestants helped pay for repairs to the dilapidated building.[106] A decade later, support came from the state legislature. A benefactor of the church died without heirs, which meant that the state could claim his property. When Catholics presented evidence that he intended to give property to the church, the legislature noted that "it would be unbecoming the liberality of the Legislature to avail itself of an accident, to the injury of said Church."[107] Protestants aided Catholic churches throughout the diocese. In the 1820s, a Catholic family in Cheraw built a church with money from non-Catholic neighbors.[108] A decade later, when a Catholic layperson started a church in Barnwell, England praised Protestants for their financial support.[109] Because church buildings could ensure regular visits by a priest, such Protestant support meant survival for rural Catholic communities.

In rural Kentucky, Protestants donated land. In 1803, Fr. Badin informed Bishop Carroll that a wealthy non-Catholic had given land for a church in Springfield. Three years later, non-Catholics in Christian County offered 1,400 acres to induce a priest and Catholics to settle in the area.[110] That same year, Fr. Nerinckx recorded a gift of two hundred acres from a Methodist minister. Two years earlier, he had reported progress on St. Clare's church in Hardin County: "Many non-Catholics have subscribed for it. God reward them with the gift of faith." Apparently they were more generous than Nerinckx's flock, for he later complained that construction was still not complete owing to the congregation's "lack of zeal."[111] Donations from non-Catholics may have reflected zeal for profit as much as for religion. Landholders realized that if they could entice a few Catholics or a priest to settle on their land it would attract other Catholics as well and so drive up the value of their property.[112]

In the cities, as well, Protestants gave their money to Catholics. In 1810, a subscription to raise funds for a church in Lexington drew as many donations from Protestants as from Catholics. Two Protestants, Nathaniel Hart and Joe H. Daviess, helped to circulate the subscription list, and St. Peter's Church opened in 1812.[113] The construction of St. Louis, the first Catholic church in Louisville, began in 1811 with 90 percent of the contributions coming from Protestants, two of whom sat on the church's board of trustees. They urged the church to buy a larger lot to accommodate a priest.[114]

Protestant generosity was so great that Flaget used it as a fund-raising tool. In an 1817 broadside to the Catholic community, he sought money to finish construction of St. Louis. He began his appeal with a tribute to Protestants: "Having on so many occasions felt the . . . generosity of those who differ from us in their religious opinion, I entertain the hope, that those who live in Louisville . . . will display the same liberality for the finishing of it."[115] Protestants provided the model for Catholics to follow.

Everywhere, Protestants seemed eager to help Catholics. In Nashville, they pledged money for a church, and the grand master of the local Masons offered Flaget a plot of land.[116] Years earlier, the governor had proposed that Badin help establish a colony of one hundred families, offering him land to support a priest.[117] The governor of Indiana sent Flaget money to subsidize the cost of stationing a priest in Vincennes.[118] Such support helped increase the number of churches in the diocese to nineteen by 1815 and thirty-five six years later.[119]

In 1825, the *Miscellany* reported that Catholics in Georgetown, South Carolina, had purchased a lot for a church "principally by the aid of their benevolent Protestant fellow citizens."[120] The same year, Catholics building a church in Beaufort benefited from "the kind and neighbourly deportment of their fellow citizens of other denominations," and the largely Protestant legislature gave the church community in Columbia permission to raise $10,000 by lottery for their building campaign. A year later, non-Catholics, including former governor Richard Irvine Manning, raised $100 for the church.[121] In North Carolina, Protestants gave money for a church in Washington and helped the Catholics of Fayetteville and Raleigh create permanent stations for priests.[122] In 1825, land commissioners in Charlotte gave Catholics a "good and convenient" plot for a church, largely at the prompting of a Protestant preacher. Just over the state line in South Carolina, the town council of Cheraw appropriated two lots for a church.[123] In Georgia, the city of Augusta gave a plot for a church.[124]

Protestants continued to sustain Catholic parishes. In 1838, a fire destroyed St. Mary's in Charleston. Donations for rebuilding came largely from non-Catholics, and included an $8,000 loan from the city. Almost forty residents of Abbeville, Kentucky, only one of whom was Catholic, sent a gift of nearly $90, and several prominent non-Catholics in Augusta also gave generously. The congregation of St. Mary's received permission to hold services in the chapel of the Medical College until they could build a new church.[125] By August, Catholics laid the cornerstone for the new church in the midst of a large crowd gathered among the ruins of the former church. "The interest manifested on the occasion by their fellow citizens, was highly gratifying to the Catholics and greatly creditable to their separated brethren," exclaimed the *Miscellany,* adding, "We have seldom seen a larger assemblage in this city!"[126] The vestry of St. Mary's thanked "our brethren in the faith, and those who differ with us in religious belief, in this city and throughout the United States, for their very kind and generous aid to us."[127] One gift deserved particular thanks. In 1814, the prominent Charleston artist John S. Cogdell painted a crucifixion that he donated to St. Mary's. When the fire destroyed this painting, Cogdell painted a second version, which he presented in 1839 with expressions of "the best feelings for your Congregation" and "respect and esteem" for England. In response, the pastor and parish committee of St. Mary's praised "the high-minded liberality of our Protestant fellow-citizens" and promised to pray for their benefactors.[128]

In Kentucky, in 1832, Senator Henry Clay and Congressman Charles Wickliffe, both friends of Flaget, helped refund import duties that Flaget had paid on gifts from European monarchs, including nine paintings for the cathedral.[129] The *Catholic Advocate,* describing the dedication of a new church at Mount Washington, Kentucky, noted that Catholics felt "encouraged" by the "good will and pecuniary aid of some of their protestant fellow citizens."[130] Elsewhere in the Diocese of Bardstown, a Catholic petitioning for a resident priest promised to build a church with the help of $200 pledged by local Protestants.[131]

Protestants helped Catholics build ever more ornate churches. They filled collection plates in the heart of Kentucky Catholicism. In 1816, they donated $10,000 to the church in Bardstown, the first cathedral west of the Alleghenies. By one estimate, this amount was 80 percent of the total of the first subscription, and Flaget expressed optimism that Protestants in other regions would contribute even more. People unable to contribute money often donated raw materials or labor. Several of the donors also sat on the board supervising construction.[132] "Monseigneur has gained the confidence not only of the Catholics, but of all the other religions, whose followers have contributed liberally to the building of the Cathedral," said David.[133] Thanks to Protestant assistance, the imposing edifice, 120 feet in length by 74 in breadth, crowned with a steeple nearly 150 feet tall, was ready for dedication before a vast concourse in 1819.[134] Those who built the cathedral also sustained it. On New Year's Day 1825, townspeople of all faiths risked their lives to save it from a fire in a nearby building. Hearing an alarm, they rushed to help as if their own homes were burning.[135]

Protestants gave money for the Cathedral of the Immaculate Conception in Mobile and the Cathedral of St. John and St. Finbar in Charleston. In Mobile, Bishop Quinlan endorsed a building society for the cathedral to solicit contributions not only from Catholics, but also from "friends of other denominations here and elsewhere."[136] In Charleston, the cathedral committee acknowledged "with great satisfaction the very liberal aid, received from their Protestant fellow-citizens."[137] Decades later, an association of Catholic women took advantage of a meeting of the Southern Rights Association of South Carolina and the National Medical Association to hold a fair for the cathedral building fund. The fair ran from 10:00 A.M. to 11:00 P.M. every day for a week in the Hibernian Hall. By midweek, the *Courier* remarked that it was becoming "one of the most popular of our many evening resorts" and that it was drawing "all classes without reference to denomination."[138] The fair offered numerous attractions. A northern visitor described the women's needlework as "the most exquisite specimens" she had ever seen.[139] The *Courier* described in great detail a bridal gown being raffled, over which stood guard "one of Eve's fairest daughters . . . closely besieged by dozens of Adam's most promising sons."[140] Lest anyone forget the fair's true purpose, a detailed model of the new cathedral stood prominently displayed. The fair netted $10,000.[141]

By the late-antebellum period, Protestants had helped Catholics establish a network of churches across the South. In 1850, Catholics worshipped in five churches in Alabama, five in Florida, eight in Georgia, four in North Carolina, three in Tennessee, fourteen in South Carolina, and forty-eight in Kentucky.[142] Within a decade, the number of churches in these states increased from 87 to 145. The value of the church's property accounted for 10 percent of the value of all church property in the South. Not all Catholic churches were as grand as the cathedrals, but, on average, each could accommodate over five hundred people.[143]

Protestants worshipped with Catholics in those new churches. In 1811, Flaget said Mass in a small chapel in Danville, Kentucky, noting afterward that almost the entire town attended, leaving a Presbyterian church opposite the chapel entirely empty.[144] In rural Kentucky, circuit-riding priests attracted mixed congregations. A priest in 1816 recalled celebrating Mass in crude cabins where "Catholics, and not infrequently Protestants too, for ten or fifteen miles around, gather together." The neighing of their horses sounded "as if a regiment of cavalry were in the vicinity."[145] In the same year, a crowd gathered in Bardstown to lay a cornerstone for the cathedral. The assembly contained, Flaget said, more Protestants than Catholics, and everyone gave "demonstrations of piety and gratitude."[146]

At places like the Trappist settlement in Casey County, Protestants attended regular services, and sometimes they formed the majority of worshippers in frontier Catholic celebrations.[147] In Alabama, Fr. Mathias Loras of Spring Hill spent weekends and vacations traveling across the state preaching to crowds of Protestants.[148] Fr. Prachensky, a professor at Spring Hill and minister to Mobile's Germans, drew congregations of all faiths and nationalities to whom he preached in French, Spanish, English, and German.[149] In some cases, the priests permitted Protestants to participate in the sacraments. In his diary, Flaget noted hearing the confessions of three Protestant women.[150] On the frontier, priests often baptized Protestant children upon their parents' request.[151]

Protestants worshipped with Catholics across the South. In 1827, Bishop Portier preached to a large crowd of all denominations while visiting St. Augustine.[152] The following year, Fr. Stokes said Mass in Darien, Georgia, to a congregation largely composed of non-Catholics, prompting him to explain the service as he performed it.[153] Protestants also attended celebrations in the Catholic community. In Charleston, in 1822, the dedication of a new church attracted "a very considerable number of highly respectable members of other Congregations," an "immense" crowd.[154] In Kentucky, the Jubilee of 1826, promulgated by Pope Leo XII the previous year, included services that Protestants attended in great numbers. The jubilee began in Bardstown, where people of all faiths crowded the cathedral for eight days. Each day included a Mass, sermon, public prayer, a second sermon in the evening, and mock debates between priests on theological questions. Protestants sometimes suggested the topics. The debates proved so popular that Flaget ordered them held in each parish. According to some Catholics, the jubilee was as notable for attracting Protestants as for stimulating the piety of Catholics.[155]

In 1835, in Charleston, non-Catholics flocked to a ceremony initiating a young woman into the Ursuline order. England noted their presence and explained that he would adjust his remarks so as to convey "to the friends by whom we are surrounded, such information as will render our ceremony fully intelligible, perhaps interesting."[156] Four years later, the *Courier* announced a public dedication for the rebuilt St. Mary's Church, praising the "handsome edifice" and noting that the pews would be "thrown open for the public accommodation."[157]

Bishop England in particular continued to draw large crowds wherever he went. In 1824, he led a series of services in Savannah, all of which drew crowds consisting "rather more of persons of other religious denominations, than of Roman Catholics." The crowning event of the visit came on St. Patrick's Day. Members of the Hibernian Society marched along with the mayor and leading citizens behind the green flag of Erin. The church was packed for the subsequent service, and on the altar sat not only Fr. Browne, the parish priest, but also an Episcopal priest and a Presbyterian minister. In keeping with the tenor of the event, England preached "that misery and ruin must be the portion of every country which creates and preserves sectional and sectarian hostility."[158]

Such hostility was noticeably absent wherever England went. One month later, in Augusta, he gave a series of lectures on revelation to "great numbers of persons of other denominations as well as Catholics" and helped raise money for an interdenominational orphanage. Civic leaders "of every creed and country" gave a public dinner in his honor.[159] The following year, he preached at the consecration of Archbishop Fenwick in Baltimore to a large crowd of people of all denominations, including public officials and Protestant clergymen.[160] The year 1827 found him holding fund-raising services in Savannah, which numerous Protestants attended.[161] A year later, he visited Washington, North Carolina, and said masses in the church that Protestants had helped Catholics build. Court was in session that week, so many visitors attended the services and behaved in a "highly becoming" manner.[162] In 1839, England said Mass at St. Peter's in Columbia before "very great numbers of respectable strangers," including a large body of college students who, as on previous occasions, behaved in a "gentlemanly and respectful" manner.[163] England's addresses left lasting impressions. A South Carolina Protestant recalled hearing as a boy an "eloquent" sermon delivered by England at a Methodist church in Georgetown to a congregation "of whom nine-tenths were Protestants accompanied by their rectors and preachers."[164]

Protestants packed cathedrals just as they had filled the ramshackle churches of earlier decades. Many attended Mass in Bardstown's cathedral on Sundays and holy days.[165] Southern Protestants also visited Catholic churches when abroad, including during the war with Mexico. The secular *Daily National Intelligencer* recorded in 1846 in the town of Parras that "at mass this morning the building was crowded with visitors from the camp . . . Protestant and Catholic, realizing for once the equality of man in the temple erected to the worship of his Creator."[166]

Catholics and Protestants worshipped together whenever and wherever they met. In 1817, Bishop Flaget, on his way to St. Louis by steamboat, reported that the craft served "successively for a synagogue, a cathedral, a theatre, an hospital . . . and what is most astonishing,—peace and harmony reign here."[167] While sailing up the Ohio River to Baltimore sixteen years later, David led evening prayers for the passengers of all faiths. He noted with pleasure that the Protestants seemed "entirely unprejudiced" and welcomed his company.[168]

Catholic churches at times provided the only venues for worship, and priests served as spiritual shepherds for Protestants as well as Catholics. A European traveler in Pensacola in the mid-1820s noted that a priest was the town's only clergyman and that "the inhabitants of whatever persuasion they may be, resort to his church."[169] In 1817, Fr. David hurried to prepare a group of missionaries for Missouri, recognizing that "the Protestants . . . not having yet any ministers of their sects, are favorably disposed to reenter the bosom of the Catholic Church."[170]

Some Protestants may have attended Catholic services without realizing it. Catholics and Protestants both worshipped in homes, ramshackle log churches, or the open air. Archbishop Spalding recalled that the first Catholic church in Kentucky was a "temporary hut . . . covered with clapboards" with holes for windows and a roughly hewed board for an altar.[171] Catholics later bought old church buildings from Protestants; they continued to be houses of God, just under new management.[172] It was easy to mistake Catholic priests and Methodist ministers, young, single men who traveled circuits on horseback and preached wherever they could assemble an audience. The often unmarried Methodist itinerants "bore an intriguingly Catholic character."[173] Catholic priests meanwhile often dressed like other ministers, as the wearing of the Roman collar and cassock was not mandatory until 1884. And Catholic parish missions had much the same tone and fervor as Protestant revivals.[174]

Even in towns with ample Protestant and Catholic churches, Protestants often attended Catholic services and associated with Catholic priests out of curiosity. While in Philadelphia, in 1787, George Mason of Virginia attended Mass "more out of Compliment than Religion, & more out of Curiosity than compliment."[175] Priests were of particular interest to many non-Catholics. A traveler to Kentucky observed that people's "curiosity to see the Priest, as also his sacred vestments, and the ceremonies performed by him, seemed insatiable."[176] Some priests became celebrities. Fr. John Thayer, a former Presbyterian minister known for his polemical style, drew so many Protestants to his preaching that the ministers looked on him with "an envious eye."[177] When word spread that Badin was traveling through Kentucky, "a party concealed themselves in the woods near the road, in order to have a peep at him. . . . They were afterwards heard to wonder that the priest was like any other man, and that he was no great show after all!"[178] As late as 1860, when Archbishop John Hughes of New York preached the baccalaureate sermon at the University of North Carolina, a trustee noted that "from appearances there will be as great a rush to see the animal as if he were the big bull of Bashan or Pope of Rome."[179] Such attention could be tiresome. Flaget, although grateful for the respect of Kentuckians, rued the time spent receiving visits "of many curious beings who have no other object in coming but to see the bishop."[180]

Religious services offered diversions to people with few other forms of entertainment. Sunday gave widely scattered neighbors a chance to gossip, court, and trade, as well as worship.[181] A foreign visitor remarked that "prayer-meetings take the place of almost all other amusements."[182] The newer and more exotic the worship, the greater the crowds. A visitor to a largely black camp meeting in South Carolina noted that "most of the white visitors were drawn there by curiosity, as there are always exhibitions of the extravagant fancies & feelings of the superstitious & ignorant."[183] Some thought the same about Catholic worship; they were "not so much alarmed as intrigued" by its growth.[184] Even in cosmopolitan areas, churchgoing remained a pastime. John Brown, a South Carolinian studying law in Louisville, admitted that the allure of the city, especially its Catholic cathedral, had distracted him from his work.[185] In 1830, when Bishop England visited New Orleans for the consecration of Bishop De Neckere, the theaters were said to be virtually deserted whenever he preached.[186] Catholic churches attracted Protestants who were pious, curious, or bored. Religion was not merely devotion; it was also entertainment.

Grand ceremonies, especially, drew large Protestant crowds. In Bardstown, Badin gave an address in 1811 on St. Patrick's Day that prompted Protestants to request a repeat performance. "Notwithstanding his foreign accent," reported a New York paper, "he had an attentive and large audience."[187] The same year, crowds flocked to the ordination of Fr. Guy Ignatius Chabrat, the first ordination west of the Alleghenies, and eight years later, a large assembly of all faiths descended on Bardstown to witness the dedication of the cathedral.[188] In September 1848, Bishop Flaget consecrated Martin John Spalding as his coadjutor. Many Protestants attended the three-hour ceremony. "We take pleasure in paying a sincere and well-merited compliment to our brethren of the different Protestant denominations, whose becoming reverence . . . and religious deportment . . . are deserving of the highest encomiums," noted the *Catholic Advocate*.[189] In Louisville, Covington, and Charleston, Protestants turned out in large numbers for the laying of cornerstones for new cathedrals.[190] In 1854, in Charleston, the "pavement in front of the church, as also the lot at the North end was blocked by a multitude." Although the service lasted nearly four hours, the crowd listened "with most decorous attention."[191]

Protestants also attended less joyous occasions. Shortly after the laying of the cathedral's cornerstone in Lousville, "multitudes of all creeds and denominations" crowded into the funeral of Bishop Flaget.[192] "To the praise of our Protestant brethren," noted the *Catholic Advocate,* they were scarcely "discernible from members of his own flock; all vied with one another in exhibiting their respect . . . to the remains of one who . . . had been respected alike by all religious denominations."[193]

Churches served as venues not only for worship but also for addresses and debates. A visit from a prelate often provided the occasion for a lecture, and addresses marked special occasions. During the Jubilee of 1825–1826, Catholic churches across Kentucky hosted public "conferences" in which one priest posed theological questions and another responded. Flaget commented on the conferences: "It is impossible for me to tell you of all the good which results from these conferences: Protestants relish them even more than Catholics. . . . But, my God! how many difficulties they have to overcome on the part of their preachers and their relations!"[194] Sometimes Catholics used public discourses to answer Protestant criticism. In 1821, Bishop David responded to Presbyterian minister Nathan Hall's attacks with talks on Catholic doctrine in Bardstown's cathedral.[195] During the jubilee, Kenrick used the conferences to take on Methodist, Episcopalian, and Presbyterian critics.[196] Such occasions continued throughout the antebellum period. In 1861, with the nation on the brink of war, Bishop John Quinlan of Mobile gave a series of Lenten lectures that many Protestants attended.[197]

Catholics noticed Protestant attendance and civility. "The congregation was considerable,—the most being Protestants, who had the patience to listen to the advice I gave them, and to two sermons from Mr. Chabrat," remarked Flaget after a Mass.[198] Badin reported that the members of "various sects" who came to hear priests preach in town halls or Protestant churches behaved in "a decent and respectful manner" and sometimes even brought children for baptism.[199] Describing several instances of sermons before non-Catholics, the *Miscellany* praised "the characteristic liberality of our fellow-citizens of other denominations; who on those occasions exhibit to the clergyman every token of kindness and benevolence, carefully attend to his discourse, and seem dispassionately to weigh his arguments."[200] Protestants but did not necessarily agree with what they heard. "I do not know the impression that my exhortation made on their spirits; but from the coldness that I observed on most of their faces, I have good reason to believe that their hearts were no warmer," noted Flaget of the Protestants at one of his masses.[201] Nor could the Protestant spectators always hold their tongues or the Catholic faithful always accept criticism. In Louisville, several Irishman threatened a Presbyterian minister who objected during a priest's lecture on celibacy. The priest restored calm, but the "too fervent zeal of the irritated Hibernians" had already driven the minister out to the street, "he in vain remonstrating on this violation of the liberty of speech and the rights of a free citizen."[202] But such cases were rare. Protestants usually wanted to hear what Catholics had to say, and Catholics were always happy to oblige.

Indeed, they reached out to Protestants. One candidate for a vacant see opined that bishops "should have much intercourse with the non-Catholics who form a large part of the population."[203] In Charleston, England forbade the practice of renting out pews for congregants' exclusive use, arguing that pew rentals created "one of the greatest obstacles to the conversion of strangers & the religious advantage of the poor."[204] To make the churches accessible to all, he decreed that they offer benches, "free for persons of all persuasions who conduct themselves with propriety."[205] Upon the opening of a new church in Charleston in 1822, the *Miscellany* advertised its "convenient benches, which are equally free to persons of all persuasions—no member of the congregation having a right of precedence to any other well conducted person who may be present."[206] Fr. Robert Abell of the Diocese of Bardstown celebrated the opening of a church by noting that Catholics would no longer have to turn away non-Catholics for lack of space. "We find ourselves in an edifice, capable of receiving the child and the stranger. An edifice, whose ample dimensions, like our affectionate hearts, expand to embrace you in the warmth of charity," he proclaimed to the assembled crowd.[207]

Lay Catholics showed similar initiative, as when a Catholic ferryman in Kentucky invited a young Protestant boy to join his family in their prayers. "Being only ten years old I knew nothing of the forms of the Catholic Church," the boy recalled, but he quickly decided "as I was in Rome, to do as Rome does." He tried to follow the ritual, but noticed that one of the ferryman's daughters laughed at his mistakes.[208] Other Catholics took greater care to explain their services. At Fr. Chabrat's ordination, Fr. Badin, noting the seats filled with Protestant visitors, "explained minutely the meaning of everything that was to be done."[209] At an ordination in Charleston, England explained the rituals "in a manner which appeared to give satisfaction to the numerous and highly respectable assembly that attended."[210]

Catholics did not dilute their theology to accommodate Protestant tastes. Saying Mass in a private house filled with Protestants, Flaget chose "the Sacrifice of the Mass" as the topic for his homily.[211] Asked in 1823 to preach in Louisville's courthouse, Bishop Dubourg of New Orleans talked about the sacrament of confession.[212] Bishop Martin John Spalding preached on the real presence of Christ in the Eucharist to a large crowd at a Confederate encampment near Bowling Green.[213] As Bishop England put it, "Liberality in religion, is the making to others the most ample concessions, which *truth* will allow. To deny known truth, is not *liberality,* it is criminal *falsehood.*"[214]

Protestants not only worshipped in Catholic churches, but they also welcomed Catholics into their own buildings. In describing the life of a priest in antebellum Kentucky, Badin boasted that "in this part of America entire liberty of conscience and religion are enjoyed." This meant that Catholics could celebrate virtually anywhere: "We march in procession around our cemeteries; we erect crosses on them; we preach in the hotels and other public places, and even in Protestant churches, for want of chapels."[215] One of the first priests in Charleston, Fr. Paulin, advertised in the *City Gazette* in 1788, that he would say Mass in the City Tavern, also a popular meeting-place for Protestant societies.[216] Likewise, the congregation of St. Mary's Church in Charleston met for worship in the city's Military Hall, without charge, while their church underwent repairs in 1851.[217]

Protestants in Kentucky offered Catholics their facilities. During the Jubilee of 1827, a priest arrived to celebrate in New Haven. Having no church, Catholics used a warehouse lent by a non-Catholic.[218] Protestants were so generous with their churches that they generated resentment. Catholics did not allow Protestants into their pulpits, complained one critic, "but let a Priest come along, and a Baptist, Methodist or Presbyterian church is at hand, and the Priest is not invited to occupy it—*Persecution* is the cry!"[219] Catholics could usually count on Protestant pulpits when they needed them.

No single source better testifies to Protestant openness than Bishop England's *Diurnal,* a record of his travels in the Diocese of Charleston between 1821 and 1823. Wherever England stopped, he addressed mixed congregations, in Catholic churches when possible, otherwise in courthouses or Protestant churches. England "received an invitation from the Pastor and Trustees of the Presbyterian Church to use their building (the best in town)." He "preached in the Evening in the Court House at the request of some of the inhabitants." He "conversed freely with the principal inhabitants, from whom I experienced much kindness."[220] In three years, England preached thirty-four times in Protestant churches, forty-seven times in courthouses, and five times in private academies in at least thirteen cities and towns in the Carolinas and Georgia. He sometimes had to decline invitations to speak in Protestant churches because he had already accepted another offer.

During the rest of the 1820s, England preached in eleven Episcopal, Presbyterian, Methodist, and Baptist churches, as well as in five courthouses and two academies in thirteen towns throughout his diocese. In one brief span in April 1829, while returning from a visitation in North Carolina, he preached at the courthouse in New Bern, a Presbyterian church in Wilmington, a Protestant church in Smithville, and the courthouse in Georgetown, South Carolina.[221] In 1826, he became the first priest to address the federal legislature. So great was the crowd, that President John Quincy Adams had trouble squeezing in and claiming his seat. England felt "extraordinary gratification" at the "intense attention" with which he was heard.[222]

Protestants went out of their way to accommodate England. In April 1824, he arrived in Warrenton, Georgia, while the Superior Court was in session. The judge adjourned the proceedings so that England could use the courthouse. Five years later, in Milledgeville, Georgia, a local Baptist society, which had arranged to use the town's Presbyterian church, gave it up so that England could preach instead.[223]

Other priests enjoyed similar hospitality from Protestants. In 1819, Fr. Nicholas Kearney preached in the courthouse in Washington, North Carolina.[224] Over the next decade, the *Miscellany* recorded that seven different priests preached fifteen times in Protestant churches, sixteen times in courthouses, and nine times in academies in twenty-three towns throughout the diocese. In 1825, in a single week, Fr. John McEncroe preached in a Presbyterian church in Walterborough, South Carolina, celebrated Mass at an academy near Coosawhatchie, preached in the courthouse, and preached again at the Baptist Tabernacle in Beaufort.[225] Such invitations became a consistent mark of southern religion.[226]

By the 1840s and 1850s, public sentiment turned against Catholicism. In some cities, animosity exploded into violence as mobs rampaged through immigrant neighborhoods, destroying Catholic churches. The South was not immune to such hatred, but southerners mostly continued to build Catholic churches rather than burn them. And Catholics responded with extravagant displays of gratitude and patriotism. Catholics of Charleston marked the Fourth of July by fastening a large flag to the cross atop the cathedral. Priests celebrated masses in each church, accompanied by readings of the Declaration of Independence, orations, and processions by the Irish and French militia companies.[227] Priests also prayed for civic leaders.[228] The implicit message was that Catholics felt at home in the American South.

Catholic Churches—"Ornaments" of the South

Some Protestants supported Catholics for reasons of civic pride. Flaget recognized that the St. Louis Church would "prove an ornament to the town" and "increase the number of its inhabitants."[229] He appealed to civic motives when asking Secretary of State Henry Clay for a remission on duties on a gift for the cathedral from the King of Naples: "For God's Sake, give me another proof of your generous friendship, & in favour of a town where, I have been told, you have been partly trained up."[230] A writer for the *Miscellany* similarly appealed to boosterism in describing the consecration of a new church. Conceding that the building was rather humble, he assured his audience that over time the Catholic community would build "a large, commodious, and ornamental Cathedral" that would advertise "the taste and public spirit of the city."[231] With the aid of Protestant donations, the Catholics of Charleston fulfilled this pledge. After the dedication of the Cathedral of Saint John the Baptist, the *Charleston Courier* extolled its civic benefits: "In our edifices of Religious Worship we can at least compare favorably with any city that could fairly challenge us."[232]

Protestant taste influenced Catholic architecture. David described the conditions for Protestant support for a cathedral in Bardstown: "they have said openly that if it were a question of a small church, they would not contribute . . . but that if we wanted to build 'a good, large substantial church' they would contribute generously."[233] Flaget preferred to build a seminary before a cathedral, but he realized that his arguments were "of no weight when compared with the ornament which Bardstown is to derive from so magnificent a building."[234] When work began on the building, Protestants provided the impetus. "The Protestants of Bardstown and its vicinity have so urged me to undertake the work," Flaget wrote, "that I should have considered myself guilty of sin had I not acceded to their solicitations." He recognized that a cathedral would offer Catholics "a character of respectability."[235] In Macon, Mississippi, a Catholic noted that a non-Catholic acquaintance had approached him and offered $500 to help build a church. A local lawyer, educated at Bardstown, promised a plot of land, and others also made pledges. The only condition they attached to their gifts was that the new church be "*attractive.*"[236]

Many saw all religious institutions as socially beneficial. Two eastern missionaries in the old Southwest noted that even the religiously indifferent appeared to be "thoroughly convinced . . . of the indispensable necessity of religion to the welfare of society."[237] A Protestant minister sailing down the Mississippi to New Orleans rejoiced at the sight of Catholic church spires "seen at the intervals of every six or seven miles," they "cheer the eyes of all," he said, "who are not skeptics or bigots."[238] A Catholic missionary in rural Kentucky recalled that a Methodist class leader asked him to preach in the local schoolhouse. When he finished, the crowd sang and prayed for his mission, leading him to speculate that they would have done the same thing for "any other preacher who might have appeared, and engaged their attention."[239] In Arkansas, Governor John Pope promised to help establish a Catholic church, in large part because he hoped to draw Catholic settlers from Kentucky. A priest reported that several Protestants in Little Rock voiced support for a church, and when fund raising began, they pledged nearly twice as much as local Catholics.[240] Catholics even claimed that Protestants owed them for building churches. In a fund-raising appeal for Charleston's cathedral, the *Miscellany* argued that not just Catholics "but a great portion of our dissenting fellow-citizens do and ought to feel an interest in the welfare of this Church, in which they themselves have frankly acknowledged, they have been frequently accommodated and edified."[241] Protestants valued churches, so they should help pay for them.

In addition to promoting social stability, churches brightened the cityscape. The 1826 *Statistics of South Carolina* noted that St. Mary's Church "is a neat and respectable building. . . . The Hebrew Synagogue is in Hazel Street opposite the Roman Catholic Church, which, with the latter building, contributes much to ornament this part of the city."[242] The *Covington Journal* described a cathedral dedicated in 1854 as "an ornament to the city" that offered "evidence of our increasing numbers and prosperity."[243] The Louisville *City Directory* referred to the new Church of St. Louis in similar terms.[244] In describing Edgefield, South Carolina, in 1859, *DeBow's Review* referred to the Catholic church as "a magnificent stone structure in the Gothic style" and judged that it would rank as "the finest ecclesiastical edifice in any village of the state."[245] A Protestant journal quoted Archbishop Maréchal of Baltimore as claiming that his city's Protestants "consider the cathedral as the ornament and honor of their city, *and frequent it with an interest almost equal to that of the Catholics*."[246] As church spires multiplied, civic pride swelled.

Catholics proclaimed their esteem for American liberality: "although our creed differs from the opinions of the great bulk of the American people, we do not know, and have not known in several thousands of miles traveling with the inhabitants of various nations, a more correct and well conducted people."[247] Religious liberty reflected the American character and set it apart from other nations. An essay in the *Miscellany* compared the United States favorably with Europe, noting that "in looking over our communications from Europe, we have frequently to congratulate ourselves upon our state of religious freedom at this side of the Atlantic. . . . The American people and the American government have done all they could or ought to do."[248] Another Catholic writer drew a clear contrast between America and Britain. Reflecting on the Revolution and the extension of liberty to Catholics, the writer noted that Americans had immediately implemented "an act of plain justice and political wisdom, which the parent country, after a lapse of nearly fifty years, has not yet had the magnanimity to perform."[249]

When intolerance flared, clerics downplayed its effects. They acknowledged bigotry but absolved southerners of responsibility. Some spoke of prejudice only as a thing of the past, a "strong tide of popular prejudice whose fury rose high; but whose last waves are now, thank God, on the ebb."[250] The opposition, they said, came only from the Protestant preachers. When vandals attacked a Catholic church in Danville, Kentucky, the *Miscellany* declared that "the citizens felt anxious to clear themselves of the unworthy act" and blamed a visiting Presbyterian minister.[251] Spalding laid the blame for "absurd prejudice" at the ministers' feet, complaining that they denounced priests for keeping Catholics in ignorance while preventing their flocks from learning about Catholicism.[252]

The *Miscellany* reasoned that Protestants could "scarcely be blamed for their prejudices against a religion which has always been to them studiously misrepresented."[253] Catholic chronicles repeated frequent anecdotes about preachers who denounced Catholicism but fell silent when a Catholic appeared to reveal their ignorance. Several anecdotes enjoyed wide currency: when a Presbyterian minister claimed that St. Paul denounced Catholicism, Kenrick was alleged to have so effectively refuted the claim that the ministers' partisans silenced him.[254] When a Catholic laywoman "of no great learning" heard a preacher denouncing the popes as the antichrist, she pointed out that "antichrist" was singular whereas "popes" was plural.[255] In such accounts, enemies of Catholicism appear more amusing than menacing, and the mass of Protestants side with truth and logic.

Catholic chroniclers even minimized a seemingly indisputable case of Protestant animosity. In the fall of 1799, while recovering from a severe cold, Fr. Anthony Salmon of Kentucky set out through the snow to visit a Protestant woman preparing for baptism. He fell from his horse about a mile from Bardstown. Badly wounded, he dragged himself to a tree and propped himself against it. Eventually a young man found him, but the man's employer refused to aid a priest who, he sneered, was probably passed out drunk. By the time friends found Salmon, there was little they could do.

Catholic chroniclers recorded the story, but no one emphasized that a Protestant left a priest to die. "This was a man of no standing in the country . . . his brutality is almost single in the early history of Kentucky," noted Spalding, who observed that the youth who wanted to aid Salmon "is now one of our most respectable citizens."[256] Badin also dismissed the incident as "in nowise American," but rather an individual failing. "Perhaps," Badin added, "he was ignorant of the extremity to which M. Salmon was reduced."[257] The *Miscellany* described the cruelty as "the *only* instance which has reached us of an act *totally at variance with the American character.*"[258] Prominent Catholic voices refused to blame anti-Catholic prejudice on Americans or southerners as a group.

Some Catholics blamed the British for the bigotry. Spalding traced early prejudice in Kentucky to "the erroneous opinions which their forefathers had inherited from England."[259] Hearing a Protestant misrepresent Catholic doctrine, England expressed his regret that "British folly and calumny should have left so much of its worst prejudice in South Carolina."[260] The *Miscellany* echoed this refrain: "the children of old England have discarded every thing English, but English intolerance."[261] The newspaper even blamed Britain for the anti-Catholic press in America.[262]

Southerners must have approved when Catholics contrasted northern intolerance to the generosity of the South. Speaking to the South Carolina Convention in 1837, England referred to the destruction of the convent in Charlestown, Massachusetts. In contrast, he said, in South Carolina, "there are vast numbers who . . . are honourably disposed to render justice to ourselves and to protect us . . . in the enjoyment of that religious freedom which is our undoubted right by the constitution of our State."[263] England urged the European press to cover attacks on Catholics in the North, giving the terms "liberality, kind feeling and honorable conduct to the Americans of the Southern States, and giving the full benefit of the terms—bigotry and intolerance—to the New England States."[264] The arrival of a contingent of Ursulines in Charleston after the destruction of the convent in Massachusetts provided an opportunity to draw contrasts. England assured them that Charleston's Protestants would never stain the city with "so foul a blot." A committee of clergy and laity explained that "though separated from us in faith, our fellow citizens are united with us in feelings of respect for female virtue." Should any danger arise, "in every

Carolinian heart you would experience sympathy, from every Carolinian hand you would find protection."[265]

Comparisons with the North hit home among southerners. In 1835, England petitioned the legislature to incorporate several convents and churches. Public opinion had turned against him because he had agreed to serve as papal legate to Haiti, so the legislature delayed his petitions while those of other denominations passed. A friendly senator arranged for him to address the Senate, which he did for over two hours. He spoke of the Charlestown convent and begged his audience "not to degrade Carolina by placing it by the side of Massachusetts." His petitions then passed without opposition.[266] In the rhetoric of southern Catholics, their Protestant neighbors bore little responsibility for American anti-Catholicism. It was a viewpoint that pleased at least some of the South's Protestants.

"Splendor Entirely Indescribable": Catholicism's Aesthetic Appeal

Lyman Beecher was no fan of Catholicism. He made it his mission to warn fellow Protestants of the danger posed by Catholic immigrants and their despotic faith. Yet for all Beecher's animosity, Catholicism seems to have gripped his imagination. He described the church as "majestic and imposing in its ceremonies, dazzling by its lights and ornaments, vestments and gorgeous drapery, and fascinating by the power of music and the breathing marble and living canvas, and all the diversified contributions of art."[267] Nothing could have dragged Beecher into a Catholic church, yet he articulated a sentiment not uncommon among American Protestants—wonder at the splendor of Catholicism's culture, art, and liturgy. For Beecher, wonder led to fear, but for others it had the opposite effect.[268]

Catholics went to great lengths to make their churches impressive. Badin boasted that Flaget had so adorned the interior of Bardstown's cathedral "as to make all the connoisseurs give it the preference before the massive cathedral of Baltimore." Particularly notable were paintings donated by Pope Leo XII and the King of Naples, which elicited from visitors "not only admiration, but sentiments of piety and religion."[269] Kentucky's Catholics owed a debt to Fr. Nerinckx, who returned from one European expedition with several tons of donated church goods, including vestments and other linens, chasubles, monstrances, a bell, and an organ for the cathedral.[270] A Protestant observer astutely noted that Catholics preferred building a single cathedral to numerous smaller churches in order to "strike and awe the minds of men."[271]

Clergy recognized that putting on a good show would impress both

Catholics and Protestants. "Nothing revives more the activity & zeal of our Catholics than that august ceremony which strikes with awe the heretics and infidels themselves," noted Badin.[272] A non-Catholic journal published a letter attributed to Archbishop James Whitfield in which he noted that music at Catholic worship produced "*a happy effect on the Protestants, whose worship is so naked and dry.*"[273] To ensure that future generations would benefit from the same style of worship, David stressed the proper conduct of religious ceremonies to Kentucky's seminarians.[274] These efforts bore fruit. A priest visiting Bardstown's cathedral reported that "the ceremonies, all performed with the greatest exactness according to the Roman rite; the chant at once grave and touching; the attendant clergy pious and modest." They made such an impression that "I almost believed myself in the midst of one of the finest churches of Rome."[275]

Priests and bishops seized every chance to host elaborate rituals. Church dedications provided perfect opportunities. In 1830, England asked several priests to join him in Columbia so that the dedication of a new church "might be as correctly & decently done as my means will permit."[276] A priest in Georgia conducted a ceremony for the blessing of a new church "with as much externity [*sic*] as our abilities enabled us to perform it" and expressed his pleasure that the "novel spectacle" seemed so pleasing.[277]

Dedicating a cathedral required an even higher level of ceremony. Flaget agonized over the most fitting way to consecrate the cathedral at Bardstown. To give the main sermon, he chose a native Kentuckian, Fr. Robert Abell, as the man most likely to impress listeners of all faiths.[278] In 1835, England urged his new coadjutor, William Clancy, to receive consecration in Charleston, knowing that the ceremony would gratify the city's residents.[279] In Kentucky, David and Flaget used missionaries passing through on their way west to conduct Holy Week liturgies with a full complement of clerics.[280] Years later, a scheduling conflict occurred when the consecration of a church in Cincinnati, a cathedral in St. Louis, and a bishop in Louisville all demanded as many priests and bishops as possible. Bishop Rosati of St. Louis, who wanted no fewer than five or six bishops at his cathedral's consecration, eventually triumphed as the others realized the importance of promoting the faith in the Mississippi Valley.[281] Flaget even turned the removal of an interdict against a rebellious church into a grand spectacle, complete with a procession, a band, speeches in French and English, and the discharge of cannons.[282]

Catholics used processions to display their faith. On the feast of Corpus Christi in 1825, they organized a procession from the church in Bardstown to a grove nearby. A standard bearing a cross and Gospel verse headed the procession. Another flag followed, with groups of young women singing hymns in between. The young women were clad in white, contrasting with the black habits of the thirty Sisters of Charity who followed them. After the women came an ornate crucifix and torches and a band of youths bearing Gospel verses, banners, and baskets of flowers. A dozen youths with smaller baskets scattered flowers along the path the sacred host would travel. Another dozen bore censers of incense, continuously replenished from two large silver plates. At the rear of the youths, four carried a large urn suspended on poles. Candidates for Holy Orders and the clergy followed, then Bishop Flaget, walking under a canopy supported by a man clad entirely in black. Twenty laymen, carrying green boughs, marched parallel to the clergy. The procession took place in the midst of an "immense multitude," among whom the utmost decorum prevailed, "though probably not half of them were Catholics."[283]

Catholic efforts paid off. The aesthetics of Catholic churches and worship attracted Protestants. Nostalgia for the past, particularly the medieval, Catholic past, was a hallmark of a romanticism that filtered through antebellum American culture. Among its religious effects was a series of high-profile conversions to Catholicism and a renewed appreciation for Catholic liturgy and architecture, particularly the Gothic style, which some Protestants had traditionally viewed as barbaric and grotesque.[284] Rev. George Lewis, a Scottish minister traveling through South Carolina, charged that Europeans had become enchanted with "the ancient architecture of the Church of Rome, and her solemn pomp of worship" without considering that "these romantic cathedrals and abbeys have been the grave of true religion."[285] But his praise of Catholic aesthetics suggested that he too had fallen under its spell. "The religion of Rome is the religion of the senses and imagination . . . she still retains her wondrous hold of mankind, overwhelming them with the magnificence of her architecture and music, the pomp of her processions . . . and her mysterious rites and symbols," he explained.[286]

A columnist in the *Miscellany,* claiming to have been "educated in a hostile creed, and sometimes inclining to skepticism," commented that it was hard to attend "the service of the Catholic church, without feeling a soothing and elevation of the mind, which no other mode of worship has ever, in the slightest degree, produced."[287] One Protestant, gazing at a painting of the crucifixion in Bardstown's cathedral, was reported to have said that the painting awakened "every sentiment of Christian piety."[288] The Catholic aesthetic could be alluring.

The *Charleston Courier* testified to the appeal in describing the city's new cathedral. Even before construction was complete, it referred to the "architectural beauties" of the "magnificent structure" that presented a "very imposing appearance."[289] The *Courier* had greater praise for the consecration of Bishop Patrick Lynch seven years later. Describing the vestments, chants, and music, the newspaper concluded that the scene was "too solemn, imposing, grand and affecting to be noted on paper . . . never before in Charleston have we witnessed the like—a ceremonial worthy, indeed, of the stern, Gothic magnificence of the edifice in which it was performed."[290] Others were still more effusive. Theodore Clapp, a Presbyterian and later Unitarian minister in New Orleans, often attended High Mass and found that "there is not on earth another ceremony so august, solemn, and impressive." He conceded that to those used to such spectacles, Protestant worship must seem "unedifying, and even irreverent."[291]

Even staunch enemies of the faith could be impressed by its aesthetics. John Brown, a South Carolinian studying law in Louisville and critic of Catholicism, described the local Catholic church as "executed with a degree of splendor entirely indescribable." He wondered: "can rational man believe there's any piety in the variegated dresses and monkey shines of the priests before the altar?" But he conceded that it required "the piety of a Socrates or the fortitude of an Alexander" to withstand the allurements of the service. Even the priests' attire elicited Brown's awe: "their dress eclipses the splendor of anything I ever saw in that way."[292]

Some Protestants visited Catholic churches purely for the aesthetics. In Maryland, Floride Clemson, a South Carolina native and granddaughter of John Calhoun, attended a service commemorating the life of Archbishop Kenrick less from esteem for the prelate than to hear Mozart's requiem.[293] Another Southern lady, the novelist Augusta Jane Evans Wilson, bemoaned the state of the arts in the South, noting that the only place to view worthwhile art in New Orleans was the Catholic cathedral.[294] Another visitor viewed the cathedral itself as a "fine thing," particularly in relation to the rest of American church architecture.[295] Catholics cultivated their reputation for high culture. Bishop England asked a colleague traveling to Italy to bring back some works of art "so as to put our Protestant Americans under a compliment to Catholic Italy."[296]

Catholic churches in the North also impressed southern tourists. "I was struck with the Solemnity of the Aparatus [*sic*], & cou'd not help remarking on how much every thing was calculated to warm the Imagination, & captivate the Senses," remarked Virginia's George Mason after attending Mass in Philadelphia.[297] William Graham, a North Carolinian who served successively as senator, governor, and secretary of the navy, noted that in

New York's cathedral "the kneeling posture, the devout appearance, the solemn chant, accompanied by music, and the lighted tapers and georgeous [*sic*] decorations . . . united to give a most imposing appearance." Graham recognized the ceremony's power, acknowledging that it "was well adapted to give solemnity to their devotions, and must operate to produce much practical morality among the ignorant," although sophisticated observers "will look on a great part of it as idle pomp."[298]

Protestants formed positive impressions of Catholicism by visiting Catholic churches abroad, especially in Rome. Southern Catholics sometimes used their contacts in Europe to facilitate these trips. England arranged introductions for a prominent non-Catholic merchant traveling to Rome with his family and found someone to explain the local customs and religious services to them.[299] St. Peter's awed the Rev. Richard Fuller, a Baptist minister from South Carolina, during his European tour in 1836.[300] William Preston, a member of the South Carolina legislature, senator, and president of South Carolina College, recalled his initial "sorrow, disgust, and horror, at the detestable superstition which had superseded the Church religion" and even discerned "the slime of the serpent everywhere, and the foul influences of his venom." But after visiting St. Peter's, he conceded that it "grows upon the imagination by successive visits . . . in its conception, its execution, and its appointments I suppose it has no equal in the world in Ancient or modern times." Preston attended Holy Week services, in which he found "an artistic perfection." Shortly thereafter, he crowded into St. Peter's along with forty thousand others to receive Pope Pius VII's benediction. Much to his own surprise, he "bent instinctively" to his knees, where he remained until the papal litter passed.[301] Catholic splendor could work strange effects on Protestants.

The wonders of Rome compelled some Protestants to reconsider their assumptions regarding popery's primitiveness and its inevitable defeat by Protestantism. The city's art and architecture "frequently overwhelmed admiring American tourists with their astonishing display of human genius and the expansive potential of the senses," undermining sureties of Protestant supremacy. The aesthetics of Catholicism on full display could spark in American Protestants "an uneasiness that threatened not the defeat but the embrace of the enemy—an embrace that led not so much to religious conversion as to an aesthetic and emotional appropriation of the enemy's powers."[302]

Montreal's churches ranked just below Rome's in their effects on southern Protestant visitors. John Short, a Kentuckian traveling in Canada, was overwhelmed by a visit to the cathedral of Montreal. "Seeing today the beautiful women kneeling as they come into church, while the divine notes of the organ (different from anything *I* ever heard before) seemed to fall from Heaven," he wrote home to his brother, "I thought my only chance of ever getting to that blessed abode, was to remain here . . . and become a devout Catholic." He mused that "we democrats and protestants are too unholy and sacriligious [*sic*]—there *must* be virtue and true religion here, or all would long since have fallen into dust."[303] During the Mexican-American War, the aesthetics of Mexican Catholicism appealed to many Protestant soldiers, and even the *Baptist Banner and Western Pioneer* noted that the beauty of a cathedral "cannot fail to impress the most insensible."[304]

Travel abroad could make America's Catholic churches seem modest by comparison. "The Catholic religion is a much more imposing affair in one of these solemn cathedrals, than it is in one of the two penny concerns in America," remarked Anna Clemson of South Carolina during a stay in Brussels.[305] But foreign visitors to America sometimes appreciated the beauty of the South's churches and worship. A German traveler who attended the cathedral in Baltimore found the music excellent "both in composition and execution" and the sermon "very edifying."[306] Frances Trollope, an Englishwoman who spent several years in America in the late 1820s, found the Baltimore cathedral to pale in comparison to its European counterparts, but she noted that all Americans considered it magnificent, and she conceded that its interior possessed "an air of neatness that amounts to elegance." Far more impressive to her eyes was the modest chapel at St. Mary's College, which with its gardens offered "something of holiness, and quiet beauty about it, that excites the imagination strangely."[307] George Lewis also felt moved by the Catholic cemetery of New Orleans, where the flowers gave an air of "sweet solemnity . . . more in accordance with the Christian's hope than the gloom and desolation of so many of the churchyards of the Old World."[308]

Conclusion

From its origins in the South, the public worship of Catholicism depended on Protestant support. In places where Catholics could not build their own churches, they worshipped in Protestant churches. Where Catholics could muster the funds to begin building, Protestants supplemented their resources. When Catholic churches stood complete, Protestants attended lectures, ceremonies, and even masses. In southern cityscapes, the steeples of Catholic churches marked the public presence of Catholicism, while the foundations of the churches rested on Protestant support. Many motives drove this support. Protestants saw Catholicism as one faith among many and recognized that, rather than threatening American society, Catholic churches sustained southern culture. They attended Catholic churches to have a place to worship, out of curiosity, or even out of boredom. Many kept coming back because they liked what they saw. Protestants helped Catholicism make a home in the South.

5
Ruling Together

In July 1835, Charleston was a powder keg. Abolitionist tracts mysteriously appeared in the city, prompting rumors and panic. The *Courier* complained that "incendiary papers and tracts" were arriving by mail—a "monstrous abuse of this national convenience"—and threatening public order.[1] Charlestonians were not known for levelheadedness even in the best of times, and these were not the best of times. Not content to direct their anger solely at northern abolitionists, some found a scapegoat closer to home—the city's Catholics.

As Bishop England later explained it, Rome's decision to send him as envoy to Haiti raised southern suspicions. "Northern sectarians" made things worse by spreading rumors that Rome arranged the mission to promote abolition. Charlestonians cast a suspicious eye on a Catholic school for free blacks. State law forbade teaching slaves to read or write but said nothing about free blacks, and other denominations ran similar schools. But it was the Catholic school that drew Charlestonians' ire. On the night of July 29, a mob broke into the city post office and seized piles of abolitionist tracts. The next night, irate citizens burned the tracts on the parade ground in front of the Citadel. As a crowd milled about the bonfire, a Catholic reportedly overheard plans to destroy the school and other Catholic institutions and to lynch Bishop England. Armed Catholics brought word to England, who raised an alarm. Irish members of the city militia grabbed their weapons and rushed to his side, putting themselves under his command.[2]

England defended Catholics through the press. In a letter to the *Courier,* he denied that any priest had received the tracts and argued that every Catholic stood "fully determined" to prevent abolitionists from disturbing the peace of the South. As for the school, he was determined "not only to keep most respectfully obedient to the law, but also in full accordance with the reasonable wishes of a large bulk of our Southern fellow citizens," and he submitted documents showing the institution's legality.[3]

Threats against Charleston's Catholics exposed an anti-Catholic bigotry in the South. But far more important than what happened during the summer of 1835 is what did not happen. Rather than handing the city over to mob rule, non-Catholics joined the forces guarding Catholic institutions, and city officials pledged their assistance in protecting Catholic property. Thanks largely to their efforts, the crisis passed without violence. Soon after, a committee approached England and asked him to close the school. England consented, but on the condition that similar schools run by other denominations also close.[4]

Rather than revealing southern antipathy to Catholicism, the incident in Charleston demonstrates how thoroughly Catholics accommodated themselves to southern mores on race and slavery and how completely they integrated themselves into southern society. England's ability to stave off a riot and his willingness to close the school demonstrated that Catholic concern for blacks, whether free or slave, was ephemeral. The deeper and enduring reality was that the Catholic Church, like the Protestant churches of the South, mirrored the racial values of its adherents. This gave the church a cultural home in southern society.[5] Southern Protestants supported the institutions—charities, schools, and churches—central to Catholicism, and Catholics supported the institution central to the South.

Catholic Opposition to Abolition

Most Catholics in both the North and the South opposed abolition. The Maryland Jesuits saw it as a product of Protestantism and the worst tendencies of the Enlightenment and wanted nothing to do with it.[6] Other Catholics associated it with liberal individualism and social disorder. They rejected the belief in human perfectibility held by some nineteenth-century reformers and saw abolition as a violation of natural property rights.[7] Some Catholics saw abolitionism as a religious movement and worried that government support would set a precedent for interference in other religious matters.[8] In Kentucky, the *Catholic Advocate* denounced abolitionists as "insidious hypocrites" for accusing Catholics of meddling in politics but then using government to impose their religious conviction that slavery was a sin: "A sect looking to Congress for a case of conscience! Politicians, have your eyes open! Patriots mind your duty, and save the liberties of your country."[9] Catholics also worried that abolitionism undermined scripture. After laying out a biblical defense of slavery, Bishop Verot concluded that "nothing more is wanted to show that the spirit of Abolitionists is not the spirit of the Angels of God, the spirit of the Bible, the spirit of truth and justice,—but the demon of anarchy, discord, stubbornness, and pride."[10] Abolitionists threatened the scriptural foundations of society.

Catholics accepted the familiar argument that abolition would harm the slaves. Bishop England denied that he was friendly to slavery but added that abolition was impossible.[11] Fr. John Grassi, a native of Italy who served as superior of the Maryland Jesuits and president of Georgetown College, saw the contradiction between slavery and American principles but viewed anything more than token manumissions as impractical. Slaves were so sunk in ignorance and sin that leaving them to their own devices would be unchristian. Other Jesuits noted that even free blacks in Maryland had few economic opportunities and drew constant suspicion from whites.[12] In Florida, Bishop Verot speculated that even voluntary manumission would be "a misfortune of appalling magnitude, more so yet for the slave than for the master."[13] In 1866, a year after the Thirteenth Amendment abolished slavery, the American bishops still wished that "a more gradual system of emancipation could have been adopted" so that the slaves "might have been in some measure prepared to make better use of their freedom, than they are likely to do now."[14] Catholic tradition had insisted that bondage existed for the good of the slave, not the benefit of the master. Turning slaves loose was an abandonment of responsibility.

To Catholics, the abolitionists seemed to be religious bigots. Such figures as Elijah Lovejoy, George Bourne, Angela Grimké, Frederick Douglass, George Cheever, and the Beechers mixed denunciations of slavery and Catholicism. One Ohio abolitionist asserted that "popery finds its appropriate ally in the institution of slavery. They are both kindred systems. One enslaves the mind, the other both mind and body."[15] Catholics observed that the mobs opposing the Fugitive Slave Act and the mobs torching Catholic churches included some of the same people.[16] No wonder Bishop Richard Whelan of Wheeling, Virginia, described abolitionists as the church's "most deadly enemies."[17] The *Miscellany* noted that Arthur Tappan, a New York abolitionist who allegedly wanted the slave to "butcher his master," had also "assailed and calumniated foreigners and catholics." Such "religious fanatics" wanted to destroy the country, caring little whether "their desired object be achieved by exciting the blacks to butcher the whites, or the citizens against each other, on account of religious difference."[18]

Bishop England, in defending his mission to Haiti to friends in the South Carolina legislature, "merely told them that they ought to know that I was opposed to the Abolitionists, who were most bitter enemies also to the Catholics."[19] A columnist for the *Miscellany* complained that the abolitionists were "totally uninformed upon the practice of our Southern States" and "wickedly prone to misrepresent the treatment of the slave."[20] The paper wondered why abolitionists, if they cared so much for blacks, did not take the money they spent denouncing Catholicism and instead use it to return free blacks to Africa.[21] Denouncing "fanatical preachers," Bishop Verot linked abolitionism to anti-Catholic riots and Know-Nothingism, and he cautioned that the South would not be as patient as the Catholic Church had been.[22] Such odium against abolitionists gained wide currency in the church.[23] Virtually all Catholics, regardless of class or national origins, mistrusted abolitionists, and not one publicly visible Catholic endorsed immediate abolition.[24]

Catholics repeated the familiar accusation that the North treated its free laborers worse than the South treated its slaves. They charged that northerners who denounced the plight of slaves ignored the horrific conditions in their own factories and cities. Verot speculated that starving families in northern cities would leap at the chance to sell themselves into slavery in exchange for the level of care that southern slaves received.[25] A young Virginia Catholic argued that southerners—at least those of "refinement and education"—treated slaves well and that "insulting epithets towards their Servants were as rare among Southerners as they are common among their fanatical and brutal friends of Yankeedom."[26] Northern Catholics made the same point. The *U.S. Catholic Intelligencer* insisted that "the slave of the South enjoys more comfort, is often more moral, and certainly more exempt from care . . . than the free black or indigent white man of the North."[27] The accusation that the North had succumbed to an unbridled capitalism that produced human misery became by 1850 a standard part of the proslavery argument in the South. The argument appealed to Catholics, who had long been suspicious of the individualism implicit in capitalist economies. In this light, slavery, even if not ideal, seemed a relatively mild social evil and vastly preferable to the schemes proposed by abolitionists.[28]

Catholic opponents of abolitionism added an ethnic dimension to the argument. They pointed out that economic greed in the North and Britain caused worse suffering among the Irish than anything slaves endured. "The general treatment of the negroes in the diocese of Charleston is kind and affectionate; far, very far more so than that of the bulk of Irish agricultural or other laborers," claimed England.[29] Two European-born Jesuits reported to Rome that southerners treated their slaves better than Europeans treated their peasants.[30] Catholic and Protestant apologists for slavery read from the same script. A Protestant minister in New Orleans argued that European peasants were "beyond all comparison more destitute, helpless, and wretched, than African bondsmen in our republic."[31] The *Alabama Planter* complained that the average Englishman "weeps for the sufferings of the negro, but allows his Irish fellow subjects to live in ignorance and filth, and often to die of starvation."[32] For the Irish, such arguments gained southern trust and struck back against their oppressors.

Emancipation implied, to Catholic writers, political radicalism. It threatened to "sunder the links of social order and national integrity."[33] Catholic concern for order and authority dictated obedience to the law, including the laws governing slavery. It was an additional benefit that such a concern deflected nativist charges that Catholics were disloyal to American institutions. Here was an instance in which the Catholic respect for hierarchical order could make sense in a nation with republican traditions, for even the most ardent republican stood for "social order." The *Miscellany* doubtless won the assent of both the friends and enemies of slavery—at least among southern whites—when it praised the "justice, wisdom and moderation" of the court that exiled or executed the conspirators in Denmark Vesey's failed uprising.[34]

Common enemies had long brought Catholic and Protestant southerners together. In the face of a perceived threat to their society—indeed to their very lives—they closed ranks. Catholics won the friendship of southern Protestants by identifying the South's enemies as their own. They not only denounced abolitionists, they appealed to order, authority, and obedience—arguments that had great resonance among the South's ruling class. And Southern Catholics went even further than condemning abolition. They supported slavery.

Catholic Support for Slavery: Rhetoric

Southern Catholics championed slavery. They drew on a tradition of moral teaching based largely on scripture, the early church fathers, Thomas Aquinas, and medieval councils that seemed to sanction the institution.[35] A parallel tradition of papal condemnations of the slave trade stretching back to the fifteenth century did not, in most interpretations, directly threaten slavery itself. When Pope Gregory XVI condemned the trade in African slaves in 1839, England used the *Miscellany* to reassure southerners.[36] He published the document and praised its condemnation of the slave trade, but he argued that it did not censure slaveholders.[37] In a series of letters to John Forsyth, former governor of Georgia and secretary of State to Martin Van Buren, he further attempted to limit the scope of Gregory's epistle. Forsyth had published Gregory's letter as a warning that foreign powers were conspiring with fanatical Whigs in the North to destroy slavery.[38] England drew on natural law and scripture to defend slavery. "There is no danger," he said, "that Catholic theology should ever be tinctured with the fanaticism of abolition. Catholics may and do differ in regard to slavery. . . . But our theology is fixed."[39] He reviewed centuries of canon law—an analysis so meticulous that when death interrupted the project after eighteen letters, he had only reached about the year 900.[40] In short, both scripture and tradition sanctioned slavery. Several subsequent defenses of slavery would follow the argument of these letters, published in pamphlet form in 1844 and again in 1847.

England was not the only southern Catholic to defend slavery. Martin Spalding, the second bishop of Louisville, worried about the pastoral needs of slaves, but he argued in the Vatican newspaper that more harm than good would come from emancipation.[41] John Mitchell, an Irish patriot and the editor of the *Southern Citizen* of Nashville, defended slavery in a debate with Henry Ward Beecher, denying that owning, selling, and flogging slaves was "a crime or a wrong or even a picadillo [*sic*]."[42]

Perhaps the strongest defense of the institution came from Bishop Augustin Verot. He was a Frenchman who studied at Issy, near Paris, joined the Sulpicians, and came to Baltimore to teach at the Sulpician college of St. Mary's. He intended to spend seven years in the United States but ended up spending the rest of his life. Indifferent in appearance, Verot was respected for his erudition and geniality. In 1857, in recognition of his attributes, he received election to the titular see of Danaba and appointment as vicar apostolic of Florida.[43]

On January 4, 1861, Verot preached a sermon in St. Augustine, taking as his text Proverbs 14:34. Ignoring the clergy's tradition of abstinence from political and social issues, Verot defended slavery so staunchly that his words circulated throughout the South as a Confederate tract. He set out to demonstrate "the conditions under which servitude is legitimate, lawful, approved by all laws, and consistent with practical religion and true holiness of life in masters who fulfil [*sic*] those conditions." He conceded that no one could own another human being, but he insisted that natural, divine, ecclesiastical, and civil law all sanctioned the right of a person to claim another's labor. He listed the ways in which one could legitimately become a slave, offered a scriptural defense, and said that attempting to prove that canon law sanctioned slavery "would be tantamount to an attempt to prove that the sun shines in the heavens, at mid-day." Verot largely echoed England's apology, but he was more inflammatory and the timing was more pivotal.

Verot devoted a third of his work to the obligations of slaveholders and to "wrongs which the South ought to acknowledge and confess." He echoed Gregory XVI's condemnation of the slave trade and insisted that "there is as much injustice in vexing the free colored population, as there would be in vexing white men." He also denounced the sexual exploitation of black women. But he insisted that he was "a sincere and devoted friend of the South."[44] Verot's sermon typified the southern Catholic stance. It insisted that owners respect slaves' natural rights, but it defended slavery.

Underlying Catholic arguments about slavery was a vision of human relationships that coincided with the southern elite worldview. Influenced by Platonic philosophy, Catholics envisioned earthly hierarchies as reflecting hierarchies in heaven. Just as the Trinity ruled in heaven, with Mary, angels, and saints of various ranks arrayed beneath, so too was hierarchical organization natural among human beings.[45] Slavery was one of many hierarchical social relationships, as natural—indeed as divinely ordained—as a parent's authority over a child and in many respects preferable to a capitalistic system in which owners exploited workers without a sense of responsibility for them.[46] For many Catholics, the French Revolution showed what happened when hierarchies collapsed. Agitation over slavery threatened to create even worse carnage, for if slaves, abolitionists, and other "worthless" whites allied with each other, "their atrocious deeds *improved* by past experience would far exceed those of a Morat or a Robespiere [*sic*]."[47] Catholics upheld an image of society as organic, corporate, and hierarchical into which not only slavery but the South's entire planter-dominated social order fit very neatly. It is no surprise that many southern intellectuals such as Thomas Dew, George Fitzhugh, and Henry Hughes found much to admire in the faith.[48]

Catholics who could not bring themselves to defend slavery evaded the issue. The Catholic *Louisville Guardian* highlighted the absence of Catholic clergy among abolitionists: "Our clergy . . . attend everywhere to religion, and let the politicians take care of themselves. This is as it should be, and as it plainly is not, among a great portion of the Protestant preachers."[49] The church's exclusive focus on religious issues meant that "it leaves slavery where it finds it, and contents itself with the endeavor to lead men to greater humility, patience and charity."[50] The *Miscellany* similarly argued that whether or not slavery could and should be abolished was "a question for the legislature and not for me."[51] The author clearly meant the state legislature, for "not only the Federal government but the respective states shall most religiously abstain from any interference . . . with the reserved rights of the individual states: and no right has been more distinctly and unequivocally reserved than that of regulating . . . slavery."[52]

Catholics shared the racial prejudices held by most white Americans. Like almost all southerners, Catholics rejected polygenesis—the view that blacks were a separate creation from whites—but they took the superiority of the white race for granted. Many white Catholics believed that blacks were incapable of controlling their passions. "The strength and violence of animal propensities is in the inverse ratio of intellectual and moral faculties, which are decidedly weaker in the African races," as Bishop Verot put it.[53] Assumptions of white superiority occasionally found expression in the *Miscellany.* "How disgraceful to find illiterate negroes in the gospel chair endeavoring to preach," fumed one writer. He thought that it was the Protestant emphasis on individual interpretation of scripture that allowed "the most ignorant slave" to view his judgment as equal to that of "eminent and pious men."[54] Placing an "illiterate negro in the station of a preacher" was an "impious burlesque," declared another writer.[55] White Catholics frequently expressed the prejudices and stereotypes that governed white-black relations.[56] One Catholic woman in South Carolina recorded the "audacity" of an "impudent demon" who dared to touch a white woman's hand.[57]

Racism alone did not explain Catholic support for slavery. The Holy See insisted on the innate equality of whites and blacks, defended interracial marriage, and opposed segregation laws. Bishop Augustin Martin of Natchitoches, Louisiana, found out just how seriously Rome held such views when he published a pastoral letter in 1861 declaring Africans fit for slavery because of the curse of Ham and their natural inferiority to whites. Authorities in Rome informed him that his views were unacceptable.[58] Unlike Martin, Verot separated race and slavery, arguing that the basis of slavery was not race, but "title."[59] A Catholic paper in New Orleans, the *Propagateur Catholique,* even argued that the justifications of slavery in scripture and tradition said nothing about race and, therefore, sanctioned the enslavement of whites as well as blacks.[60]

Northern Catholic views of race and slavery mirrored those of their southern coreligionists. Northerners were hardly less racist than southerners were. Relations between white Catholics, particularly immigrants, and blacks were often tense and occasionally led to violence.[61] In 1853, a black Catholic woman in New York, Harriet Thompson, wrote to Pope Pius IX in protest against Catholic treatment of blacks. She singled out Archbishop John Hughes, claiming that he hated blacks so much that "he cannot bear them to come near him."[62] Northern Catholic soldiers did not join the Civil War army out of love for blacks. An Irishman serving with the Massachusetts Volunteers recorded that "the feeling against nigars [*sic*] is intensely strong in this army . . . and this feeling is especially strong in the Irish regiments."[63]

Northern Catholics also echoed the southern Catholic hierarchy's voice on slavery. The *Boston Pilot* declared that "Irish Catholics, whatever they may think of slavery, generally sustain the law because it is the law of the land, unwarranted by no law of God—of the Church."[64] The *U.S. Catholic Intelligencer* maintained that it was not for Catholics to judge the propriety of identifying slaves as property but denounced "any attempt, direct or indirect, that would tend to alienate property acknowledged as such by law" as "tantamount to flagrant injustice, to criminal theft, and evidently calculated to sunder the links of social order."[65]

Francis Patrick Kenrick, bishop of Philadelphia and later archbishop of Baltimore, wrote in his *Theologia Moralis,* a textbook for seminarians, that "all men are by the law of nature equal . . . yet by the law of nations not only the dominion of jurisdiction, but also the dominion of property is granted to man over man." He regretted "that in the present fullness of liberty . . . there should be so many slaves," but conceded that "nothing should be attempted against the laws, nor anything be done or said that would make them bear their yoke unwillingly."[66]

The few Catholics sympathetic to abolition were the exceptions that proved the rule. Henry Kemp, probably the only Catholic member of the Massachusetts Anti-Slavery Society, claimed at an 1855 meeting that the popes had condemned slavery and, therefore, that any Catholic who sympathized with slavery was a heretic. But he conceded that "he thought himself about the only representative of the true Catholic Church in this country."[67] Northern Catholics displayed a broader range of opinions than southerners did—although still falling short of outright abolitionism—but in the end, they too conceded that the theological position of the church was clear: slavery *per se* was no evil. As a result, they resolved to obey the law.[68]

The church was anxious to duck the divisive issue. Catholics shared the defensiveness of a beleaguered minority, intent on proving their loyalty and hoping to be left alone. Their chief political impulse was to uphold the Constitution and the religious liberty it guaranteed and to abstain from a debate that threatened stability.[69] As a result, none of the ten church councils that met between 1829 and 1852 offered an opinion on slavery, although the council of 1843 issued a pastoral urging "obedience to the laws of the nation," a point reiterated in an 1852 pastoral that commanded Catholics to "obey the public authorities, not only for wrath but for conscience sake."[70] It would not have taken much imagination for Catholics to see these statements as subtle condemnations of abolitionism.

Catholics stressed that their church was law-abiding and more concerned with unity than with meddling in the issue of slavery. "The spirit of the Catholic Church is eminently conservative, and while her ministers rightfully feel a deep and abiding interest in all that concerns the welfare of the country, they do not think it their province to enter the political arena," claimed a pastoral letter to the Archdiocese of Cincinnati.[71] One historian has summarized the Catholic stance as "tolerating what could not be corrected, and patiently waiting."[72] This assessment overlooks Catholics' involvement with slavery and their defenses of the institution but rightly emphasizes that their primary impulse was to keep quiet. Southerners took note.

The Protestant churches of the South, like the Catholic Church, yielded to social and political pressures. Although some early evangelicals criticized slavery as part of their attack on elite society, a desire for prestige and respectability led them to embrace slavery to preserve their own status. Rather than condemning slavery, they argued that their ability to convert and control slaves earned them "a special claim upon the conscience of the South."[73]

Evangelicals also maintained racial boundaries in order to avoid alienating members and potential converts.[74] The Methodists, for example, denounced slavery in 1784, but they quickly retreated in the face of fierce opposition. When results of the conference appeared in pamphlet form in Charleston, a mob burned the leaflets, assaulted one Methodist preacher, and threatened another. When the next edition of the Methodist *Discipline* appeared four years later, copies distributed south of Virginia omitted any condemnation of slavery. Like Catholics, evangelicals concluded that their mission was spiritual, not political, and that their goal was individual conversion, not social reform.[75]

Virtually all southern Protestant churches, even those with antislavery factions, accommodated the institution. Kentuckians, for example, owned relatively few slaves and prided themselves on their mild treatment of those they held. As a result, an antislavery movement, led by the churches, emerged around 1792. Inspired by David Rice's moral and pragmatic arguments, Presbyterians adopted a mild emancipatory platform. In 1794, the Transylvania Presbytery called for slaveholders to educate slaves to prepare them for freedom. But emancipationist church members seemed content to improve the quality of slaves' lives while waiting for slavery to die out gradually.

Concern for church unity stifled any attempt to condemn the institution. In 1796, the Presbytery declared slaveholding a matter for individual consciences and the civil authorities, not the church. Other churches made even the Presbyterians' timid steps seem bold by comparison. Kentucky Methodists produced a few abolitionist ministers, most notably Peter Cartwright, but followed the lead of the national body, which by 1808 had almost completely given up on emancipation.

The Baptists' congregationalism created more space for dissent, but the results were the same. Antislavery Baptist churches and ministers, ostracized by their brethren, formed The Baptized Licking-Locust Association, Friends of Humanity in 1807, taking their name from a church near the Ohio River. This defensive measure testified to the dominance of the mainstream Baptists' argument that slavery was a political issue best left alone and served to further marginalize the antislavery wing. In 1811, a traveler estimated that only about 300 of 17,511 Baptists in Kentucky were emancipationists. The Kentucky Abolition Society, organized by Baptists in 1808, drew from all denominations but struggled to attract more than a few hundred members. Denied access to the regular press, the society established a monthly paper but could only sustain it for one year. By 1827, the society ceased to exist, and the few remaining members drifted into state chapters of the American Colonization Society. Individuals in Kentucky had some freedom to discuss slavery critically, but the majority felt equally free to ignore them.[76]

If even Kentucky proved so hostile to antislavery forces that its churches accommodated the institution, there was little chance that religious opposition could exist at all in other southern states. If even powerful churches such as the Presbyterians, Methodists, and Baptists felt compelled to toe the southern line, there was no chance that Catholics could resist. The Catholic Church inherited an ambiguous stance toward slavery as did the evangelicals and followed a similar trajectory of accommodation. In response to social pressures, but also in keeping with its own tradition and principles, it adopted a southern view on social issues.[77]

Catholic attitudes toward race reflected economic interests, for unskilled immigrants viewed blacks as unwelcome competitors.[78] In some cases, immigrants filled an economic niche even below slaves, performing dangerous labor for which masters deemed their slaves too valuable. When a northern traveler asked a steamboat operator why he used only

Irish workers to load the cotton, the man replied that "'the niggers are worth too much to be risked here; if the Paddies are knocked overboard, or get their backs broke, nobody loses anything!'"[79] Over time, as Europe replaced Africa as a source of labor, white workers supplanted blacks in many industries.[80] In Orleans Parish in 1810, slaves and free blacks made up 67 percent of the labor force. Half a century later, their share had decreased to 14 percent. In Mobile, competition for jobs between immigrants and blacks increased throughout the antebellum period. By 1860, half the free male labor force was foreign-born, and the percentage of slaves among the population had declined by 7 percent from a decade earlier.[81] A visitor reported that "the Irish and the Germans seem to do nearly all the work of the streets. Here, as in New Orleans, I was surprised to see how effectually free labor seems to have driven slave labor from the wharves and streets." He added that white servants were replacing house slaves and that he expected the trend to continue: "I think that but a few years will pass away ere nearly all of the colored population will be removed from the *cities* of the South."[82] The situation was the same in Louisville, where slaves constituted 26 percent of the population in 1820 but less than 8 percent in 1860.[83] Whites drove blacks out of some industries. By the late 1850s, white women in Richmond and Petersburg had largely replaced slaves in the tobacco factories.[84] Irishwomen in Mobile competed with free black women in washing and ironing services and wrested control of the dressmaking and seamstress businesses.[85]

Economic competition and the precariousness of their own social status heightened immigrants' racism. Some observers believed it increased their fealty to slavery. "No native even can exceed, in idolatry to Slavery, the mass of the ignorant foreign-born laborers," remarked one commentator, speculating that "their hatred of the negro is proportionate to the equality of their intellect and character to his: and their regard for Slavery, to their disinclination to compete with him, in a fair field."[86] In fact, the attitudes of immigrant workers toward slavery were complex, and some saw slavery as a threat to their own freedom. Most, however, viewed the institution as protecting their liberty and ensuring their elevated position in the labor market. When they complained about slavery, it was generally to increase their share of the workforce, not to demand abolition. White workers opposed slaves, not slavery.[87]

For most Catholics, acceptance of slavery followed logically from the church's teaching, but it was also part of a strategy to survive as a foreign and minority population. Catholics were not the only ones to employ this strategy. Northern and foreign merchants in Mobile soon found that attitudes toward slavery largely determined their reception by locals and that owning a slave or two strengthened their credentials. Virtually all the major slaveholders were southern-born, but Yankee and British transplants often bought, inherited, or hired slaves. Dissenters learned to keep their opinions to themselves. In 1856, public sentiment forced two booksellers, one a native of England, the other of Connecticut, to leave the city for selling abolitionist tracts even though they had owned slaves and even accepted slaves as payment.[88]

By 1850, there were almost two hundred thousand northerners in the South, many socially prominent, including newspaper editors in Louisville, Mobile, and Charleston. Very few opposed slavery, either because they were too prudent or because they saw abolition was too dangerous.[89] Foreigners in the South, including many Catholics, provided a potential basis for dissent, but most conformed to southern mores. In 1847, Henry Ruffner proved a rare exception when he gave an antislavery speech in Lexington, Kentucky, but he was careful to distance himself from northern abolitionists and to make his argument on economic and social grounds. Even radicals fleeing the 1848 revolutions proved accommodating, despite their antipathy toward slavery. When Adolph Douai, the editor of the *San Antonio Zeitung,* expressed his antislavery views in 1854, most Germans in Texas disavowed him even though they employed free labor almost exclusively. The Irish in the South produced only one notable antislavery spokesman—James G. Birney, the son of Irish Protestant expatriates.[90]

Acquiescence to slavery was often the first step toward support for the system. A Scottish traveler in Savannah encountered a countryman who had learned "to accommodate himself to the evils around him, and even to plead their cause" to the extent that he interrogated the traveler about whether he had come to spy on the South. It was hard for outsiders not to honor the color line, for "nothing strikes a stranger so much in Savannah as the extraordinary jealousy which is had of any intercourse between strangers and the coloured population."[91] But southern society enforced its prejudices with carrots as well as sticks. Outsiders in the South found it difficult to resist.

For some Catholics, such as the refugees from Santo Domingo, acceptance of slavery was a foregone conclusion. For others, however, it was more complex. The Irish, for example, had a long tradition of antislavery and reasons to sympathize with the plight of slaves. Nonetheless, within a short time, they stood among the defenders of human bondage. When, in 1843, the Irish patriot Daniel O'Connell attacked American slavery, Irish Catholics in Savannah complained that he had acceded to the teaching of northern abolitionists, "the dire enemies of real liberties, and the notorious enemies of Ireland's religion."[92] O'Connell's stance had earlier drawn rebukes from Bishop England, and his comments in 1843 led to more criticism from Bishop John Hughes of New York and to a decrease in contributions to Ireland.[93] American Catholics were not about to confirm nativist fears that they were pawns of European leaders. "I am no friend of slavery, but I am still less friendly to any attempt of *foreign origin* to abolish it," declared Hughes.[94]

The construction of race in antebellum America allowed the Irish and other Catholic immigrants to derive material and psychological benefits from identifying themselves as white.[95] Slavery raised them from the bottom of society and allowed them to become part of the ruling race.[96] "We can have a healthy State of society with but two classes—white and slave," argued the *Mobile Register.*[97] Slavery denied the immigrants any possibility of an alliance with blacks, but it also tempered Protestant nativism. Elites recognized that order depended on reducing ethnic tensions among whites in favor of a clear black/white dichotomy.[98] Even Catholics in the North accepted slavery to prove that they were no threat to American institutions. The need for racial solidarity was even greater in the South. As a result, religious differences faded as race became the boundary between insiders and outsiders.

Catholic Opposition to Slavery

The Southern Catholic stance on slavery was not unambiguous. Some prelates, priests, and laity recoiled from the system's excesses. A few interpreted scripture and tradition to condemn it entirely. Protestant distrust of Catholics often focused, particularly in the colonial period, on the church's perceived eagerness to conspire with blacks. In Maryland, rumors that priests plotted with slaves and Indians to overthrow the government dated back to 1689.[99] South Carolinians and Georgians were no doubt aware that Spanish authorities in Florida offered freedom to slaves who escaped from the English colonies, provided they converted to Catholicism.[100] This policy ended with Spain's cession of Florida to Britain in 1763, but distrust lingered.

Throughout the colonial period, rumors that Catholics were inciting slave revolts swept British America.[101] Around 1755, a Virginia minister warned slaves that "at one time or other it will probably be suggested to you that the French will make better Masters than the English" and urged them to resist such overtures.[102] In 1775, a mob attacked two Irish Catholics in Charleston on the grounds that they had conspired with slaves.[103] During the antebellum period, some Protestants worried that Catholics, many of whom lived and worked alongside slaves, would develop sympathies for them. By the 1850s, the dominant force in southern politics was the planters' attempt "not only to counter subversion from without but also subversion from within."[104]

Southerners were acutely sensitive to anything that smacked of abolitionism. Controversy followed Pope Gregory XVI's 1839 apostolic letter *In Supremo Apostolatus,* which condemned the slave trade and asserted the moral dangers of slavery.[105] Bishop Benedict Fenwick put things mildly when he noted that the letter would place the southern bishops "in no very pleasant situation."[106] Slavery sympathizers were quick to exaggerate the letter's impact. One government official argued that it not only contained a "deep Censure upon the institution of Slavery" but also called on Catholics "to use their utmost exertions to destroy it." This was, at least, "the Construction put upon it by the fanatics of the north."[107] Abolitionists, who ordinarily had little love for Catholics, seized on the letter and lionized Gregory, trying to convince Catholics that they had a duty to support emancipation.[108]

In the North, nativists accused Catholics of buttressing slavocracy; some even argued that Catholics had been responsible for American slavery from the start.[109] "The Catholic clergy are on the side of slavery. They find the dominant power and pay court thereto that they may rise by its help," argued Theodore Parker, a Unitarian minister and abolitionist, in an 1854 sermon. He charged that Catholics found slavery "thoroughly congenial to them, consistent with the first principles of their church."[110] The movement of northern evangelicals out of the Whig Party and into the American Party in 1854 and the Republican Party in 1856 produced a stream of complaints about "the alliance between an ancient and powerful Church and the slave interests of America."[111] The loyalty of Catholic immigrants to the Democratic Party prompted a Republican state senator to charge that they constituted "the cornerstone of American slavery."[112] Antislavery nativists in the North argued that slavery and Catholicism were two sides of the same coin. Both opposed political liberty, education, and free speech. Slavery followed naturally from Catholicism: "Protestants who tolerated slavery betrayed their principles . . . while Catholics who tolerated slavery applied them."[113]

Southern nativists and bigots, however, denounced Catholics as abolitionists.[114] In the early 1840s, the defrocked priest William Hogan received a commission from the State Department to investigate the aims of the Mexican government and church regarding slavery. He dispatched reports of nefarious conspiracies, with Irish priests working for "that *Arch Abolitionist* the Pope." In a letter to Senator Calhoun, he claimed that the church had instructed him "*to never cease* in trying to abolish Slavery & overthrow this *heretical* government, nor is there now in the United States a single Catholic priest or Bishop who is not engaged in the same work." The only way to prevent abolition, "that darling object of England & the Pope of Rome," was for native Americans to "unite as a body against foreigners."[115] Another of Calhoun's correspondents confirmed that Catholics were "to a man opposed to slavery. The Irish portion of them were made Abolitionists by [Daniel] O'Connel[l] before they came here."[116]

Calhoun was not convinced, but some southerners were. The *Lexington (VA) Gazette* complained that "ninety-nine out of every hundred of the immigrants" were abolitionists devoted to "an uncompromising warfare upon Southern institutions." The *Sumter County (AL) Whig* argued that the immigrants' preference for the North demonstrated "their aversion to our institutions" and their view of slavery "as a sin and an evil."[117] John Berrien, president of the American Party in Georgia, warned a crowd, in 1855, that Catholic immigrants, "flocking to the North, from their abolition tendencies . . . are rapidly increasing the majority against you in Congress and will, unless checked . . . place the Constitution and the institutions of the South at the mercy of fanaticism."[118] Such arguments created doubts in southern minds.

The fears were not entirely unfounded. Some clergy and laymen had reservations about how slavery was practiced, even if they justified it in principle. John Carroll reported that some American priests had begun to emancipate their slaves in order "to suppress censure, which some are always glad to affix to the priesthood." But he added that emancipation would be gradual, for freeing slaves too quickly "would not be either humanity towards the Individuals, nor doing justice to the trust, under which the estates have been transmitted and received."[119] A Maryland Jesuit expressed his frustration: "I sincerely regret that slaves were ever introduced into the United States, but as we have them, we know not how to get rid of them."[120]

In Kentucky, Fr. John Thayer, a New England convert serving as a missionary, asked Carroll in 1794 to allow him to transfer away from the slave territory. Carroll refused, but confessed that he, too, was far from "easy in my mind" about enslavement. He advised Thayer to remedy the excesses and then to bear "the many disorders" that would remain.[121] Five years later, Badin reported that Thayer "enervates the authority of masters over the negroes by being blindly and publicly devoted to their cause & even saying now & then that they are fully as virtuous as the white people of his congregation."[122] Thayer soon left Kentucky, his refined New England upbringing having ill-equipped him for ministry in Kentucky. Badin also accused Protestants of hypocrisy for treating slaves "almost like animals" without "giving them either instruction or compensation."[123] Badin's superior, Bishop Flaget, praised Ohio for prohibiting the institution.[124]

In Charleston, England struggled with slavery. He resolved to stay in obedience to the pope "no matter how great may be my disgust with the condition of the slaves, brought into my Diocess [*sic*] under a system which perhaps is the greatest moral evil that can desolate any part of the civilized world."[125] England's coadjutor, William Clancy, also admitted that his conscience opposed slavery.[126] The *Miscellany* was generally proslavery but it revealed the ambivalence, with occasional columns arguing that slavery was incompatible with a country's moral improvement or insisting that slaves should have special protection under the law.[127] At least one priest carried his views into the pulpit. In 1862, Fr. Claude Pascal Maistre, pastor of St. Rose of Lima Church in New Orleans, preached against slavery. Ordered to stop by the archbishop, he refused and eventually established a schismatic church in which the register no longer distinguished between whites and blacks.[128]

Some lay Catholics shared the opposition to slavery. Robert Carter, a scion of one of Virginia's aristocratic families and a convert to Catholicism, grew uncomfortable with slaveholding and filed a deed providing for his slaves' gradual emancipation.[129] Another convert, the English-born poet Richard Realf, who spent most of his time in New Orleans, where he wrote for the *Bee* and the *Catholic Standard*, published violently antislavery verse and supported John Brown's raid.[130] Cradle Catholics could be equally critical. "The constitutions of the United States, say it is self evident that all men are born free; and their laws which are said to be founded on reason and justice, permit some to be held in slavery every hour of their lives," wrote a layman in the *Miscellany*.[131] Two wealthy laymen in Maryland, Charles Carroll and Roger B. Taney, served as officers of the Colonization Society and freed some of their slaves. Although Taney, as chief justice of the Supreme Court, earned notoriety for his decision in *Dred Scott*, he also supported the rights of free blacks and served as counsel for a Methodist minister on trial for making antislavery comments in a sermon.[132] Judge William Gaston denounced the institution in an 1832 address at the University of North Carolina, condemning it as "the worst evil" of the South.[133] Some working-class immigrants also viewed slavery as a threat to their liberty and recognized that it depressed wages. The planters reminded them of the landlords they had fled in Europe.[134]

In voicing their unease with slavery, southern Catholics echoed a chorus of opposition from the rest of the Catholic world. "I say to myself, My God died upon the cross for all mankind, and yet there are men who still are crucified. He died to deliver all from bondage, and there . . . are millions of men who are still in slavery," wrote a French bishop to his priests while the Civil War raged in the United States.[135] France had abolished slavery in its colonies in 1848.[136] Some Latin American nations had abolished slavery decades earlier. In Ireland, Daniel O'Connell, as noted, attacked American slavery in 1843, referring to Gregory XVI's letter.[137] All signs suggested that global Catholic opinion was turning, and the shift made itself felt even in the South.

Catholics raised suspicions not only with their antislavery pronouncements but also with their ministry to blacks. This ministry took some time to develop. Although some Catholic immigrants came from slave-owning societies, such as the French colony of Santo Domingo, most had no experience with the institution. "I will not tell how amused I was at the Southern ladies and their black slaves," recalled an Irishwoman who joined the Sisters of Mercy in Charleston.[138] "There are neither towns nor villages, you see no peasantry nor servants, all the work is done by negro slaves, who are very numerous," remarked an Italian priest newly arrived in Kentucky.[139] For the immigrant clergy, it was not always self-evident how the church should reach out to the slave population. Most believed that the church should include slaves in its ministry, but it was not clear how.

Church leaders groped with the issues arising from their new setting. In an 1814 letter to Archbishop Carroll, Badin asked permission to refer to the head of the newly established Sisters of Charity as "superior" rather than "sister servant." He explained that Kentuckians used the term "servant" for their slaves and that such a title would subject the superior to contempt. Carroll acquiesced.[140] In 1813, Nerinckx and Flaget asked the prefect of the Congregation for the Propagation of the Faith whether Catholics could sell slaves, especially to non-Catholics. Nerinckx later asked whether they could sell slaves to "infidels and heretics" and sought guidance on how to treat slaves who lived together as married.[141] The church struggled especially with slavery and marriage. Bishop DuBourg pointed out to Propaganda that the slaves could not legally marry without permission. If owners withheld it, as they often did, DuBourg wondered whether church teaching required slaves to remain celibate.[142]

Despite the conundrums, Catholics insisted that they saw blacks, free and slave, as children of God and rightful claimants to the church's ministries. It is difficult to know how many black Catholics lived in the antebellum South because the church did not conduct a systematic survey of black Catholics until 1888.[143] In 1785, John Carroll put the number of Catholic slaves in Maryland at three thousand, roughly one-fifth of the Catholic population.[144] The slaves of Catholic refugees from Santo Domingo increased the number. In July 1793, fifty-three ships arrived in Baltimore carrying a thousand refugees and five hundred blacks.[145] Other prelates offered estimates, but these often seem implausible. For example, in an 1833 report to the Leopoldine Association of Vienna, England speculated that there were five thousand Catholic slaves in Charleston alone, almost certainly an exaggeration.[146] Most scholars estimate that at emancipation, one hundred thousand black Catholics lived in the South, although at least one historian has speculated that two hundred thousand, or roughly 5 percent, of the four million slaves in the United States at the time of emancipation were Catholic. Free black Catholics would have significantly increased this number.[147]

"The soul of the most humble slave is as dear to the Catholic church, as is that of the most powerful monarch." So spoke the *Miscellany* in response to a non-Catholic who thanked a priest for ministering to his slaves.[148] Bishop Verot insisted that a slave possessed "an immortal soul, made to the image and likeness of God, and redeemed by the blood of Christ," the loss of which was "a greater misfortune than the destruction of the whole world."[149] He and other bishops ordered that the masters allow their slaves to receive religious instruction. Badin instructed catechists to attend to children and slaves.[150]

A visitor to Bardstown's cathedral noticed a room decorated with "a painting of a coloured Saint, whom they call St. Benedict, (the Moor)" and dedicated to the instruction of slaves.[151] The room typified the church's interest in the religious instruction of blacks. England catechized blacks in the Carolinas and reported on his converts, who were joined by "a few black children baptized under the promise of the owner that they shall be sent to the Catholic congregation for instruction."[152] In 1839, he reported from Halifax, North Carolina, that he had confirmed ten black converts who were "remarkably well instructed."[153] The obituary of Fr. Peter Vergani, a priest in New Orleans, observed "the great moral improvement that his exhortations and precepts" had produced in his slave converts.[154]

To be a Catholic was to gain access to the sacraments, even if owners objected. This access dated back to the colonial slave systems of Catholic nations. Laws in both the French and Spanish colonies required that owners permit religious instruction and worship. In 1788, Don Cirilo de Barcelona, auxiliary bishop of Havana, arrived in St. Augustine on a visitation and threatened to excommunicate slave owners who did not baptize and instruct their slaves.[155] In 1794, Bishop Carroll urged Badin to "use all means in your power to prevent any masters from hiring their negroes and much more of selling them, so as to leave them no means of frequenting the exercise of their religion."[156] When a Catholic slave complained to Badin that his master had sold him to a non-Catholic, Badin bought the man.[157] Marriage was a point of contestation. In 1814, Flaget preached to almost five hundred slaves at St. Genevieve. Finding that masters had kept many from marrying, he threatened to excommunicate the owners.[158]

The church had success in opening the sacraments to the slaves. The parish of Our Lady of the Port in Louisville baptized twenty-five blacks, primarily slaves, between 1839 and 1865.[159] St. Theresa's in Meade County, Kentucky, baptized over two hundred between 1826 and 1865.[160] The register from St. Mary's in Calvary reveals 5 slave children of 13 total baptized in 1807, 7 slaves of 39 in 1819, and 21 of 110 in 1832.[161] The parish church (later the Cathedral of the Immaculate Conception) in Mobile recorded even more slave and free black baptisms than the Kentucky parishes. Under Spanish rule, the church baptized 524 from 1790 to 1805, and in 1813, the year of the American occupation, 27 slaves and 12 free blacks received baptism. The numbers then fluctuated, peaking in 1843, when priests baptized 32 slaves and 43 free blacks.[162] In the sacramental register of the Church of Saint John the Baptist in Savannah, between 1796 and 1808, the 107 baptism entries included 42 black infants, slave and free.[163]

Blacks received other sacraments. In Charleston, Fr. Clorivière gave Communion to seventeen blacks at Easter 1818.[164] Years later, England noted that "a very considerable number of coloured people presented themselves to be prepared for their first communion" during a jubilee in Savannah.[165] The church also administered last rites. When cholera broke out in Kentucky in 1833, Flaget knelt on the ground to administer the sacrament to a dying slave, moving a corpse to make room.[166] In happier times, blacks joined in the sacrament of marriage. Catholic clergy at least tried, with a fair amount of success, to ensure that blacks received the sacraments.

They also attended to blacks in their daily ministries. Unlike some Protestant denominations, Catholics generally accepted blacks into white churches rather than establishing separate parishes.[167] The sight of blacks and whites worshipping together sometimes surprised non-Catholic visitors.[168] In Charleston, England regularly visited black parishioners, especially during outbreaks of fever. According to tradition, many Protestant masters allowed him to instruct their slaves.[169] At times, he gave priority to the ministry to blacks. He normally preached three times each Sunday, including once to a largely black congregation, and when time constraints allowed only one sermon, he usually preached to the blacks.[170]

Such ministries extended beyond the spiritual realm. The rules of several orders, particularly of women, stipulated that they were to educate black children as well as poor whites. Orders pursued this duty even in the face of public opposition.[171] Orders that featured nursing ministered to the sick regardless of race. The Sisters of Charity hospital in St. Louis, for example, cared for black cholera victims, particularly during the epidemic of 1832. When the Daughters of Charity opened a new hospital in New Orleans in 1859, their first patients included 285 slaves and several free blacks.[172] Priests also nursed sick blacks during epidemics. In Kentucky, Fr. Byrne died in this ministry during the cholera outbreak of 1833.[173]

In a few instances, free blacks formed their own religious orders. In 1829 in Baltimore, a Sulpician named Jacques Hector Nicolas Joubert de la Muraille, a Frenchman who had served as a government official in Haiti before coming to the United States and receiving ordination, founded an order for free women of color called the Oblate Sisters of Providence. The sisters' mission was to educate young black women, but three years after their founding, they also took up nursing.[174] In 1842, in New Orleans, two free women of color, Henriette Delille and Juliette Gaudin, established a community called the Presentation Sisters, soon renamed the Sisters of the Holy Family. The two women ran a school that the daughters of free people of color attended by day and slaves at night. They cared for orphans and the aged and nursed epidemic victims, but they struggled against hostility from both whites and slaves. Although they won permission to wear religious garb, they never received public recognition.[175]

Black female orders drew opposition from those who viewed blacks as unfit for religious life, but they also won praise from other southerners. Archibald Sterling, secretary for the Trustees for the Poor in Baltimore, wrote Fr. Joubert to express the board's thanks "for the assistance kindly and charitably rendered" by the sisters.[176] Although small in number, the orders ministered to neglected communities, publicized the black Catholic community, and helped lay the groundwork for future growth.[177]

England recorded that the "well instructed and pious" slaves of his diocese were "fond of entering little sodalities of devotion and of assembling in the afternoon in the church for prayer and singing."[178] In 1818, black Catholics in New Orleans established the Christian Doctrine Society to honor the Blessed Virgin and evangelize other blacks.[179] In the 1840s, in Baltimore, a society of 150 to 200 black Catholics met weekly in the parish hall next to the cathedral. As the Holy Family Society, they sponsored hymn singing, took up collections for the cathedral fund, and sponsored a lending library. At times, Protestants attended the meetings.[180] Four "colored societies"—the St. Joseph's Benevolent Society, the St. Peter's Society, and the Francis Xavier Society of Charleston and the St. Paul's Society of Columbia—contributed to the construction of the cathedral in Charleston in 1848.[181]

Blacks participated in the life of the church, but Catholic leaders took it for granted that whites had first claim on its resources. Slaves were the "chief anxiety" of Bishop William Elder of Natchez, but they often went unattended because Elder's priests could not leave their parishes to minister on the plantations.[182] Archbishop Eccleston of Baltimore pleaded for help from Europe, highlighting the slave population as a mission field: "Purchased by the blood of the same Redeemer, and destined for the same happy immortality, their souls are not less precious in the eyes of God than those of their masters . . . in many cases their simplicity constitutes a better preparation to profit of the assistance of divine grace than the superior knowledge of the latter." Protestant and Catholic masters called for missionaries, but Eccleston had no one to send.[183] When Maryland's Jesuits abandoned slaveholding, they also shifted their attention to immigrants.[184] Given the church's limited resources, ministry to blacks depended on initiatives from individual churchmen.[185]

The ministry carried paternalistic overtones. One apologist noted that the church's Magisterium offered knowledge of salvation "to the most illiterate slave no less than to the most enlightened scholar."[186] Praising the virtue of a Catholic slave named "Uncle Harry," Martin John Spalding, future bishop of Louisville and archbishop of Baltimore, concluded by noting that "God often chooses the humblest individuals as His most special favourites."[187] Bishop Elder of Natchez begged for priests to come from Europe to minister to blacks. He described them as "every one of them immortal, made to the image and likeness of God," but also as "fickle," "very much creatures of feeling," and "naturally inclined to be dependent on others."[188] In the family of God, race distinguished the parents from the children.

Caught between the belief that blacks were coheirs to the kingdom and the assumption of white superiority, church leaders encouraged black participation within limits. Religious orders educated blacks, but separately from whites. Catholics policed racial boundaries. The Spring Hill College register noted that a student from New Orleans did not return from vacation in 1849 "because it seems he had some negro blood in him."[189] England ordered the Dames de la Retraite to expel a member he claimed was a mulatto, although the order's superior refused.[190] White southern Catholic attitudes toward black coreligionists were complex. Many white Catholics, particularly among the clergy, welcomed blacks into the church and insisted on their right to worship, but only from the balconies or back benches. This mentality was one accommodation to southern mores, but Catholics found a far more explicit way to signal their support for the South's racial caste system.

Catholic Complicity in Slavery: Practice

In 1833, Bishop England estimated that a thousand Catholic slaves in his diocese belonged to Protestant masters, for "the Catholics are generally too poor to possess this or any other kind of property."[191] England was correct that the immigrants could not afford slaves, but he overlooked wealthier Catholics. Many older Catholic families were slave owners. The first federal census (1790) revealed that five of the nine Marylanders who owned 150 or more slaves were Catholics, as were at least a quarter of those owning 50.[192] Refugees from Santo Domingo brought slaves with them or purchased new ones. The old Spanish and French families along the Gulf Coast had often owned slaves for generations.[193] Catholic planters in Maryland took their slaves with them when they migrated to Kentucky. One of them, Nicholas Miles, settled near Bardstown in 1796 with his family and at least twelve slaves (his son, Richard, would become the first bishop of Nashville).[194] A few southern Catholics joined the ranks of the largest slave holders. Charles March and his wife, planters on Hutchinson Island, South Carolina, owned some four hundred slaves, most of whom they baptized Catholic.[195] Harriet Elizabeth Crider Bellinger, the Catholic wife of a Methodist planter, owned 123 slaves in Colleton District and 27 in Barnwell District. William McKenna, an Irish-born merchant and planter, who was active in state government, owned 151 slaves in Barnwell District.[196]

Catholic schools, orders, and clergy bought and sold slaves and received slaves as donations. The Jesuits of Maryland were among the first large-scale Catholic slaveholders in America. Jesuit slaveholding probably began as a means of replacing indentured servants in the early eighteenth century. Like later clerical slave owners, the Jesuits received slaves as gifts from lay patrons. By 1765, they owned 192 slaves, a number that increased to 400 in 1831 before the society began a series of sales culminating in the 1838 selling of the remaining 272 slaves. In the colonial period, the Jesuits used slave ownership to stake their claim to full civil rights as English subjects and used slave labor to recreate the self-sufficient English manors. Like most Catholic clergy, the Jesuits insisted on their slaves' right to worship as Catholics, receiving the sacraments, and they stressed a responsibility to take care of them, often at great expense. The Jesuits resolved to divest themselves of slaves in 1814, but over two decades passed before they put this plan into effect.[197]

Jesuits in Missouri picked up where their predecessors in Maryland left off. One of the Missouri Jesuits, Brother Mathew Smith, had served as overseer of slaves on his brother's plantation in South Carolina.[198] The Missouri Jesuits, like their colleagues in Maryland, realized that slave owning was a financial drain and sought to replace slaves with hired help.[199] The Vincentians, who settled south of St. Louis in 1818, held onto their slaves longer than the Jesuits did, arguing that they needed them for domestic work so that they could concentrate on running their seminary. By 1830, they were the largest slaveholders in the area.[200]

Slaves helped build Catholic institutions. In Kentucky, Thomas Howard, a layman whose legacy to the diocese established the foundation for St. Thomas's Seminary, donated his house, his plantation, and his slaves.[201] Fr. Edward Fenwick, the Kentucky Dominican, brought inherited slaves from Maryland.[202] Even such priests as Fr. Badin, who objected to the institution, owned slaves.[203] On one occasion, he gave Fr. Fournier a young house slave whom he had received as a gift from a parishioner.[204] When Flaget and David left Maryland for Kentucky, they took with them a slave given by their Sulpician colleagues in Baltimore.[205] Years later, Flaget tried to reciprocate. He wrote that "it would be easy for me to give a very fine country-place at a league from Bardstown to the Sulpicians with enough slaves to cultivate it."[206] As late as 1839, the College of St. Joseph in Bardstown depended on slave labor.[207] Priests in Kentucky often relied on slave labor to run the plantations that supported their missions. In South Carolina, Fr. Jeremiah O'Connell had a slave who made sure things ran smoothly whenever he lectured.[208] In Mobile, the marriage register recorded the union of several slaves owned by Bishop Portier.[209]

All three female orders in Kentucky employed slave labor. In 1811, Flaget reported that his plans for establishing a female religious order in Kentucky had received a boost from a Catholic who offered a plantation and several slaves for the endeavor.[210] The following year, the sale of a slave by an aspiring Sister of Loretto helped the order buy land for their school and home.[211] Around 1817, Flaget sent the Sisters of Nazareth two slaves to relieve them of hard labor, and when he inducted four young women into the Sisterhood of Loretto, he rejoiced that their family of slaves would help ensure the order's financial stability.[212] Four years later, the Sisters of Nazareth received assistance from a widow who joined the order and donated $3,000 and a slave family.[213] The Dominican Sisters struggled to sustain themselves until the acquisition of slaves as part of the dowries of new members gave them time for study and teaching.[214] Of the twelve communities established in the United States between 1790 and 1829, eight survived, seven of which acquired slaves. Of the communities that failed, none seemed to own slaves.[215] Slaves freed the sisters from labor and gave them a financial footing.

Priests and nuns received, bought, and sold slaves. In 1840, Fr. Edward McMahon of St. Peter's Church in Lexington, Kentucky, sold a female slave and her son to Henry Clay for $600.[216] Flaget's diary included a receipt for a teenage slave girl named Henney, whom Flaget sold for $400.[217] In 1863, Bishop Lynch of Charleston purchased a slave for $740.[218] Catholic orders occasionally tried to divest themselves of slaves but generally on economic rather than moral grounds. The directors of St. Thomas seminary hired free workers for their plantation in order to rid themselves of the "evil breed of Negroes that we have here who steal from us and deceive us in every way."[219] They ended slavery not because they thought blacks should be free but because they deemed them unworthy even of being slaves.

Fully complicit in the slave system, Catholics argued that they at least treated their slaves well. "There is . . . one great duty which is obvious. The obligation of the master to treat his servant with kindness," noted the *Miscellany.* It added that "amongst us it is generally practiced."[220] Religious orders took steps to ensure that slaves received proper treatment.[221] Orders tried to avoid selling slaves and at times purchased the spouses of slaves to keep families together. To sell slaves, particularly to Protestants, was to put their souls at risk, and separating husbands and wives exposed them to adultery.[222] Authorities in Rome recalled the Jesuit superior in Maryland responsible for divesting the order of slaves in 1838 because he had sold them without attempting to keep their families intact.[223] Some Catholics believed that the burden of slavery fell more heavily on the masters than on the slaves. "It is truly remarkable," observed Verot, "how gay, cheerful, and sprightly are the slaves of the South. I do not hesitate to say, that they seem to be better contented than their masters."[224]

Catholics claimed that they treated their slaves well. They would not "conscientiously get out of the slaves all the advantage" that other slaveholders derived.[225] Some liked to say that the church made Catholics treat slaves "humanely" under threat of being "barred from the sacraments."[226] One asserted that wealthy masters knelt alongside their slaves "at the confessional and before the altar . . . Between the Catholic masters and their slaves there most generally existed real sympathy and affection."[227]

Earlier Catholic historians echoed these self-assessments. One explained that a "'priest's negro,' was a proverbial expression for a slave who could, to a great extent, do much as he pleased."[228] Another depicted the slaves of Catholics as being "happy as the day is long, toiling long."[229] Bishop David's biographer notes that ten slaves carried him "reverently" to Nazareth to die because they "knew and loved him" for having been "a true spiritual father to them and theirs."[230]

There is no evidence to suggest that Catholics managed their slaves and plantations much differently than non-Catholics. Some clergy felt some paternal responsibilities, but Catholic laity were typical masters. The treatment of slaves varied in older and newly settled regions and on small farms or large plantations. Religion had little to do with it.[231]

Southerners could be confident that Catholics' insistence on the spiritual equality of all people would not translate into demands for material equality. They knew that, whatever hesitations Catholics might harbor in their hearts or voice among themselves, at the end of the day they would fall in line behind slavery.

White Southerners' Gratitude toward Catholics

Catholics highlighted their abstinence from politics in contrast to the meddling of northern Protestants. Thomas Semmes of New Orleans noted that a protest against the Kansas-Nebraska Act signed by three thousand Protestant ministers included not a single signature of a Catholic priest.[232] Verot pointed out that Catholics "scrupulously adhered" to separation of church and state and intervened "only by praying for the republic." Protestants, especially the clergy, bore responsibility for the "deplorable state" of the Union.[233] This argument struck home among southerners: "A tribute of warm commendation is due to the Catholic Church" wrote the *Richmond Dispatch,* "for the entire abstinence of its clergy from all intermeddling . . . with national troubles."[234]

Southerners contrasted Catholics with northern Protestants. Ex-President John Tyler thanked priests for their "example of non-interference in politics which furnishes an example most worthy of imitation on the part of the clergy of the other sects at the North."[235] Georgia Congressman A. H. Stephens defended Catholics against Know-Nothing critics: "as a church," he said, "they have never warred against us or our peculiar institutions.

No man can say as much of the New England Baptists, Presbyterians or Methodists."[236] Fitzwilliam Brydsall, a friend of John C. Calhoun, complained that northern Protestant ministers were the ones who meddled in slavery "to the manifest neglect of the most sacred duties of Gospel Christianity." In contrast, he noted, Bishop Hughes of New York devoted his energy to establishing an institution for impoverished women.[237] As southern Protestants saw their coreligionists in the North crusading against slavery, they appreciated Catholic loyalty. England reported that he had gained public favor by denouncing O'Connell's attack on slavery.[238] Upon his death, the *Courier* called him a friend of the South who used his gifts to defend "her much misunderstood and much reviled domestic institutions."[239]

Catholic support for slavery helped diffuse nativism in the South. Organized political opposition to foreigners and Catholics began around 1843, when New Yorkers, disgruntled over Democratic control of the city—control that immigrant support helped ensure—organized the American Republican Party, soon known as the Native American Party. Although it quickly faded from the political scene, in 1849, Charles B. Allen established a secretive patriotic society called the Order of the Star-Spangled Banner to exploit fear of immigration and Catholicism. It took off in 1852 under the leadership of James W. Barker, a merchant with a talent for organization. The order held its first national conventions in 1854.

The order's success stemmed from its ability to combine opposition to foreigners with opposition to Catholics. Members had to be native-born and of Protestant parents, and they could not be married to a Catholic. The leadership had to pledge to use all legal means to remove Catholics and foreigners from public office. Gaining in strength and numbers, the organization soon ran its own candidates in local elections. The established parties repeatedly saw their candidates lose to political unknowns who did not even appear on the ballots, but who won through write-in votes.

The order took the name of the American Party, although it became known as the Know-Nothing Party because of the evasive answers that members gave when asked about their activities. Elections in the fall of 1854 brought triumphs, and the party sent 75 congressmen to Washington and in Massachusetts won the governorship, every seat in the state Senate, and 376 of 378 seats in the state House of Representatives. The following year, the party took control of Rhode Island, New Hampshire, Connecticut, Maryland, and Kentucky and nearly carried several other states. It seemed inevitable that 1856 would see the election of a Know-Nothing president.

The Know-Nothings were highly effective as candidates but proved inept as legislators, and nationally they never controlled the House or the Senate. Many Democrats and Republicans refused to join in attacks on Catholics that would alienate potential voters and run afoul of the constitutional protection of religion. The Know-Nothings found some support for their efforts to curtail immigration, but the bills they introduced died in committee. Even in state governments, the results were the same, and the few victories proved costlier than the defeats. In Massachusetts, they established a "Nunnery Committee" to examine Catholic institutions, but the group spent as much time drinking as investigating. Legislative ineptitude exposed the party to ridicule, many took to calling it the "Do-Nothing" party, and its secrecy became a liability.

In the South, nativist parties enjoyed some success, but their influence was largely limited to regions with relatively high immigration and to border states conscious of the swelling populations of their free state neighbors. In New Orleans, a nativist party formed as early as 1835. By 1850, the city trailed only New York in the number of immigrants admitted to the country, and the seventh census recorded an almost equal number of native- and foreign-born residents. Maryland, which also drew a high percentage of immigrants, also became a center for nativism, along with Kentucky. In 1854, Alabama was one of the few southern states represented at the party's national council, and two months later, its candidates won offices in Mobile after an election in which mobs severely beat several Irishmen. Twenty-five percent of Mobile's population was foreign-born, exceeding all other southern cities but New Orleans. In 1855, southerners sent two Know-Nothings to the Senate and thirty to the House of Representatives.[240]

Success in the South varied by region. In Arkansas, the party had virtually no support. In South Carolina, it fared even more poorly, winning only a few local elections, including the contest for mayor of Charleston in 1855. South Carolina welcomed roughly forty thousand immigrants between 1840 and 1860, making the white population nearly 30 percent foreign-born, but the Democratic Party kept the Know-Nothings at bay.[241] The party had vocal critics in states where its presence was strong. The *Florence (AL) Gazette* labeled it an "infamous band of treasonable conspirators."[242]

Nativists in the South won few votes but they instigated their share of mob violence. Election day violence was a fact of life in New Orleans, with five major riots between 1854 and 1858. In 1855, armed bands roamed the city for a week, killing people and paralyzing the civil authorities. Two months later, citizens brave enough to vote went to the polls armed with pistols and knives. Democrats and Know-Nothings accused each other of fraud and intimidation. Before the municipal election of 1858, opponents of the Know-Nothings, largely foreign-born, pillaged a state arsenal, hauled cannons into Jackson Square, and encamped in military style. An opposing band fortified Lafayette Square, less than a mile away. The two sides faced off for several days before going home.[243]

Baltimore endured similar violence. Gangs such as the Rip Raps, Plug Uglies, Bloody Eights, and Calithumpians ruled the city. The Blood Tubs carried tubs of blood from slaughter houses and daubed it on foreign voters or immersed them headfirst. Open warfare broke out between the gangs, who killed dozens and injured hundreds.[244]

Louisville suffered some of the worst violence. Almost one-third of the city's white population was foreign-born by the 1850s, and the *Louisville Daily Courier* warned for years that the city risked being overrun with immigrants. In 1855, ex-priest Giacinto Achilli gave a series of addresses at the YMCA entitled "Popery Opposed to Civil and Religious Liberty." Three months later, the city chose a Know-Nothing mayor, city attorney, auditor, assessor, and treasurer in an election marred by rioting.

A closely contested election ignited a conflagration. On August 6, 1855, citizens went to the polls to choose state officers and congressmen. American Party thugs controlled many of the polling stations. The editor of the *Louisville Daily Journal,* George Prentice, published incendiary attacks on Catholics and immigrants. Although it remains unclear what started the violence, by the afternoon, riots engulfed the city. Thwarted in its attempt to destroy St. Martin's Catholic Church by the intercession of the mayor, who also protected the cathedral by declaring it free of weapons, the mob turned on Irish and German neighborhoods. The violence flared out quickly, but not before claiming at least twenty-two lives.[245]

Civic leaders denounced the violence of "Bloody Monday." The *Courier* attributed the atrocities to "the malice, wickedness and every evil work that naturally spring from a combination of political and religious hatred" and insisted that "No Christian, no peaceable citizen of Louisville, can think upon these things without feeling the awful wickedness of the times." The paper's editor, a former Know-Nothing, turned on the party: "However we may regret and shudder to hear of such outrages, they are the sure results of Know Nothism [*sic*], wherever its proscriptive and unhallowed principles have been urged."[246]

Political nativism and anti-Catholicism often overlapped but should not be taken as synonymous.[247] Nativist parties attracted many by promising entertainment, novelty, and the allure of mystery. Some joined after the collapse of the Whigs left them without a political home. Others wanted a party committed to both unionism and states' rights. Still others feared the economic competition, disorder, political radicalism, and poverty that accompanied immigration. Often religion had nothing to do with it.

In the South, many Know-Nothings argued that the party should focus on immigration, not Catholicism. When the national party refused to amend its platform, some southern chapters seceded, abolished religious tests, and even nominated Catholics for office. The 1855 platform of the Tennessee council acknowledged the right of all people to worship as they chose, whereas the Alabama platform pledged the party to protect all people in "the inestimable privilege of worshipping God in the manner most agreeable to their consciences." That same year, William Alexander of Maryland, speaking to the national council, urged the party to welcome Catholics.[248]

Little of the anti-Catholic propaganda published during the 1850s came out of the South. To the extent that anti-Catholicism figured in southern nativism, it was "very mild and indirect."[249] Maryland delegates to the national convention of the American Republican Party, an early nativist party organized in the mid-1840s, stressed that they would not attack others' religious beliefs.[250] Meeting in 1855, the Virginia Know-Nothings insisted that the party's platform did not exclude anyone from public office purely on account of religion, but rather, only those with a paramount loyalty to a foreign power.[251] John Berrien, president of the Georgia chapter, similarly argued that the party's anti-Catholic principles applied only to disloyal and foreign Catholics: "I would not feel that native American Romanists, trained in the principles of civil liberty, of reverence to the Constitution and laws, and devoted to the Union, would come within its scope."[252] This echoed the party's official stance, which opposed only Catholics who gave temporal allegiance to the pope.[253] The American Party included Catholic members. Some elite Catholics, particularly in Louisiana and southern Maryland, shared the party's concern that mobs of immigrants threatened social stability.[254] One did not need to be anti-Catholic to be a nativist.

The belief that immigrants supported slavery spurred the rise of Know-Nothingism in the North, and fears that they opposed slavery (or at least gave the North a demographic advantage) stimulated its rise in the South.[255] But slavery could unify the party only as long as its northern and southern branches ignored the fact that they held diametrically opposed positions. All that southern foes of Know-Nothingism had to do was point out this incongruity. The Democratic Party condemned northern Know-Nothings as abolitionists and damned their southern allies by association. By 1857, the party had disappeared in Virginia and South Carolina and in all the Gulf states but Louisiana. Only in Missouri, North Carolina, Kentucky, Maryland, and Louisiana did it maintain any organization, often by allying with any opponents of the Democrats it could find.[256]

Southerners turned against Know-Nothingism with a vengeance. "Never did I see such an intolerant, arrogant, insolent, overbearing, inconsistent, vindictive party as this," complained Augustus Longstreet.[257] Robert Toombs of Georgia described the party as a group of "miserable wretches who expect to govern a great country like this with imbecility, if they can only cover it with secrecy." When asked to respond to reports that he had donated money for a Catholic church, he said that he "responded to their calls just as I have those of other denominations," adding that the inquirer could "tell people that the distribution of my money is none of their business."[258] In Maryland, an investigative committee denounced the party's secrecy as un-American. In Buncombe County, North Carolina, a grand jury asked for an indictment of the party on the grounds that it controlled voting by requiring secret oaths. In Virginia, the *Richmond Examiner* published copies of the party's ritual and constitution.[259] Even a supporter in North Carolina conceded in 1856 that a barrage of "denunciations and abuses" had left the party greatly weakened and that many potential members had stayed away because they disliked its secrecy and viewed it as a threat to religious liberty.[260]

With Know-Nothings damned as abolitionists, Catholics appeared to be allies, not enemies, of the South.[261] They recognized that slavery would soon overshadow nativism. Fr. William Murphy, president of Spring Hill College, reassured Catholics that Know-Nothingism was "merely a local disturbance" and that "slavery must finally lead to the war which is to decide whether or not the United States can endure."[262] Alexander Stephens said that he would "much sooner risk my civil rights with the American Catholics" than with Know-Nothings.[263] He argued that the menace came not from foreigners or Catholics, but rather from abolitionists, "those native born traitors at the North who are disloyal to the Constitution of that country which gave them birth."[264] The voters of Georgia signaled their approval by sending him to Congress.[265] Senator Fitzpatrick of Alabama agreed that southerners had far more to fear from native abolitionists than from immigrant Catholics. Sharing opposition to abolitionism, southern Protestants began to describe Catholics as "the friends of the Constitution and of the South."[266] John Fletcher of Louisiana responded to William Ellery Channing's denunciation of the burning of Pennsylvania Hall by antiabolitionists in 1833 by pointing out that Channing had "nowhere, in all his works, said one word about the burning of the Convent on Mount Benedict, by his own townsmen, the good people of Boston."[267]

The slavery debate had been central to the rise of political nativism but it proved even more crucial to its demise. As public interest in the slavery debate grew, fears about immigrants and Catholics faded. As the institution's supporters and opponents hardened their positions, the party's attempts to cling to a middle ground, so long an important asset, quickly became a liability. Southern members charged that northern members were drifting into abolitionism, and many northern members criticized the party for going too far in accommodating the southern wing. In the words of one historian, "the party succumbed partially because it was not founded on sectional issues in a period when only sectional issues could hold mass allegiance."[268] The rising importance of the slavery question proved to be the nail in the American Party's coffin.[269]

Catholic Confederates

Years before secession, some southern Catholics anticipated that the South might one day go its separate way. Their responses fell along a wide spectrum. Edward Bermudez, a student at Spring Hill College who later became chief justice of the Louisiana Supreme Court, denounced agitators on both sides and urged all southerners to preserve the Union.[270] Most southern Catholics were less restrained. Bishop England contemplated disunion as early as 1828, with a clear idea that he would support it.[271] Catholics found many ways to express their pro-South sentiments. When Catholic women in Charleston held a fundraising fair in 1851, they timed it to coincide with a meeting of the Southern Rights Association of South Carolina. Among the items they offered for sale was a "southern rights quilt," dedicated to the members of the convention.[272]

As North and South drifted apart, southern Catholics sided with their states. An Alabama priest hoped for a "peaceable separation," but he acknowledged that if Lincoln refused to recognize secession, "war must come."[273] Others were less reserved. Following the 1860 election, Fr. James Corcoran, who had edited the *Miscellany* since 1850, noted that Lincoln's triumph was merely the culmination of "long years of menace, insult, outrage and unconstitutional aggression." He praised "the calm, determined attitude of our people" and predicted a resolution to the conflict that would "leave untouched the honor and happiness of the South."[274] Soon after South Carolina seceded, Corcoran explained that he had removed from the heading of the *Miscellany* "two obnoxious words": "United States." The paper was now the *Charleston Catholic Miscellany*.[275]

Catholics usually based their support for the Confederacy on constitutional grounds rather than on a defense of slavery. Bishop Quinlan of Mobile insisted that he would not "purchase Union at the expense of Justice."[276] Bishop John McGill of Richmond declared that the Republican Party was "organized on principles *unconstitutional*" and wondered whether anyone could join the Union army without committing a sin.[277] But Catholics' dislike of abolitionism also shaped their view of the conflict. Four months after the war began, Bishop Auguste Marie Martin of Natchitoches described it as a war of "enslavement and extermination" brought about by "those thousands of preachers" in the North "who from their pestilential pulpits have breathed on the people a spirit of hatred and discord." He urged Catholics to enlist.[278] Bishop Patrick Lynch set the blame for the conflict entirely on the "fanatical party spirit" of the abolitionists: "Taking up anti-slavery, making it a religious dogma, and carrying it into politics," he wrote, "they have broken up the Union."[279] Fr. William James Barry, writing from Moundsville, Virginia, in 1861, shared Lynch's views. "I am with the *South and the Right,* now and forever," he proclaimed, denouncing the North for the "blind fanaticism" driving it to wage a war of "total subjugation."[280] John Dooley, a Virginia Catholic wounded at Gettysburg, insisted that the slaves had been "happy creatures" and lamented that "the restless spirit of New England has spread its wings on the blast, and its envenomed breath has gone forth to poison the happiness of black and white." Although Dooley was the son of Irish immigrants, he identified much more strongly with the South than with fellow Irishmen. On meeting a "Yanko-Irish" soldier who had fought in the Irish rebellion of 1848, Dooley bitterly asked him how he could "turn his back on his principles" and "engage in the cause of tyranny, fighting against honesty, Justice and right."[281]

Southern Catholics served in the Confederacy in any way they could. Catholic laymen from across the South hurried to enlist, and many priests took on new assignments as chaplains in the Confederate army. Several companies of Irish volunteers left Charleston for the battlefields of Virginia, marching under a banner with the Irish harp on one side and a palmetto and crescent on the other, presented to them by the students at the Academy of Our Lady of Mercy.[282] Bishop Whelan of Virginia denounced northern bishops for flying the flag over their churches and spoke so boldly in favor of the Confederacy that Union forces threatened to arrest him for treason.[283] Bishop Lynch of Charleston served as a Confederate envoy to the European powers. Having run the blockade in a steamer crammed with cotton bales, he preached the gospel of states' rights throughout Ireland and France, trying to win international recognition for the Confederacy. Fr. John B. Bannon, an Irish-born priest from St. Louis, also became a Confederate agent and traveled to Europe with the dual task of winning papal recognition of the Confederacy and dissuading the Irish from emigrating to the North.[284]

Catholic women and other civilians also did their part. Catholic women religious nursed in Confederate hospitals, winning renown for their sacrifices. Mary Boykin Chesnut of South Carolina demonstrated her respect for them by using "Sister of Charity" as a shorthand for any woman who nursed the sick.[285] In 1863, the vestry of St. Mary's in Charleston sold the church's bank stocks to purchase Confederate war bonds.[286] Pauline DeCaradeuc, the South Carolina belle, who not only prayed for the South but also made cartridges at the Augusta arsenal, spoke for such Catholics when she insisted that "God who is justice, will accept the sacrifice of the lives of the Chivalry of the South, and give their land its own proud place among nations."[287]

Conclusion

The Confederacy never won its "own proud place among the nations," but not for lack of sacrifices on the part of southern Catholics. Catholics were devoted to the South and to the South's peculiar institution. Church tradition, scripture, economic interests, the desire to fit in, dislike of abolitionists, and their own racism pushed them toward accommodation. In time, southern Catholics not only reconciled themselves to slavery but championed it. Catholic support for the southern way of life and southerners' support for Catholic hospitals, schools, and churches were not unrelated. Southerners welcomed Catholics as fellow citizens and Catholics demonstrated that southern faith in them was well placed.

Conclusion

Few antebellum buildings survive in downtown Atlanta. Of those that escaped the destruction of the Civil War, many fell to the wrecking ball as the city raced to reinvent itself as the commercial capital of the New South. But in the midst of downtown's hotels, skyscrapers, and parking decks, a few old churches still stand. Unknown to most passersby, they are not only places of worship, but also monuments to a forgotten religious world.

In 1861, an Irish-born priest named Fr. Thomas O'Reilly came to Atlanta, which until 1850 was part of the Diocese of Charleston, to minister at Immaculate Conception Catholic Church. Three years later, he found himself in the middle of a war zone as the Union army under General William Tecumseh Sherman laid siege to the city. Throughout the battle, O'Reilly cared for soldiers of both sides, saying Mass, hearing confessions, and administering last rites. Soon after the Union army occupied Atlanta, O'Reilly learned of Sherman's plan to lay waste to the city. He protested, arguing that the destruction of churches in particular constituted a monstrous breach of the laws of war. He also reminded Sherman that his army contained a large number of Catholics who would not take kindly to church burning. As a result of his intervention, Sherman eventually relented and, at O'Reilly's urging, spared not only Immaculate Conception, but also Central Presbyterian, St. Philip's Episcopal, Second Baptist, and Trinity Methodist.

Fr. O'Reilly's actions during the waning of the Old South were the least that a southern Catholic priest could do for his Protestant neighbors. Throughout the antebellum period, Catholics had benefited from Protestant support. Protestants had welcomed them as coworkers, friends, and even spouses and had shown their priests and bishops every mark of courtesy and respect. Protestants had funded, patronized, and endorsed their hospitals, orphanages, and schools. Most remarkably, Protestants had helped build their churches, had attended their services, and had welcomed them into their own places of worship. It is no exaggeration to say that in some communities, Catholicism would not have survived without Protestant support. The South also saw its share of religious conflict. Ancient prejudices and new resentments led to bitter denunciations, antipathy, and even violence. But these instances were exceptions; cooperation was the rule.

Catholics reciprocated when they could, although rarely with gestures as grand as Fr. O'Reilly's. They occasionally gave to Protestant-run institutions and charities, and they lent their support to causes endorsed by Protestant leaders. They seldom had the means to contribute much financially, but they could give something that southerners valued even more: support for slavery. The path by which Catholics reached an accommodation with chattel bondage was circuitous. Many harbored reservations about slavery, but almost without exception, they kept their concerns to themselves. Officially, the church proclaimed that slavery was none of its business. In the South, many clergy and laity went even further, actively defending the institution and even participating in it.

Catholics bought their place in the South in part by acquiescing to slavery, but that was not the only reason for Protestant support. Protestants admired the character and sacrifices of many Catholics, especially among the clergy. They appreciated the ways in which Catholic institutions met pressing social needs. Some even felt drawn to Catholic worship. Catholics proved themselves to be useful citizens, true Americans, and loyal Southerners, and their Protestant neighbors approvingly took note.

Catholicism's growth in the Old South reveals a great deal about the nature of the church in America. First, it testifies to the energy of the Catholic clergy and laity. The European-born priests and nuns left their homes and families, sometimes forever, in order to toil among a people whose language they often did not speak and whose customs were strange and foreign to them. They and their native-born colleagues often traveled thousands of miles through wilderness to reach scattered congregations. They established churches, schools, hospitals, and newspapers where none had existed before. They rushed to aid the victims of epidemics, in many cases at the cost of their own lives. For their part, the laity maintained their faith, often over years spent without regular access to the sacraments, and they helped the church grow. The church in the South also bore its share of incompetent, disloyal, and malicious members. Rifts between clergy and laity, and among the clergy themselves, threatened the church's stability. But in the long run, Catholics managed to overcome their differences. Protestant support would have been meaningless had not a unified Catholic community been ready and willing to receive it.

But there is an even larger lesson about American Catholicism to be learned from the experiences of these southerners. Contrary to conventional wisdom, in the South at least, Catholics accommodated themselves to American culture quite easily. Some lay people agitated to make the church more republican in its governance, and some European-born clergy recoiled from the excesses of American liberty and individualism, but these tensions were relatively minor. In general, laypeople were content to live in a republican state and to worship in a monarchical church. The clergy, especially the foreign-born, were quick to identify themselves as American patriots and to adapt to American tastes and practices. Catholic institutions grafted the holidays of American civil religion onto the church's liturgical calendar. In the South, being both American and Catholic posed no great dilemma.

Catholicism's growth in the South also sheds light on the Old South itself. It reveals that, despite the numerical and cultural dominance of evangelical Protestantism, other faiths could also take root and flourish. The southern religious landscape was remarkably fluid, as people drifted into and out of churches for reasons of belief, taste, or whim. Catholics could compete more or less as equals in the religious marketplace.

But southerners' acceptance of Catholicism also reveals a darker aspect of their society. Although white believers of all faiths cooperated with each other, it was precisely because they were white that they could do so. The Catholic experience demonstrates how conclusively race obliterated all other distinctions in the Old South.

Finally, the Old South's reception of Catholics points to important commonalities between Catholicism and southern culture. Southerners, particularly among elites, recognized elements of their own worldview in Catholic teaching. Both Protestant planters and Catholic prelates believed that hierarchies were the natural form of social organization. Hierarchies bound all members of society into a series of relationships, rights, and responsibilities. This understanding shaped all elements of Catholic culture from church polity to architecture to defenses of slavery and helped southern Protestants relate to an otherwise foreign faith.

The Old South died on the day Atlanta fell. The city was one of the Confederacy's final manufacturing and transportation centers, and its capture helped ensure Lincoln's reelection. For the city itself, defeat meant utter destruction. Yet thanks to Fr. O'Reilly, a few vestiges survived. In 1945, the city of Atlanta, the Atlanta Historical Society, and the five churches spared by Sherman dedicated a monument to O'Reilly outside City Hall. It is a fitting epitaph, not only to O'Reilly, but to a society in which people of all faiths worked together to create and sustain a way of life.

Notes

Introduction

1. *Charleston Courier,* April 12, 1842; *Charleston Patriot,* April 18, 1842.

2. Bernard Code, *Dictionary of the American Catholic Hierarchy* (New York: Longmans, Green, 1940), 97–98. The most thorough and authoritative biography of England is Peter Guilday, *The Life and Time of John England, First Bishop of Charleston,* 2 vols. (New York: The America Press, 1927).

3. Alvan F. Sanborn, ed., *Reminiscences of Richard Lathers: Sixty Years of a Busy Life in South Carolina, Massachusetts and New York* (New York: Grafton Press, 1907), 15–16.

4. *Patriot,* April 18, 1842.

5. *Courier,* April 12, 1842.

6. In addition to the prominence of anti-Catholic violence in surveys of American religious history, numerous studies focus on Protestant antipathy toward Catholics. These include: Mary Augustina, *American Opinion of Roman Catholicism in the Eighteenth Century* (New York: Columbia University Press, 1936); Ray Billington, *The Protestant Crusade: 1800–1860* (New York: MacMillan, 1938); and John J. Kane, *Catholic-Protestant Conflicts in America* (Chicago: Regnery, 1955). Mary Augustina found deep roots for American anti-Catholicism, building a case that religious intolerance faded only gradually in the nineteenth and twentieth centuries. Ray Billington defined his topic as nativism, but his interest was anti-Catholicism, which he traced from its roots in Europe through its culmination in the riots of the 1840s and the success of the Know-Nothing Party in the 1850s. Although he described lulls in anti-Catholic viciousness, he wrote a narrative of increasing acrimony, heightened by anti-Catholic propaganda and punctuated by violence. John Kane argued that the anti-Catholicism of the mid-twentieth century mirrored the religious prejudice of a century earlier. More recent works demonstrating the lingering effects of the anti-Catholic temper include: Philip Jenkins, *The New Anti-Catholicism: The Last Acceptable Prejudice* (Oxford: Oxford University Press, 2003) and Mark Stephen Massa, *Anti-Catholicism in America: The Last Acceptable Prejudice* (New York: Crossroad, 2003). For examples of the centrality of

anti-Catholicism in surveys of American Catholicism, see John Tracy Ellis, *American Catholicism,* 2nd ed. (Chicago: University of Chicago Press, 1969); Andrew M. Greeley, *The Catholic Experience* (New York: Image, 1969); and Charles R. Morris, *American Catholic: The Saints and Sinners Who Built America's Most Powerful Church* (New York: Random House, 1997).

7. John England, *Works of the Right Rev. John England, First Bishop of Charleston,* ed. Ignatius Aloysius Reynolds, vol. 1 (Baltimore: John Murphy & Co., 1849), 52; Samuel J. Mills and Daniel Smith, *Report of a Missionary Tour through That Part of the United States Which Lies West of the Allegany Mountains* (Andover, MA: Flagg and Gould, 1815), 11. Flaget did insist that the missionaries allow him to examine the translation first.

8. Ellis, *American Catholicism,* 42, 63; Greeley, *Catholic Experience,* 19, 28.

9. Morris, *American Catholic.*

10. John R. Dichtl, *Frontiers of Faith: Bringing Catholicism to the West in the Early Republic* (Lexington: University Press of Kentucky, 2008). Quotation p. 180.

11. David Brion Davis, "Some Themes of Counter-Subversion: An Analysis of Anti-Masonic, Anti-Catholic, and Anti-Mormon Literature," *The Mississippi Valley Historical Review* 47, no. 2 (Sept. 1960), 205–24; Philip Jenkins, *Mystics and Messiahs: Cults and New Religions in American History* (New York: Oxford University Press, 2000), 28–31; Nancy Lusignan Schultz, *Veil of Fear: Nineteenth-Century Convent Tales by Rebecca Reed and Maria Monk* (West Lafayette, IN: Perdue University Press, 1999).

12. Jenny Franchot, *Roads to Rome: The Antebellum Protestant Encounter with Catholicism* (Berkeley: University of California Press, 1994). Although Franchot focused primarily on New Englanders, her analysis is useful for understanding Protestants' reactions to Catholicism in the South as well.

13. Joseph Agonito, "Ecumenical Stirrings: Catholic-Protestant Relations during the Episcopacy of John Carroll," *Church History* 45 (1967): 358–73; Jay P. Dolan, *The American Catholic Experience: A History from Colonial Times to the Present* (Notre Dame: University of Notre Dame Press, 1992), 102.

14. William R. Hutchison, *Religious Pluralism in America: The Contentious History of a Founding Ideal* (New Haven, CT: Yale, 2003), 58. Hutchison argued that although America has been religiously diverse from the early nineteenth century, it only became pluralistic in the second half of the twentieth (4).

15. Of the surveys of American Catholicism, only one devotes significant space to southern Catholicism: John Gilmary Shea, *History of the Catholic Church in the United States,* vols. 1–4 (New York: J. G. Shea, 1886–1892). Several other exceptions to this rule are early histories by prominent southern Catholics: Thomas F. Hopkins, *St. Mary's Church, Charleston, S.C.: The First Catholic Church in the Original Diocese of Charleston: An Historic Sketch of the Church from Its Beginning to the Present Time* (Charleston: Walker, Evans, & Cogswell, 1898); J. J. O'Connell, *Catholicity in the Carolinas and Georgia: Leaves of Its History* (s.l.: Sadlier, 1879); Martin John Spalding, *Sketches of the Early Catholic Missions of Kentucky; from Their Commencement in 1787 to the Jubilee of 1826–7* (Louisville: B. J. Webb, 1844). More reliable are a handful of relatively contemporary regional studies: Clyde F. Crews, *Presence and Possibility: Louisville Catholicism and*

its Cathedral (s.1.: s.n., 1973); Gerald P. Fogarty, *Commonwealth Catholicism: A History of the Catholic Church in Virginia* (Notre Dame: University of Notre Dame Press, 2001); Michael Kenny, *Catholic Culture in Alabama: Centenary Story of Spring Hill College, 1830–1930* (New York: The America Press, 1931); Richard C. Madden, *Catholics in South Carolina: A Record* (New York: University Press of America, 1985); Sister Mary Ramona Mattingly, *The Catholic Church on the Kentucky Frontier (1785–1812),* The Catholic University of America Studies in American Church History 25 (Washington, DC: Catholic University Press, 1936); Thomas W. Spalding, *The Premier See: A History of the Archdiocese of Baltimore, 1789–1989* (Baltimore: The Johns Hopkins Press, 1989). I know of only one work that deals with Catholics throughout the antebellum South: Randall Miller and Jon Wakelyn, eds., *Catholics in the Old South* (Macon: Mercer University Press, 1999). Another work shedding important light on antebellum southern Catholics, in particular French missionary priests serving in what is today the Deep South, is Michael Pasquier's *Fathers on the Frontier: French Missionaries and the Roman Catholic Priesthood in the United States, 1789–1870* (New York: Oxford University Press, 2010).

16. J. F. Regis Canevin, "Loss and Gain in the Catholic Church in the United States, 1800–1916," *Catholic Historical Review,* January 1917, 380–81.

17. Code, *Dictionary,* 417–21. South here refers to the states that joined the Confederacy plus the border states of Missouri, Kentucky, and Maryland, whereas North refers to the states that joined the Union. Dioceses west of those states bordering the Mississippi plus Texas are excluded. Kenneth Zanca gives the ratio of northern to southern dioceses in 1860 as 24:18, but his criteria for determining northern and southern is unclear (Kenneth J. Zanca, *American Catholics and Slavery: 1789–1866* [New York: University Press of America, 1994], 47). The fifteen southern dioceses were Baltimore (1789), New Orleans (1793, originally detached from the see of Havana and established as the diocese of Louisiana and the Floridas), Bardstown (1808, transferred to Louisville in 1841), Richmond (1820), Charleston (1820), St. Louis (1826), Mobile (1829), Natchez (1837), Nashville (1837), Little Rock (1843), Galveston (1847), Savannah (1850), Wheeling (1850), Natchitoches (1853), and Covington (1853).

18. These schools were not only the first founded but also proved to be the most long-lasting. Of the fourteen Catholic men's colleges founded by 1819, the four that are still in operation today are all in the South: Spring Hill College, St. Louis University, Georgetown University, and Mount St. Mary's College.

19. Ira Berlin and Herbert Gutman, "Natives and Immigrants, Free Men and Slaves: Urban Workingmen in the Antebellum American South," *American Historical Review* 88, no. 5 (Dec. 1983), 1178, 1187; Richard R. Duncan, "Catholics and the Church in the Antebellum Upper South," in Miller and Wakelyn, *Catholics in the Old South,* 92.

20. Samuel S. Hill, ed., *Religion in the Southern States* (Macon: Mercer University Press, 1983). Donald Mathews similarly traced the ascendancy and eventual dominance of Evangelical Protestantism in the South in his *Religion in the Old South* (Chicago: University of Chicago Press, 1977). See also Charles Reagan Wilson, ed., *Religion in the South* (Jackson: University Press of Mississippi, 1985). This work includes David Edwin Harrell Jr.'s "Religious Pluralism: Catholics, Jews, and Sectarians" (59–82) on Catholic,

Jews, and sectarians, which argued that each group felt at home in the South but focused on sectarians and the postwar period. The final article in this volume, Edwin Gaustad's "Regionalism in American Religion" (155–72), buttressed the view of Protestant hegemony by identifying Baptists as the "culture religion" of the South.

21. Randall Miller, "Catholic in a Protestant World: The Old South Example," in *Varieties of Southern Religious Experience,* ed. Samuel S. Hill (Baton Rouge: Louisiana State University Press, 1988), 130.

22. Studies of particular regions of the South often pay more attention to Catholics. See, for example: John B. Boles, *Religion in Antebellum Kentucky* (Lexington: University Press of Kentucky, 1976). Jon F. Sensbach discussed the importance of Catholics along the Gulf Coast to early southern religious history in an essay titled "Before the Bible Belt: Indians, Africans, and the New Synthesis of Eighteenth-Century Southern Religious History." The title of the volume in which the essay appeared, however, aptly summarizes historians' views of southern religious history: Beth Barton Schweiger and Donald Mathews, eds., *Religion in the American South: Protestants and Others in History and Culture* (Chapel Hill: University of North Carolina Press, 2004).

23. These dioceses included Cincinnati (1821); Detroit (1833); Vincennes, Indiana (1834); and Nashville (1837).

24. George H. Yater, *Two Hundred Years at the Falls of the Ohio: A History of Louisville and Jefferson County* (Louisville, KY: Filson Club, 1987), 62.

25. Although this and the following map both date from the 1870s, the churches they depict were almost all built during the antebellum period. The maps show all the Catholic churches and a majority of the Protestant churches.

26. "Report of Bishop England to the Cardinal Prefect of Propaganda (Rome, 1833)," *Records of the American Catholic Historical Society of Philadelphia* 8, no. 3 (Sept. 1897), 321 (hereafter cited as *ACHS*). In 1850, Georgia became a separate diocese with the see at Savannah.

27. Walter J. Fraser Jr., *Charleston! Charleston!: The History of a Southern City* (Columbia: University of South Carolina Press, 1989), 196–97, 220–23, 235; Robert N. Rosen, *A Short History of Charleston* (Columbia: University of South Carolina Press, 1997), 86–95.

28. Fraser, *Charleston,* 174, 214.

29. Ibid., 235. In terms of manufacturing, Charleston ranked only eighty-fifth among the nation's cities in 1860 despite the fact that in population it ranked twenty-second (241).

30. Ibid., 228–29. The economic gap between rich and poor was enormous with roughly 3 percent of the households owning about half of the city's wealth (240).

31. All of Florida with the exception of the western part of the panhandle became part of the newly created diocese of Savannah in 1850.

32. Cited in Harriet E. Amos, *Cotton City: Urban Development in Antebellum Mobile* (Tuscaloosa: The University of Alabama Press, 1985), xiii.

33. Ibid., 216–17.

34. Ibid., 81, 93. Industrial might rarely translated into political clout. Only 3 per-

cent of city leaders whose religious affiliations are known belonged to Catholic congregations. In contrast, over 60 percent were Episcopalian (67).

35. Ibid., 107, 110.

36. Joseph Belcher, *The Religious Denominations of the United States: their History, Doctrine, Government and Statistics* (Philadelphia: J. E. Potter, 1854), 764; *Catholic Advocate* (Louisville), May 7, 1853; Jay P. Dolan, ed., *The American Catholic Parish: A History from 1850 to the Present,* vol. 1 (New York: Paulist Press, 1987); Duncan, "Catholics and the Church," 92; Kenny, *Catholic Culture in Alabama,* 48, 110; Mattingly, *Catholic Church on the Kentucky Frontier,* 103; O'Connell, *Catholicity in the Carolinas,* 37, 88, 111, 114; V. F. O'Daniel, "Bishop Flaget's Report of the Diocese of Bardstown to Pius VII, April 10, 1815," *Catholic Historical Review* 1 (April 1915–Jan. 1916), 313–19; Oscar Hugh Lipscomb, "The Administration of John Quinlan, Second Bishop of Mobile, 1859–1883" *ACHS* 78, nos. 1–4 (March–Dec. 1967), 8, 21; E. Rameur, "The Progress of the Church in the United States," *The Catholic World* 1, no. 1 (April 1865), 1–19; "Report of Bishop England," 321; Joseph Salzbacher, *Miene Reise Nach Nord-Amerika im Jahre 1842* (Vienna: Wimmer, Schmidt & Leo, 1845), 388–89, 398; J. Herman Schauinger, *Cathedrals in the Wilderness* (Milwaukee: Bruce Publishing Company, 1952), 18, 54, 232, 307; Raymond H. Schmidt, "An Overview of Institutional Establishments in the Antebellum Southern Church," in Miller and Wakelyn, *Catholics in the Old South,* 63, 64, 68; Martin John Spalding, *Life, Times, and Character of the Right Reverend Benedict Joseph Flaget* (Louisville: Webb & Levering, 1852), 98; Spalding, *Sketches of Early Catholic Missions,* 192.

37. Amos, *Cotton City,* 67; Yater, *Two Hundred Years at the Falls,* 71. The difficulties in accurately estimating the numbers of Catholics also apply to Protestants, because denominations defined membership in different ways. Evangelicals, for example, tended to count as members only those who had undergone a conversion experience, thus minimizing their numbers relative to denominations that counted all baptized believers as members.

38. Billington, *Protestant Crusade,* 1–18.

39. Ibid., 9–10; Leonard Levy, *The Establishment Clause: Religion and the First Amendment* (Chapel Hill: University of North Carolina Press, 1994), 5; Sydney Ahlstrom, *A Religious History of the American People* (New Haven, CT: Yale, 1972), 197. For several specific acts of the colonial assembly, see Madden, *Catholics in South Carolina,* 7–9.

40. Billington, *Protestant Crusade,* 18. Madden offered a different account of the same event. In his account, a sort of puppet show took place with the effigy of the pope being made to bow before two hated British officials (14).

41. Hopkins, *St. Mary's Church,* 1; Madden, *Catholics in South Carolina,* 14; Rosen, *Short History,* 92.

42. Dolan, *American Catholic Experience,* 69–76.

43. Billington, *Protestant Crusade,* 11.

44. Madden, *Catholics in South Carolina,* 7, 9–10, 13–15.

45. Ruth Allison Hudnut and Hayes Baker-Crothers, "Acadian Transients in South Carolina," *American Historical Review* 43, no. 3 (April 1938), 500–13. The treatment of the Acadians was itself an interesting episode in the history of Catholic-Protestant re-

lations. Protestant South Carolinians greatly feared and resented their presence due to the financial burden they posed, the possibility of civil disturbance, and religious bigotry. Despite these sentiments, however, both the assembly and Governor James Glen demonstrated significant concern for the Acadians' well-being. See also Madden, *Catholics in South Carolina,* 11–12.

46. Billington, *Protestant Crusade,* 22.

47. For some notable exceptions in South Carolina see Madden, *Catholics in South Carolina,* 14.

48. See Dolan, *American Catholic Experience,* 97–124.

49. Levy, *Establishment Clause,* 6–9, 52; Billington, *Protestant Crusade,* 21.

50. Billington, *Protestant Crusade,* 21–23; Levy, *Establishment Clause,* 58; Ahlstrom, *Religious History,* 380.

Chapter 1

1. J. Hector St. John de Crèvecoeur, *Letters from an American Farmer; Describing Certain Provincial Situations, Manners, and Customs, Not Generally Known* (Dublin: John Exshaw, 1782), 47–48.

2. Ibid., 48–51.

3. Reynolds to Purcell, Charleston, March 5, 1850, CACI II-4-K, Archives of the University of Notre Dame (hereafter cited as UNDA).

4. *Charleston Courier,* October 16, 1827.

5. Cited in *United States Catholic Miscellany* (Charleston), October 20, 1827.

6. Mary D. Robertson, ed., *A Confederate Lady Comes of Age: The Journal of Pauline DeCaradeuc Hayward, 1861–1888* (Columbia: University of South Carolina Press, 1992), quotations on 81, 86.

7. "The Beginning and Progress of Catholicity in Washington, Wilkes Co, GA," *American Catholic Historical Researches* 11, no. 1 (Jan. 1894), 17–24 (hereafter cited as *ACHR*). In Virginia, Mary Otis Weed played a role similar to that of Semmes in Georgia. Weed converted in 1855 and then entered the Ursulines, establishing their convent in Tuscaloosa, Alabama. Her two brothers also converted, one of whom, Ambler J. Weed, had been an Episcopal priest. After his conversion, he received ordination in the Catholic Church. Gerald P. Fogarty, *Commonwealth Catholicism: A History of the Catholic Church in Virginia* (Notre Dame: University of Notre Dame Press, 2001), 136–37.

8. Mary Boykin Chesnut, *A Diary from Dixie,* ed. Ben Ames Williams (Cambridge, MA: Harvard University Press, 1980), 351.

9. Theodore Clapp, *Autobiographical Sketches and Recollections: During a Thirty-Five Year Residence in New Orleans,* 2nd ed. (Boston: Phillips, Samson & Co., 1858), 66, 237.

10. Reprinted in the *Miscellany,* June 16, 1827.

11. *Miscellany,* October 7 and 14, 1826.

12. Ibid., July 19, 1828.

13. Ibid., November 16, 1825.

14. Oscar Penn Fitzgerald, *Fifty Years: Observations—Opinions—Experiences* (Nashville: Publishing House of the Methodist Episcopal Church, South, 1903), 173. By no means were all Irish immigrants Catholic, but in their praise for the Irish, southern Protestants either failed to distinguish between Catholics and Protestants or praised Catholics specifically.

15. Clapp, *Autobiographical Sketches,* 248, 249.

16. *Alabama Planter* (Mobile), December 28, 1846.

17. Ibid., January 18, 1847.

18. Nerinckx and Flaget to Cardinal Michele de Pietro, Prefect of the Congregation for the Propagation of the Faith, Bardstown, 1813, in Augustin Wand and M. Lilliana Owens, eds., *Documents: Nerinckx—Kentucky—Loretto, 1804–1851 in Archives Propaganda Fide, Rome* (Nerinx, KY: Loretto Literary and Benevolent Institution, 1972), 35, Filson Historical Society, Louisville (hereafter cited as Filson).

19. Nerinckx to Cardinal Litta, Prefect of the Congregation for the Propagation of the Faith, Bardstown, 1816, in ibid., 170.

20. *Miscellany,* December 22, 1827.

21. M. J. Spalding to Purcell, Louisville, December 3, 1849, CACI 11-4-k, UNDA.

22. John Lyons, "Cathedral of the Assumption, Marriages to 1875," Filson. The register listed forty-nine marriages involving a non-Catholic and eight "mixed" marriages. The distinction is unclear.

23. "Register of the Prefect of Classes and Studies 1847–1859," Spring Hill College Archives. Of roughly 129 families recorded between 1847 and 1854, the period for which the most details are available, approximately 13 percent had parents of different faiths.

24. *Catholic Advocate* (Louisville), April 2, 1836.

25. *Miscellany,* April 7, 1827.

26. Ibid., October 18, 1828.

27. Ibid., September 20, 1828.

28. Ibid., June 6, 1829; Madden estimates the total amount raised in South Carolina for Irish relief as $20,000 (55).

29. *Miscellany,* September 27, 1828.

30. *Alabama Planter,* February 15, and March 1, 1847.

31. *The Life and Speeches of Henry Clay,* vol. 2 (Philadelphia: Leary & Getz, 1859), 599.

32. *Alabama Planter,* March 8, 1847.

33. *Miscellany,* January 21 and 28, 1824.

34. Ibid., February 4, 1824.

35. *Courier,* August 29, 1840.

36. *Miscellany,* October 7, 1826.

37. Walter Brownlow Posey, *Frontier Mission: A History of Religion West of the Southern Appalachians to 1861* (Lexington: University Press of Kentucky, 1966), 316–17.

38. *Statuta Synodi Baltimorensis, anno 1791, celebratae* (Baltimore: s.n., 1817), [25–26].

39. "Flaget to Plessis, The North East Shore, February 21, 1819," *Records of the American Catholic Historical Society of Philadelphia* 18, no. 1 (March 1907), 34 (hereafter cited as *ACHS*).

40. Martin John Spalding, *Sketches of the Early Catholic Missions of Kentucky; from Their Commencement in 1787 to the Jubilee of 1826–7* (Louisville: B. J. Webb, 1844), 69.

41. "Badin to Carroll, Washington Cnty, May 5, 1801," *ACHS* 23, no. 3 (Sept. 1912), 145.

42. Cited in J. Herman Schauinger, *Cathedrals in the Wilderness* (Milwaukee: Bruce Publishing Company, 1952), 19.

43. Cited in Sister Mary Ramona Mattingly, *The Catholic Church on the Kentucky Frontier (1785–1812),* The Catholic University of America Studies in American Church History 25 (Washington: Catholic University Press, 1936), 128.

44. John F. Schermerhorn and Samuel J. Mills, *A Correct View of That Part of the United States Which Lies West of the Alleghany Mountains, with Respect to Religion and Morals* (Hartford, CT: Cleason and Co., 1814), 35, 51.

45. Samuel J. Mills and Daniel Smith, *Report of a Missionary Tour through That Part of the United States Which Lies West of the Allegany Mountains* (Andover, MA: Flagg and Gould, 1815), 11, 36, 60.

46. Thomas W. Spalding, *The Premier See: A History of the Archdiocese of Baltimore, 1789–1989* (Baltimore: The Johns Hopkins Press, 1989), 59–60.

47. Clapp, *Autobiographical Sketches,* 202.

48. Harriet E. Amos, *Cotton City: Urban Development in Antebellum Mobile* (Tuscaloosa: The University of Alabama Press, 1985), 64.

49. Ibid., 124–25, 137.

50. Ibid., 13.

51. Mattingly, *Catholic Church on the Kentucky Frontier,* 166; Spalding, *Sketches of Early Catholic Missions,* 26, 118–19.

52. Chalmers Gaston Davidson, *The Last Foray: the South Carolina Planters of 1860: A Sociological Study* (Columbia: University of South Carolina Press, 1971), 85, 225. During the late colonial period, another prominent Catholic Dr. James Fallon had played an important role in Charleston politics. Fraser, *Charleston,* 171.

53. *Miscellany,* September 16, 1826.

54. Ibid., August 14, 1822. The *Miscellany*'s reprinting of this correspondence reveals a desire to ensure that Americans would indeed remember Catholics' "patriotic part."

55. "Carroll to Washington, Doughoregan, July 29, 1798," *ACHS* 18, no. 4 (Dec. 1907), 391.

56. Amos, *Cotton City,* 64.

57. Frederick Law Olmsted, *A Journey in the Seaboard Slave States* (New York: Dix & Edwards, 1856), 404.

58. Michael Kenny, *Catholic Culture in Alabama: Centenary Story of Spring Hill College, 1830–1930* (New York: The America Press, 1931), 34; *Miscellany,* February 2, 1828.

59. *Miscellany,* April 7, 1824.

60. "England to Cullen, Charleston, February 23, 1836," *ACHS* 8, no. 2 (June 1897), 227.

61. Mattingly, *Catholic Church on the Kentucky Frontier,* 32, 35; Spalding, *Sketches of Early Catholic Missions,* 38–40.

62. Cited in Mattingly, *Catholic Church on the Kentucky Frontier,* 36.

63. Martin John Spalding, *Life, Times, and Character of the Right Reverend Benedict Joseph Flaget* (Louisville: Webb & Levering, 1852), 130.

64. "Speech on the War with Mexico," February 9, 1847, *The Papers of John C. Calhoun,* vol. 24, ed. Clyde Wilson and Shirley Cooks (Columbia: University of South Carolina Press, 1998), 131.

65. "Waddy Thompson to John Calhoun, Greenville, October 22, 1847," in ibid., 616.

66. "W[illia]m Eveliegh to John Calhoun and others, Statesburgh, SC, February 7, 1848," *The Papers of John C. Calhoun,* vol. 25, ed. Clyde Wilson and Shirley Cooks (Columbia: University of South Carolina Press, 1999), 183. Calhoun had made a similar argument in a speech before the Senate, in which he stated that the Mexican priesthood was uniformly opposed to republicanism (61).

67. "Geo[rge] H. Thatcher to John Calhoun, Ballston Centre [NY], August 10, 1848," *Papers,* vol. 25, 674.

68. William B. Hesseltine, ed., *Dr. J. G. M. Ramsey: Autobiography and Letters* (Nashville: Tennessee Historical Commission, 1954), 169.

69. Isaac McDaniel, *Impact of the Mexican War on Anti-Catholicism in the United States* (Ann Arbor: University Microfilms International, 1991), 103–4.

70. Cited in ibid., 151.

71. McDaniel, *Impact of the Mexican War,* 48, 77. Positive reactions to the aesthetics of Mexican Catholicism emphasize both the appeal of different forms of religion and the importance of churches as civic "ornaments."

72. Cited in ibid., 208.

73. Cited in ibid., 65.

74. "John G. Tod to Calhoun, City of Mexico, April 6, 1848," *Papers,* vol. 25, 302.

75. See Ray Billington, *The Protestant Crusade: 1800–1860* (New York: MacMillan, 1938), 238–39.

76. David T. Gleeson, *The Irish in the South: 1815–1877* (Chapel Hill: University of North Carolina Press, 2001), 134–35.

77. Clapp, *Autobiographical Sketches,* 231.

78. "The Church at Norfolk, VA. 1819," *ACHR* 9, no. 3 (July 1892), 129; *Miscellany,* May 31, 1828.

79. C. J. Jeronimus, ed., *Travels by His Highness Duke Bernhard of Saxe-Weimar-Eisenach through North America in the Years 1825 and 1826* (Lanham, MD: University Press of America, 2001), 48.

80. *Miscellany,* February 2, 1828.

81. Fitzgerald, *Fifty Years,* 169–70.

82. *Miscellany,* June 8, 1825.

83. Ibid., December 15, 1827.

84. Ibid., December 22, 1827.

85. Cited in Spalding, *Premier See,* 61, 99.

86. John B. Boles, *Religion in Antebellum Kentucky* (Lexington: University Press of Kentucky, 1976), 64–65; Schauinger, *Cathedrals in the Wilderness,* viii, 48, 58; Spalding, *Life, Times, . . . Flaget,* 60 (quotation), 240, 272.

87. Cited in Spalding, *Life, Times, . . . Flaget,* 195.

88. Schermerhorn and Mills, *Correct View,* 34.

89. *Alabama Planter,* January 4, 1847.

90. Wilson and Cooks, *Papers,* vol. 25, 260.

91. "D[aniel] Jenifer to Calhoun, Vienna, January 20, 1845," *The Papers of John C. Calhoun,* vol. 21, ed. Clyde Wilson (Columbia: University of South Carolina Press, 1993), 163.

92. Cited in Mattingly, *Catholic Church on the Kentucky Frontier,* 109. For an analysis of French priests' assimilation in America, see Michael Pasquier, *Fathers on the Frontier: French Missionaries and the Roman Catholic Priesthood in the United States, 1789–1870* (New York: Oxford University Press, 2010). Pasquier describes the challenges French priests faced, and he argues that they tended to maintain a transnational identity, but he also concludes that the majority had become thoroughly American by about the 1840s.

93. Cited in Peter Guilday, *The Life and Time of John England, First Bishop of Charleston,* vol. 2 (New York: The America Press, 1927), 139.

94. Augustin Verot, *A Tract for the Times: Slavery and Abolitionism, Being the Substance of a Sermon, Preached in the Church of St. Augustine, Florida, on the 4th Day of January, 1861, Day of Public Humiliation, Fasting and Prayer* (New Orleans: Catholic Propagator, 1861), 17–18.

95. "Flaget to Henry Clay, April 19, 1827," *The Papers of Henry Clay,* vol. 5, "*Secretary of State,*" ed. Mary Hargreaves and James Hopkins (Lexington: University Press of Kentucky, 1981), 463.

96. Spalding, *Life, Times, . . . Flaget,* 264.

97. Cited in ibid., 56.

98. V. F. O'Daniel, "Bishop Flaget's Report of the Diocese of Bardstown to Pius VII, April 10, 1815," *Catholic Historical Review* 1 (April 1915–Jan. 1916), 314 (hereafter cited as *CHR*).

99. Cited in Kenny, *Catholic Culture in Alabama,* 77.

100. Stephen Badin, "Origin and Progress of the Mission of Kentucky," translated and reprinted in *Catholic World* 21, no. 126 (Sept. 1875),831. Filson.

101. Cited in Schauinger, *Cathedrals in the Wilderness,* 151.

102. Spalding, *Life, Times, . . . Flaget,* 31.

103. W. J. Howlett, "Bishop Flaget's Diary," *ACHS* 29, no. 3 (Sept. 1918), 245.

104. Spalding, *Life, Times, . . . Flaget,* 237.

105. Ibid., 335.

106. John England, *Diurnal of the Right Rev. John England, D.D., first Bishop of Charleston, S.C.* (Philadelphia: American Catholic Historical Society, 1895), 60.

107. *Miscellany,* July 13, 1825.

108. Ibid., April 14, 1827.

109. Ibid., April 7, 1824.

110. "England to Gaston, Charleston, February 24, 1838," *ACHS* 19, no. 2 (June 1908), 167–68.

111. *Miscellany,* November 17, 1827.

112. Clapp, *Autobiographical Sketches,* 223, 232, 234.

113. Fenwick to Concanen, Lexington, July 10, 1808 in V. F. O'Daniel, "A Long Misunderstood Episode in American History," *CHR* 6 (April 1920–Jan. 1921), 44; Mattingly, *Catholic Church on the Kentucky Frontier,* 199; Schauinger, *Cathedrals in the Wilderness,* 16, 27–28.

114. "Badin to Carroll, Priestland, Marden's Creek, March 2, 1797," *ACHS* 19, no. 4 (Dec. 1908), 458. In an obituary for Badin, the *Catholic Telegraph and Advocate* emphasized that he had been "a most interesting companion even to persons not of our Holy Religion" (April 23, 1853).

115. "England to Cullen, Charleston, February 23, 1836," *ACHS* 8, no. 2 (June 1897), 222. Rome chose England to negotiate a concordat between the Holy See and Jean Boyer, Haiti's dictator. England was reluctant to accept the mission, aware of the damage it would do to his standing in South Carolina, but he ultimately concluded that obedience to the pope compelled him to accept. For Haiti's place in the southern imagination, see Alfred N. Hunt, *Haiti's Influence on Antebellum America: Slumbering Volcano in the Caribbean* (Baton Rouge: Louisiana State University Press, 1988).

116. Richard C. Madden, *Catholics in South Carolina: A Record* (New York: University Press of America, 1985), 38.

117. Boles, *Religion in Antebellum Kentucky,* 58; Schauinger, *Cathedrals in the Wilderness,* 30–31. When Daviess died during the Battle of Tippecanoe in 1811, David poured out his grief in a long Latin poem written to honor "Heroic Daviess." For an English translation see Spalding, *Sketches of Early Catholic Missions,* 304–6.

118. Schauinger, *Cathedrals in the Wilderness,* 116; Spalding, *Life, Times, . . . Flaget,* 135.

119. Spalding, *Life, Times, . . . Flaget,* 237; Spalding, *Sketches of Early Catholic Missions,* 26.

120. "Luke Tiernan to Clay, Baltimore, May 27, 1828," *The Papers of Henry Clay,* vol. 7, ed. Robert Seager II (Lexington: University Press of Kentucky, 1982), 303.

121. "Clay to Demetrius Gallitzin, Washington, February 8, 1837," *The Papers of Henry Clay,* vol. 9, ed. Robert Seager II (Lexington: University Press of Kentucky, 1988), 24. Gallitzin was a scion of a prominent European family who converted to Catholicism and became one of the first priests ordained in America.

122. "Clay to James Simpson, Lexington, August 15, 1843," *Papers,* vol. 9, 845.

123. Cited in Schauinger, *Cathedrals in the Wilderness,* 268, 270.

124. "Flaget to Badolet, [Bardstown], January 18, 1825," *ACHR* 9, no. 3 (July 1894), 134–37.

125. Cited in Mattingly, *Catholic Church on the Kentucky Frontier,* 92.

126. Quinlan to Purcell, Summerville, May 22, 1860, CACI 11–5-a, UNDA.

127. *Courier,* April 12, 1842; *Charleston Patriot,* April 18, 1842.

128. Cited in Kenny, *Catholic Culture in Alabama,* 210.

129. Spalding, *Sketches of Early Catholic Missions,* 284.

130. *Miscellany,* April 27, 1825. The timing of this publication seems odd, given that Dehon, a native of Massachusetts who first came to South Carolina for his health and received election as bishop in 1812, died in 1817. See also ibid., October 13, 1827.

131. J. J. O'Connell, *Catholicity in the Carolinas and Georgia: Leaves of Its History* (s.l.: Sadlier, 1879), 89–93.

132. Diary of Anita Dwyer Withers, July 20, 1861, 1746-Z, Southern Historical Collection, University of North Carolina-Chapel Hill (hereafter cited as SHC).

133. Peter William Hairston Papers, SHC.

Chapter 2

1. Charles C. Jones Jr., *Memorial History of Augusta, Georgia* (Syracuse, NY: D. Mason, 1890), 255.

2. Barry had already earned a reputation for charity by his service during a fever seven years earlier. In 1854, he would again turn his parsonage into a hospital for fever victims. Barry became bishop of Savannah in 1857 but died less than three years later. J. J. O'Connell, *Catholicity in the Carolinas and Georgia: Leaves of Its History* (s.l.: Sadlier, 1879), 529–35; Jones, *Memorial History of Augusta,* 383; John Donald Wade, *Augustus Baldwin Longstreet: A Study of the Development of Culture in the South* (New York: MacMillan, 1924), 233.

3. Oscar Penn Fitzgerald, *Judge Longstreet: A Life Sketch* (Nashville: Publishing House of the Methodist Episcopal Church, South, 1891), 67–68. Longstreet was a native of Georgia who had studied at Yale and Litchfield Law School before returning to Georgia, where he gained renown as a lawyer, author, and member of the Georgia legislature. After the death of his son in 1838, he entered the Methodist ministry and went on to serve as the president of Emory College, Centenary College in Louisiana, and the University of Mississippi.

4. Fitzgerald, *Judge Longstreet,* 68.

5. *United States Catholic Miscellany* (Charleston), November 16, 1839.

6. Ibid., November 16, 1839.

7. Ibid.

8. Richard Harrison Shryock, *Medicine and Society in America, 1660–1860* (New York: New York University Press, 1960), 117–18. For Shryock's continuing importance to the study of medicine in the Old South see Ronald L. Numbers and Todd L. Savitt, eds., *Science and Medicine in the Old South* (Baton Rouge: Louisiana State University Press, 1989), 147–48. Numbers and Savitt also note that facets of southern health care, particularly hospitals and medical societies and journals, remain unexplored by historians (150–51).

9. John Duffy, "Medical Practice in the Ante Bellum South," *Journal of Southern History* 25, no. 1 (Feb. 1959), 53.

10. Shryock, *Medicine and Society,* 86, 89; K. David Patterson, "Disease Environments of the Antebellum South," in Numbers and Savitt, *Science and Medicine,* 157.

Patterson argues that most white southerners probably ate about as well as northerners or Europeans did, but he cites deficiencies of several vitamins and iron as major problems.

11. Patterson, "Disease Environments," 152–53, 158, 160. Slavery affected virtually every aspect of life in the South, including epidemiology.

12. Yellow fever severely limited the South's economic development by discouraging immigration and investment and by decimating the labor force. Because whites were more susceptible than blacks were, many viewed the fever as a threat to the ruling race's security against revolt. Margaret H. Warner, "Public Health in the Old South," in Numbers and Savitt, *Science and Medicine,* 229–30, 232.

13. Richard Harrison Shryock, *Medicine in America: Historical Essays* (Baltimore: Johns Hopkins Press, 1966), 49, 52. An 1840 study of infant mortality rates gave one indication of the unhealthiness of the South. The study calculated the number of babies, out of a hundred, still alive after five years. It found 94 in New Hampshire, 79.7 in North Carolina, and only 72.5 in Mississippi (52). For a comparison of mortality rates in major northern and southern cities, see Warner, "Public Health," 237.

14. James H. Cassedy, "Medical Men and the Ecology of the Old South," in Numbers and Savitt, *Science and Medicine,* 169. Americans had noted differences between northern and southern health since the colonial period, but the decline of yellow fever in the North after 1822, coupled with its increase in the South, made the contrast even starker. See Warner, "Public Health," 226.

15. Cited in Warner, "Public Health," 236.

16. Shryock, *Medicine and Society,* 132. One such innovative surgeon was Ephraim McDowell, a pioneer in ovariotomy in Kentucky. Shryock warns, however, against attributing too much weight to this "frontier hypothesis."

17. Shryock, *Medicine in America,* 56.

18. Ibid. Some southern doctors where truly outstanding as practitioners and scholars, even by European standards. For example, Dr. John Lining of Charleston conducted original research on metabolism as early as 1740. See Shryock, *Medicine and Society,* 62.

19. Shryock, *Medicine and Society,* 58. Medical training produced tangible benefits. For example, Dr. Ramsey noted significant improvements in infant mortality in the half century after 1750 (99).

20. Ibid., 139; Shryock, *Medicine in America,* 56–58.

21. John Hanley Warner, "A Southern Medical Reform: the Meaning of the Antebellum Argument for Southern Medical Education," in Numbers and Savitt, *Science and Medicine,* 217.

22. Shryock, *Medicine in America,* 58–59. The growth of urban areas also created new disease environments. See Warner, "Public Health," 231.

23. Shryock, *Medicine and Society,* 132. Shryock notes, for example, that probably the most useful achievement of American surgery was a successful operation for vaginal fistula by J. Marion Sims of Mobile in 1849. Some southerners contributed to the growth of national medical institutions, for example, Dr. Richard Arnold, a professor

at a medical school in Savannah, who was one of the two first secretaries of the American Medical Association (143).

24. John Hanley Warner, "The Idea of Southern Medical Distinctiveness: Medical Knowledge and Practice in the Old South," in Numbers and Savitt, *Science and Medicine,* 180, 189–95.

25. Cassedy, "Medical Men," 176.

26. Ibid., 177–78.

27. Warner, "Medical Reform," 221–22.

28. Ibid., 207, 216; Warner, "Medical Distinctiveness," 198–99, 216.

29. Harriet E. Amos, *Cotton City: Urban Development in Antebellum Mobile* (Tuscaloosa: The University of Alabama Press, 1985), 218; Warner, "Medical Distinctiveness," 180, 197.

30. *Miscellany,* November 18, 1826. In later years, the *Miscellany* continued to support the college by advertising its commencements and other public events.

31. Cited in Peter Guilday, *The Life and Time of John England, First Bishop of Charleston,* vol. 2 (New York: The America Press, 1927), 162.

32. In 1857, Dr. Richard Arnold singled out for criticism the low standards of Oglethorpe and Atlanta College. See Shryock, *Medicine and Society,* 143.

33. John R. Thelin, *A History of American Higher Education* (Baltimore: The Johns Hopkins University Press, 2004), 55–56. Northern medical schools also admitted many students without college degrees, but these schools still tended to be of a higher quality than their southern counterparts.

34. Robert F. Pace, *Halls of Honor: College Men in the Old South* (Baton Rouge: Louisiana State University Press, 2004), 12.

35. Shryock, *Medicine and Society,* 105.

36. Ibid., 13; Shryock, *Medicine in America,* 68–69.

37. Amos, *Cotton City,* 154, 156; David R. Goldfield, "The Business of Health Planning: Disease Prevention in the Old South," *Journal of Southern History* 42, no. 4 (Nov. 1976), 559–62, 566; Warner, "Public Health," 228, 236, 239, 254.

38. Shryock, *Medicine and Society,* 9, 15–16.

39. Bernard Code, *Dictionary of the American Catholic Hierarchy* (New York: Longmans, Green, 1940), 71–72; Columba Fox, *The Life of the Right Reverend John Baptist Mary David* (New York: United States Catholic Historical Society, 1925), 49, 79–80 (quotation on 79); J. Herman Schauinger, *Cathedrals in the Wilderness* (Milwaukee: Bruce Publishing Company, 1952), 66, 179, 193; Martin John Spalding, *Life, Times, and Character of the Right Reverend Benedict Joseph Flaget* (Louisville: Webb & Levering, 1852), 67, 207, 241. In 1819, David received consecration as bishop of the titular see of Mauricastro and appointment as auxiliary bishop of Bardstown. He served as bishop of Bardstown for a brief interlude between 1832 and 1833.

40. Schauinger, *Cathedrals in the Wilderness,* 107.

41. Cited in Duffy, "Medical Practice," 57.

42. Elizabeth Barnaby Keeney, "Unless Powerful Sick: Domestic Medicine in the Old South," in Numbers and Savitt, *Science and Medicine,* 276–87. Regarding access to

doctors, Keeney notes that although the number of physicians in the South increased dramatically between 1790 and 1850, in keeping with a national trend, many clustered in urban areas. The percentage of southerners who lived in urban areas, however, increased much more slowly, from roughly 4 to 7 percent. As a result, many southerners remained without access to professional medical care (281).

43. Shryock, *Medicine and Society,* 20, 140. Dr. Arnold criticized the practice at many schools of "taking a winter student, hurrying him through a summer course, & turning him out a doctor in less than a year" (143).

44. Ibid., 149.

45. Warner, "Medical Reform," 208.

46. Shyrock, *Medicine in America,* 62. Americans did not hesitate to take advantage of the medical profession's openness. In 1848, the American Medical Association reported with chagrin that the ratio of "physicians" to population was five times higher in the United States than in France (147). This situation persisted for decades. In 1890, a commentator bemoaned that in Georgia, despite regulations on the medical profession, "the officers of the law are derelict in arresting and prosecuting those prowling quacks, mountebanks, and charlatans who from time to time peregrinate the country, robbing the ignorant and unwary, and leaving in their trail untold agony." Jones, *Memorial History of Augusta,* 254.

47. In those cases where Catholics ran pay hospitals, they did so in order to subsidize their charitable work. The same pattern appeared in Catholic schools, which generally charged tuition for the wealthy in order to support poor students.

48. Shryock, *Medicine and Society,* 154.

49. Ibid., 15, 146.

50. *Miscellany,* September 28, 1825.

51. Shryock, *Medicine and Society,* 147.

52. Keeney, "Unless Powerful Sick," 288, 291.

53. Fox, *Life of . . . David,* 50.

54. Stephen Badin, "Origin and Progress of the Mission of Kentucky," translated and reprinted in *Catholic World* 21, no. 126 (Sept. 1875), 831. Filson.

55. W. J. Howlett, "Bishop Flaget's Diary," *Records of the American Catholic Historical Society of Philadelphia* 29, no. 3 (Sept. 1918), 39–42 (hereafter cited as *ACHS*).

56. Michael Kenny, *Catholic Culture in Alabama: Centenary Story of Spring Hill College, 1830–1930* (New York: The America Press, 1931), 188.

57. *Miscellany,* September 8, 1827, August 2, 1828.

58. Howlett, "Diary," 40.

59. Theodore Clapp, *Autobiographical Sketches and Recollections: During a Thirty-Five Year Residence in New Orleans,* 2nd ed. (Boston: Phillips, Samson & Co., 1858), 233.

60. Schauinger, *Cathedrals in the Wilderness,* 2.

61. Flaget to unknown, Bordeaux, May 28, 1810, Filson; Schauinger, *Cathedrals in the Wilderness,* 120.

62. Flaget to Maréchal, Loretto, July 10, 1817, Filson Historical Society, Louisville (hereafter cited as Filson).

63. Christopher J. Kauffman, *Ministry and Meaning: A Religious History of Catholic Health Care in the United States* (New York: Crossroad, 1995), 2, 27–28.

64. Barbara Lawatsch-Boomgaarden with Josef IJsewijn, trans. and ed., *Voyage to Maryland (1663): Relatio Itineris in Marilandiam* (Wauconda, IL: Bolchazy-Carducci, 1995), 7–8.

65. Robert Emmett Curran, *American Jesuit Spirituality: The Maryland Tradition, 1634–1900* (Mahwah, NJ: Paulist Press, 1988), 64–65.

66. Ibid., 70–71.

67. Schauinger, *Cathedrals in the Wilderness,* 94.

68. "Badin to Carroll, Washington County, August 4, 1796," *ACHS* 19, no. 3 (Sept. 1908), 268. In an appeal to Cuba for funds, Catholics in South Carolina noted the "melancholy fact" that many Catholics in the diocese died without receiving the last sacraments. *Miscellany,* November 24, 1827.

69. Martin John Spalding, *Sketches of the Early Catholic Missions of Kentucky; from Their Commencement in 1787 to the Jubilee of 1826–7* (Louisville: B. J. Webb, 1844), 230. David was well qualified to help establish the order, having served as superior of the Sisters of Charity of Emmitsburg. For the origins and first members of the Sisters of Charity, see Fox, *Life of . . . David,* chap. 8. The sisters moved their motherhouse to Nazareth, Kentucky, in 1822 and as a result are sometimes known as the Sisters of Charity of Nazareth or simply Sisters of Nazareth. I will use the term Sisters of Nazareth to avoid confusion with other orders.

70. The Sisters of Nazareth received the rule in a form adapted by St. Elizabeth Ann Seton. I would like to thank Sister Betty Ann McNeil for clarifying this point.

71. Cited in Mary Ewens, *The Role of the Nun in Nineteenth Century America* (New York: Arno Press, 1978), 89.

72. Fox, *Life of . . . David,* 70; Schauinger, *Cathedrals in the Wilderness,* 104.

73. *Miscellany,* February 17, 1827.

74. Schauinger, *Cathedrals in the Wilderness,* 271–73.

75. "Report of Bishop England to the Cardinal Prefect of Propaganda (Rome, 1833)," *ACHS* 8, no. 3 (Sept. 1897), 323. Religious orders in the United States often chose very similar names. Sources generally refer to England's order as the Sisters of Mercy, or alternately as the Sisters of Our Lady of Mercy. Their official name, however, is the Sisters of Charity of Our Lady of Mercy. This may explain why the citizens of Augusta, in their letters of thanks, referred to Sisters of Charity. This order is not to be confused with the Sisters of Mercy, established in Ireland in 1831 and in the United States in 1843. Nor should the Charleston order be confused with the Sisters of Charity of Our Lady of Mercy founded in Holland and established in the United States in 1874 (see Ursala M. Stepsis and Dolores Liptak, eds., *Pioneer Healers: The History of Women Religious in American Healthcare* [New York: Crossroad, 1989], 31, 254). Finally, they are distinct from the Sisters of Charity of Emmitsburg, Maryland, established by Elizabeth Ann Seton in 1809. The Sisters of Charity of Emmitsburg merged with the Daughters of Charity, established in France in 1633, in 1850 and took the name Daughters of Charity of St. Vincent de Paul (see Kauffman, *Ministry and Meaning,* 23; Stepsis, *Pioneer Healers,* 24–28). England clearly wanted the order in Charleston to be indepen-

dent of the Maryland order (see England to Gaston, February 25, 1830, cited in Guilday, *Life and Time . . . England,* vol. 2, 135).

76. The Catholic community published an announcement of the ceremonies surrounding the laying of the cornerstone in the *Charleston Courier* of March 25, 1840.

77. Cited in Prior F. Felix, "The Sisters of Our Lady of Mercy," *American Ecclesiastical Review* 20, no. 5 (March 1899), 457.

78. Ibid., 457–58; Ewens, *Role of the Nun,* 103, 138.

79. *Miscellany,* March 28, 1840.

80. The sisters had raised the same amount at another fair two years earlier. See *Miscellany,* April 17, 1841, and May 1, 1841.

81. Oscar Hugh Lipscomb, "The Administration of John Quinlan, Second Bishop of Mobile, 1859–1883," *ACHS* 78, nos. 1–4 (March–Dec. 1967), 11.

82. Portier to Eccleston, Mobile, September 18, 1845. Archives of the Archdiocese of Baltimore P.11.

83. England to Whitfield, Dublin, September 18, 1832, cited in Guilday, *Life and Time . . . England,* vol. 1, 522. England had previously tried to recruit Uruslines from Boston, during a visit in December 1825. Failure in this attempt led him to turn his sights toward Europe. See Guilday, *Life and Time . . . England,* vol. 2, 137.

84. "Report of Bishop England," 323. Europe supplied not only the personnel but the funding as well. England's $4,000 had been a gift from the Leopoldine Association of Vienna.

85. Cited in Guilday, *Life and Time . . . England,* vol. 2, 143.

86. *Miscellany,* May 23, 1835. In 1841, the Superioress of the Ursulines, Mother Borgia McCarthy, accompanied England on another trip to Ireland in order to recruit more members for the community. Despite these reinforcements, the community suffered after England's death in 1842, and in the late 1840s, they left Charleston. Guilday argues that Bishop Reynolds asked the Ursulines to leave because he did not see the utility of having two orders in the city and because he planned to take the Ursulines' house as his residence (*Life and Time . . . England,* vol. 2, 171–72). Other historians assign different causes to their departure. Madden argues that the Ursulines had never been as popular as the Sisters of Mercy and only remained in Charleston as long as they did out of deference to Bishop England (*Catholics in South Carolina,* 56). O'Connell disputes this view, arguing that their departure was widely unpopular, but absolves Reynolds of blame, attributing the decision to preoccupation with building a new cathedral (*Catholicity in the Carolinas,* 111). Bishop Lynch, whose sister was a member of the Ursulines, invited them back to the diocese in the late 1850s. They returned in 1858, establishing a school and convent in Columbia.

87. Kauffman, *Ministry and Meaning,* 15, 20–27. English colonists were much slower to establish hospitals. Except for a brief attempt in Virginia in the early 1600s, no true hospitals existed in the English colonies for over a century after first settlement. This was due in large part to the fact that the Church of England had abandoned the hospital tradition of the Middle Ages that the Catholic Church perpetuated. See Shryock, *Medicine and Society,* 21.

88. Ewens, *Role of the Nun,* 22–23.

89. Between 1829 and 1860, the Sisters of Charity alone opened eighteen hospitals, and other Catholic organizations opened roughly seven more. Ibid., 103. Laypeople were also important in establishing and sustaining Catholic hospitals. In Norfolk, for example, a wealthy Catholic named Ann Behan Plume Herron gave her house to the Daughters of Charity for use as a hospital before she herself died while nursing her sick slaves during an epidemic in 1855. Gerald P. Fogarty, *Commonwealth Catholicism: A History of the Catholic Church in Virginia* (Notre Dame: University of Notre Dame Press, 2001), 128–29.

90. Fox, *Life of . . . David* 133; Penelope Papangelis, "Hospitals," *Encyclopedia of Louisville* (Lexington: University Press of Kentucky, 2001). The Marine Hospital became the city hospital in 1836. St. Vincent's moved to a new location and was renamed the St. Joseph Infirmary in 1853.

91. *Miscellany,* August 23, 1838.

92. Guilday, *Life and Time . . . England,* vol. 2, 160, 165.

93. *Miscellany,* October 27, 1838; Madden, *Catholics in South Carolina,* 48. Overall, four hundred residents of Charleston died of the fever.

94. *Miscellany,* September 22, 1838.

95. Felix, "Sisters," 456; Madden, *Catholics in South Carolina,* 64.

96. Amos, *Cotton City,* 161.

97. Sister Mary Margaret to Blanc, City Hospital, Mobile, November 18, 1852, CANO VI-I-d, Archives of the University of Notre Dame (hereafter cited as UNDA). Such was not the case at all hospitals staffed by sisters. In New Orleans, a sister working at the Charity Hospital complained that she and her colleagues spent a great deal of time dealing with administrators and doctors who interfered with the sisters' work. Sister Regina Smith to unknown, Charity Hospital, New Orleans, April 24, 1852, CANO VI-I-c, UNDA.

98. Amos, *Cotton City,* 226; Kenny, *Catholic Culture in Alabama,* 210; Lipscomb, "Administration of Quinlan," 11; Quinlan to Purcell, Summerville, May 22, 1860, CACI 11–5-a, UNDA (quotation).

99. Kauffman, *Ministry and Meaning,* 3–4.

100. Ibid., 49.

101. Ibid., 36.

102. Cited in ibid., 39–40.

103. Ewens, *Role of the Nun,* 21–22.

104. Fox, *Life of . . . David,* 132–33.

105. Ewens, *Role of the Nun,* 104; Spalding, *Life, Times, . . . Flaget,* 336–38.

106. "Orphanages," *Encyclopedia of Louisville.*

107. *Miscellany,* September 14, 1825, October 13, 1827; Schauinger, *Cathedrals in the Wilderness,* 214.

108. Code, *Dictionary,* 290–91; Kenny, *Catholic Culture in Alabama,* 31; *Spring Hill College, Mobile, Ala., 1830–1905* (Mobile: Commercial Printing Company, 1906), 15, 94–95.

109. Vernice McKeever Spotswood, *Legacy of Love: History of St. Mary's Home, 1838–1988* (Mobile: s.n., 1988).

110. *Alabama Planter,* January 4, 1847.

111. Spotswood, *Legacy of Love,* 3–7.

112. *Alabama Planter,* December 21, 1846.

113. Spotswood, *Legacy of Love,* 3–7.

114. "Records of the Names, Ages, Parents, Nations, &c of Orphans Received in the Catholic Male Orphan Asylum of Mobile since the Opening of the Institution December 24th 1838," Archives of the Diocese of Mobile. In an 1845 letter, Portier referred to an order called the Brothers of Christian Instruction, who cared for thirty male orphans in their house in Mobile. It is unclear whether this was the male orphan asylum established in 1838 or an independent institution. See Portier to Eccleston, Mobile, September 18, 1845, Archives of the Archdiocese of Baltimore.

115. Lipscomb, "Administration of Quinlan," 11. The Sisters of Charity preferred to limit their ministrations to female orphans, although they often accepted orphaned boys as well when no separate facilities existed for their care. In 1845, however, the sisters began to prepare for affiliation with the French Daughters of Charity, which involved bringing their practices into conformity with the original rule of St. Vincent de Paul and ceasing to care for male orphans over five years of age. Ewens, *Role of the Nun,* 125–26.

116. *Miscellany,* June 22, 1825.

117. "England to the Cardinal Prefect of Propaganda, Rome, 1833," *ACHS* 8, no. 3 (1897), 323–24; Guilday, *Life and Time . . . England,* vol 2, 171.

118. *Miscellany,* April 21, 1824.

119. Schauinger, *Cathedrals in the Wilderness,* 214. Spalding identifies the priest as M. Hosten. Schauinger uses both spellings and also notes that some referred to him as Fr. Austin.

120. Ibid.; Fox, *Life of . . . David,* 93–94.

121. Flaget to Rev. Louis Regis Deluol, July 5, 1833, Filson.

122. *Miscellany,* September 15, 1838.

123. Spotswood, *Legacy of Love,* 8.

124. Schauinger, *Cathedrals in the Wilderness,* 4, 259, 274. Fenwick was born in 1768 to an old Catholic family of Maryland. He studied in Belgium, and when forced to flee by the French Revolution, he studied and taught in England for several years. He conducted missionary work in Maryland, Kentucky, and Ohio from 1804 until his election to the newly erected see of Cincinnati in 1821. In 1831, he established the *Catholic Telegraph,* with which the *Catholic Advocate* of Kentucky merged in 1850. Fenwick was the cousin of Benedict Joseph Fenwick, vicar general of Charleston from 1820 and second Bishop of Boston from 1825. See Code, *Dictionary,* 104–6.

125. Michael J. McNally, "A Peculiar Institution: A History of Catholic Parish Life in the Southeast (1850–1980)," in *The American Catholic Parish: A History from 1850 to the Present,* ed. Jay P. Dolan, vol. 1 (New York: Paulist Press, 1987), 165. Born in Ireland, Gartland studied at Mount St. Mary's College and Seminary, Emmitsburg, Maryland. He received consecration as the first Bishop of Savannah on November 10, 1850 (Code, *Dictionary,* 127).

126. Lipscomb, "Administration of Quinlan," 8.

127. "Letter of the Rt. Rev. John Carroll to the Congregation of Baltimore, August 26, 1800 Relative to Services of Priests During the Yellow Fever Epidemic," *American Catholic Historical Researches* 9, no. 4 (Oct. 1892), 150 (hereafter cited as *ACHR*).

128. Bernard U. Campbell, "Desultory Sketches of the Catholic Church in Maryland, No. VII: Memoir of the Rev. John Francis Moranvillé," *Religious Cabinet: A Monthly Periodical* 1, no. 12 (Dec. 1842), 622–36. News of Moranvillé's deeds spread as far as Kentucky, where David and Flaget praised his work among the sick and recommended him for the newly created Diocese of Charleston. See Schauinger, *Cathedrals in the Wilderness,* 192.

129. Fogarty, *Commonwealth Catholicism,* 127–28; McNally, "Peculiar Institution," 128. Quotation in Joseph Margi, "Catholicity in Virginia during the Episcopate of Bishop McGill (1850–1872)," *ACHR* 2 (April 1916–June 1917), 418–19.

130. Camillus Paul Maes, *The Life of the Reverend Charles Nerinckx* (Cincinnati: Robert Clarke, 1880).

131. Spalding, *Sketches of Early Catholic Missions,* 140–42.

132. Schauinger, *Cathedrals in the Wilderness,* 223.

133. *Miscellany,* December 1, 1824.

134. Kauffman, *Ministry and Meaning,* 60. During the same epidemic, four Sisters of St. Joseph, who had arrived from France in 1836, nursed the sick in a village just south of St. Louis. Three of the four died of the disease.

135. John Lyons, "Historical Sketches of Old St. Theresa's," Filson.

136. Spalding, *Life, Times, . . . Flaget,* 82.

137. "Badin to Carroll, Coxe's Creek, February 28, 1804," *ACHS* 23, no. 3 (Sept. 1912), 150.

138. Schauinger, *Cathedrals in the Wilderness,* 29–30.

139. Spalding, *Life, Times, . . . Flaget,* 141.

140. Ibid., 142. Schauinger, *Cathedrals in the Wilderness,* 117. Flaget's visitation to Illinois and Missouri alone lasted six months and required, in his estimate, nine hundred miles of travel (118).

141. Spalding, *Life, Times, . . . Flaget,* 104.

142. M. J. Spalding to Purcell, March 29, 1858, CACI 11-4-n, UNDA.

143. Schauinger, *Cathedrals in the Wilderness,* 170. This visitation to Michigan, which included a trip to Canada, lasted over a year and involved 2,100 miles of travel (175).

144. *Miscellany,* February 21, 1829.

145. Spalding, *Sketches of Early Catholic Missions,* 76–77. This incident became well-known to antebellum Catholics, particularly due to reports that a Protestant farmer had failed to help Salmon. This aspect of the incident will be discussed in greater detail.

146. "Correspondent of Society for the Propagation of the Faith, Philadelphia, October 10, 1854," *ACHR* 11, no. 4 (Oct. 1894), 186.

147. Cited in Kauffman, *Ministry and Meaning,* 33.

148. Clapp, *Autobiographical Sketches,* 71–72.

149. Cited in Guilday, *Life and Time . . . England,* vol. 2, 166.

150. Cited in Kauffman, *Ministry and Meaning,* 55.

151. Cited in Spalding, *Premier See,* 114.

152. Ewens, *Role of the Nun,* 139. Priests and nuns continued to use public transportation in New Orleans without charge until an American Civil Liberties Union lawsuit in 1988.

153. Clapp, *Autobiographical Sketches,* 210, 240.

154. Sarah Mytton Maury, *An Englishwoman in America* (London: Thomas Richardson and Son, 1848), 126.

155. George Lewis, *Impressions of America and of the American Churches* (Edinburgh: W. P. Kennedy, 1845), 249.

156. Oscar Penn Fitzgerald, *Fifty Years: Observations—Opinions—Experiences* (Nashville: Publishing House of the Methodist Episcopal Church, South, 1903), 171–72. Fitzgerald was born in Caswell County, North Carolina in 1829. He received his license to preach from the Methodist Church in 1853. Two years later, his church in North Carolina sent him as a missionary to California, where he labored for most of his life. He was elected bishop in 1890 and died in Tennessee in 1911.

157. Charles Henry Jones, *History of the Campaign for the Conquest of Canada in 1776, from the Death of Montgomery to the Retreat of the British Army under Sir Guy Carleton* (Philadelphia: Porter and Coates, 1882), 78.

158. Ewens, *Role of the Nun,* 44.

159. Reprinted in the *Miscellany,* January 12, 1828.

160. *Miscellany,* January 26, 1828.

161. Ewens, *Role of the Nun,* 137.

162. Among these was an Irishman named Dr. Hart. Hart was probably the first physician in the territory of Kentucky, settling near Harrod's Station with one of the first bands of Catholic immigrants from Maryland in 1775 (John B. Boles, *Religion in Antebellum Kentucky* [Lexington: University Press of Kentucky, 1976], 52; Schauinger, *Cathedrals in the Wilderness,* 10).

163. Fitzgerald, *Fifty Years,* 169.

164. Jones, *Memorial History of Augusta,* 273–75. The archives of the University of Georgia, the Augusta Historical Society, and the Medical College of Georgia all contain information on Dugas but nothing regarding his religious affiliation, if any. Given his background, it is safe to assume that he was at least nominally Catholic. In addition, the *Miscellany* of May 23, 1835, mentions that he played an important role in building a Catholic church in Augusta.

165. Bullit family papers, Diana Gwathmey Bullit miscellaneous papers, Filson.

166. "Clancy to Dr. Cullen, Charleston, November 23, 1836," *ACHS* 8, no. 3 (Sept. 1897), 301.

167. *Miscellany,* November 24, 1827.

168. Ibid., September 15, 1838.

169. Spalding, *Sketches of Early Catholic Missions,* 156.

170. *Miscellany,* September 22, 1824.

171. Such charges appeared in William Hogan's *Popery! As It Was and Is* (1853) and Samuel B. Smith's *Renunciation of Popery* (1833) and *The Downfall of Babylon* (1834). See Ewens, *Role of the Nun,* 189.

172. *Miscellany,* May 24, 1828.

173. Lewis, *Impressions of America,* 408.

174. Clapp, *Autobiographical Sketches,* 241.

175. Frederick Law Olmsted, *A Journey in the Seaboard Slave States* (New York: Dix & Edwards, 1856), 582.

176. Maury, *Englishwoman in America,* 79.

177. *Miscellany,* August 31, 1825.

178. Cited in Kauffman, *Ministry and Meaning,* 57.

179. Cited in ibid., 28.

180. Curran, *American Jesuit Spirituality,* 64–65.

181. Flaget to unknown, Bordeaux, May 28, 1810, Filson.

182. *Miscellany,* October 3, 1829.

183. "Clancy to Cullen, Charleston, November 23, 1826," *ACHS* 8, no. 3 (Sept. 1897), 301.

184. Ewens, *Role of the Nun,* 139–40.

185. *Miscellany,* December 16, 1826.

186. Charles E. Rosenberg, *The Cholera Years: the United States in 1832, 1849, and 1866* (Chicago: University of Chicago Press, 1962), 4–5, 40.

187. Shryock, *Medicine and Society,* 162. These findings reinforced the southern ideology of agrarianism, which viewed the growth of urbanism and industry as a threat to the region's traditional agricultural society. See Warner, "Public Health," 247.

188. Kauffman, *Ministry and Meaning,* 61.

189. Warner, "Public Health," 235. Bishop John McGill of Richmond took a different view. He argued in a public sermon that the epidemics were God's punishment for "the sin of Know-Nothingism," sparking a fierce exchange with the editors of several Richmond papers. Fogarty, *Commonwealth Catholicism,* 125–26.

190. Broadside "To the Freemen of the Eighth Congressional District," Frankfort, July 28, 1849, Filson.

191. Ray Billington, *The Protestant Crusade: 1800–1860* (New York: MacMillan, 1938), 411.

192. Ibid., 323–24; Fraser, *Charleston,* 235.

193. *Miscellany,* September 1, 1838.

194. Ibid. For the importance of immigrant labor to southern cities, see Amos, *Cotton City,* 81, 211; Ira Berlin and Herbert Gutman, "Natives and Immigrants, Free Men and Slaves: Urban Workingmen in the Antebellum American South," *American Historical Review* 88, no. 5 (Dec. 1983), 1175–2000.

195. Guilday, *Life and Time . . . England,* vol. 2, 163, 165. Catholics cared for hardworking immigrants in other cities as well. In Savannah, the Hibernian Society cared for Irish injured while working on canals near the city (*Miscellany,* January 6, 1827).

196. O'Connell, *Catholicity in the Carolinas,* 112.

197. Fitzgerald, *Judge Longstreet,* 68–69.

Chapter 3

1. *New Orleans Bee,* December 28, 1831, in Michael Kenny, *Catholic Culture in Alabama: Centenary Story of Spring Hill College, 1830–1930* (New York: The America Press, 1931), 79–80.

2. Ellwood P. Cubberly, *Public Education in the United States: A Study and Interpretation of American Educational History* (Boston: Houghton Mifflin, 1947), 94–104. Cubberly provides an excellent state-by-state summary of constitutions and laws regarding education.

3. For the act's specific provisions see John Furman Thomason, *Foundations of the Public Schools of South Carolina* (Columbia: The State Company, 1925), 127–31. Charleston continued to lead the way in South Carolina education. By the outbreak of the Civil War, the city had four public schools educating over four thousand students. Most of this growth, however, had only come about in the 1850s (161–65).

4. Meriwether Colyer, *History of Higher Education in South Carolina* (Washington: Government Printing Office, 1889), 109–12.

5. Thomason, *Foundations of the Public Schools,* 134–37, 142.

6. Cited in Colyer, *History of Higher Education,* 114.

7. Cubberly, *Public Education,* 102–3, 414–15.

8. Harriet E. Amos, *Cotton City: Urban Development in Antebellum Mobile* (Tuscaloosa: The University of Alabama Press, 1985), 179–91.

9. Seventh Census of the United States (1850).

10. Cited in Robert F. Pace, *Halls of Honor: College Men in the Old South* (Baton Rouge: Louisiana State University Press, 2004), 14.

11. Samuel J. Mills and Daniel Smith, *Report of a Missionary Tour through That Part of the United States Which Lies West of the Allegany Mountains* (Andover, MA: Flagg and Gould, 1815), 20.

12. Edgar Wallace Knight, who laid the foundations for southern educational history in dozens of books and articles between 1913 and 1953, took as his constant theme the view that southerners were making great strides toward establishing public schools before the Civil War interrupted. In this view, he stood opposed to Ellwood Cubberly and others, who argued that Reconstruction pulled a backward South into modernity in terms of education. In the half century since his death, Knight has come under criticism by historians, particularly for his use of sources and attitudes toward blacks. Knight's most enduring contribution to the study of southern educational history was his editing of documents, on which many later historians have based their works. See *A Documentary History of Education in the South before 1860,* 5 vols. (Chapel Hill: University of North Carolina Press, 1949–1953). See also *Public Education in the South* (Boston: Ginn and Company, 1922). For a critical appraisal of Knight's work see Clinton B. Allison, "The Appalling World of Edgar Wallace Knight," *History of Education in the South,* a special topic edition of the *Journal of Interdisciplinary Thought* 18, no. 3 (Fall 1983), 7–14.

13. Colyer, *History of Higher Education,* 51.

14. Thomason, *Foundations of the Public Schools,* 89. Churches, societies, and com-

munities all sponsored academies, which could be either single-sex or coeducational. Academies generally offered a broader range of courses than schools of the colonial period and, in some cases, survived to become high schools in later state systems (78).

15. John R. Thelin, *A History of American Higher Education* (Baltimore: The Johns Hopkins University Press, 2004), 46.

16. Pace, *Halls of Honor,* 19–20.

17. Seventh Census of the United States (1850). South Carolina's libraries were by far the largest, with an average of over four thousand volumes. Kentucky's averaged under one thousand and Alabama's, less than four hundred.

18. George Lewis, *Impressions of America and of the American Churches* (Edinburgh: W. P. Kennedy, 1845), 110; Thomason, *Foundations of the Public Schools,* 22.

19. Cited in Colyer, *History of Higher Education,* 115–16.

20. *Charleston Courier,* December 17, 1839.

21. Thelin, *History of American Higher Education,* 47, 52, 68; Pace, *Halls of Honor,* 1, 3–4. Denominational colleges tended to be less exclusive and expensive than state schools but were still beyond the means of most southerners.

22. *United States Catholic Miscellany* (Charleston), September 19, 1829.

23. Christie Anne Farnham, *The Education of the Southern Belle: Higher Education and Student Socialization in the Antebellum South* (New York: New York University Press, 1994), 2, 7, 18.

24. Cited in ibid., 13.

25. Ibid., 3, 20, 28.

26. Columba Fox, *The Life of the Right Reverend John Baptist Mary David* (New York: United States Catholic Historical Society, 1925), 93; J. Herman Schauinger, *Cathedrals in the Wilderness* (Milwaukee: Bruce Publishing Company, 1952), 182.

27. V. F. O'Daniel, "Bishop Flaget's Report of the Diocese of Bardstown to Pius VII, April 10, 1815," *Catholic Historical Review* 1 (April 1915–Jan. 1916), 315 (hereafter cited as *CHR*).

28. Cited in Mary Ewens, *The Role of the Nun in Nineteenth Century America* (New York: Arno Press, 1978), 135.

29. Ewens, *Role of the Nun,* 47; Thomas W. Spalding, *The Premier See: A History of the Archdiocese of Baltimore, 1789–1989* (Baltimore: The Johns Hopkins Press, 1989), 57; Vernice McKeever Spotswood, *Legacy of Love: History of St. Mary's Home, 1838–1988* (Mobile: s.n., 1988), 8.

30. Ewens, *Role of the Nun,* 48, 65. Not all orders followed this pattern. The Sisters of Loretto in Kentucky, for example, educated rich and poor students together.

31. *Miscellany,* December 13, 1834.

32. Ibid., January 28, 1837.

33. Fox, *Life of . . . David,* 50; Schauinger, *Cathedrals in the Wilderness,* 71.

34. Nor did all opposition to the schools come from non-Catholics. In 1823, Flaget dispatched a group of nuns to a disgruntled community of Catholics in central Kentucky, praising their fortitude, "for these poor children know that scarcely any one in that county is pleased to see them come. The road from Nazareth to St. Pius Church will be for them a real Via Crucis." Fox, *Life of . . . David,* 106.

35. *Register of Debates in Congress Comprising the Leading Debates and Incidents of the First Session of the Twenty-Second Congress,* vol. 8 (Washington: Gales and Seaton, 1833), 2201–03.

36. Richard C. Madden, *Catholics in South Carolina: A Record* (New York: University Press of America, 1985), 25, 32.

37. *Miscellany,* November 10, 1827.

38. John Peyre Thomas, *The History of the South Carolina Military Academy* (Charleston: Walker, Evans, & Cogswell, 1893), 69–72.

39. John England, *Works of the Right Rev. John England, First Bishop of Charleston,* ed. Ignatius Aloysius Reynolds, vol. 1 (Baltimore: John Murphy & Co., 1849), 52.

40. Fox, *Life of . . . David,* 39; Sister Mary Ramona Mattingly, *The Catholic Church on the Kentucky Frontier (1785–1812),* The Catholic University of America Studies in American Church History 25 (Washington: Catholic University Press, 1936), 143–45; Joseph T. Merkt, "Catholic Schools," *Encyclopedia of Louisville* (Lexington: University Press of Kentucky, 2001). The Coomes family later moved to Bardstown, where Jane continued to teach.

41. Schauinger, *Cathedrals in the Wilderness,* 127. At the extreme northern end of the Diocese of Bardstown, Fr. Gabriel Richard not only held several professorial chairs at the University of Michigan, but also served as the school's first vice president. The president at the time was a Protestant minister (226).

42. Ewens, *Role of the Nun,* 34.

43. Ibid., 35–40.

44. Ibid., 22–23, 42–43.

45. The Sulpicians are not technically an order, but rather a community of diocesan priests. They take their name from the church of St. Sulpice in Paris, where their founder, Jean Jacques Olier, first convoked the community.

46. Schauinger, *Cathedrals in the Wilderness,* 5–7.

47. Trent allowed exceptions to this rule, permitting poor dioceses to combine their resources to support a single seminary. See H. J. Schroeder, trans., *Canons and Decrees of the Council of Trent* (Rockford, IL: Tan Books, 1978), 175–79.

48. Chabrat to Rt. Rev. Joseph Rosati, Bishop of St. Louis, Bardstown, February 10, 1837, Filson Mss. BA/B245/2.

49. Schauinger, *Cathedrals in the Wilderness,* 212. Benedict Joseph Webb, *Centenary of Catholicity in Kentucky* (Louisville: C. A. Rogers, 1884), 344–45.

50. Flaget to Maréchal, Bardstown, January 7, 1820, Filson Historical Society, Louisville, Mss. Ba/B245/5 (hereafter cited as Filson).

51. "An Imposter 'Bishop' in Illinois and Kentucky in 1827," *American Catholic Historical Researches* 9, no. 2 (April 1892), 81–83 (hereafter cited as *ACHR*).

52. "Badin to Carroll, Priestland, Harden's Creek, Washington County, April 28, 1796," *Records of the American Catholic Historical Society of Philadelphia* 19, no. 3 (Sept. 1908), 265 (hereafter cited as *ACHS*).

53. John R. Dichtl, *Frontiers of Faith: Bringing Catholicism to the West in the Early Republic* (Lexington: University Press of Kentucky, 2008), 73–74. Dichtl devotes much of the third chapter of his work to chronicling the misdeeds of clergy and laypeople.

54. Fogarty, *Commonwealth Catholicism,* 133–34.

55. "Report of Bishop England to the Cardinal Prefect of Propaganda (Rome, 1833)," *ACHS* 8, no. 3 (Sept. 1897), 321; "England to Gaston, Charleston, February 25, 1830," *ACHS* 19, no. 2 (June 1908), 145; "England to Petit De Villers, Charleston, May 27, 1829," *ACHS* 19, no. 1 (March 1908), 119.

56. John Carroll to Charles Plowden, Maryland, March 1, 1788, in Thomas O'Brien Hanley, ed., *The John Carroll Papers,* vol. 1, *1755–1791* (Notre Dame: University of Notre Dame Press, 1976), 275.

57. Dolan, *American Catholic Experience,* 249.

58. Fox, *Life of . . . David,* 10, 19–20; Schauinger, *Cathedrals in the Wilderness,* 66.

59. Flaget to Henry Clay, Bardstown, April 19, 1827, Filson.

60. Schauinger, *Cathedrals in the Wilderness,* 3, 22, 42–44; Spalding, *Life, Times, . . . Flaget,* 82.

61. The Howards had come from Maryland in 1787. Thomas Howard, in whose patron saint's honor the seminary was named, left half the property outright, with the other half to pass to the church after his wife's death. Mrs. Howard, however, offered immediate use of the entire property and retired to a small house that the seminarians built for her. Flaget to Carroll, Mrs. Howard's plantation, August 22, 1811, Archives of the Archdiocese of Baltimore (hereafter cited as BCA).

62. Fox, *Life of . . . David,* 56–57; Schauinger, *Cathedrals in the Wilderness,* 163; Webb, *Centenary of Catholicity,* 272–73.

63. Schauinger, *Cathedrals in the Wilderness,* 74–75. The schedule varied somewhat depending on the season. For a similar account of the schedule, based on David's letters to the superior-general of the Sulpicians in Paris, in which he stresses the Kentucky school's conformity to the standards of St. Sulpice, see Fox, *Life of . . . David,* 52–53.

64. Schauinger, *Cathedrals in the Wilderness,* 125.

65. John B. Boles, *Religion in Antebellum Kentucky* (Lexington: University Press of Kentucky, 1976), 67; Schauinger, *Cathedrals in the Wilderness,* 105, 140, 176, 180.

66. Flaget to the Sacred Congregation for the Propagation of the Faith, 1824, cited in Fox, *Life of . . . David,* 54.

67. For a list of forty-seven men ordained during Fr. David's administration, see Webb, *Centenary of Catholicity,* 348.

68. Fox, *Life of . . . David,* 42. The Trappists arrived in Kentucky in the fall of 1805 and left in the spring of 1809.

69. Spalding, *Life, Times, . . . Flaget,* 345.

70. Boles, *Religion in Antebellum Kentucky,* 63; Mattingly, *Catholic Church on the Kentucky Frontier,* 83–84. The college seems to have closed by the early 1820s. Spalding notes that the college opened around 1809 and "continued to flourish for about ten years," during which time it educated both Catholics and Protestants (*Sketches of the Early Catholic Missions,* 160).

71. Schauinger, *Cathedrals in the Wilderness,* 219.

72. Ibid., 181–83; Fox, *Life of . . . David,* 92.

73. Flaget first appealed for Jesuits in 1815, just one year after Pope Pius VII reinstated the order. The following year, Fr. Nerinckx succeeded in securing eight Bel-

gian Jesuits for Georgetown University. In 1820, he recruited another band that passed through Kentucky before settling in Missouri in 1823. These Jesuits soon became involved in education and established St. Louis University. Boles, *Religion in Antebellum Kentucky,* 69. Once again, the church in America benefited from events in Europe. The Jesuits' expulsion from France in 1830 freed personnel for the American mission. One of the Jesuits to settle in Kentucky, Peter Chazelle, was a native of France. The other, Nicholas Petit, was born in Haiti. After his father's death during the island's revolution, he and his family joined the flood of refugees to America. They settled in Baltimore, where his mother conducted a school. Although Petit moved to France at age twelve, his early years in America served him well upon his return. Whereas Chazelle had to study English at St. Mary's, Flaget immediately appointed Petit to the cathedral, where he worked alongside another priest for several months. Schauinger, *Cathedrals in the Wilderness,* 265.

74. Boles, *Religion in Antebellum Kentucky,* 70; Schauinger, *Cathedrals in the Wilderness,* 266, 298–99. Kenny gives the year of the Jesuits' takeover of St. Mary's as 1833 (126).

75. Boles, *Religion in Antebellum Kentucky,* 71–72.

76. Schauinger, *Cathedrals in the Wilderness,* 181.

77. David to Bruté, September 24, 1825, MSGB, Archives of the University of Notre Dame (hereafter cited as UNDA).

78. Ibid.; David to Fenwick, Bardstown, November 19, 1825, ACI 11–4-d, UNDA. The number of boarders continued to increase, reaching 107 by 1827, although the number of day students declined somewhat. See Flaget to Maréchal, June 1827, BCA 16 V20. A decade later, enrollment had dropped somewhat with between seventy and eighty boarders and forty day students. David to Deloul, Bardstown, December 13, 1837. Cited in Fox, *Life of . . . David,* 212.

79. Thelin, *History of American Higher Education,* 65.

80. Bishop Chabrat to Rt. Rev. Joseph Rosati, Bardstown, May 28, 1839, Filson; Schauinger, *Cathedrals in the Wilderness,* 299. According to Schauinger, the debt still stood at $23,000 a decade later (309). Bishop Rosati painted a very different picture of the college in a letter written almost two years after the fire: "The College is in a flourishing condition. They have . . . more than a hundred and fifty scholars; the college has no debts, is well furnished, has a number sufficient of servants, and every advantage that can be wished for." He seems to have received his information during a visit to Kentucky before the fire, however, and so may not have been aware of the new conditions. Rosati to Timon, St. Louis, November 27, 1839, CVIN IV-3-L-5, UNDA. Chabrat's letter to Rosati of May, 1839, referred to a fire but not to debts. Chabrat to Rosati, May 28, 1839, Filson.

81. Schauinger, *Cathedrals in the Wilderness,* 299, 308. Flaget had considered transferring the college to the Jesuits almost two decades earlier. At that time, he decided against it, but by 1848, the circumstances were more conducive (265).

82. Fox, *Life of . . . David,* 169.

83. Emphasizing education no doubt seemed natural, given that several women, including Rhodes, Stuart, and one of the first postulants, Nellie Morgan, taught before joining the order. See Schauinger, *Cathedrals in the Wilderness,* 79.

84. Schauinger, *Cathedrals in the Wilderness,* 71, 77–79, 138. In early 1849, a colony of French Trappists purchased a large farm at Gethsemane from the Sisters of Loretto, where they established their famous abbey.

85. Ibid., 166, 222–23; *Miscellany,* December 8, 1824, and September 14, 1825.

86. David mentioned these students in a letter dated July 12, 1813. This indicates that Schauinger is mistaken when he notes that classes began in September 1814. See David to Bruté, St. Thomas's Seminary, July 12, 1813, CRCL 11-3-N, UNDA; Schauinger, *Cathedrals in the Wilderness,* 105.

87. Fox, *Life of . . . David,* 71, 75, 86, 99; Schauinger, *Cathedrals in the Wilderness,* 81–82, 104–5; Spalding provides an overview of the order's establishment and growth in *Sketches of the Early Catholic Missions,* 229–41.

88. Flaget to Maréchal, Bardstown, August 10, 1820, Filson.

89. Schauinger, *Cathedrals in the Wilderness,* 165. To make more efficient use of their resources, the sisters consolidated their school system in the early 1830s, closing a number of struggling institutions. See Fox, *Life of . . . David,* 131.

90. David to Bruté, September 13, 1816, CRCL 11–3-N, UNDA.

91. Fox, *Life of . . . David,* 100–3; Schauinger, *Cathedrals in the Wilderness,* 185. The roots of the confusion regarding the land lay in a long dispute over property between Flaget and Badin.

92. David to Bruté, February 4, 1823; March 30, 1825; and June 5, 1826, MSGB, UNDA; David to Fenwick, Bardstown, November 19, 1825, ACI 11–4-d, UNDA.

93. David to Deloul, Bardstown, December 13, 1837, cited in Fox, *Life of . . . David,* 212.

94. Spalding, *Sketches of Early Catholic Missions,* 240–41.

95. Webb, *Centenary of Catholicity,* 341–42.

96. Mary Antonella Hardy, "Loretto, Bishop Flaget and Sister Eulalie Flaget," *ACHS* 36, no. 2 (June 1925), 192–201. Schauinger gives a slightly different account of this incident, depicting Eulalia (as he gives the spelling) as traveling to France with the intent of learning how to teach the deaf and dumb. He also notes that she left without the formal approval of the Sisters of Nazareth, who expelled her upon her return (302). The asylum did not remain open long, although advertisements for it appeared as late as 1843. See Anna Catherine Minogue, *Loretto: Annals of the Century* (New York: The American Press, 1912), 97.

97. Merkt, "Catholic Schools"; Schauinger, *Cathedrals in the Wilderness,* 309.

98. Schauinger, *Cathedrals in the Wilderness,* 87, 267.

99. Kenny, *Catholic Culture in Alabama,* 33.

100. Ibid. 35; Oscar Hugh Lipscomb, "The Administration of John Quinlan, Second Bishop of Mobile, 1859–1883," *ACHS* 78, nos. 1–4 (March–Dec. 1967), 8. Shortly after opening, the school already enrolled over 200 students (*Spring Hill College, Mobile, Ala., 1830–1905* [Mobile: Commercial Printing Company, 1906], 4).

101. Kenny, *Catholic Culture in Alabama,* 50. Kenny disagrees on this point with the authors of *Spring Hill College,* who claim that Portier initially only purchased thirty-five acres (8). The confusion may arise from two separate transactions.

102. Kenny, *Catholic Culture in Alabama,* 53–54, 60; *Spring Hill College,* 10, 12. Spring

Hill is the oldest existing college in Alabama, predating the opening of the University of Alabama by one year. In the Gulf states, only Centenary of Louisiana and Mississippi College are older. Among Catholic colleges, Spring Hill trails only Georgetown and Mount St. Mary's, Maryland.

103. Kenny, *Catholic Culture in Alabama,* 55.

104. Ibid., 76; *Spring Hill College,* 13–14. In 1869, a fire destroyed many of these earliest buildings.

105. Kenny, *Catholic Culture in Alabama,* 104, 110–11.

106. Portier to Eccleston, Mobile, September 18, 1845, BCA 25 P. 11.

107. Seventh Census of the United States (1850). The census did not identify Spring Hill by name but referred to a college in Mobile County that could only have been Spring Hill.

108. Amos, *Cotton City,* 184; Lipscomb, "Administration of Quinlan," 11; Spotswood, *Legacy of Love,* 4, 7, 8. Although most Catholic education took place in Mobile, Portier also helped establish schools for boys in Pensacola and St. Augustine. Austin Carroll, *A Catholic History of Alabama and the Floridas* (Freeport, NY: Books for Libraries Press, 1970), 205.

109. *Miscellany,* December 5, 1829.

110. Ibid., May 16, 1829.

111. Ibid., June 5, 1822.

112. Guilday, *Life and Time . . . England,* vol. 1, 485, 503. Unfortunately for England, few seem to have contributed to the general fund, leaving the seminary, and other projects, chronically short of funds. See Guilday, *Life and Time . . . England,* vol. 1, 511.

113. Ibid., 486; England to Maréchal, Charleston, June 26, 1823, BCA 16 J10. The first ordination of a seminarian took place in January, 1823. The seminary continued to produce candidates for the priesthood until it closed in 1851. Madden, *Catholics in South Carolina,* 35, 63.

114. "A Southern Teaching Order: The Sisters of Mercy of Charleston, S.C., A.D. 1829–1904; by a Member of the Order," *ACHS* 15, no. 3 (Sept. 1904), 249–58.

115. *Miscellany,* October 8, 1836.

116. Madden, *Catholics in South Carolina,* 65.

117. *Miscellany,* December 20, 1834.

118. "England to Gaston, Charleston, February 24, 1838," *ACHS* 19, no. 2 (1908), 169.

119. Guilday, *Life and Time . . . England,* vol. 2, 141–42, 170–71. For England's uncertainty regarding the standing of the Dames de la Retraite, see "England to O'Connor, Charleston, April 7, 1835," *ACHS* 8, no. 2 (June 1897), 210–11; "England to Cullen, Charleston, February 23, 1836," *ACHS* 8, no. 2 (June 1897), 232–33.

120. *Miscellany,* November 23, 1839.

121. "England to Cullen, Charleston, February 23, 1836," *ACHS* 8, no. 2 (June 1897), 223; "Report of Bishop England," 327.

122. *Miscellany,* May 11, 1825.

123. "Judge Gaston on Slavery," *ACHR* 8, no. 2 (April 1891), 71; Spalding to W. Prescott Smith, Louisville, December 23, 1853, Filson.

124. Schauinger, *Cathedrals in the Wilderness,* 79–80.

125. Fox, *Life of . . . David,* 101–3; Schauinger, *Cathedrals in the Wilderness,* 185.

126. Fox, *Life of . . . David,* 41, 96. Like many prominent Kentucky Catholics, the Gardiners had originally emigrated from Maryland. At least three women of the family joined the Sisters of Nazareth.

127. "England to Gaston, Charleston, February 25, 1830," *ACHS* 19, no. 2 (June 1908), 146. England repeatedly voiced this complaint, both in letters to colleagues and in public addresses.

128. Fox, *Life of . . . David,* 42.

129. Flaget to Rev. Louis Regis Deloul, January 26, 1831, Filson Mss. BA/B245/4.

130. Pace, *Halls of Honor,* 4–5, 6–7, 17. Pace defines southern honor in the following terms: "Being a man of honor in the South meant that one exhibited a persona that conformed to society's expectations. . . . In public, southern men had to exhibit behavior that held them to be dutiful to their responsibilities, respectful of their peers, and, most of all, honest in their public declarations. . . . Any public hint that a southern man was anything contrary to this definition had to be challenged rapidly and publicly in order to maintain the identity of a man of honor" (5). For the classic study on honor in the South, see Bertram Wyatt-Brown, *Southern Honor: Ethics and Behavior in the Old South* (New York: Oxford, 1982).

131. Flaget to Maréchal, Bardstown, August 10, 1820, Filson Mss. Ba/B245/5.

132. "Register of the Prefect of Classes and Studies 1847-48-49," Spring Hill College Archives.

133. Schauinger, *Cathedrals in the Wilderness,* 229. Things could have been much worse for Reynolds. Violence between students and faculty could be lethal. In 1840, at the University of Virginia, for instance, a masked student shot and killed a professor during an altercation. Pace, *Halls of Honor,* 91.

134. Mattingly, *Catholic Church on the Kentucky Frontier,* 128.

135. Varina Jefferson Davis, *Jefferson Davis: Ex-President of the Confederate States of America, a Memoir by His Wife,* vol. 1 (New York: Belford, 1890), 14.

136. Guilday, *Life and Time . . . England,* vol. 1, 509. Madden notes that the Lyon Society gave the diocese $1,000 annually after 1830 and the Leopold Foundation contributed even more. Madden, *Catholics in South Carolina,* 35.

137. Lipscomb, "Administration of Quinlan," 12; *Spring Hill College,* 5.

138. Spalding, *Life, Times, . . . Flaget,* 255.

139. Schauinger, *Cathedrals in the Wilderness,* 250.

140. *Miscellany,* August 15, 1829.

141. Samuel F. B. Morse, *Foreign Conspiracy Against the Liberties of the United States* (New York: Leavitt, Lord, & Co., 1835), 21–23.

142. Mattingly, *Catholic Church on the Kentucky Frontier,* 101.

143. Spalding, *Life, Times, . . . Flaget,* 303. Flaget declined the offer, citing a lack of manpower.

144. Annemond Dupuy to Bishop Joseph Rosati, August 11, 1835, cited in F. G. Holweck, "The Beginnings of the Church in Little Rock," *CHR* 6, no. 2 (July 1920), 161–62.

Holweck notes that Ashley probably offered the land at a favorable price, not for free. Rosati ultimately declined the offer, citing a lack of personnel. The Sisters of Loretto finally opened a school in Little Rock in 1841, three years after they opened one in Pine Bluff.

145. Spalding, *Sketches of Early Catholic Missions,* 239.

146. Kenny, *Catholic Culture in Alabama,* 50, 133. Kenny argues that this Protestant donated the twenty acres in addition to selling Portier several hundred acres based on an 1846 contract in which the diocese ceded twenty acres to the Jesuits but claimed that the rest of the land had been purchased with church funds and thus belonged to the diocese. Church officials later dropped this claim.

147. Dichtl, *Frontiers of Faith,* 96.

148. Robert Emmett Curran, *The Bicentennial History of Georgetown University,* vol. 1 (Washington, DC: Georgetown University Press, 1993), 407–14.

149. Lewis, *Impressions of America,* 253. Lewis calculated the Catholic schools' enrollment as 1,056, the common schools' as about 500, and the private teachers' as perhaps 600 (256).

150. James J. Pillar, *The Catholic Church in Mississippi, 1837–1865* (New Orleans: Hauser Press, 1964), 104.

151. Spalding, *Sketches of Early Catholic Missions,* 160; Fox, *Life of . . . David,* 130. Badin had worried that the high tuition at St. Thomas would prevent Catholics from attending and that the Dominicans' labor would almost exclusively benefit members of other denominations. "Badin to Carroll, near Bardstown, October 5, 1805," *CHR* 6 (April 1920–Jan. 1921), 70.

152. Nerinckx to Pietro, Loretto, October 2, 1818, in *Documents: Nerinckx—Kentucky—Loretto, 1804–1851 in Archives Propaganda Fide, Rome.* Edited by Augustin Wand and M. Lilliana Owens (Nerinx, KY: Loretto Literary and Benevolent Institution, 1972), 45.

153. Pillar, *Catholic Church in Mississippi,* 22.

154. Flaget to unknown, Bardstown, October 12, 1839, Filson Maa. BA/B245/7.

155. "Short History of St. Peter's Parish from 1824 to 1958," PHC, 95/01, UNDA.

156. "England to Gaston, Charleston, September 21, 1822," *ACHS* 18, no 4 (1907), 382. With perhaps a touch of hyperbole, O'Connell claimed that the school educated "professional men of all grades, even the clergy of the various denominations, generals of armies, statesmen, judges, senators, and governors of States" (70).

157. J. Richard Beste, *The Wabash: or Adventure of an English Gentleman's Family in the Interior of America,* vol. 1 (Freeport, NY: Books for Libraries Press, 1970), 222.

158. Lewis, *Impressions of America,* 232. Lewis claimed to have seen an advertisement stipulating that students bring silver forks for use at mealtimes.

159. Ewens, *Role of the Nun,* 40, 66.

160. Curran, *Bicentennial History,* 47; Kenny, *Catholic Culture in Alabama,* 33.

161. Ewens, *Role of the Nun,* 48. Catholics were not shy about publicizing European orders' reputations as educators. Upon the Ursulines' arrival in Charleston, the *Miscellany* proclaimed that their house in Ireland "has been for very many years known as one of the best regulated in Europe, and its pupils are found decorating the first circles

of polished society" (December 13, 1834). Given that many Catholic educators had European backgrounds, it is not surprising that they enjoyed particular renown for language instruction. For example, an endorsement of a candidate for a position in the legation to Chile included a note that he had studied at St. Mary's, Baltimore, where, "the Spanish Language is probably better taught than in any other seminary of learning in the United States." "V[irgil] Maxcy to John C. Calhoun, Tulip Hill [Maryland], June 28, 1823," *The Papers of John C. Calhoun,* vol. 8, ed. Edwin Hemphill (Columbia: University of South Carolina Press, 1975), 138.

162. Lewis, *Impressions of America,* 252.

163. Schauinger, *Cathedrals in the Wilderness,* 225, 299.

164. Flaget to unknown, Bardstown, October 12, 1839, Filson Mss. BA/B245/7.

165. Flaget to Maréchal, St. Thomas, February 23, 1818, Filson Mss. BA/B245/5.

166. Schauinger, *Cathedrals in the Wilderness,* 226.

167. "Report of Bishop England," 327.

168. *Miscellany,* March 16, 1825. Several months later in a letter to Archbishop Maréchal, Flaget added that the legislature had also assisted the college financially. Flaget to Maréchal, Bardstown, May 13, 1825, Filson Mss. Ba/B245/5.

169. Fox, *Life of . . . David,* 215, 217.

170. Schauinger, *Cathedrals in the Wilderness,* 298.

171. Kenny, *Catholic Culture in Alabama,* 96.

172. Thelin, *History of American Higher Education,* 43.

173. "Letter of Rev. John S. Bazin, Spring Hill, October 7, 1831," in Kenny, *Catholic Culture in Alabama,* 77.

174. Cited in Ewens, *Role of the Nun,* 43.

175. H. S. Spalding, "Pottinger's Creek Settlement—Kentucky, 1785," *Mid-America* 13, no. 4 (April 1931), 310.

176. *Alabama Planter,* December 21, 1846.

177. Kenny, *Catholic Culture in Alabama,* 53; *Spring Hill College,* 11.

178. *Miscellany,* September 14, 1825.

179. Fox, *Life of . . . David,* 217.

180. Ibid., 117; Schauinger, *Cathedrals in the Wilderness,* 231. The quality of Catholic education seems to have impressed Clay. Years later, in response to a friend's request for information on education for young women, he recommended the Catholic college at Bardstown and a Catholic girls' school in Lexington. "Clay to Joshua Folsom, Zanesfield, Ohio, December 20, 1839," *The Papers of Henry Clay,* vol. 9, ed. Robert Seager II (Lexington: University Press of Kentucky, 1988), 368.

181. Kenny, *Catholic Culture in Alabama,* 148–49.

182. Ibid., 134; Schauinger, *Cathedrals in the Wilderness,* 298.

183. Spalding, *Sketches of Early Catholic Missions,* 283–84.

184. Kenny, *Catholic Culture in Alabama,* 206.

185. "Report of Bishop England," 322–23.

186. Cited in *Miscellany,* October 13, 1827.

187. Judge S. S. Nicholas charge to the jury, May 2, 1846, Bullitt Family papers—Oxmoor collection, Filson.

188. Cooper to England, May 30, 1826, Archives of the Diocese of Charleston.

189. *Alabama Planter,* December 21, 1846.

190. Cited in *Miscellany,* October 13, 1827; Fox, *Life of . . . David,* 217.

191. Wand and Owens, *Documents,* 189. For similar assurances regarding Catholic schools in Kentucky, see *Miscellany,* October 13, 1827.

192. O'Connell, *Catholicity in the Carolinas,* 70.

193. *Miscellany,* December 13, 1834.

194. Kenny, *Catholic Culture in Alabama,* 142.

195. See, for example, *Miscellany,* June 19 and July 3, 1822.

196. *Miscellany,* January 12, 1825.

197. Kenny, *Catholic Culture in Alabama,* 99.

198. "Spring Hill College Charter," Spring Hill College Archives.

199. Kenny, *Catholic Culture in Alabama,* 72.

200. "Letter of Rev. John S. Bazin, Spring Hill, October 7, 1831," in Kenny, *Catholic Culture in Alabama,* 77. For additional praise of Protestant students, see "Register of the Prefect of Classes and Studies 1847–1873," Spring Hill College Archives.

201. Davis, *Jefferson Davis,* 13–14.

202. *Miscellany,* July 31, 1822.

203. Ibid., August 14, 1822.

204. Ewens, *Role of the Nun,* 157; Josephine M. Bunkley, *Testimony of an Escaped Novice* (New York: Harper, 1855). Such tales appeared well after the antebellum period. In the early 1900s, two women from Kentucky claimed to have been imprisoned in a convent in Louisville. Their tale followed the pattern of earlier accounts in describing exploitation, beatings, and complete isolation from their families. C. K. Richardson and Lillie E. Burch, *A Kentucky Hell* (Milan, IL: Rail Splitter Press, 1904).

205. David Brion Davis, "Some Themes of Counter-Subversion: An Analysis of Anti-Masonic, Anti-Catholic, and Anti-Mormon Literature," *Mississippi Valley Historical Review* 47, no. 2 (Sept. 1960), 205, 209, 214, 219; Nancy Lusignan Schultz, *Veil of Fear: Nineteenth-Century Convent Tales by Rebecca Reed and Maria Monk* (West Lafayette, IN: Perdue University Press, 1999), xxiv.

206. Jenny Franchot, *Roads to Rome: The Antebellum Protestant Encounter with Catholicism* (Berkeley: University of California Press, 1994), 120. For overviews of anxiety about gender roles and the construction of the cult of domesticity see: Ann Douglas, *The Feminization of American Culture* (New York: Knopf, 1977); Barbara Welter, "The Cult of True Womanhood: 1820–1860," *American Quarterly* 18, no. 2 (Summer 1966), 151–74. Welter described the cult of domesticity as the idea that women were to be guardians of the purity and sacredness of the home, their proper sphere, while remaining submissive to their husbands and freeing them to engage in the rough-and-tumble world of nineteenth-century America.

207. Billington, *Protestant Crusade,* 99.

208. Ibid., 68–69.

209. Ewens, *Role of the Nun,* 86. Ewens notes that twenty-eight of these foundations were offshoots of European institutions.

210. Guilday, *Life and Time . . . England,* vol. 2, 143.

211. Ewens, *Role of the Nun,* 152, 153.

212. Ibid.; Madden, *Catholics in South Carolina,* 74.

213. Ewens, *Role of the Nun,* 74. Schauinger, *Cathedrals in the Wilderness,* 127–28. The timing of the protests against Nerinckx and the sisters reveals a great deal about Americans' fears. No one protested when older women joined the order, but when socially useful women of marriageable age began to join, the alarm spread. The fact that the girls had come into contact with the sisters through Catholic schools confirmed the belief that the schools' purpose was to steal away daughters and future spouses.

214. Schauinger, *Cathedrals in the Wilderness,* 165.

215. Fox, *Life of . . . David,* 180–81; Schauinger, *Cathedrals in the Wilderness,* 78, 302.

216. Ignatius Loyola Robertson, *Sketches of Public Characters Drawn from the Living and the Dead* (s.l.: Knapp, 1830), cited in *ACHR* 9, no. 3 (July 1894), 128.

217. David to Carroll, St. Thomas's Seminary, September 17, 1814, BCA 8A F1.

218. Cited in Ewens, *Role of the Nun,* 112.

219. Ewens, *Role of the Nun,* 32.

220. Lewis, *Impressions of America,* 251.

221. Schauinger, *Cathedrals in the Wilderness,* 238. The academy, like most Catholic schools, did require Protestant students to submit to its general regulations, including attendance at daily prayers and services on Sundays and holy days.

222. Deposition of Frances Gardiner (Mother Frances), Principal of Nazareth, December 29, 1845, Bullitt Family papers—Oxmoor collection, Filson; Flaget and David, "An Abbreviated History of the Sisters of Charity of Nazareth, Kentucky, United States of America," in Wand and Owens, *Documents,* 55–56.

223. *Miscellany,* October 10, 1829.

224. Guilday, *Life and Time . . . England,* vol. 2, 141; *Miscellany,* December 13, 1834.

225. Flaget to Rev. Louis Regis Deluol, July 5, 1833, Filson Mss. BA/B245/4; Nerinckx and Flaget to Cardinal Michele de Pietro, Prefect of the Congregation for the Propagation of the Faith, Bardstown, 1813, in Wand and Owens, *Documents,* 33. Nerinckx and Flaget let slip that conversions may not have been an unintended side effect of the school, arguing that "it was founded to easily and appropriately nourish our sacred religion among Catholics *and to scatter and sow it among non-Catholics*" [italics mine].

226. Fox, *Life of . . . David,* 153–54.

227. Curran, *Bicentennial History,* 407–14.

228. Fox, *Life of . . . David,* 204n8.

229. "Register of the Prefect of Classes and Studies 1847–1873," Spring Hill College Archives. These conversions include cases listed as such; cases of non-Catholic students receiving baptism; and the case of one Protestant alumnus who called for a priest, confessed, and received extreme unction on his deathbed.

230. "Register of the Prefect of Classes and Studies 1850–1873," Spring Hill College Archives.

231. Flaget to unknown, Bardstown, October 12, 1839, Filson Maa. BA/B245/7.

232. Cited in Fox, *Life of . . . David,* 182.

233. Ibid.

234. "Constitutions of the Associates of Mary at the Foot of the Cross: Part I, Chapter 1," in Wand and Owens, *Documents.*

235. Nerinckx and Flaget to Cardinal Michele de Pietro, Prefect of the Congregation for the Propagation of the Faith, Bardstown, 1813, in ibid., 33. "Letter of Rev. John S. Bazin, Spring Hill, October 7, 1831," in Kenny, *Catholic Culture in Alabama,* 77.

236. "Register of the Prefect of Classes and Studies Dec. 1849–May 1854," Spring Hill College Archives.

237. "Eccleston to the Committee of the Propagation of the Faith, Paris, Baltimore, January 31, 1838," *ACHR* 9, no. 3 (July 1892), 141. Eccleston knew firsthand the influence one's teachers and classmates could have. Raised an Episcopalian, he converted while a student at St. Mary's College in Maryland. When he was made Archbishop of Baltimore in 1834, he was the first convert in the American hierarchy.

238. Spalding, *Life, Times, . . . Flaget,* 300.

239. Flaget and David, "Abbreviated History of the Sisters of Charity of Nazareth," 55.

240. "Notices of the Papal Church in the United States," *Quarterly Register of the American Education Society* 3, no. 2 (Nov. 1830), 98.

241. "Report of Bishop England," 323.

242. "England to Gaston, Charleston, December 18, 1824," *ACHS* 19, no. 1 (March 1908), 102. In an earlier letter, England had noted that Presbyterians in particular had begun attacking the school: "England to Gaston, September 21, 1822," *ACHS* 18, no. 4 (Dec. 1907), 382. This incident clearly galled England, as evidenced by his repeated references to it in later years. See "England to Petit de Villers, Charleston, May 27, 1829," *ACHS* 19, no. 1 (March 1908), 119; "Report of Bishop England," 322.

243. "England to Gaston, Charleston, February 25, 1830," *ACHS* 19, no. 2 (June 1908),.145, 147. Five years later, the situation had not improved. "We manage to keep our opponents in check. But here they treat us worse than you can imagine. . . . Education is in their hands, they will not give us a scholar, and then prejudices are kept up and the means for supporting our institutions are kept from us," complained England. "England to Rosati, Charleston, March 3, 1835," *Illinois Catholic Historical Review* 9, no. 3 (Jan. 1927) 368. England had also hoped to use profits from the *Miscellany* to fund priests' educations, but conceded that if this plan became public, "I would have not only our great enemy but all his namesakes in the printers' offices at open war with me." The fact that the *Miscellany* chronically lost money rendered this problem moot. "England to Gaston, Charleston, January 9, 1823," *ACHS* 18, no. 4 (Dec. 1907), 384.

244. Schauinger, *Cathedrals in the Wilderness,* 18; Carroll, *Catholic History,* 150.

245. "Report of Bishop England," 323–24.

246. Janet Duitsman Cornelius, "*When I Can Read My Title Clear*": *Literacy, Slavery, and Religion in the Antebellum South* (Columbia: University of South Carolina Press, 1991), 43–44.

247. Lyman Beecher, *A Plea for the West,* 2nd ed. (Cincinnati, Truman & Smith, 1835), 160.

248. Ibid., 90–91.

249. Ibid., 182–83.

250. Ibid., 143.

251. Beecher referred to the riot in his *Plea for the West,* noting that it was regarded "with regret and abhorrence by Protestants and patriots throughout the land" (65). It is doubtful whether the Ursulines and their students, who received no compensation from Beecher or anyone else, took much comfort in his words.

252. "Notices of the Papal Church in the United States," *Quarterly Register of the American Education Society* 3, no. 2 (Nov. 1830), 100. Emphasis in the original.

253. Lewis, *Impressions of America,* 205.

254. "Circular to American Protestants," Big Spring, Meade County, KY, J. W. Kasey, Secretary, ca. 1853, Filson.

255. Madden, *Catholics in South Carolina,* 71.

256. Cited in John R. Bodo, *The Protestant Clergy and Public Issues* (Princeton: Princeton University Press, 1954), 66.

257. Beecher, *Plea for the West,* 188.

258. Schauinger, *Cathedrals in the Wilderness,* 298.

259. *Miscellany,* August 3, 1839.

260. Kenny, *Catholic Culture in Alabama,* 162–65.

261. *Miscellany,* September 26, 1829, reprinted from the *Columbian Gazette,* September 17, 1829. In fact, during much of the antebellum period, many Georgetown faculty members were foreign-born.

262. Kenny, *Catholic Culture in Alabama,* 60, 134, 163.

263. "England to Gaston, Charleston, December 2, 1823," *ACHS* 19, no. 1 (March 1908), 100.

264. Cited in Thomas F. Hopkins, *St. Mary's Church, Charleston, S.C.: The First Catholic Church in the Original Diocese of Charleston: An Historic Sketch of the Church from Its Beginning to the Present Time* (Charleston: Walker, Evans, & Cogswell, 1898), 13.

265. "England to Dr. M. O'Connor, Paris, September 7, 1834," *ACHS* 8, no. 2 (June 1897), 201.

266. Hugh Nolan, ed., *Pastoral Letters of the American Hierarchy, 1792–1970* (Huntington, IN: Our Sunday Visitor, 1971), 57.

267. *Miscellany,* December 5, 1829.

268. Ibid., November 18, 1826.

269. Fox, *Life of . . . David,* 118.

270. Guilday, *Life and Time . . . England,* vol. 1, 476.

271. *Miscellany,* November 17, 1824.

272. Kenny, *Catholic Culture in Alabama,* 32; Fox, *Life of . . . David,* 20.

273. Kenny, *Catholic Culture in Alabama,* 86; Schauinger, *Cathedrals in the Wilderness,* 149.

274. Fox, *Life of . . . David,* 161–62.

275. *Miscellany,* November 18, 1826.

276. Fox, *Life of . . . David,* 217–19.

277. William Henry Sparks, *The Memories of Fifty Years,* 3rd ed. (Philadelphia: Claxton, Remsen & Haffelfinger, 1872), 99.

Chapter 4

1. Cited in Clyde F. Crews, *Presence and Possibility: Louisville Catholicism and its Cathedral* (s.1.: s.n., 1973), 21.

2. Jon Butler, *Awash in a Sea of Faith: Christianizing the American People* (Cambridge, MA: Harvard University Press, 1990), 256. Some historians have estimated that only 5 to 10 percent of colonists in the South and on the frontier affiliated with a church.

3. Richard Hofstadter, *America at 1750: A Social Portrait* (New York: Knopf: 1971), xv–xvi. Like Butler and others, Hofstadter noted that southerners joined churches to an even lower degree than other colonists did (181).

4. Patricia U. Bonomi and Peter R. Eisenstadt, "Church Adherence in the Eighteenth-Century British American Colonies," *William and Mary Quarterly* 39, no. 2 (April 1982), 248, 253, 273.

5. Ibid., 247.

6. Ibid., 273. The authors draw on Edwin S. Gaustad's survey of churches for 1750 in *Historical Atlas of Religion in America,* rev. ed. (New York: Harper & Row, 1976), app. B.

7. Bonomi and Eisenstadt, "Church Adherence," 275.

8. Christine Leigh Heyrman, *Southern Cross: The Beginnings of the Bible Belt* (Chapel Hill: University of North Carolina Press, 1997).

9. John B. Boles, *Religion in Antebellum Kentucky* (Lexington: University Press of Kentucky, 1976), 16–17.

10. Ibid., 25–29, 32, 51.

11. Sydney Ahlstrom, *A Religious History of the American People* (New Haven, CT: Yale, 1972), 436, 445.

12. Elizabeth Corliss to Father Bourbon, September 1, 1827, Filson Historical Society, Louisville (hereafter cited as Filson).

13. John F. Schermerhorn and Samuel J. Mills, *A Correct View of That Part of the United States Which Lies West of the Alleghany Mountains, with Respect to Religion and Morals* (Hartford, CT: Cleason and Co., 1814), 23.

14. Samuel J. Mills and Daniel Smith, *Report of a Missionary Tour through That Part of the United States Which Lies West of the Allegany Mountains* (Andover, MA: Flagg and Gould, 1815), 27, 29, 47.

15. D. C. Blood to Rev. Sylvester Dana, Cincinnati, January 10, 1832, Filson.

16. Cited in Frederick Law Olmsted, *A Journey in the Seaboard Slave States* (New York: Dix & Edwards, 1856), 510.

17. Cited in Sister Mary Ramona Mattingly, *The Catholic Church on the Kentucky Frontier (1785–1812),* The Catholic University of America Studies in American Church History 25 (Washington: Catholic University Press, 1936), 195.

18. V. F. O'Daniel, "Bishop Flaget's Report of the Diocese of Bardstown to Pius VII, April 10, 1815," *Catholic Historical Review* 1 (April 1915–Jan. 1916), 318 (hereafter cited as *CHR*). Five years later, another observer estimated that seven-eighths of Kentuckians belonged to no particular denomination. See Martin John Spalding, *Sketches of the Early Catholic Missions of Kentucky; from Their Commencement in 1787 to the Jubilee of 1826–7* (Louisville: B. J. Webb, 1844), 108–9.

19. Frances Trollope, *Domestic Manners of the Americans,* ed. Donald Smalley (New York: Knopf, 1949), 110.

20. J. T. Brett to unknown, December 16, 1820, Archives of the Diocese of Charleston, Wallace Papers.

21. See, for example, the analysis of the Anglican itinerant Charles Woodmason's journal in Bonomi and Eisenstadt, "Church Adherence," 267.

22. W. J. Howlett, "Bishop Flaget's Diary," *Records of the American Catholic Historical Society of Philadelphia* 29, no. 3 (Sept. 1918), 248 (hereafter cited as *ACHS*).

23. "Anonymous to Carroll, Augusta, GA, December 26, 1805," *ACHS* 19, no. 2 (June 1908), 225.

24. *United States Catholic Miscellany* (Charleston), March 31, 1827.

25. Mary D. Robertson, ed., *A Confederate Lady Comes of Age: The Journal of Pauline DeCaradeuc Hayward, 1861–1888* (Columbia: University of South Carolina Press, 1992), 72. A few months later, DeCaradeuc pretended to be Jewish when she overheard anti-Semitic remarks aimed at southern Jews (82).

26. Mills and Smith, *Report of a Missionary Tour,* 19.

27. Elizabeth Blackwell, "Letter from Elizabeth Blackwell, July, 1846," *Pioneer Work in Opening the Medical Profession to Women* (New York: Longmans, 1985), 265.

28. William Bodley to Ellen Bodley, Tuscaloosa, December 22, 1845, Filson. See also Peter William Hairston Papers, Southern Historical Collection, University of North Carolina-Chapel Hill (hereafter cited as SHC).

29. Cited in Ann Ashby Manigault, *Extracts from the Journal of Mrs. Ann Manigault,* ed. Mabel J. Webber (Charleston: South Carolina Historical Society, 1920), 61.

30. Olmsted, *Journey,* 451.

31. Diary of Elizabeth Ann March (Mrs. William Robertson), 1849–1856, Eliza Anne Marsh Robertson Papers, SHC. Robertson's husband often attended Know-Nothing meetings, making her openness to the Catholic Church all the more notable.

32. Spring Hill College Register, Spring Hill College Archives.

33. Douglas Miln in St. Louis to Rev. William Beckett in Scotland, February 26, 1840, Filson.

34. George Lewis, *Impressions of America and of the American Churches* (Edinburgh: W. P. Kennedy, 1845), 397.

35. Trollope, *Domestic Manners,* 107, 109.

36. John Cleves Short to Charles Wilkins Short, Shorthill, January 18, 1845, Filson.

37. Lewis, *Impressions of America,* 127.

38. Ibid., 141.

39. Ibid., 268, 303.

40. Ibid., 237.

41. Ibid., 240–41, 245.

42. Seventh Census of the United States (1850).

43. B. B. Smith, *The Temper and Conduct Proper on the Part of Episcopalians Towards their Fellow-Christians Who are not Episcopalians: A Charge to the Clergy of the Diocese of Kentucky, Delivered in Christ Church, Lexington, on Thursday, the 11th of May, 1843* (Lexington: James Virden, 1843).

44. Olmsted, *Journey,* 453.

45. Charles C. Jones Jr., *Memorial History of Augusta, Georgia* (Syracuse, NY: D. Mason, 1890), 380.

46. Heyrman, *Southern Cross,* 64, 226–28.

47. Ibid., 231.

48. Ibid., 152; Schermerhorn and Mills, *Correct View,* 41.

49. D. C. Blood to Rev. Sylvester Dana, Cincinnati, January 10, 1832, Filson.

50. John Cleves Short to Charles Wilkins Short, Shorthill, January 18, 1845, Filson.

51. James J. Pillar, *The Catholic Church in Mississippi, 1837–1865* (New Orleans: Hauser Press, 1964), 91.

52. Martin John Spalding, *Life, Times, and Character of the Right Reverend Benedict Joseph Flaget* (Louisville: Webb & Levering, 1852), 246.

53. "Badin to Carroll, Pottinger's Creek, February 25, 1801," *ACHS* 23, no. 3 (Sept. 1912), 143.

54. "Report of Bishop England to the Cardinal Prefect of Propaganda (Rome, 1833)," *ACHS* 8, no. 3 (Sept. 1897), 321.

55. Cited in J. Herman Schauinger, *Cathedrals in the Wilderness* (Milwaukee: Bruce Publishing Company, 1952), 38.

56. See E. Brooks Holifield, "Theology as Entertainment: Oral Debate in American Religion," *Church History* 67, no. 3 (Sept. 1998): 499–520.

57. R. T. Allison to John C. Bullitt, Lexington, November 1843, Filson.

58. Spalding, *Sketches of Early Catholic Missions,* 128–29.

59. Ibid., 254.

60. Columba Fox, *The Life of the Right Reverend John Baptist Mary David* (New York: United States Catholic Historical Society, 1925), 111. David was a prolific writer. For a summary of his major works see Fox, 174–75.

61. John England, *Works of the Right Rev. John England, First Bishop of Charleston,* ed. Ignatius Aloysius Reynolds (Baltimore: John Murphy & Co., 1849), vol. 2, 333; vol. 3, 1.

62. "Badin to Carroll, Washington County, June 3, 1799," *ACHS* 19, no. 4 (Dec. 1908), 474.

63. Oscar Hugh Lipscomb, "The Administration of John Quinlan, Second Bishop of Mobile, 1859–1883," *ACHS* 78, nos. 1–4 (March–Dec. 1967), 26.

64. "Report of Bishop England," 325.

65. *Miscellany,* June 5, 1822; "England to O'Connor, Charleston, April 7, 1835," *ACHS* 8, no. 2 (June 1897), 209.

66. Schauinger, *Cathedrals in the Wilderness,* 297–98.

67. "Report of Bishop England," 326.

68. Augustus Baldwin Longstreet, *Know Nothingism Unveiled* (Washington, DC: Office of the Congressional Globe, 1855), 2.

69. "The Temper and Conduct Proper on the Part of Episcopalians Towards their Fellow-Christians Who are not Episcopalians." Being the Third Charge to the Clergy of the Diocese of Kentucky, delivered in Christ Church, Lexington, on Thursday, the 11th of May 1843, by the Rt. Rev. B.B. Smith, Bishop of the Diocese of Kentucky, Lexington, 1843, Filson.

70. Stephen Badin, "Origin and Progress of the Mission of Kentucky," translated and reprinted in *Catholic World* 21, no. 126 (Sept. 1875), 828.

71. Robertson, *Confederate Lady,* 88.

72. *The Old Pine Farm: or, The Southern Side. Comprising Loose Sketches from the Experience of a Southern Country Minister, S.C.* (Nashville: Southwestern Publishing House, 1860), 97, 110.

73. England, *Works,* vol. 4, 420.

74. "Report of Bishop England," 325.

75. "England to Gaston, Wilmington, May 17, 1821," *ACHS* 18, no. 4 (Dec. 1907), 368–69.

76. "England to Gaston, Fayetteville, January 29, 1826," *ACHS* 19, no. 1 (March 1908), 106. See also *Miscellany,* June 5, 1822.

77. Cited in Mattingly, *Catholic Church on the Kentucky Frontier,* 183.

78. Letter of April 12, 1856, [2], James Graham Ramsey Papers, SHC.

79. "Report of Bishop England," 320–21.

80. "Clancy to Cullen, Charleston, November 23, 1836," *ACHS* 8, no. 3 (Sept. 1897), 300.

81. "Flaget to Plessis, Baltimore, March 31, 1811," *ACHS* 18, no. 1 (March 1907), 14. The fact that neither Archbishop Carroll nor the Sulpicians had money to loan Flaget testifies to the state of American Catholicism at the time. Badin offered to raise the necessary funds in Kentucky, but Flaget did not want to begin his tenure on a negative note. "I would a thousand times prefer to go on foot rather than to cause the slightest murmur," he explained. Cited in Badin, "Origin and Progress," 832; Fox, *Life of . . . David,* 45; Schauinger, *Cathedrals in the Wilderness,* 52–53.

82. Flaget to Rev. Messrs. Garnier and Nagot at St. Sulpice, Paris, Bardstown, September 6, 1811, Filson Mss. BA/B245/6.

83. Almost a decade after taking charge of the diocese, Flaget was still uncertain of its exact boundaries. "Flaget to Plessis, The North East Shore, January 22, 1818," *ACHS* 18, no. 1 (March 1907), 31.

84. Schauinger, *Cathedrals in the Wilderness,* 13.

85. "Badin to Carroll, Washington, August 9, 1799," *ACHS* 19, no. 4 (Dec. 1908), 480.

86. Spalding, *Life, Times, . . . Flaget,* 114.

87. Spalding, *Sketches of Early Catholic Missions,* 46–47.

88. Schauinger, *Cathedrals in the Wilderness,* 13.

89. "Badin to Carroll, Rolling-Fork, August 24, 1796," *ACHS* 19, no. 3 (Sept. 1908), 265.

90. Richard still enjoyed wide public support, as evidenced by his election to the United States Congress while in prison. Richard's superior, Bishop Flaget, found the whole affair to be rather humorous. He once remarked that Richard "was more interesting in the obscurity of his prison lying on his bed of straw than in the center of the light of Congress seated on a velvet-covered chair." Schauinger, *Cathedrals in the Wilderness,* 226–28.

91. Congregation for Propagation of the Faith to Bishop Flaget, October 5, 1816, cited in *Documents: Nerinckx—Kentucky—Loretto, 1804–1851 in Archives Propaganda Fide, Rome.* Edited by Augustin Wand and M. Lilliana Owens (Nerinx, KY: Loretto Literary and Benevolent Institution, 1972), 129, Filson.

92. Madden, *Catholics in South Carolina,* 26–27. Guilday discusses the conflict in great detail in *The Life and Time of John England, First Bishop of Charleston,* vol. 1 (New York: The America Press, 1927), 164–280. England noted that trustees often had an advantage over priests in that they had generally been in America longer and were more familiar with laws governing religious associations and church property. "Report of Bishop England," 318. For an analysis of the relationship between French priests and the American Catholic laity, see Michael Pasquier, *Fathers on the Frontier: French Missionaries and the Roman Catholic Priesthood in the United States, 1789–1870* (New York: Oxford University Press, 2010).

93. Edward Lynch to Neale, Charleston, October 7, 1816, Archives of the Archdiocese of Baltimore 12A I2 (hereafter cited as BCA). Clorivière was not only a monarchist, but he had been a member of a conspiracy to assassinate Napoleon. In Charleston, his views greatly incensed the French Bonapartists and Irish Republicans in his congregation. See Thomas W. Spalding, *The Premier See: A History of the Archdiocese of Baltimore, 1789–1989* (Baltimore: The Johns Hopkins Press, 1989), 53.

94. Fenwick to Maréchal, Charleston, February 19, 1821, BCA 16 P33.

95. Richard C. Madden, *Catholics in South Carolina: A Record* (New York: University Press of America, 1985), 33.

96. Gerald P. Fogarty, *Commonwealth Catholicism: A History of the Catholic Church in Virginia* (Notre Dame: University of Notre Dame Press, 2001), 33–53; Spalding, *Premier See,* 67–70, 81–83.

97. Lipscomb, "Administration of Quinlan," 11.

98. Boles, *Religion in Antebellum Kentucky,* 74.

99. Spalding, *Life, Times, . . . Flaget,* 247.

100. Flaget to Maréchal, Loretto, July 10, 1817, Filson Mss. Ba/B245/5.

101. Schauinger, *Cathedrals in the Wilderness,* 84.

102. For example, Lyman Beecher included a section on the hierarchy's attempt to limit trusteeism in his *A Plea for the West,* 2nd ed. (Cincinnati, Truman & Smith, 1835), 164–65; Ray Billington, *The Protestant Crusade: 1800–1860* (New York: MacMillan, 1938), 39–40.

103. "Papers Relating to the Church in America: From the Portfolios of the Irish College at Rome," *ACHS* 8, no. 4 (1897), 458.

104. *Miscellany,* March 24, 1824.

105. Ibid., November 11, 1826.

106. Hopkins, *St. Mary's Church,* 9.

107. Ibid., 19.

108. O'Connell, *Catholicity in the Carolinas,* 134.

109. England, *Works,* vol. 4, 332.

110. Badin to Carroll, January 16, 1803, BCA case A special; September 26, 1810, BCA I J10.

111. Mattingly, *Catholic Church on the Kentucky Frontier,* 89, 96, 98; John A. Lyons, "The Sesquicentennial of St. Clare's Church on Clear Creek in Hardin County Kentucky, 1808–1958," PHC, 44/14 UNDA.

112. John Grassi, "The Catholic Religion in the United States in 1818," in *Documentary Reports on Early American Catholicism,* ed. Phillip Gleason (New York: Arno Press, 1978), 22–24.

113. Mattingly, *Catholic Church on the Kentucky Frontier,* 89; Spalding, *Sketches of Early Catholic Missions,* 262.

114. Crews, *Presence and Possibility,* 17; Mattingly, *Catholic Church on the Kentucky Frontier,* 92. Spalding estimates the total amount raised at $3,000 and notes that the Protestants were the major donors (262). Protestants also served as members of the corporation, the chartered body of Charleston Catholics. This, however, became a source of controversy when England clashed with the corporation, and as a result, it was decided in January 1822 to require all members to subscribe to articles of faith "as only Roman Catholics can with a safe conscience subscribe to." See Thomas F. Hopkins, *St. Mary's Church, Charleston, S.C.: The First Catholic Church in the Original Diocese of Charleston: An Historic Sketch of the Church from Its Beginning to the Present Time* (Charleston: Walker, Evans, & Cogswell, 1898), 47–48.

115. Benedict Joseph Flaget, "Subscription for Funds to Finish the Building of the St. Louis Church in Louisville," February 26, 1817, Library of Congress.

116. Spalding, *Life, Times, . . . Flaget,* 236–37.

117. "Badin to Carroll, Washington C'ty, June 7, 1799," *ACHS* 19, no. 4 (Dec. 1908), 477.

118. Howlett, "Diary," 51, 59.

119. "Bishop Flaget's Report," 313; Badin, "Origin and Progress," 833.

120. *Miscellany,* January 5, 1825.

121. Ibid., February 16, 1825; May 11, 1825; December 23, 1826.

122. Ibid., March 10, 1824; February 11, 1824; Stephen Worsley, "Catholicism in Antebellum North Carolina," *North Carolina Historical Review,* 1983, 419.

123. Ibid., October 26, 1825; November 11, 1826.

124. Jones, *Memorial History of Augusta,* 381.

125. Hopkins, *St. Mary's Church,* 54; *Miscellany,* August 11, September 15, and November 17, 1838.

126. *Miscellany,* August 18, 1838.

127. Cited in Hopkins, *St. Mary's Church,* 53.

128. Charleston *Courier,* June 10, 1839; *Miscellany,* June 8, 1839.

129. Schauinger, *Cathedrals in the Wilderness,* 267–68.

130. *Catholic Advocate* (Louisville), October 24, 1846, cited in Betty Darnell, "St. Francis Xavier Parish," Filson.

131. David to Bruté, St. Joseph's Seminary, June 15, 1834, MSGB, Archives of the University of Notre Dame (hereafter cited as UNDA).

132. "Flaget to Joseph Octavius Plessis, Bishop of Quebec, Loretto, June 18, 1816," *ACHS* 18, no. 1 (March 1907), 24; Schauinger, *Cathedrals in the Wilderness,* 70; Spalding estimates the total amount raised in the first subscription at $12,000–14,000 (*Sketches of Early Catholic Missions,* 243).

133. David to "Tres cher Confrere," St. Thomas Seminary, October 20, 1816, Filson Mss. BA/B235/3.

134. Spalding, *Sketches of Early Catholic Missions,* 244–45.

135. Flaget to Bruté, January 3, 1825, MSGB, UNDA.

136. Lipscomb, "Administration of Quinlan," 25.

137. *Miscellany,* September 26, 1829.

138. *Courier,* May 7, 1851.

139. J. H. Easterby, "South Carolina through New England Eyes: Almira Coffin's Visit to the Low Country in 1851," *South Carolina Historical and Genealogic Magazine* 45, no. 3 (1944), 127.

140. *Courier,* May 7, 1851.

141. Madden, *Catholics in South Carolina,* 63.

142. Seventh Census of the United States (1850).

143. Eighth Census of the United States (1860). This is a surprising statistic; the census offers no explanation of how its agents calculated church capacity.

144. Schauinger, *Cathedrals in the Wilderness,* 63.

145. Cited in Fox, *Life of . . . David,* 62.

146. Flaget to Babade, August 1, 1816, CRCL 11-3-n, UNDA.

147. Crews, *Presence and Possibility,* 100.

148. Michael Kenny, *Catholic Culture in Alabama: Centenary Story of Spring Hill College, 1830–1930* (New York: The America Press, 1931), 60.

149. Ibid., 179.

150. Howlett, "Diary," 46–48. Unfortunately, Flaget provided no details.

151. John R. Dichtl, *Frontiers of Faith: Bringing Catholicism to the West in the Early Republic* (Lexington: University Press of Kentucky, 2008), 137.

152. *Miscellany,* September 29, 1827.

153. Ibid., January 26, 1828.

154. Ibid., June 5, 1822.

155. Ibid., May 5, 1827; Schauinger, *Cathedrals in the Wilderness,* 234–35.

156. England, *Works,* vol. 4, 197.

157. *Courier,* June 8, 1839.

158. *Miscellany,* March 24, 1824.

159. Ibid., April 7, 21, 1824.

160. Ibid., November 9, 1825.

161. Ibid., February 10, 1827.

162. Ibid., March 1, 1828.

163. Ibid., June 1, 1839.

164. Alvan F. Sanborn, ed., *Reminiscences of Richard Lathers: Sixty Years of a Busy Life in South Carolina, Massachusetts and New York* (New York: Grafton Press, 1907), 15.

165. Spalding, *Sketches of Early Catholic Missions,* 250.

166. Cited in Isaac McDaniel, *Impact of the Mexican War on Anti-Catholicism in the United States* (Ann Arbor: University Microfilms International, 1991), 151.

167. Cited in Spalding, *Life, Times, . . . Flaget,* 174.

168. John Baptist Mary [David] to Martin John Spalding, St. Joseph's, Bardstown, December 2, 1833, Filson Mss. BA/B245/3.

169. C. J. Jeronimus, ed., *Travels by His Highness Duke Bernhard of Saxe-Weimar-Eisenach through North America in the Years 1825 and 1826* (Lanham, MD: University Press of America, 2001), 330–31.

170. David to unknown, St. Thomas, July 14, 1817, Filson Mss. BA/B245/3.

171. Spalding, *Sketches of Early Catholic Missions,* 66.

172. In Charleston, Catholics first met in a building previously occupied by a Protestant preacher, and this pattern continued throughout the period. In 1850, they bought a Methodist church in Sumter for use as a parish, and as late as 1861, when they opened a new parish in Charleston, they used a building that had served as a Presbyterian church. Madden, *Catholics in South Carolina,* 19, 65, 78.

173. Butler, *Awash in a Sea of Faith,* 237.

174. See, for example, Jay P. Dolan, *Catholic Revivalism: The American Experience 1830–1900* (Notre Dame: University of Notre Dame Press, 1978).

175. George Mason to George Mason Jr., Philadelphia, May 20, 1787, in *The Papers of George Mason, 1725–1792,* ed. Robert A. Rutland, vol. 3 (Chapel Hill, University of North Carolina Press, 1970), 881.

176. *Miscellany,* July 28, 1827.

177. "Badin to Carroll, Washington C'ty, June 3, 1799," *ACHS* 19, no. 4 (Dec. 1908), 473.

178. Spalding, *Sketches of Early Catholic Missions,* 70, 141.

179. Clement Eaton, *Freedom of Thought in the Old South* (Durham, NC: Duke University Press, 1940), 303.

180. Flaget to Carroll, Mrs. Howard's plantation, August 22, 1811, Filson Mss. BA/B245/7. David also testified to Protestants' "extreme curiosity" regarding Flaget. See David to Bruté, St. Stephen's, September 16, 1811, CRCL 11-3-n, UNDA.

181. Boles, *Religion in Antebellum Kentucky,* 15.

182. Trollope, *Domestic Manners,* 110.

183. *The Diaries of Donald Macdonald: 1824–1826* (Clifton, NJ: Augustus M. Kelley, 1973), 372.

184. John R. Bodo, *The Protestant Clergy and Public Issues* (Princeton: Princeton University Press, 1954), 66.

185. John Brown to Dr. Wilson, Louisville, October 1821, Filson.

186. Spalding, *Life, Times, . . . Flaget,* 283.
187. Mattingly, *Catholic Church on the Kentucky Frontier,* 109.
188. Schauinger, *Cathedrals in the Wilderness,* 68, 178; Spalding, *Life, Times, . . . Flaget,* 257.
189. Cited in Crews, *Presence and Possibility,* 27.
190. Robert T. Krebs, *The Celestial City: A History of the Cathedral Basilica of the Assumption* (Covington: Diocese of Covington, 1991), 29, Filson; Spalding, *Life, Times, . . . Flaget,* 346.
191. *Courier,* April 7, 1854.
192. Spalding, *Life, Times, . . . Flaget,* 357.
193. Cited in Crews, *Presence and Possibility,* 28.
194. Flaget to Badin, September 29, 1826, cited in Spalding, *Sketches of Early Catholic Missions,* 292.
195. Schauinger, *Cathedrals in the Wilderness,* 186–87; Spalding, *Sketches of Early Catholic Missions,* 253.
196. Spalding, *Sketches of Early Catholic Missions,* 298.
197. Whelan to Purcell, Summerville [AL], March 19, 1861, CACI 11–4-k, UNDA.
198. Howlett, "Diary," 240.
199. Badin, "Origin and Progress," 830–31.
200. *Miscellany,* September 23, 1826.
201. Cited in Schauinger, *Cathedrals in the Wilderness,* 63.
202. *Miscellany,* November 25, 1826.
203. Cited in Fox, *Life of . . . David,* 165.
204. "England to Gaston, Charleston, February 25, 1830," *ACHS* 19, no. 2 (June 1908), 145.
205. "England to Gaston, Charleston, January 9, 1823," *ACHS* 18, no. 4 (Dec. 1907), 385–86.
206. *Miscellany,* June 5, 1822.
207. Ibid., August 29, 1829.
208. "Transcribed Journal of Samuel Haycroft, Jr (1849–1878) (with Some Additions by a Daughter, 1878–1880)," Filson.
209. Flaget to Carroll, January, 1812, Filson Mss. BA/B245/7.
210. *Miscellany,* December 18, 1822.
211. Howlett, "Diary," 244.
212. Spalding, *Life, Times, . . . Flaget,* 249.
213. Robert Winn to his sister, Camp Bristow, Bowling Green, September 24, 1863, Filson.
214. *Miscellany,* August 11, 1824.
215. Badin, "Origin and Progress," 830–31.
216. Cited in Madden, *Catholics in South Carolina,* 18.
217. Hopkins, *St. Mary's Church,* 59.
218. *Miscellany,* December 22, 1827.

219. James Cain, "The Reviewer Reviewed; or, an Expose of the Late Billingsgate Production of Mr. 'William Sim' M'Atee Elder, against the Rev. N. L. Rice, his Counsel, and Part of the Jury," (Bardstown, 1837), 18, Filson.

220. John England, *Diurnal of the Right Rev. John England, D.D., first Bishop of Charleston, S.C.* (Philadelphia: American Catholic Historical Society, 1895), 18, 27, 63.

221. *Miscellany,* April 11, 1829.

222. "England to Gaston, Fayetteville, January 29, 1826," *ACHS* 19, no. 1 (March 1908), 105.

223. *Miscellany,* April 21, 1824; February 28, 1829.

224. Ibid., March 10, 1824.

225. Ibid., February 16, 1825.

226. Ibid., July 28, and August 11, 1827; March 29, 1828.

227. Ibid., July 10, 1822.

228. Ibid., March 9, 1825.

229. Flaget, "Subscription."

230. *The Papers of Henry Clay,* vol. 5, ed. Mary Hargreaves and James Hopkins (Lexington: University Press of Kentucky, 1981), 463.

231. *Miscellany,* June 5, 1822.

232. *Courier,* August 6, 1854.

233. David to Bruté, July 18, 1811, CRCL 11–3-n, UNDA.

234. Flaget to Carroll, Mrs. Howard's plantation, August 22, 1811, Filson Mss. BA/B245/7.

235. "Flaget to Joseph Octavius Plessis, Bishop of Quebec, Loretto, June 18, 1816," *ACHS* 18, no. 1 (March 1907), 24; "Flaget to Plessis, St. Thomas, September 19, 1816," *ACHS* 18, no. 1 (March 1907), 29.

236. Henry C. Ferris to Bishop John Chanche, Macon, Noxubee County, Mississippi, June 17, 1852, DNT, UNDA.

237. Mills and Smith, *Report of a Missionary Tour,* 18.

238. Clapp, *Autobiographical Sketches,* 68.

239. *Miscellany,* August 18, 1827.

240. F. G. Holweck, "The Beginnings of the Church in Little Rock," *CHR* 6, no. 2 (July 1920), 157, 164.

241. *Miscellany,* September 5, 1829.

242. Cited in Hopkins, *St. Mary's Church,* 20.

243. Robert Krebs, "The Celestial City," 29, Filson.

244. Cited in Clyde F. Crews, *An American Holy Land: A History of the Archdiocese of Louisville* (Louisville: Ikonographics, 1987), 115; George H. Yater, *Two Hundred Years at the Falls of the Ohio: a History of Louisville and Jefferson County* (Louisville: Filson Club, 1987), 48.

245. Cited in Madden, *Catholics in South Carolina,* 75.

246. "Notices of the Papal Church in the United States," *Quarterly Register of the American Education Society* 3, no. 2 (Nov. 1830), 97.

247. *Miscellany,* August 25, 1824.

248. Ibid., August 7, 1822.

249. Ibid., July 3, 1822.

250. Ibid., September 16, 1826.

251. Ibid., September 27, 1828.

252. Spalding, *Sketches of Early Catholic Missions,* 70, 124–25.

253. *Miscellany,* December 31, 1823.

254. Spalding, *Life, Times, . . . Flaget,* 258–59.

255. Spalding, *Sketches of Early Catholic Missions,* 120. Spalding's work offers numerous similar anecdotes.

256. Ibid., 76–77.

257. Badin, "Origin and Progress."

258. *Miscellany,* December 1, 1824.

259. Spalding, *Sketches of Early Catholic Missions,* 44.

260. *Miscellany,* December 8, 1827. See also *Miscellany,* January 12, 1825, and September 9, 1826.

261. Ibid., September 29, 1827.

262. Ibid., September 23, 1826.

263. Guilday, *Life and Time . . . England,* vol. 2, 158.

264. "England to Cullen, Charleston, May 25, 1835," *ACHS* 8, no. 2 (June 1897), 214.

265. *Miscellany,* December 20, 1834.

266. "England to Cullen, Charleston, May 25, 1835," *ACHS* 8, no. 2 (June 1897), 224.

267. Beecher, *Plea for the West,* 143.

268. Jenny Franchot analyzed what she termed the "Attraction of Repulsion" throughout her work: *Roads to Rome: The Antebellum Protestant Encounter with Catholicism* (Berkeley: University of California Press, 1994), especially 197–220. Many nineteenth-century Protestants were so enamored of Catholic art and architecture that they incorporated "Catholic" devices such as crosses and stained-glass windows into their own churches. See Ryan K. Smith, *Gothic Arches, Latin Crosses: Anti-Catholicism and American Church Designs in the Nineteenth Century* (Chapel Hill: University of North Carolina Press, 2006). Lyman Beecher's first church in Boston, Hanover Street Congregational Church, was an excellent example of the Gothic Revival style. When the church burned down in 1830, Beecher and his congregation rebuilt it in exactly the same style (117).

269. Cited in Fox, *Life of . . . David,* 150.

270. Schauinger, *Cathedrals in the Wilderness,* 155.

271. Lewis, *Impressions of America,* 356.

272. Cited in Mattingly, *Catholic Church on the Kentucky Frontier,* 126. Archbishop Carroll disagreed with this view, fearing that too much pomp and show on the part of Catholics would become a source of dissension with Protestantism. But he was in the minority. Spalding, *Premier See,* 62.

273. *Quarterly Register of the American Education Society* 3, no. 2 (Nov. 1830), 97.

274. Schauinger, *Cathedrals in the Wilderness,* 179.

275. Cited in Spalding, *Sketches of Early Catholic Missions,* 214.

276. "England to Gaston, Charleston, November 6, 1830," *ACHS* 19, no. 2 (June 1908), 149.

277. "Rev. Robert Browne to Archbishop Carroll, May 24, 1813," *ACHS* 18, no. 4 (Dec. 1907), 420.

278. Schauinger, *Cathedrals in the Wilderness,* 176.

279. "England to O'Connor, March 7, 1835," *ACHS* 8, no. 2 (June 1897), 204.

280. Schauinger, *Cathedrals in the Wilderness,* 152.

281. Ibid., 286.

282. Spalding, *Life, Times, . . . Flaget,* 187.

283. *Miscellany,* September 28, 1825.

284. Ahlstrom, *Religious History,* 589, 623. A Kentuckian revealed the extent to which Americans associated the Gothic style with Catholicism when he wrote to his brother that the Gothic windows in his brother's house led passers-by to inquire what Catholic gentleman resided there. John Cleves Short to Charles Wilkins Short, Shorthill, January 18, 1845, Filson.

285. Lewis, *Impressions of America,* 133.

286. Ibid., 356.

287. *Miscellany,* May 18, 1825.

288. Ibid., April 13, 1825.

289. *Courier,* May 6 and 7, 1851.

290. Ibid., March 15, 1858.

291. Theodore Clapp, *Autobiographical Sketches and Recollections: During a Thirty-Five Year Residence in New Orleans,* 2nd ed. (Boston: Phillips, Samson & Co., 1858), 227, 228. In particular, Clapp described the sight of an entire congregation kneeling at the moment of transubstantiation to be "thrillingly, ineffably sublime."

292. Diary of John Brown, October 24, 1821, 16, Filson.

293. Charles M. McGee Jr. and Ernest M. Lander Jr., eds., *A Rebel Came Home: The Diary of Floride Clemson* (Columbia: University of South Carolina Press, 1961), 37.

294. Rebecca Grant Sexton, ed., *A Southern Woman of Letters: The Correspondence of Augusta Jane Evans Wilson* (Columbia: University of South Carolina Press, 2002), 14.

295. Olmsted, *Journey,* 582.

296. John Rothensteiner, "Bishop England's Correspondence with Bishop Rosati," *Illinois Catholic Historical Review* 9, no. 3 (Jan. 1927), 268.

297. "George Mason to George Mason Jr., Philadelphia, May 20, 1787," in Rutland, *Papers of George Mason,* vol. 3, 881.

298. William Alexander Graham, *The Papers of William Alexander Graham,* vol. 1, ed. J. G. de Roulhac Hamilton (Raleigh: State Department of Archives and History, 1957), 211.

299. "England to Cullen, Charleston, March 19, 1835," *ACHS* 8, no. 2 (June 1897), 208.

300. Lawrence S. Rowland, Alexander Moore, and George C. Rogers Jr., *History of Beaufort County, South Carolina,* vol. 1, 1514–1861 (Columbia: University of South Carolina Press, 1996), 411.

301. William C. Preston, *The Reminiscences of William C. Preston,* ed. Minnie Clare Yarborough (Chapel Hill: University of North Carolina Press, 1933), 79–81, 86–87.

302. Franchot, *Roads to Rome,* 16, 20.

303. John Cleves Short to Charles Wilkins Short, Montreal, June 17, 1849, Filson.

304. Cited in McDaniel, *Impact of the Mexican War,* 208.

305. "Anna [Maria Calhoun Clemson] to John C. Calhoun, Brussels, December 5, 1844," *The Papers of John C. Calhoun,* vol. 20, ed. Clyde Wilson (Columbia: University of South Carolina Press, 1991), 467.

306. Jeronimus, *Travels,* 219.

307. Trollope, *Domestic Manners,* 206, 208.

308. Lewis, *Impressions of America,* 219.

Chapter 5

1. *Charleston Courier,* July 30, 1835.

2. *United States Catholic Miscellany* (Charleston), August 1, 1835; "England to Cullen, Charleston, February 23, 1836," *Records of the American Catholic Historical Society of Philadelphia* 8, no. 2 (June 1897), 217–21 (hereafter cited as *ACHS*).

3. *Charleston Courier,* July 31, 1835.

4. "England to Cullen, Charleston, February 23, 1836," *ACHS* 8, no. 2 (June 1897), 217–21. O'Connell claimed that civic leaders had "connived at the gathering storm," and only came to Catholics' aid when it became clear that "any attempt at violence would have buried the proud city in its ruins." Such an interpretation is absent in England's account. See J. J. O'Connell, *Catholicity in the Carolinas and Georgia: Leaves of Its History* (s.l.: Sadlier, 1879), 81.

5. Randall M. Miller, "The Failed Mission: The Catholic Church and Black Catholics in the Old South," in *Catholics in the Old South,* ed. Randall Miller and Jon Wakelyn (Macon: Mercer University Press, 1999), 157.

6. Thomas Murphy, *Jesuit Slaveholding in Maryland, 1717–1838* (New York: Routledge, 2001), xxi, 155–57.

7. Madeleine Hooke Rice, *American Catholic Opinion in the Slavery Controversy* (New York: Columbia University Press, 1944), 97–98. German Catholics, for example, although generally inclined to oppose slavery, denounced abolitionism when they saw the radical revolutionaries among their countrymen supporting it (102).

8. Rice, *American Catholic Opinion,* 74.

9. Cited in ibid., 75. The fact that three thousand antislavery Protestant ministers signed a protest against the Kansas-Nebraska Act particularly incensed Catholics and many non-Catholic southerners.

10. Augustin Verot, *A Tract for the Times: Slavery and Abolitionism, Being the Substance of a Sermon, Preached in the Church of St. Augustine, Florida, on the 4th Day of January, 1861, Day of Public Humiliation, Fasting and Prayer* (New Orleans: Catholic Propagator, 1861), 8.

11. *Miscellany,* February 17, 1841.

12. Murphy, *Jesuit Slaveholding,* 80–82. Concern for the condition of free blacks in America led many Catholics to support the colonization movement. See Rice, *American Catholic Opinion,* 53.

13. Verot, *Tract for the Times,* 22.

14. Hugh Nolan, ed., *Pastoral Letters of the American Hierarchy, 1792–1970* (Huntington, IN: Our Sunday Visitor, 1971), 157. As late as 1929, Catholic historian John T. Gillard, Society of Saint John, while acknowledging that emancipation "was in one sense a great boon to the colored people," still maintained that "the new-found freedom was too much," citing an exodus of blacks from the church as evidence. *The Catholic Church and the American Negro* (Baltimore: St. Joseph's Society Press, 1929), 33.

15. Cited in John McGreevy, *Catholicism and American Freedom* (New York: Norton, 2003), 57. See also 58–59.

16. McGreevy, *American Freedom,* 60–61.

17. Cited in Rice, *American Catholic Opinion,* 98. For an analysis of abolitionist anti-Catholicism, see Peter Walker, *Moral Choices: Memory, Desire, and Imagination in Nineteenth-Century American Abolition* (Baton Rouge: Louisiana State University Press, 1978), 161–66.

18. *Miscellany,* September 12, 1835.

19. "England to Cullen, Charleston, February 23, 1836," *ACHS* 8, no. 2 (June 1897), 222.

20. *Miscellany,* November 17, 1838. The columnist conceded that he would not introduce slavery where it did not exist; he insisted that a legislature could face no task more difficult than trying to abolish it once in place.

21. Ibid., October 15, 1831.

22. Verot, *Tract for the Times,* 4–5, 13–14.

23. Rice, *American Catholic Opinion,* 76–77.

24. Ibid., 79; McGreevey, *American Freedom,* 51; "Pastoral Letter of R. Rev. Félix Antoine Philibert Dupanloup, Bishop of Orleans, to his Clergy on the subject of the Civil War in the United States, April 6, 1862," *ACHS* 25, no. 1 (March 1914), 21.

25. Verot, *Tract for the Times,* 6.

26. John Dooley, *John Dooley, Confederate Soldier: His War Journal,* ed. Joseph T. Durkin (Notre Dame: University of Notre Dame Press, 1963), 141.

27. Reprinted in the *Miscellany,* October 15, 1831.

28. *Catholic Advocate (Louisville)*, April 26, 1837.

29. Cited in S. L. Theobold, "Catholic Missionary Work among the Colored People of the United States (1776–1866)," *ACHS* 15, no. 4 (Dec. 1914), 341; See also *Miscellany,* August 26, 1826.

30. Murphy, *Jesuit Slaveholding,* 80.

31. Theodore Clapp, *Autobiographical Sketches and Recollections: During a Thirty-Five Year Residence in New Orleans,* 2nd ed. (Boston: Phillips, Samson & Co., 1858), 377.

32. *Alabama Planter* (Mobile), December 28, 1846. Southerners emphasized the suffering of many British subjects besides the Irish. The *Catholic Mirror* of Baltimore argued that southern slaves lived in "Paradise" compared to the "wretched subjects of Great Britain in India." Cited in Rice, *American Catholic Opinion,* 106–7.

33. *Miscellany,* October 15, 1831; McGreevy, *American Freedom,* 52–56.

34. *Miscellany,* July 31, 1822.

35. Murphy, *Jesuit Slaveholding,* 41, 66–67, 131, 147–48. For Thomas Aquinas and slav-

ery, see also Stephen F. Brett, *Slavery and the Catholic Tradition: Rights in the Balance* (New York: Peter Lang, 1994). Brett argues that Aquinas saw any sort of servitude as opposed to God's plan and human wisdom. He contrasts Aquinas with the sixteenth-century theorists Francisco Vitoria and Domingo de Soto for whom belief in the authority of civil legislation obscured the first principles Aquinas had discerned through metaphysics.

36. Gregory issued his letter at the urging of the British government, which hoped that it would convince Spain and Portugal to enforce laws against the slave trade. See John F. Quinn, "'Three Cheers for the Abolitionist Pope!': American Reaction to Gregory XVI's Condemnation of the Slave Trade, 1840–1860," *Catholic Historical Review* 90, no. 1 (Jan. 2004), 67–69.

37. *Miscellany,* March 14, and October 3, 1840.

38. Quinn, "Three Cheers," 76–77.

39. John England, *Letters of the Late Bishop England to the Hon. John Forsyth, on the Subject of Domestic Slavery* (Baltimore: John Murphy, 1844), v.

40. According to O'Connell, England had contemplated tracing the duties of masters and rights of slaves according to natural, divine, and ecclesiastical law in an addendum to his letters, but he died before he could do so. See *Catholicity in the Carolinas,* 71–72.

41. Martin Spalding, "Dissertation on the American Civil War," cited in Kenneth J. Zanca, *American Catholics and Slavery: 1789–1866* (New York: University Press of America, 1994), 209.

42. Cited in William G. Bean, "An Aspect of Know-Nothingism—The Immigrant and Slavery," *South Atlantic Quarterly* 23, no. 4 (Oct. 1924), 326n24. Mitchell's stance won the respect of South Carolina Senator Andrew P. Butler, who worried that immigrants did not understand "our institutions" but named Mitchell as an exception (325–26).

43. Michael V. Gannon, *Rebel Bishop: The Life and Era of Augustin Verot* (Milwaukee: Bruce Publishing Company, 1964). In 1861, Verot transferred to the See of Savannah. Nine years later, he returned to St. Augustine, now elevated to a see, where he died in 1876.

44. Verot, *Tract for the Times,* 5–18. Verot not only wanted slave owners to regulate themselves, but he also hoped that the Confederacy would implement a "servile code" enshrining in law the rights and duties of slaves and masters.

45. Murphy, *Jesuit Slaveholding,* 142.

46. McGreevy, *American Freedom,* 53.

47. *U.S. Catholic Intelligencer,* reprinted in the *Miscellany,* October 15, 1831.

48. Elizabeth Fox-Genovese and Eugene Genovese, *The Mind of the Master Class: History and Faith in the Southern Slaveholders' Worldview* (Cambridge: Cambridge University Press, 2005), 321–24; Eugene Genovese, *The Slaveholders' Dilemma: Freedom and Progress in Southern Conservative Thought, 1820–1860* (Columbia: University of South Carolina Press, 1992), 6–7. Southern intellectuals' attitudes toward Catholicism were clear in their assessments of the Middle Ages. They saw medieval society as primitive, but they bemoaned the costs of progress, particularly the deterioration of social ties between rulers and subjects. They saw the medieval church as a stabilizing force

that used its resources to advance civilization. This affinity with Catholicism was true of some twentieth-century southern intellectuals as well. Allen Tate, for example, saw the South's great failure as one of religion. He argued that southerners had constructed a European-style feudal society but without the necessary religious underpinnings, as they had mistakenly adopted Protestantism—a nonagrarian religion of merchants. The South's ultimate defeat—the collapse of its social structure during and soon after the Civil War—was due to its failure to choose a fitting religion. Tate did not explicitly identify Catholicism as the religion that could have saved southern feudalism, but it is not unreasonable to draw such an inference, especially given his eventual conversion. Allen Tate, "Religion in the Old South," in *Essays of Four Decades* (Chicago: Swallow Press, 1968).

49. *Louisville Guardian,* January 14, 1860, cited in Zanca, *Catholics and Slavery,* 133.

50. *Guardian,* November 24, 1860, cited in Rice, *American Catholic Opinion,* 137.

51. *Miscellany,* February 17, 1841. England's argument was not innovative. As early as 1606, Robert Parsons, an English Jesuit political philosopher, had assigned slavery to the temporal realm. Murphy, *Jesuit Slaveholding,* 12.

52. *Miscellany,* August 22, 1835.

53. Verot, *Tract for the Times,* 19.

54. *Miscellany,* December 15, 1827.

55. Ibid., September 10, 1831.

56. Ibid., July 19, 1828.

57. Mary D. Robertson, ed., *A Confederate Lady Comes of Age: The Journal of Pauline DeCaradeuc Hayward, 1861–1888* (Columbia: University of South Carolina Press, 1992), 34.

58. Maria Genoino Caravaglios, *The American Catholic Church and the Negro Problem in the XVIII–XIX Centuries,* ed. Ernest L. Unterkoefler (Charleston: s.n., 1974), 183–200; Cyprian Davis, *The History of Black Catholics in the United States* (New York: Crossroad, 1990), 51, 56–57. Joseph Mobberly, a Maryland Jesuit, also held the view that Africans were the descendants of Ham, a son of Noah who had incurred his father's curse for his disrespectful behavior. Like many Protestant apologists for slavery, Mobberly believed that black skin was a sign of sin and a product of the curse on Ham. He argued that because Ham had rebelled against his rightful superior, his father, God had sentenced his descendents to eternal servitude. Unlike Martin, however, Mobberly confined his views to his private diary and thus escaped censure. See Murphy, *Jesuit Slaveholding,* 149–50.

59. Verot, *Tract for the Times,* 16.

60. McGreevy, *American Freedom,* 55–56.

61. Noel Ignatiev, *How the Irish Became White* (New York: Routledge, 1995), 106–38.

62. Cited in Davis, *History of Black Catholics,* 96.

63. Peter Welsh, *Irish Green and Union Blue: The Civil War Letters of Peter Welsh, Color Sergeant, 28th Regiment, Massachusetts Volunteers,* ed. Lawrence Frederick Kohl (New York: Fordham University Press, 1986), 62, 66.

64. Cited in Bean, "Aspect of Know-Nothingism," 321n8.

65. Reprinted in the *Miscellany,* October 15, 1831.

66. Cited in Rice, *American Catholic Opinion,* 70–71. Kenrick's work seems to re-

flect the influence of Italian neo-Thomists, whose writings he studied during several years spent in Rome. Like Kenrick, the neo-Thomists saw great problems with the actual practice of slavery but argued that it was permissible in the abstract and stressed the importance of social order. McGreevy, *American Freedom,* 53.

67. Cited in McGreevy, *American Freedom,* 60.

68. Rice, *American Catholic Opinion,* 152. For a summary of northern Catholic attitudes, see Rice, 110–30. Once the Civil War began, the gap between pro and antislavery Catholics in the North deepened and some of those opposed to slavery came closer to calling for abolition. See McGreevy, *American Freedom,* 76–79; Rice, *American Catholic Opinion,* 118–30.

69. Murphy, *Jesuit Slaveholding,* 138–39.

70. Cited in Rice, *American Catholic Opinion,* 64. See also Peter Guilday, *A History of the Councils of Baltimore (1791–1884)* (New York: MacMillan, 1932), 141, 169–70. The Ninth Provincial Council of Baltimore in 1858 reiterated these views, instructing clergy to avoid interfering with people's social or political views as long as those views were within the scope of Christian principles.

71. Cited in Rice, *American Catholic Opinion,* 94.

72. Richard C. Madden, *Catholics in South Carolina: A Record* (New York: University Press of America, 1985), 68.

73. *Religion in the Old South* (Chicago: University of Chicago Press, 1977), 136. See also xvii, 184.

74. Christine Leigh Heyrman, *Southern Cross: The Beginnings of the Bible Belt* (Chapel Hill: University of North Carolina Press, 1997), 69, 93.

75. Janet Duitsman Cornelius, "*When I Can Read My Title Clear*": *Literacy, Slavery, and Religion in the Antebellum South* (Columbia: University of South Carolina Press, 1991), 26–28. Among themselves, evangelicals rationalized their accommodation of slavery by arguing that they needed to maintain slaveholders' trust in order to bring the gospel to the slaves. Opposing slavery would thus imperil the slaves' souls.

76. John B. Boles, *Religion in Antebellum Kentucky* (Lexington: University Press of Kentucky, 1976), 104–22.

77. Randall Miller, "Some Speculations on Catholic Identity in the Old South," in Miller and Wakelyn, *Catholics in the Old South,* 14.

78. Rice, *American Catholic Opinion,* 103.

79. Frederick Law Olmsted, *A Journey in the Seaboard Slave States* (New York: Dix & Edwards, 1856), 551. Olmsted had gotten a similar reply when he asked a Virginia planter why he used Irish workers rather than slaves to drain his fields (90–91).

80. For the dominance of immigrant labor in southern cities, and the consequences for blacks, see Ira Berlin and Herbert Gutman, "Natives and Immigrants, Free Men and Slaves: Urban Workingmen in the Antebellum American South," *American Historical Review* 88, no. 5 (Dec. 1983), 1175–1200.

81. Harriet E. Amos, *Cotton City: Urban Development in Antebellum Mobile* (Tuscaloosa: The University of Alabama Press, 1985), 91–92, 143.

82. John S. C. Abbott, *South and North; or, Impressions Received during a Trip to Cuba and the South* (New York: Abbey & Abbott, 1860), 112–13, 210.

83. Mary O'Brien, "Slavery in Louisville 1820–1860," in *Encyclopedia of Louisville* (Lexington: University Press of Kentucky, 2001).

84. Ulrich Bonnell Phillips, *Life and Labor in the Old South* (Boston: Little, Brown, and Company, 1946), 186–87.

85. Amos, *Cotton City,* 98.

86. Olmsted, *Journey,* 512.

87. Berlin and Gutman, "Natives and Immigrants," 1195.

88. Amos, *Cotton City,* 62.

89. Clement Eaton, *Freedom of Thought in the Old South* (Durham, NC: Duke University Press, 1940), 241, 246.

90. Ibid., 218, 220, 227, 229.

91. George Lewis, *Impressions of America and of the American Churches* (Edinburgh: W. P. Kennedy, 1845), 127, 130.

92. Thomas Paul Thigpen, "Aristocracy of the Heart: Catholic Lay Leadership in Savannah, 1820–1870" (PhD diss., Emory University, 1995), 591.

93. McGreevy, *American Freedom,* 51; Rice, *American Catholic Opinion,* 83.

94. Cited in Rice, *American Catholic Opinion,* 84.

95. David Roediger, *The Wages of Whiteness: Race and the Making of the American Working Class* (London: Verson, 1991), 133–86.

96. David T. Gleeson, *The Irish in the South: 1815–1877* (Chapel Hill: University of North Carolina Press, 2001), 121; Eaton, *Freedom of Thought,* 228. For the colonial roots of the connection between whiteness and freedom, see Edmund Morgan, *American Slavery, American Freedom: The Ordeal of Colonial Virginia* (New York: W. W. Norton, 1975).

97. Cited in Amos, *Cotton City,* 99.

98. Ignatiev, *How the Irish,* 159.

99. Gillard, *Catholic Church,* 14.

100. Davis, *History of Black Catholics,* 30.

101. Winthrop Jordan, *White Over Black: American Attitudes toward the Negro, 1550–1812* (Chapel Hill: University of North Carolina Press, 1968), 116–19.

102. Carter G. Woodson, *The Education of the Negro Prior to 1861: A History of the Education of the Colored People of the United States from the Beginning of Slavery to the Civil War* (New York: G. P. Putnam, 1915), 351–52.

103. Thomas F. Hopkins, *St. Mary's Church, Charleston, S.C.: The First Catholic Church in the Original Diocese of Charleston: An Historic Sketch of the Church from Its Beginning to the Present Time* (Charleston: Walker, Evans, & Cogswell, 1898), 1.

104. Berlin and Gutman, "Natives and Immigrants," 1196–1200, quotation on 1198.

105. This document continued a centuries-old papal critique of slavery's excesses. The slave trade had come under papal censure two centuries earlier when Urban VIII condemned it and forbade Christian participation. For an overview of papal pronouncements on slavery, see Rice, *American Catholic Opinion,* 11–24. For a history of papal condemnations of slavery stretching back to 1435, see Joel S. Panzer, *The Popes and Slavery* (New York: Alba House, 1996). Contrary to most scholars, Panzer argues that Gregory

XVI's work condemned not only the slave trade but also slavery itself (44–48). Although the letter's antislavery language could be seen as a denunciation of the institution, Gregory said nothing about emancipation. For an overview of the historiographical debate regarding Gregory's intent, see Quinn, "Three Cheers," 71n19.

106. Cited in Quinn, "Three Cheers," 74.

107. "Ch[arles] H. Winder [Clerk, Department of State], to John C. Calhoun, [Washington, April?, 1844]," *The Papers of John C. Calhoun,* vol. 28, ed. Clyde Wilson (Columbia: University of South Carolina Press, 1988), 381.

108. Quinn, "Three Cheers," 85, 89, 91.

109. Bean, "Aspect of Know-Nothingism." This view did not die with the nineteenth century. As late as 1957, a work appeared claiming that "there can be no doubt that the whole system of slavery as known in America . . . was introduced, nurtured, promoted, protected, and justified by the Roman Catholic Church and her communicants." Richard Roscoe Miller, *Slavery and Catholicism* (Durham, NC: North State Publishers, 1957), 256.

110. Theodore Parker, *Additional Speeches, Addresses, and Occasional Sermons* (Boston: Little, Brown and Company, 1855), vol. 2, 244.

111. Charles Buxton Going, *David Wilmot, Free-Soiler* (New York: D. Appleton and Company, 1924), 736. Although the Republican Party generally denounced nativism, the anti-Catholic comments of state and local leaders led many Catholics to perceive it as little better than the American Party. McGreevy, *American Freedom,* 64.

112. Bean, "Aspect of Know-Nothingism," 323–24.

113. McGreevy, *American Freedom,* 57.

114. W. Darrell Overdyke, *The Know-Nothing Party in the South* (Baton Rouge: Louisiana State University Press, 1950), 198–200.

115. "William Hogan to John C. Calhoun, Boston, November 1844," *The Papers of John C. Calhoun,* vol. 20, ed. Clyde Wilson (Columbia: University of South Carolina Press, 1991), 190; "Hogan to Calhoun, Boston, November 12, 1844," ibid., 237–38. Calhoun's predecessor as Secretary of State, Abel P. Upshur, a native of Virginia, had grown concerned about Catholic aims regarding slavery in the United States. He had sent Hogan abroad to gather more information. Upshur also asked a Catholic member of the State Department to secure an official repudiation of the abolitionist reading of *In Supremo Apostolatus,* but Archbishop Eccleston refused the request (381–82).

116. George H. Thatcher to Calhoun, Ballston Center, August 10, 1848, *The Papers of John C. Calhoun,* vol. 25, ed. Clyde Wilson and Shirley Cooks (Columbia: University of South Carolina Press, 1999), 674.

117. Cited in Bean, "Aspect of Know-Nothingism," 329.

118. John Macpherson Berrien, "To the People of Georgia," Rockingham, Georgia, September 4, 1855, cited in Stephen F. Miller, *The Bench and Bar of Georgia: Memoirs and Sketches* (Philadelphia: J. B. Lippincott, 1858), 94. Southern Democrats offered a number of responses to the nativist argument. Some insisted that European Catholics settled in the North only because they found the climate more congenial. Others proposed encouraging immigration to the South as a way of balancing the demographics.

A paper in Georgia even suggested that because immigrants were so poor and ignorant they weakened the North and thus indirectly strengthened the South. Overdyke, *Know-Nothing Party,* 89, 204.

119. "Carroll to Archbishop Troy, undated," *ACHS* 20, no. 1 (March 1909), 69.

120. Cited in Murphy, *Jesuit Slaveholding,* 55.

121. "Carroll to Thayer, Baltimore, July 15, 1794," *ACHS* 20, no. 1 (March 1909), 58–59.

122. "Badin to Carroll, Washington County, July 5, 1799," *ACHS* 19, no. 4 (Dec. 1908), 478. Sympathy for blacks was just one of Thayer's problems. Allegations of propositioning and threatening female parishioners in the confessional—allegations to which Badin gave credence—also dogged him during his brief time in Kentucky. John R. Dichtl, *Frontiers of Faith: Bringing Catholicism to the West in the Early Republi*c (Lexington: University Press of Kentucky, 2008), 74–76.

123. Cited in Mattingly, *Catholic Church on the Kentucky Frontier,* 173. Presumably Badin's objection was to the form of Protestant slaveholding, not slavery itself, because he also owned slaves.

124. W. J. Howlett, "Bishop Flaget's Diary," *ACHS* 29, no. 3 (Sept. 1918), 246.

125. "Report of Bishop England to the Cardinal Prefect of Propaganda (Rome, 1833)," *ACHS* 8, no. 3 (Sept. 1897), 329.

126. "England to Cullen, Charleston, February 23, 1836," *ACHS* 8, no 2 (June 1897), 224.

127. *Miscellany,* September 29, 1827; November 17, 1838. The second column concerned a case in which Governor Pierce Butler refused, despite public pressure, to pardon a white man who had murdered a slave boy. The column approvingly cited Butler's decision as evidence that whites were held to account when they violated slaves' rights.

128. Davis, *History of Black Catholics,* 65.

129. Phillips, *Life and Labor,* 226.

130. Michael Kenny, *Catholic Culture in Alabama: Centenary Story of Spring Hill College, 1830–1930* (New York: The America Press, 1931), 187. During the war, Realf served as a colonel in the Union army. He committed suicide in San Francisco in 1878.

131. *Miscellany,* May 25, 1825. The layman made the point not in support of abolitionism, but rather to demonstrate the insufficiency of reason in contrast to the promise of infallibility given by God to the church.

132. Rice, *American Catholic Opinion,* 133, 141. Economic, social, and legal restrictions made manumission much less common as the antebellum era progressed.

133. "Judge Gaston on Slavery," *American Catholic Historical Researches* 8, no. 2 (April 1891), 71 (hereafter cited as *ACHR*). Madeleine Rice argued that Gaston's outspokenness reflected a legacy of antislavery sentiment in North Carolina and that the topic was safer in that state than in other southern states (136). But surely Gaston would have suspected that news of such a speech by a man of his stature would spread beyond North Carolina. Indeed it did, with published editions of the speech soon appearing in Alabama and Virginia.

134. Berlin and Gutman, "Natives and Immigrants," 1195, 1197.

135. "Pastoral Letter of R. Rev. Félix Antoine Philibert Dupanloup, Bishop of Or-

leans, to his Clergy on the subject of the Civil War in the United States, April 6, 1862," *ACHS* 25, no. 1 (March 1914), 19–20.

136. France had abolished slavery in 1794, but Napoleon reestablished it in 1802. On the second period of French abolitionism, including the role of the Catholic Church, see Lawrence C. Jennings, *French Anti-Slavery: The Movement for the Abolition of Slavery in France, 1802–1848* (New York: Cambridge University Press, 2000), 213–46.

137. Quinn, "Three Cheers," 83–85

138. Cited Prior F. Felix, "The Sisters of Our Lady of Mercy," *American Ecclesiastical Review* 20, no. 5 (March 1899), 263.

139. Cited in Columba Fox, *The Life of the Right Reverend John Baptist Mary David* (New York: United States Catholic Historical Society, 1925), 62.

140. David to Carroll, September 17, 1814, Archives of the Archdiocese of Baltimore.

141. Nerinckx and Flaget to Cardinal Michele de Pietro, Prefect of the Congregation for the Propagation of the Faith, Bardstown, 1813; Nerinckx to Cardinal Francesco Luigi Fontana, Prefect of the Sacred Congregation for the Propagation of the Faith, Mechlin, Belgium 1821 in Augustin Wand and M. Lilliana Owens, eds., *Documents: Nerinckx—Kentucky—Loretto, 1804–1851 in Archives Propaganda Fide, Rome* (Nerinx, KY: Loretto Literary and Benevolent Institution, 1972), 161–70.

142. Davis, *History of Black Catholics,* 42.

143. The first authoritative statistics for the number of black Catholics in the United States came from the Commission for Catholic Missions among the Colored People and Indians in 1888 which put the total number at 138,213. See Gillard, *Catholic Church,* 1.

144. Davis, *History of Black Catholics,* 35.

145. Gillard, *Catholic Church,* 15.

146. Guilday, *Life and Time . . . England,* vol. 2, 191.

147. Gillard, *Catholic Church,* 33; Rice, *American Catholic Opinion,* 39.

148. *Miscellany,* August 25, 1827. Catholic historians often boasted that non-Catholics preferred to have their slaves instructed by Catholic priests, often to the exclusion of Protestant ministers. See O'Connell, *Catholicity in the Carolinas,* 56.

149. Verot, *Tract for the Times,* 21.

150. Badin, "Origin and Progress," 828; J. Herman Schauinger, *Cathedrals in the Wilderness* (Milwaukee: Bruce Publishing Company, 1952), 18.

151. *Miscellany,* April 13, 1824.

152. "England to Gaston, Washington, NC, June 13, 1821," *ACHS* 8, no. 4 (Dec. 1907), 371.

153. "England to Gaston, Halifax, NC, July 8, 1839," *ACHS* 19, no. 2 (June 1908), 173.

154. *Miscellany,* August 9, 1828.

155. Davis, *History of Black Catholics,* 69, 73; Gillard, *Catholic Church,* 17.

156. Cited in Mattingly, *Catholic Church on the Kentucky Frontier,* 105.

157. Martin John Spalding, *Sketches of the Early Catholic Missions of Kentucky; from Their Commencement in 1787 to the Jubilee of 1826–7* (Louisville: B. J. Webb, 1844), 116.

158. Martin John Spalding, *Life, Times, and Character of the Right Reverend Benedict*

Joseph Flaget (Louisville: Webb & Levering, 1852), 138. Bishop England and Bishop McGill of Richmond were also outspoken defenders of the sanctity of slave marriages. See Eaton, *Freedom of Thought.*

159. Our Lady of the Port, Louisville, Church Register, Filson Historical Society, Louisville (hereafter cited as Filson). One of the baptized slaves was the property of the Sisters of Loretto. The number of black baptisms pales in comparison to white baptisms, which totaled over nine hundred for the same period.

160. John Lyons, "Historical Sketches of Old St. Theresa's," Filson.

161. "St. Mary's Church Records, Calvary, Kentucky," Filson.

162. In 1853, twenty-four slaves and thirty-five free blacks received baptism, but by 1860, these numbers had fallen to eleven and sixteen. *Baptisma Negorum*, vol. 1, 1781–1805 and vol. 2, 1806–1828, Archives of the Diocese of Mobile; Baptismal Register for Colored People of the Cathedral of the Immaculate Conception at Mobile, AL 1843–1855, 1855–1863, Archives of the Diocese of Mobile. In several cases it is unclear whether the baptized were free or slaves. I have counted these cases as free blacks, generally because the records do not list an owner or list the parents by first and last names.

163. Davis, *History of Black Catholics,* 81.

164. *Miscellany,* August 1, 1829.

165. Ibid., February 10, 1827.

166. Spalding, *Life, Times, . . . Flaget,* 276.

167. Amos, *Cotton City,* 110; McGreevy, *American Freedom,* 50; Albert J. Raboteau, *Slave Religion: The "Invisible Institution" in the Antebellum South,* updated ed. (New York: Oxford University Press, 2004). Raboteau points out that integration was not necessarily a blessing for black Catholics because it restricted black leadership (275).

168. Olmsted, *Journey,* 582.

169. Joseph L. O'Brien, *John England—Bishop of Charleston: The Apostle to Democracy* (New York: Edward O'Toole, 1934), 204.

170. Felix, "Sisters," 258–59. O'Connell also describes England's prioritizing ministry to blacks. See *Catholicity in the Carolinas,* 71.

171. For an overview of Catholic efforts to educate blacks in the Old South, see Gillard, *Catholic Church,* 134–141.

172. Christopher J. Kauffman, *Ministry and Meaning: A Religious History of Catholic Health Care in the United States* (New York: Crossroad, 1995), 57, 79.

173. Fox, *Life of . . . David,* 93.

174. Davis, *History of Black Catholics,* 99–105; Kauffman, *Ministry and Meaning,* 54–55. For the antebellum history of the Oblate Sisters of Providence, see Diana Batts Morrow, *Persons of Color and Religious at the Same Time: The Oblate Sisters of Providence, 1828–1860* (Chapel Hill: University of North Carolina Press, 2002).

175. Davis, *History of Black Catholics,* 105–10; Kauffman, *Ministry and Meaning,* 79.

176. Cited in Kauffman, *Ministry and Meaning,* 55.

177. Davis, *History of Black Catholics,* 114–15.

178. Cited in Gillard, *Catholic Church,* 25.

179. Gillard, *Catholic Church,* 18–19.

180. Davis, *History of Black Catholics,* 86–88.

181. Madden, *Catholics in South Carolina,* 59, 68. In some cases, blacks may have joined predominantly white associations. One woman listed on the roll of the Confraternity of the Holy Name, established at St. Charles Church, Hardin's Creek, Kentucky in 1809, had the designation "Nigra" placed after her name. Mattingly, *Catholic Church on the Kentucky Frontier,* 125.

182. John Tracy Ellis, *Documents of American Catholic History,* rev. ed., vol. 1 (Chicago: H. Regnery Co., 1967), 327.

183. "Eccleston to the Committee of the Propagation of the Faith, Paris, Baltimore, January 31, 1838," *ACHR* 9, no. 3 (July 1892), 141.

184. Murphy, *Jesuit Slaveholding,* 164.

185. Gillard, *Catholic Church,* 13; Rice, *American Catholic Opinion,* 55.

186. *Miscellany,* November 24, 1827.

187. Spalding, *Sketches of Early Catholic Missions,* 117.

188. Ellis, *Documents,* vol. 1, 328.

189. "Register of the Prefect of Classes and Studies 1847–48–49," Spring Hill College Archives.

190. "England to Cullen, Charleston, February 23, 1836," *ACHS* 8, no. 2 (June 1897), 232.

191. "Report of Bishop England," 321.

192. Thomas W. Spalding, *The Premier See: A History of the Archdiocese of Baltimore, 1789–1989* (Baltimore: The Johns Hopkins Press, 1989), 57.

193. For an overview of slavery in the Spanish and French colonies, see Davis, *History of Black Catholics,* 28–33, 68–77.

194. Gillard, *Catholic Church,* 19.

195. Madden, *Catholics in South Carolina,* 66; Chalmers Gaston Davidson, *The Last Foray: the South Carolina Planters of 1860: A Sociological Study* (Columbia: University of South Carolina Press, 1971), 227. Davidson only mentions 258 slaves owned by the March family in Colleton District. Madden got his estimate from Davidson and Jeremiah O'Connell, who spelled the family name Marsh. See *Catholicity in the Carolinas,* 182.

196. Davidson, *Last Foray,* 106, 225.

197. Curran, R. Emmett, "Splendid Poverty: Jesuit Slaveholding in Maryland, 1805–1838" in Miller and Wakelyn, *Catholics in the Old South,* 125–46; Murphy, *Jesuit Slaveholding,* xv–78; Spalding, *Premier See,* 113.

198. Gilbert J. Garraghan, *The Jesuits of the Middle United States,* vol. 1 (New York: American Press, 1938), 617.

199. Ibid., 617–19.

200. Davis, *History of Black Catholics,* 37–38.

201. Flaget to Carroll, Mrs. Howard's Plantation, August 22, 1811, Filson Mss. BA/B245/7.

202. Mattingly, *Catholic Church on the Kentucky Frontier,* 81.

203. Ibid., 105. One of Badin's slaves was a gift from Ann Rhodes, who was later the first superior of the Sisters of Loretto.

204. Schauinger, *Cathedrals in the Wilderness,* 22.

205. Fox, *Life of . . . David,* 46.

206. Flaget to unknown, Bardstown, February 22, 1820, Filson Mss. BA/B245/7.

207. Rosati to Timon, St. Louis, November 27, 1839, CVIN IV-3-1-5, Archives of the University of Notre Dame (hereafter cited as UNDA).

208. O'Connell, *Catholicity in the Carolinas,* 333–35.

209. Davis, *History of Black Catholics,* 79.

210. Schauinger, *Cathedrals in the Wilderness,* 71.

211. Mary Ewens, *The Role of the Nun in Nineteenth Century America* (New York: Arno Press, 1978), 49.

212. Schauinger, *Cathedrals in the Wilderness,* 154.

213. Fox, *Life of . . . David,* 101.

214. Ewens, *Role of the Nun,* 61.

215. Ibid., 68.

216. *The Papers of Henry Clay,* vol. 9, ed. Robert Seager II (Lexington: University Press of Kentucky, 1988), 218.

217. W. J. Howlett, "Bishop Flaget's Diary," *ACHS* 29, no. 1 (March 1918), 38; no. 2 (June 1918), 164.

218. Archives of the Diocese of Charleston. Madden notes that the bill of sale indicates that the slave was in poor health and suggests that Lynch's motive in purchasing her may have been humanitarian (*Catholics in South Carolina,* 69).

219. Schauinger, *Cathedrals in the Wilderness,* 153.

220. *Miscellany,* November 17, 1838.

221. Garraghan, *Jesuits,* vol. 1, 617.

222. Verot, *Tract for the Times,* 19.

223. Rice, *American Catholic Opinion,* 47–48.

224. Verot, *Tract for the Times,* 6.

225. Garraghan, *Jesuits,* vol. 1, 618. Such a mentality also characterized Jesuit slaveholding in Maryland. See Murphy, *Jesuit Slaveholding,* xx, 119.

226. Theobold, "Catholic Missionary Work," 340.

227. Cited in ibid., 340–41.

228. Austin Carroll, *A Catholic History of Alabama and the Floridas* (Freeport, NY: Books for Libraries Press, 1970), 72. Gillard was one of the historians who repeated this claim, arguing that the Jesuit slaves were "slaves in name rather than fact" and that the term "Priest's Negroes" indicated the "enviable treatment they received" (15). With the exception of one letter by Bishop John Carroll, I have not come across this expression in any primary source. See Thomas O'Brien Hanley, ed., *The John Carroll Papers,* vol. 1, *1755–1791* (Notre Dame: University of Notre Dame Press, 1976), 343. However, Curran cited a letter from a Maryland Jesuit who used a similar expression—"priest's slave"—in a complaint about the Jesuits' failure to discipline their slaves. "Splendid Poverty," 132–33.

229. *Spring Hill College, Mobile, Ala., 1830–1905* (Mobile: Commercial Printing Company, 1906), 12–13. This chronicler may have borrowed from a letter written in 1830 by Fr. Loras, the first president of Spring Hill. Loras noted seeing from his window "a joyous company of negroes naked to the waist, toiling bravely and gaily in the broiling heat of the summer sun, at a work whose importance they are far from realizing." Cited in Kenny, *Catholic Culture in Alabama,* 55.

230. Fox, *Life of . . . David,* 187.

231. Rice, *American Catholic Opinion,* 41–42.

232. McGreevy, *American Freedom,* 61.

233. Verot, *Tract for the Times,* 15.

234. Cited in Zanca, *Catholics and Slavery,* 106.

235. John Tyler to Robert Tyler, July 17, 1854, cited in McGreevy, *American Freedom,* 65.

236. A. H. Stephens, "Letter to Judge Thomas W. Thomas, on the Subject of Know-Nothingism," Crawfordville, GA, May 9, 1855, in Henry Cleveland, *Alexander Stephens in Public and Private* (Philadelphia: National Publishing Company, 1866), 464. Catholics contrasted their own unity and loyalty on slavery with the geographical divisions among Protestants. The *Louisville Guardian* noted: "There is no Catholic Church North and South. The Church is everywhere the same, both for bond and free" (cited in Rice, *American Catholic Opinion,* 139).

237. Fitzwilliam Byrdsall to John C. Calhoun, New York, June 6, 1847, *The Papers of John C. Calhoun,* vol. 14, ed. Clyde N. Wilson (Columbia: University of South Carolina Press, 1981), 391.

238. "England to Cullen, Charleston, February 23, 1836," *ACHS* 8, no. 2 (June 1897), 218.

239. *Charleston Courier,* April 12, 1842, cited in John England, *Works of the Right Rev. John England, First Bishop of Charleston,* vol. 1, ed. Ignatius Aloysius Reynolds (Baltimore: John Murphy & Co., 1849), 22.

240. Overdyke, *Know-Nothing Party,* 5–11, 19, 32, 63, 91, 101, 154, 163. For statistics on foreigners in the South, see Berlin and Gutman, "Natives and Immigrants," 1178–88. By 1860, foreign-born whites accounted for 64 percent of the adult free workingmen in Mobile.

241. Overdyke, *Know-Nothing Party,* 33, 70, 95–96, 113.

242. Cited in Overdyke, *Know-Nothing Party,* 63.

243. Overdyke, *Know-Nothing Party,* 240–52.

244. Ray Billington, *The Protestant Crusade: 1800–1860* (New York: MacMillan, 1938), 421; Overdyke, *Know-Nothing Party,* 252–58.

245. Boles, *Religion in Antebellum Kentucky,* 77–78; Overdyke, *Know-Nothing Party,* 105, 106, 258–59; George H. Yater, "Bloody Monday," *Encyclopedia of Louisville*; George H. Yater, *Two Hundred Years at the Falls of the Ohio: a History of Louisville and Jefferson County* (Louisville: Filson Club, 1987), 65–70.

246. *Louisville Daily Courier,* Wednesday, August 8, 1855.

247. Billington's failure to distinguish between the two mars his otherwise excellent study.

248. Overdyke, *Know-Nothing Party,* 38, 75, 90, 129, 218–24.

249. Overdyke, *Know-Nothing Party,* 86. Given the differences of opinion among nativists, Overdyke concluded that "after the emergence of Know-Nothingism no dogmatic statement of its policy toward Roman Catholicism nationally, sectionally, or in any given state could be made, because it varied greatly" (213).

250. Spalding, *Premier See,* 135.

251. Gerald P. Fogarty, *Commonwealth Catholicism: A History of the Catholic Church in Virginia* (Notre Dame: University of Notre Dame Press, 2001), 125.

252. Berrien, "To the People of Georgia," 96.

253. Overdyke, *Know-Nothing Party,* 213.

254. Ibid., 219, 229; Eaton, *Freedom of Thought,* 303; Rice, *American Catholic Opinion,* 91; Spalding, *Premier See,* 135.

255. Bean, "Aspect of Know-Nothingism," 319–20.

256. Overdyke, *Know-Nothing Party,* 203, 209, 261, 271, 281.

257. Augustus Baldwin Longstreet, *Know Nothingism Unveiled* (Washington, DC: Office of the Congressional Globe, 1855), 5.

258. Cited in Pleasant A. Stovall, *Robert Toombs: Statesman, Speaker, Soldier, Sage* (New York: Cassell, 1892), 124–25.

259. Billington, *Protestant Crusade,* 417–19, 434 n.60; Overdyke, *Know-Nothing Party,* 78. In the face of such criticism, several state councils of the party abandoned secrecy and the national party eventually followed suit (80).

260. James Graham Ramsey letter of April 26, 1856, [35], James Graham Ramsey Papers, Southern Historical Collection, University of North Carolina-Chapel Hill.

261. A common interest in defending slavery worked the same effects among Protestants, tempering sectarianism and division. Eaton, *Freedom of Thought,* 292.

262. Kenny, *Catholic Culture in Alabama,* 211.

263. Stephens, "Letter," in Cleveland, *Alexander Stephens,* 464.

264. Cited in Bean, "Aspect of Know-Nothingism," 333.

265. Stovall, *Robert Toombs,* 123.

266. Cited in Bean, "Aspect of Know-Nothingism," 333.

267. John Fletcher, *Studies on Slavery, in Easy Lessons* (Natchez: Jackson Warner, 1852), 214.

268. Overdyke, *Know-Nothing Party,* 294.

269. Billington, *Protestant Crusade,* 423.

270. Kenny, *Catholic Culture in Alabama,* 147.

271. England to Bruté, Charleston, June 4, 1828, MSGB, UNDA.

272. *Charleston Courier,* May 9, and 10, 1851.

273. Whelan to Purcell, Summerville [AL], March 19, 1861, CACI 11–4-k, UNDA.

274. *Miscellany,* November 10, 1860.

275. Ibid., December 29, 1860.

276. Ibid., March 2, 1861.

277. Cited in Fogarty, *Commonwealth Catholicism,* 148. McGill even contemplated

denying Catholic chaplains in the Union army faculties to hear confessions in Virginia because they were agents of an illegitimate and aggressive force.

278. Cited in Davis, *History of Black Catholics,* 51. For an analysis of how French Catholic priests in the South supported the Confederacy, and the connections between that support and their endorsement of slavery, see Michael Pasquier, *Fathers on the Frontier: French Missionaries and the Roman Catholic Priesthood in the United States, 1789–1870* (New York: Oxford University Press, 2010), chap. 5.

279. Patrick Lynch, "Letter to Archbishop John Hughes, August 4, 1861," in Ellis, *Documents,* vol. 1, 359. Bishop McGill of Richmond expressed a similar view, blaming secession on "the fanaticism of abolitionists." Cited in Fogarty, *Commonwealth Catholicism,* 143.

280. Cited in Lipscomb, "Administration of Quinlan," 38.

281. Dooley, *Confederate Soldier,* 115, 205. Fr. James Corcoran, editor of the *Miscellany,* similarly condemned Irish Catholics in the North for failing to fight back during anti-Catholic riots but then being all too eager to join a war against the one part of the country where nativism had failed to take root. *Miscellany,* May 11, 1861.

282. Madden, *Catholics in South Carolina,* 81. For more examples of Catholic soldiers and chaplains, see Fogarty, *Commonwealth Catholicism,* 148–62.

283. Fogarty, *Commonwealth Catholicism,* 145–47.

284. Ibid., 162–63. In December 1863, Pope Pius IX sent a warm letter to Jefferson Davis that many in Europe, the South, and the North construed as tacitly recognizing the Confederacy.

285. Mary Boykin Chesnut, *A Diary from Dixie,* ed. Ben Ames Williams (Cambridge, MA: Harvard University Press, 1980), 70, 116, 124. Catholics likewise praised Protestant ministers who showed courage in aiding the wounded. James Dooley described one Protestant chaplain as being "held in high esteem by all, whether members of religion or not; for, they say, in times of action, he is as bold as the bravest as is to be seen in the first and fiercest battles consoling and assisting the wounded" (58).

286. Hopkins, *St. Mary's Church,* 61.

287. Robertson, *Confederate Lady,* 75.

Bibliography

Primary sources

Newspapers

Alabama Planter (Mobile)
Catholic Advocate (Kentucky)
Charleston Courier
Charleston Patriot
United States Catholic Miscellany (Charleston)

Archives

Archives of the Archdiocese of Baltimore (BCA)
Archives of the Diocese of Charleston
Archives of the Diocese of Mobile
Archives of the University of Notre Dame (UNDA)
Filson Historical Society, Louisville (Filson)
Southern Historical Collection, University of North Carolina-Chapel Hill (SHC)
Spring Hill College Archives, Mobile

Journal Reproductions of Primary Sources

American Catholic Historical Researches (ACHR)
Catholic Historical Review (CHR)
Illinois Catholic Historical Review
Quarterly Register of the American Education Society
Records of the American Catholic Historical Society of Philadelphia (*ACHS*)

Published Primary Sources

Abbott, John S. C. *South and North; or, Impressions Received during a Trip to Cuba and the South.* New York: Abbey & Abbott, 1860.

Badin, Stephen. "Origin and Progress of the Mission of Kentucky." *Catholic World* 21, no. 126 (Sept. 1875): 825–835.

Beecher, Lyman. *A Plea for the West.* 2nd ed. Cincinnati: Truman & Smith, 1835.

Belcher, Joseph. *The Religious Denominations of the United States: Their History, Doctrine, Government and Statistics.* Philadelphia: J. E. Potter, 1854.

Beste, J. Richard. *The Wabash: or Adventure of an English Gentleman's Family in the Interior of America.* 2 vols. Freeport, NY: Books for Libraries Press, 1970.

Blackwell, Elizabeth. "Letter from Elizabeth Blackwell, July, 1846." *Pioneer Work in Opening the Medical Profession to Women.* New York: Longmans, 1985.

Bunkley, Josephine M. *Testimony of an Escaped Novice.* New York: Harper, 1855.

Calhoun, John C. *The Papers of John C. Calhoun.* 28 vols. Columbia: University of South Carolina Press, 1959–2003.

Chesnut, Mary Boykin. *A Diary from Dixie.* Edited by Ben Ames Williams. Cambridge, MA: Harvard University Press, 1980.

Clapp, Theodore. *Autobiographical Sketches and Recollections: During a Thirty-Five Year Residence in New Orleans.* 2nd ed. Boston: Phillips, Samson & Co., 1858.

Clay, Henry. *The Papers of Henry Clay.* 11 vols. Lexington: University of Kentucky Press, 1959–1992.

"Constitutions of the Associates of Mary at the Foot of the Cross: Part I, Chapter 1." In *Documents: Nerinckx—Kentucky—Loretto, 1804–1851 in Archives Propaganda Fide, Rome.* Edited by Augustin Wand and M. Lilliana Owens, 72–73. Nerinx, KY: Loretto Literary and Benevolent Institution, 1972.

Davis, Varina Jefferson. *Jefferson Davis: Ex-President of the Confederate States of America, a Memoir by His Wife.* 2 vols. New York: Belford, 1890.

The Diaries of Donald Macdonald: 1824–1826. Clifton, NJ: Augustus M. Kelley, 1973.

Dooley, John. *John Dooley, Confederate Soldier: His War Journal.* Edited by Joseph T. Durkin. Notre Dame: University of Notre Dame Press, 1963.

Easterby, J. H. "South Carolina through New England Eyes: Almira Coffin's Visit to the Low Country in 1851." *South Carolina Historical and Genealogic Magazine* 45, no. 3 (1944): 127–136.

Ellis, John Tracy. *Documents of American Catholic History.* Rev. ed. 2 vols. Chicago: H. Regnery Co., 1967.

England, John. *Diurnal of the Right Rev. John England, D.D., First Bishop of Charleston, S.C.* Philadelphia: American Catholic Historical Society, 1895.

———. *Letters of the Late Bishop England to the Hon. John Forsyth, on the Subject of Domestic Slavery.* Baltimore: John Murphy, 1844.

———. *Works of the Right Rev. John England, First Bishop of Charleston.* Edited by Ignatius Aloysius Reynolds. 5 vols. Baltimore: John Murphy & Co., 1849.

Fitzgerald, Oscar Penn. *Fifty Years: Observations—Opinions—Experiences.* Nashville: Publishing House of the Methodist Episcopal Church, South, 1903.

Flaget, Joseph Benedict. "Subscription for Funds to Finish the Building of the St. Louis Church in Louisville." February 26, 1817. Library of Congress.

Fletcher, John. *Studies on Slavery, in Easy Lessons.* Natchez: Jackson Warner, 1852.

Gleason, Phillip, ed. *Documentary Reports on Early American Catholicism.* New York: Arno Press, 1978.

Graham, William Alexander. *The Papers of William Alexander Graham.* Vol. 1. Edited by J. G. de Roulhac Hamilton. Raleigh: State Department of Archives and History, 1957.

Hanley, Thomas O'Brien, ed. *The John Carroll Papers.* Notre Dame: University of Notre Dame Press, 1976.

Hesseltine, William B., ed. *Dr. J. G. M. Ramsey: Autobiography and Letters.* Nashville: Tennessee Historical Commission, 1954.

Jeronimus, C. J., ed. *Travels by His Highness Duke Bernhard of Saxe-Weimar-Eisenach through North America in the Years 1825 and 1826.* Lanham, MD: University Press of America, 2001.

Lawatsch-Boomgaarden, Barbara, with Josef Ijsewjin, trans. and ed. *Voyage to Maryland (1663): Relatio Itineris in Marilandiam.* Wauconda, IL: Bolchazy-Carducci, 1995.

Lewis, George. *Impressions of America and of the American Churches.* Edinburgh: W. P. Kennedy, 1845.

The Life and Speeches of Henry Clay. Vol. 2. Philadelphia: Leary & Getz, 1859.

Longstreet, Augustus Baldwin. *Know Nothingism Unveiled.* Washington, DC: Office of the Congressional Globe, 1855.

Manigault, Ann Ashby. *Extracts from the Journal of Mrs. Ann Manigault.* Edited by Mabel J. Webber. Charleston: South Carolina Historical Society, 1920.

Maury, Sarah Mytton. *An Englishwoman in America.* London: Thomas Richardson and Son, 1848.

McGee, Charles M., Jr., and Ernest M. Lander Jr., eds. *A Rebel Came Home: The Diary and Letters of Floride Clemson, 1863–1866.* Columbia: University of South Carolina Press, 1989.

Mills, Samuel J., and Daniel Smith. *Report of a Missionary Tour through That Part of the United States Which Lies West of the Allegany Mountains.* Andover, MA: Flagg and Gould, 1815.

Morse, Samuel F. B. *Foreign Conspiracy Against the Liberties of the United States.* New York: Leavitt, Lord, & Co., 1835.

Nolan, Hugh, ed. *Pastoral Letters of the American Hierarchy, 1792–1970.* Huntington, IN: Our Sunday Visitor, 1971.

"Notices of the Papal Church in the United States." *Quarterly Register of the American Education Society* 3, no. 2 (Nov. 1830): 98.

O'Connell, J. J. *Catholicity in the Carolinas and Georgia: Leaves of Its History.* S.l.: Sadlier, 1879.

The Old Pine Farm: or, The Southern Side. Comprising Loose Sketches from the Experience of a Southern Country Minister, S.C. Nashville: Southwestern Publishing House, 1860.

Olmsted, Frederick Law. *A Journey in the Seaboard Slave States.* New York: Dix & Edwards, 1856.

Parker, Theodore. *Additional Speeches, Addresses, and Occasional Sermons.* Vol. 2. Boston: Little, Brown and Company, 1855.

Preston, William C. *The Reminiscences of William C. Preston.* Edited by Minnie Clare Yarborough. Chapel Hill: University of North Carolina Press, 1933.

Rameur, E. "The Progress of the Church in the United States." *Catholic World* 1, no. 1 (April 1865): 1–19.

Register of Debates in Congress Comprising the Leading Debates and Incidents of the First Session of the Twenty-Second Congress. Vol. 8. Washington: Gales and Seaton, 1833.

"Report of Bishop England to the Cardinal Prefect of Propaganda (Rome, 1833)." *American Catholic Historical Studies* 8, no. 3 (Sept. 1897): 317–329.

Richardson, C. K., and Lillie E. Burch. *A Kentucky Hell.* Milan, IL: Rail Splitter Press, 1904.

Robertson, Mary D., ed. *A Confederate Lady Comes of Age: The Journal of Pauline DeCaradeuc Heyward, 1863–1888.* Columbia: University of South Carolina Press, 1992.

Rothensteiner, John. "Bishop England's Correspondence with Bishop Rosati." *Illinois Catholic Historical Review* 9, no. 3 (Jan. 1927): 268–368.

Rutland, Robert A., ed. *The Papers of George Mason, 1725–1792.* 3 vols. Chapel Hill: University of North Carolina Press, 1970.

Salzbacher, Joseph. *Miene Reise Nach Nord-Amerika im Jahre 1842.* Vienna: Wimmer, Schmidt & Leo, 1845.

Sanborn, Alvan F., ed. *Reminiscences of Richard Lathers: Sixty Years of a Busy Life in South Carolina, Massachusetts and New York.* New York: Grafton Press, 1907.

Schermerhorn, John F., and Samuel J. Mills. *A Correct View of That Part of the United States Which Lies West of the Alleghany Mountains, with Respect to Religion and Morals.* Hartford, CT: Cleason and Co., 1814.

Schroeder, H. J., trans. *Canons and Decrees of the Council of Trent.* Rockford, IL: Tan Books, 1978.

Sexton, Rebecca Grant, ed. *A Southern Woman of Letters: The Correspondence of Augusta Jane Evans Wilson.* Columbia: University of South Carolina Press, 2002.

Smith, B. B. *The Temper and Conduct Proper on the Part of Episcopalians Towards their Fellow-Christians Who are not Episcopalians: A Charge to the Clergy of the Diocese of Kentucky, Delivered in Christ Church, Lexington, on Thursday, the 11th of May, 1843.* Lexington: James Virden, 1843.

Spalding, Martin John. *Life, Times, and Character of the Right Reverend Benedict Joseph Flaget.* Louisville: Webb & Levering, 1852.

———. *Sketches of the Early Catholic Missions of Kentucky; from Their Commencement in 1787 to the Jubilee of 1826–7.* Louisville: B. J. Webb, 1844.

Sparks, William Henry. *The Memories of Fifty Years.* 3rd ed. Philadelphia: Claxton, Remsen & Haffelfinger, 1872.

St. John de Crèvecoeur, J. Hector. *Letters from an American Farmer; Describing Certain Provincial Situations, Manners, and Customs, Not Generally Known.* Dublin: John Exshaw, 1782.

Statuta Synodi Baltimorensis, anno 1791, celebratae. Baltimore: s.n., 1817.

Trollope, Frances. *Domestic Manners of the Americans.* Edited by Donald Smalley. New York: Knopf, 1949.

Verot, Augustin. *A Tract for the Times: Slavery and Abolitionism, Being the Substance of a Sermon, Preached in the Church of St. Augustine, Florida, on the 4th Day of January,*

1861, Day of Public Humiliation, Fasting and Prayer. New Orleans: Catholic Propagator, 1861.

Wand, Augustin, and M. Lilliana Owens, eds. *Documents: Nerinckx—Kentucky—Loretto, 1804–1851 in Archives Propaganda Fide, Rome.* Nerinx, KY: Loretto Literary and Benevolent Institution, 1972.

Welsh, Peter. *Irish Green and Union Blue: The Civil War Letters of Peter Welsh, Color Sergeant, 28th Regiment, Massachusetts Volunteers.* Edited by Lawrence Frederick Kohl. New York: Fordham University Press, 1986.

Secondary Sources

Agonito, Joseph. "Ecumenical Stirrings: Catholic-Protestant Relations during the Episcopacy of John Carroll." *Church History* 45 (1967): 358–373.

Ahlstrom, Sydney. *A Religious History of the American People.* New Haven, CT: Yale, 1972.

Allison, Clinton B. "The Appalling World of Edgar Wallace Knight." *History of Education in the South,* a special topic edition of the *Journal of Interdisciplinary Thought* 18, no. 3 (Fall 1983): 7–14.

Amos, Harriet E. *Cotton City: Urban Development in Antebellum Mobile.* Tuscaloosa: The University of Alabama Press, 1985.

Augustina, Mary. *American Opinion of Roman Catholicism in the Eighteenth Century.* New York: Columbia University Press, 1936.

Bean, William G. "An Aspect of Know-Nothingism—The Immigrant and Slavery." *South Atlantic Quarterly* 23, no. 4 (Oct. 1924): 319–334.

"The Beginning and Progress of Catholicity in Washington, Wilkes Co, GA." *American Catholic Historical Review* 11, no. 1 (Jan. 1894): 17–24.

Berlin, Ira, and Herbert Gutman. "Natives and Immigrants, Free Men and Slaves: Urban Workingmen in the Antebellum American South." *American Historical Review* 88, no. 5 (Dec. 1983): 1175–1200.

Billington, Ray. *The Protestant Crusade: 1800–1860.* New York: MacMillan, 1938.

Bodo, John R. *The Protestant Clergy and Public Issues.* Princeton: Princeton University Press, 1954.

Boles, John B. *Religion in Antebellum Kentucky.* Lexington: University Press of Kentucky, 1976.

Bonomi, Patricia U., and Peter R. Eisenstadt. "Church Adherence in the Eighteenth-Century British American Colonies." *William and Mary Quarterly* 39, no. 2 (April 1982): 245–286.

Brett, Stephen F. *Slavery and the Catholic Tradition: Rights in the Balance.* New York: Peter Lang, 1994.

Butler, Jon. *Awash in a Sea of Faith: Christianizing the American People.* Cambridge, MA: Harvard University Press, 1990.

Campbell, Bernard U. "Desultory Sketches of the Catholic Church in Maryland, No. VII: Memoir of the Rev. John Francis Moranvillé." *Religious Cabinet: A Monthly Periodical* 1, no. 12 (Dec. 1842): 18–37.

Canevin, J. F. Regis. "Loss and Gain in the Catholic Church in the United States, 1800–1916." *Catholic Historical Review,* Jan. 1917, 377–385.

Caravaglios, Maria Genoino. *The American Catholic Church and the Negro Problem in the XVIII–XIX Centuries.* Edited by Ernest L. Unterkoefler. Charleston: s.n., 1974.

Carroll, Austin. *A Catholic History of Alabama and the Floridas.* Freeport, NY: Books for Libraries Press, 1970.

Cassedy, James H. "Medical Men and the Ecology of the Old South." In Numbers and Savitt, *Science and Medicine in the Old South,* 166–178. Baton Rouge: Louisiana State University Press, 1989.

Cleveland, Henry. *Alexander Stephens in Public and Private.* Philadelphia: National Publishing Company, 1866.

Code, Bernard. *Dictionary of the American Catholic Hierarchy.* New York: Longmans, Green, 1940.

Colyer, Meriwether. *History of Higher Education in South Carolina.* Washington, DC: Government Printing Office, 1889.

Cornelius, Janet Duitsman. "*When I Can Read My Title Clear": Literacy, Slavery, and Religion in the Antebellum South.* Columbia: University of South Carolina Press, 1991.

Crews, Clyde F. *An American Holy Land: A History of the Archdiocese of Louisville.* Louisville: Ikonographics, 1987.

———. *Presence and Possibility: Louisville Catholicism and its Cathedral.* S.1.: s.n., 1973.

Cubberly, Ellwood P. *Public Education in the United States: A Study and Interpretation of American Educational History.* Boston: Houghton Mifflin, 1947.

Curran, Robert Emmett. *American Jesuit Spirituality: The Maryland Tradition, 1634–1900.* Mahwah, NJ: Paulist Press, 1988.

———. *The Bicentennial History of Georgetown University.* Vol. 1. Washington, DC: Georgetown University Press, 1993.

Davidson, Chalmers Gaston. *The Last Foray: The South Carolina Planters of 1860: A Sociological Study.* Columbia: University of South Carolina Press, 1971.

Davis, Cyprian. *The History of Black Catholics in the United States.* New York: Crossroad, 1990.

Davis, David Brion. "Some Themes of Counter-Subversion: An Analysis of Anti-Masonic, Anti-Catholic, and Anti-Mormon Literature." *Mississippi Valley Historical Review* 47, no. 2 (Sept. 1960): 205–224.

Dichtl, John R. *Frontiers of Faith: Bringing Catholicism to the West in the Early Republic.* Lexington: University Press of Kentucky, 2008.

Duncan, Richard R. "Catholics and the Church in the Antebellum Upper South." In Miller and Wakelyn, *Catholics in the Old South,* 77-98.

Dolan, Jay P. *The American Catholic Experience: A History from Colonial Times to the Present.* Notre Dame: University of Notre Dame Press, 1992.

———, ed. *The American Catholic Parish: A History from 1850 to the Present.* Vol. 1. New York: Paulist Press, 1987.

———. *Catholic Revivalism: The American Experience 1830–1900.* Notre Dame: University of Notre Dame Press, 1978.

Douglas, Ann. *The Feminization of American Culture.* New York: Knopf, 1977.
Duffy, John. "Medical Practice in the Ante Bellum South." *Journal of Southern History* 25, no. 1 (Feb. 1959): 53–72.
Eaton, Clement. *Freedom of Thought in the Old South.* Durham, NC: Duke University Press, 1940.
Ellis, John Tracy. *American Catholicism.* 2nd ed. Chicago: University of Chicago Press, 1969.
Encyclopedia of Louisville. Lexington: University Press of Kentucky, 2001.
Ewens, Mary. *The Role of the Nun in Nineteenth Century America.* New York: Arno Press, 1978.
Farnham, Christie Anne. *The Education of the Southern Belle: Higher Education and Student Socialization in the Antebellum South.* New York: New York University Press, 1994.
Felix, Prior F. "The Sisters of Our Lady of Mercy." *American Ecclesiastical Review* 20, no. 5 (March 1899): 255–26.
Fitzgerald, Oscar Penn. *Judge Longstreet: A Life Sketch.* Nashville: Publishing House of the Methodist Episcopal Church, South, 1891.
Flaget, Benedict Joseph, and John Baptist Mary David. "An Abbreviated History of the Sisters of Charity of Nazareth, Kentucky, United States of America." In *Documents: Nerinckx—Kentucky—Loretto, 1804–1851 in Archives Propaganda Fide, Rome.* Edited by Augustin Wand and M. Lilliana Owens. 55–56. Nerinx, KY: Loretto Literary and Benevolent Institution, 1972.
Fogarty, Gerald P. *Commonwealth Catholicism: A History of the Catholic Church in Virginia.* Notre Dame: University of Notre Dame Press, 2001.
Fox, Columba. *The Life of the Right Reverend John Baptist Mary David.* New York: United States Catholic Historical Society, 1925.
Fox-Genovese, Elizabeth, and Eugene Genovese. *The Mind of the Master Class: History and Faith in the Southern Slaveholders' Worldview.* Cambridge: Cambridge University Press, 2005.
Franchot, Jenny. *Roads to Rome: The Antebellum Protestant Encounter with Catholicism.* Berkeley: University of California Press, 1994.
Fraser, Walter J., Jr. *Charleston! Charleston!: The History of a Southern City.* Columbia: University of South Carolina Press, 1989.
Gannon, Michael V. *Rebel Bishop: The Life and Era of Augustin Verot.* Milwaukee: Bruce Publishing Company, 1964.
Garraghan, Gilbert J. *The Jesuits of the Middle United States.* Vol. 1. New York: American Press, 1938.
Gaustad, Edwin. "Regionalism in American Religion." In *Religion in the South.* Edited by Charles Reagan Wilson. 155–172. Jackson: University Press of Mississippi, 1985.
Genovese, Eugene. *The Slaveholders' Dilemma: Freedom and Progress in Southern Conservative Thought, 1820–1860.* Columbia: University of South Carolina Press, 1992.
Gillard, John T. *The Catholic Church and the American Negro.* Baltimore: St. Joseph's Society Press, 1929.

Gleeson, David T. *The Irish in the South: 1815–1877.* Chapel Hill: University of North Carolina Press, 2001.

Going, Charles Buxton. *David Wilmot, Free-Soiler.* New York: D. Appleton and Company, 1924.

Goldfield, David R. "The Business of Health Planning: Disease Prevention in the Old South." *Journal of Southern History* 42, no. 4 (Nov. 1976): 557–570.

Greeley, Andrew M. *The Catholic Experience.* New York: Image, 1969.

Guilday, Peter. *A History of the Councils of Baltimore (1791–1884).* New York: MacMillan, 1932.

———. *The Life and Time of John England, First Bishop of Charleston.* 2 vols. New York: The America Press, 1927.

Hardy, Mary Antonella. "Loretto, Bishop Flaget and Sister Eulalie Flaget." *American Catholic Historical Studies* 36, no. 2 (June 1925): 192–201.

Harrell, David Edwin, Jr. "Religious Pluralism: Catholics, Jews, and Sectarians." In *Religion in the South.* Edited by Charles Reagan Wilson. 59–82. Jackson: University Press of Mississippi, 1985.

Heyrman, Christine Leigh. *Southern Cross: The Beginnings of the Bible Belt.* Chapel Hill: University of North Carolina Press, 1997.

Hill, Samuel S., ed. *Religion in the Southern States.* Macon: Mercer University Press, 1983.

———. *Varieties of Southern Religious Experience.* Baton Rouge: Louisiana State University Press, 1988.

Historical Atlas of Religion in America. Rev. ed. New York: Harper & Row, 1976.

Hofstadter, Richard. *America at 1750: A Social Portrait.* New York: Knopf: 1971.

Holifield, E. Brooks. "Theology as Entertainment: Oral Debate in American Religion." *Church History* 67, no. 3 (Sept. 1998): 499–520.

Holweck, F. G. "The Beginnings of the Church in Little Rock." *Catholic Historical Review* 6, no. 2 (July 1920): 161–178.

Hopkins, Thomas F. *St. Mary's Church, Charleston, S.C.: The First Catholic Church in the Original Diocese of Charleston: An Historic Sketch of the Church from Its Beginning to the Present Time.* Charleston: Walker, Evans, & Cogswell, 1898.

Howlett, W. J. "Bishop Flaget's Diary." *American Catholic Historical Studies* 29, no. 3 (Sept. 1918): 237–60.

Hudnut, Ruth Allison, and Hayes Baker-Crothers. "Acadian Transients in South Carolina." *American Historical Review* 43, no. 3 (April 1938): 500–513.

Hunt, Alfred N. *Haiti's Influence on Antebellum America: Slumbering Volcano in the Caribbean.* Baton Rouge: Louisiana State University Press, 1988.

Hutchison, William R. *Religious Pluralism in America: The Contentious History of a Founding Ideal.* New Haven, CT: Yale, 2003.

Ignatiev, Noel. *How the Irish Became White.* New York: Routledge, 1995.

Jenkins, Philip. *Mystics and Messiahs: Cults and New Religions in American History.* New York: Oxford University Press, 2000.

———. *The New Anti-Catholicism: The Last Acceptable Prejudice.* Oxford: Oxford University Press, 2003.

Jennings, Lawrence C. *French Anti-Slavery: The Movement for the Abolition of Slavery in France, 1802–1848.* New York: Cambridge University Press, 2000.

Jones, Charles C., Jr. *Memorial History of Augusta, Georgia.* Syracuse: D. Mason, 1890.

Jones, Charles Henry. *History of the Campaign for the Conquest of Canada in 1776, from the Death of Montgomery to the Retreat of the British Army under Sir Guy Carleton.* Philadelphia: Porter and Coates, 1882.

Jordan, Winthrop. *White Over Black: American Attitudes toward the Negro, 1550–1812.* Chapel Hill: University of North Carolina Press, 1968.

Kane, John J. *Catholic-Protestant Conflicts in America.* Chicago: Regnery, 1955.

Kauffman, Christopher J. *Ministry and Meaning: A Religious History of Catholic Health Care in the United States.* New York: Crossroad, 1995.

Keeney, Elizabeth Barnaby. "Unless Powerful Sick: Domestic Medicine in the Old South." In Numbers and Savitt, *Science and Medicine in the Old South,* 276–294.

Kenny, Michael. *Catholic Culture in Alabama: Centenary Story of Spring Hill College, 1830–1930.* New York: The America Press, 1931.

Knight, Edgar Wallace. *A Documentary History of Education in the South before 1860.* 5 vols. Chapel Hill: University of North Carolina Press, 1949–1953.

———. *Public Education in the South.* Boston: Ginn and Company, 1922.

Krebs, Robert T. *The Celestial City: A History of the Cathedral Basilica of the Assumption.* Covington: Diocese of Covington, 1991.

Levy, Leonard. *The Establishment Clause: Religion and the First Amendment.* Chapel Hill: University of North Carolina Press, 1994.

Lipscomb, Oscar Hugh. "The Administration of John Quinlan, Second Bishop of Mobile, 1859–1883." *Records of the American Catholic Historical Society of Philadelphia* 78, nos. 1–4 (March–Dec. 1967): 2–40.

Madden, Richard C. *Catholics in South Carolina: A Record.* New York: University Press of America, 1985.

Maes, Camillus Paul. *The Life of the Reverend Charles Nerinckx.* Cincinnati: Robert Clarke, 1880.

Margi, Joseph. "Catholicity in Virginia during the Episcopate of Bishop McGill (1850–1872)." *American Catholic Historical Researches* 2 (April 1916–June 1917): 410–425.

Massa, Mark Stephen. *Anti-Catholicism in America: The Last Acceptable Prejudice.* New York: Crossroad, 2003.

Mathews, Donald. *Religion in the Old South.* Chicago: University of Chicago Press, 1977.

Mattingly, Sister Mary Ramona. *The Catholic Church on the Kentucky Frontier (1785–1812).* The Catholic University of America Studies in American Church History 25. Washington: Catholic University Press, 1936.

McDaniel, Isaac. *Impact of the Mexican War on Anti-Catholicism in the United States.* Ann Arbor: University Microfilms International, 1991.

McGreevy, John. *Catholicism and American Freedom.* New York: Norton, 2003.

Miller, Randall. "Catholic in a Protestant World: The Old South Example." In *Va-*

rieties of Southern Religious Experience. Edited by Samuel S. Hill, 128–145. Baton Rouge: Louisiana State University Press, 1988.

———. "The Failed Mission: The Catholic Church and Black Catholics in the Old South." In Miller and Wakelyn, *Catholics in the Old South,* 149–170.

———. "Some Speculations on Catholic Identity in the Old South." In Miller and Wakelyn, *Catholics in the Old South,* 11–52.

Miller, Richard Roscoe. *Slavery and Catholicism.* Durham, NC: North State Publishers, 1957.

Miller, Randall, and Jon Wakelyn, eds. *Catholics in the Old South.* Macon: Mercer University Press, 1999.

Miller, Stephen F. *The Bench and Bar of Georgia: Memoirs and Sketches.* Philadelphia: J. B. Lippincott, 1858.

Minogue, Anna Catherine. *Loretto: Annals of the Century.* New York: The American Press, 1912.

Morgan, Edmund. *American Slavery, American Freedom: The Ordeal of Colonial Virginia.* New York: W. W. Norton, 1975.

Morris, Charles R. *American Catholic: The Saints and Sinners Who Built America's Most Powerful Church.* New York: Random House, 1997.

Morrow, Diana Batts. *Persons of Color and Religious at the Same Time: The Oblate Sisters of Providence, 1828–1860.* Chapel Hill: University of North Carolina Press, 2002.

Murphy, Thomas. *Jesuit Slaveholding in Maryland, 1717–1838.* New York: Routledge, 2001.

Numbers, Ronald L., and Todd L. Savitt, eds. *Science and Medicine in the Old South.* Baton Rouge: Louisiana State University Press, 1989.

O'Brien, Joseph L. *John England—Bishop of Charleston: The Apostle to Democracy.* New York: Edward O'Toole, 1934.

O'Daniel, V. F. "Bishop Flaget's Report of the Diocese of Bardstown to Pius VII, April 10, 1815." *Catholic Historical Review* 1 (April 1915–Jan. 1916): 313–319.

———. "A Long Misunderstood Episode in American History." *Catholic Historical Review* 6 (April 1920–Jan. 1921): 15–45.

Overdyke, W. Darrell. *The Know-Nothing Party in the South.* Baton Rouge: Louisiana State University Press, 1950.

Pace, Robert F. *Halls of Honor: College Men in the Old South.* Baton Rouge: Louisiana State University Press, 2004.

Panzer, Joel S. *The Popes and Slavery.* New York: Alba House, 1996.

Pasquier, Michael. *Fathers on the Frontier: French Missionaries and the Roman Catholic Priesthood in the United States, 1789–1870.* New York: Oxford University Press, 2010.

Patterson, David K. "Disease Environments of the Antebellum South." In Numbers and Savitt, *Science and Medicine in the Old South,* 152–165.

Phillips, Ulrich Bonnell. *Life and Labor in the Old South.* Boston: Little, Brown, and Company, 1946.

Pillar, James J. *The Catholic Church in Mississippi, 1837–1865.* New Orleans: Hauser Press, 1964.

Posey, Walter Brownlow. *Frontier Mission: A History of Religion West of the Southern Appalachians to 1861.* Lexington: University Press of Kentucky, 1966.

Quinn, John F. "'Three Cheers for the Abolitionist Pope!': American Reaction to Gregory XVI's Condemnation of the Slave Trade, 1840–1860." *Catholic Historical Review* 90, no. 1 (Jan. 2004): 67–93.

Raboteau, Albert J. *Slave Religion: The "Invisible Institution" in the Antebellum South.* Updated ed. New York: Oxford University Press, 2004.

Rice, Madeleine Hooke. *American Catholic Opinion in the Slavery Controversy.* New York: Columbia University Press, 1944.

Robertson, Ignatius Loyola Robertson. *Sketches of Public Characters Drawn from the Living and the Dead.* s.l.: Knapp, 1830.

Roediger, David. *The Wages of Whiteness: Race and the Making of the American Working Class.* London: Verso, 1991.

Rosen, Robert. *A Short History of Charleston.* Columbia: University of South Carolina Press, 1997.

Rosenberg, Charles E. *The Cholera Years: The United States in 1832, 1849, and 1866.* Chicago: University of Chicago Press, 1962.

Rowland, Lawrence S., Alexander Moore, and George C. Rogers Jr. *History of Beaufort County, South Carolina.* Vol. 1. Columbia: University of South Carolina Press, 1996.

Schauinger, J. Herman. *Cathedrals in the Wilderness.* Milwaukee: Bruce Publishing Company, 1952.

Schmidt, Raymond H. "An Overview of Institutional Establishments in the Antebellum Southern Church." In Miller and Wakelyn, *Catholics in the Old South,* 53–76.

Schultz, Nancy Lusignan. *Veil of Fear: Nineteenth-Century Convent Tales by Rebecca Reed and Maria Monk.* West Lafayette, IN: Perdue University Press, 1999.

Schweiger, Beth Barton, and Donald Mathews, eds. *Religion in the American South: Protestants and Others in History and Culture.* Chapel Hill: University of North Carolina Press, 2004.

Sensbach, Jon F. "Before the Bible Belt: Indians, Africans, and the New Synthesis of Eighteenth-Century Southern Religious History." In *Religion in the American South: Protestants and Others in History and Culture.* Edited by Beth Barton Schweiger and Donald Mathews. 5–30. Chapel Hill: University of North Carolina Press, 2004.

Shea, John Gilmary. *History of the Catholic Church in the United States.* 4 vols. New York: J. G. Shea, 1886–1892.

Shryock, Richard Harrison. *Medicine and Society in America, 1660–1860.* New York: New York University Press, 1960.

———. *Medicine in America: Historical Essays.* Baltimore: Johns Hopkins Press, 1966.

Smith, Ryan K. *Gothic Arches, Latin Crosses: Anti-Catholicism and American Church Designs in the Nineteenth Century.* Chapel Hill: University of North Carolina Press, 2006.

"A Southern Teaching Order: The Sisters of Mercy of Charleston, S.C., A.D. 1829–1904; by a Member of the Order." *American Catholic Historical Studies* 15, no. 3 (Sept. 1904): 249–265.

Spalding, H. S. "Pottinger's Creek Settlement—Kentucky, 1785." *Mid-America* 13, no. 4 (April 1931): 307–323.

Spalding, Thomas W. *The Premier See: A History of the Archdiocese of Baltimore, 1789–1989.* Baltimore: The Johns Hopkins University Press, 1989.

Spotswood, Vernice McKeever. *Legacy of Love: History of St. Mary's Home, 1838–1988.* Mobile: s.n., 1988.

Spring Hill College, Mobile, Ala., 1830–1905. Mobile: Commercial Printing Company, 1906.

Stepsis, Ursala M., and Dolores Liptak, eds. *Pioneer Healers: The History of Women Religious in American Healthcare.* New York: Crossroad, 1989.

Stern, Andrew. "Roman Catholicism: Catholics in the Atlantic Colonies." *Encyclopedia of Religion in America.* Vol 4. Edited by Charles H. Lippy and Peter Williams, 1960–1963. Washington, DC: CQ Press, 2010.

———. "Southern Harmony: Catholic-Protestant Relations in the Antebellum South." *Religion and American Culture* 17, no. 2 (2007): 165–190.

Stovall, Pleasant A. *Robert Toombs: Statesman, Speaker, Soldier, Sage.* New York: Cassell, 1892.

Tate, Allen. *Essays of Four Decades.* Chicago: Swallow Press, 1968.

Thelin, John R. *A History of American Higher Education.* Baltimore: The Johns Hopkins University Press, 2004.

Theobold, S. L. "Catholic Missionary Work among the Colored People of the United States (1776–1866)." *Records of the American Catholic Historical Society of Philadelphia* 25, no. 4 (Dec. 1914): 330–342.

Thigpen, Thomas Paul. "Aristocracy of the Heart: Catholic Lay Leadership in Savannah, 1820–1870." PhD diss., Emory University, 1995.

Thomas, John Peyre. *The History of the South Carolina Military Academy.* Charleston, SC: Walker, Evans, & Cogswell, 1893.

Thomason, John Furman. *Foundations of the Public Schools of South Carolina.* Columbia, SC: The State Company, 1925.

Wade, John Donald. *Augustus Baldwin Longstreet: A Study of the Development of Culture in the South.* New York: MacMillan, 1924.

Walker, Peter. *Moral Choices: Memory, Desire, and Imagination in Nineteenth-Century American Abolition.* Baton Rouge: Louisiana State University Press, 1978.

Warner, John Hanley. "The Idea of Southern Medical Distinctiveness: Medical Knowledge and Practice in the Old South." In Numbers and Savitt, *Science and Medicine in the Old South,* 179–205.

———. "A Southern Medical Reform: the Meaning of the Antebellum Argument for Southern Medical Education." In Numbers and Savitt, *Science and Medicine in the Old South,* 206–225.

Warner, Margaret H. "Public Health in the Old South." In Numbers and Savitt, *Science and Medicine in the Old South*, 226–255.

Webb, Benedict Joseph. *Centenary of Catholicity in Kentucky.* Louisville: C. A. Rogers, 1884.

Welter, Barbara. "The Cult of True Womanhood: 1820–1860." *American Quarterly* 18, no. 2 (Summer 1966): 151–174.

Wilson, Charles Reagan, ed. *Religion in the South.* Jackson: University Press of Mississippi, 1985.

Woodson, Carter G. *The Education of the Negro Prior to 1861: A History of the Education of the Colored People of the United States from the Beginning of Slavery to the Civil War.* New York: G. P. Putnam, 1915.

Worsley, Stephen. "Catholicism in Antebellum North Carolina." *North Carolina Historical Review* 61 (Oct. 1983): 399–430.

Wyatt-Brown, Bertram. *Southern Honor: Ethics and Behavior in the Old South.* New York: Oxford, 1982.

Yater, George H. *Two Hundred Years at the Falls of the Ohio: A History of Louisville and Jefferson County.* Louisville: The Filson Club, 1987.

Zanca, Kenneth J. *American Catholics and Slavery: 1789–1866.* New York: University Press of America, 1994.

Index